CAMBRIDGE STUDIES IN ITALIAN HISTORY AND CULTURE

FLORENTINE TUSCANY

Florence has often been studied in the past for its distinctive urban culture and society, while insufficient attention has been paid to the important Tuscan territorial state that was created by Florence in the fourteenth and fifteenth centuries. Comprising a handful of formerly independent city-states and numerous smaller communities in the plains and mountains, the Florentine 'empire' in Tuscany supplied the markets and fiscal coffers of the Renaissance republic, while providing lessons in statecraft that nourished the political thought of Machiavelli and Guicciardini.

This volume comprises seventeen original essays representing the new directions being taken by historians of the Florentine Renaissance. It offers new and exemplary approaches towards state-building, political vocabulary, political economy, civic humanism, local history and social patronage in what is one of the most interesting and well documented of the states of late medieval and Renaissance Europe.

WILLIAM J. CONNELL holds the Joseph M. and Geraldine C. La Motta Chair in Italian Studies, Seton Hall University.

ANDREA ZORZI is Researcher in Medieval History, University of Florence.

CAMBRIDGE STUDIES IN ITALIAN HISTORY AND CULTURE

Edited by GIGLIOLA FRAGNITO, Università degli Studi, Parma
CESARE MOZZARELLI, Università Cattolica del Sacro Cuore, Milan
ROBERT ORESKO, Institute of Historical Research, University of London
and GEOFFREY SYMCOX, University of California, Los Angeles

This series comprises monographs and a variety of collaborative volumes, including translated works, which concentrate on the period of Italian history from late medieval times up to the Risorgimento. The editors aim to stimulate scholarly debate over a range of issues which have not hitherto received, in English, the attention they deserve. As it develops, the series will emphasize the interest and vigour of current international debates on this central period of Italian history and the persistent influence of Italian culture on the rest of Europe.

For a list of titles in the series, see end of book

Florentine coats-of-arms on the Palace of the Vicars, Scarperia. Photo: Alinari.

FLORENTINE TUSCANY

Structures and Practices of Power

EDITED BY
WILLIAM J. CONNELL
AND
ANDREA ZORZI

CAMBRIDGE
UNIVERSITY PRESS

PUBLISHED BY THE PRESS SYNDICATE OF THE UNIVERSITY OF CAMBRIDGE
The Pitt Building, Trumpington Street, Cambridge, United Kingdom

CAMBRIDGE UNIVERSITY PRESS
The Edinburgh Building, Cambridge CB2 2RU, UK   www.cup.cam.ac.uk
40 West 20th Street, New York, NY 10011–4211, USA   www.cup.org
10 Stamford Road, Oakleigh, Melbourne 3166, Australia
Ruiz de Alarcón 13, 28014 Madrid, Spain

First published 2000

Printed in the United Kingdom at the University Press, Cambridge

Typeset in Bembo 11/12.5pt   [CE]

A catalogue record for this book is available from the British Library

Library of Congress cataloguing in publication data
Florentine Tuscany: structures and practices of power / edited by
William J. Connell and Andrea Zorzi.
p.   cm.
ISBN 0 521 59111 2 hb
1. Tuscany (Italy) – Politics and government – 1434–1737.
2. Tuscany (Italy) – Politics and government – To 1434.
3. Tuscany (Italy) – Economic conditions – 1434–1737.
4. Tuscany (Italy) – Economic conditions – To 1434.
I. Connell, William J.   II. Zorzi, Andrea.
DG737.4.F59 2000
945'.505–dc21   99–33441 CIP

ISBN 0 521 59111 2 hardback

CONTENTS

FIGURES

TABLES

ABBREVIATIONS USED FOR ARCHIVAL SOURCES

ACSM	San Miniato, Archivio del comune
Delib.	Deliberazioni della comunità
Dipl. SSIL	Diplomatico del convento dei Ss. Iacopo e Lucia
Ent. usc. vic.	Entrate e uscite del vicariato
ASA	Arezzo, Archivio di Stato
Provv.	Deliberazioni del magistrato dei priori e del consiglio generale
ASCV	Volterra, Archivio storico del comune
ASF	Florence, Archivio di Stato
Bal.	Balìe
CCP	Camera del comune. Provveditori e massai. Campioni di entrata e uscita
CdB	Carte del Bene
Cap. Pop.	Atti del Capitano del Popolo
Capitoli	Capitoli. Registri
Catasto	Archivio del catasto
Cento	Consiglio del Cento
Corp. rel. sopp.	Corporazioni religiose soppresse
CP	Consulte e pratiche
CPGNR	Capitani di Parte Guelfa, Numeri rossi
CS	Carte strozziane
DAC	Dogana di Firenze. Dogana antica e campioni (sec. XIV–1808)
DG	Decima granducale
Dipl.	Diplomatico
EOG	Atti dell'Esecutore degli Ordinamenti di Giustizia
GA	Giudice degli appelli e nullità
LF	Libri fabarum

MAP	Archivio mediceo avanti il principato
MC	Monte comune o delle graticole
Merc.	Mercanzia
Misc. rep	Miscellanea repubblicana
Miss. I canc.	Signoria. Carteggi. Missive. Prima cancelleria
Miss. II canc.	Signoria. Carteggi. Missive. Seconda cancelleria
NA	Notarile antecosimiano
OGBR	Otto di guardia e balìa. Periodo repubblicano.
PR	Provvisioni. Registri
Pod.	Atti del Podestà
SA	Sei ufficiali di Arezzo, Cortona e Pistoia
SCAS	Statuti delle comunità 'autonome' e 'soggette'
SC Delib. ord.	Signoria. Collegi. Deliberazioni fatte in forza di ordinaria autorità
SC Delib. spec.	Signoria. Collegi. Deliberazioni fatte in forza della loro speciale autorità
SCLC	Signoria. Collegi. Legazioni e commissarìe
SCLCRROF	Signoria. Carteggi. Legazioni e commissarìe. Rapporti e relazioni di oratori fiorentini
Stat. com.	Statuti del comune di Firenze
Tratte	Archivio delle Tratte
Zecca	Archivio della Zecca
ASPe	Pescia, Archivio di Stato
Com.	Comune di Pescia preunitario
Delib. e rif.	Deliberazioni e riforme
Lett. Sig. Fir.	Lettere della Signoria di Firenze ai Vicari della Valdinievole
ASPi	Pisa, Archivio di Stato
ASPt	Pistoia, Archivio di Stato
Com.	Archivio del comune
Provv. e rif.	Provvisioni e riforme
SO	Statuti e ordinamenti
ASS	Siena, Archivio di Stato
Colle	Archivio del comune di Colle
Delib.	Deliberazioni
ASV	Vatican City, Archivio Segreto del Vaticano
RV	Registra Vaticana
BAV	Vatican City, Biblioteca Apostolica Vaticana
BFPt	Pistoia, Biblioteca Comunale Forteguerriano
FF	Fondo Forteguerriano
BNF	Florence, Biblioteca Nazionale Centrale
BRF	Florence, Biblioteca Riccardiana

INTRODUCTION

WILLIAM J. CONNELL

In the century that followed the Black Death of 1348, the republic of Florence became the dominant power in Tuscany, absorbing within its dominion a large number of formerly independent communes and their rural territories, so that the area controlled by Florence nearly tripled in size. The plague itself seems to have contributed to Florentine expansion, for, although the disease roughly halved the population of all of the Tuscan urban centres, Florence, as the region's largest city, still commanded resources that permitted her to capitalise on the new weakness of her neighbours. Florentine growth was accomplished through a steady series of purchases, conquests and alliances (see Map on p. 3) and it was accompanied by important efforts to integrate newly acquired lands into the Florentine state. The century of dramatic territorial expansion had important and lasting consequences for the political and economic history of Florence and Tuscany. It also corresponded with the first flourishing of the cultural phenomenon we know as the Florentine Renaissance.

It used to be thought that the Renaissance was an affair strictly for cities. A distinguished scholarly tradition has long held that the distinctive urban society of late medieval Italy made possible the political and philosophical speculation of humanist scholars as well as the masterpieces of Renaissance artists. As for the countryside, its historians tended to work in demographic or agrarian history, fields that were interested in long-term trends, against which the political changes of a ruling centre like Florence were simply ephemera, of interest only insofar as they affected the surviving documentary evidence.

The first sustained effort to integrate the study of the Florentine territory with the political and institutional history of Renaissance Florence was made by Marvin Becker, who, in the second volume of his *Florence in Transition*, published in 1968, and also in several preliminary articles, argued that the dramatic annexations of the fourteenth

I

century resulted in a changed consciousness or mentality at Florence, which he termed a 'harsh paideia'.[1] The exigencies of defending and administering a much larger territory resulted in the adoption by the Florentine elite of an aggressive and calculating approach to statecraft, so that the republic shed its communal traditions and emerged as a 'territorial state'. 'Territoriality' had long been common currency among historians of feudalism in northern Europe. Marc Bloch, Jan Dhondt, Jean-François Lemarignier, and Georges Duby ascribed vast social and cultural consequences to the assumption of responsibility over territorial holdings by northern warlords in the eleventh and twelfth centuries. But Becker was the first historian to attribute this sort of aggressive territoriality to an Italian republic. That he did so at a time when a number of historians were lauding Florentine foreign policy in the fourteenth century as pacific and defensive makes his effort all the more notable.

Subsequent research has modified Becker's findings to a certain extent. Thus, it has been shown that there was significant and eloquent opposition by some members of the Florentine ruling class to a policy of territorial expansion.[2] Some of the harshest aspects of Florentine rule, especially the high fiscal exactions Becker criticised, were concentrated during periods of military conflict with foreign powers.[3] This in no way diminishes the general argument, however, that the extension of Florentine control over a significant portion of Tuscany caused changes in the practices and the ways of thinking of a medieval commune as it attempted to satisfy the requirements of a territorial state.[4]

An emphasis on territoriality in the work of Becker, and on the institutional history of Florence in the work of other English and American historians, such as Gene Brucker, Lauro Martines, Anthony Molho, and Nicolai Rubinstein, anticipated in certain respects a new

---

[1] M. B. Becker, *Florence in Transition*, II, *Studies in the Rise of the Territorial State* (Baltimore, 1968); Becker, 'Problemi della finanza pubblica fiorentina della seconda metà del Trecento e dei primi del Quattrocento', *Archivio storico italiano*, 123 (1965), pp. 433–66; Becker, 'Economic Change and the Emerging Florentine Territorial State', *Studies in the Renaissance*, 13 (1986), pp. 7–39; Becker, 'The Florentine Territorial State and Civic Humanism in the Early Renaissance', in N. Rubinstein (ed.), *Florentine Studies: Politics and Society in Renaissance Florence* (London, 1968), pp. 109–39.

[2] G. A. Brucker, *The Civic World of Early Renaissance Florence* (Princeton, 1977), p. 344.

[3] D. Hay and J. Law, *Italy in the Age of the Renaissance* (London, 1989), pp. 112–19.

[4] L. Martines, *Lawyers and Statecraft in Renaissance Florence* (Princeton, 1968), esp. pp. 220–45; A. Molho, *Florentine Public Finances in the Early Renaissance, 1400–1433* (Cambridge, Mass., 1971); Brucker, *Civic World*, pp. 187–247; A. Brown, 'Florence, Renaissance and Early Modern State', in Brown, *The Medici in Florence: The Exercise and Language of Power* (Florence, 1992), pp. 307–26.

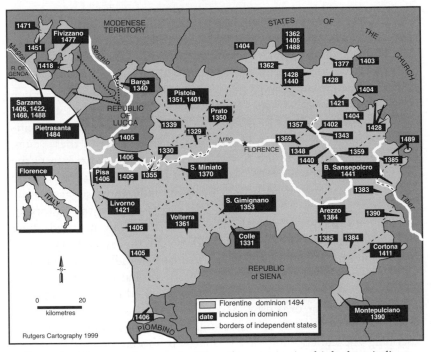

Florentine Tuscany, fourteenth–fifteenth centuries (multiple dates indicate
subsequent reacquisition)

interest in political and institutional history that was developed by
several Italian scholars in the 1960s and 70s.[5] The blueprint for this
approach – which involved <u>an emphasis on regions rather than nation-
states</u> – was laid out in notable essays by <u>Giorgio Chittolini</u> and <u>Elena
Fasano Guarini</u>.[6] State building in early modern Europe had been
discussed for a long time with reference to a few large, geographically

---

[5] On the Italian historiography, see J. S. Grubb, *Firstborn of Venice: Vicenza in the Early
Renaissance State* (Baltimore, 1988), pp. ix–xvi; J. Kirshner, 'Introduction: The State is
"Back In"', in Kirshner (ed.), *The Origins of the State in Italy, 1300–1600* (Chicago,
1995), pp. 1–10.

[6] See especially Giorgio Chittolini, 'Alcune considerazioni sulla storia politico-istituzio-
nale del tardo Medioevo: alle origini degli "stati regionali"', *Annali dell'Istituto Italo-
Germanico in Trento*, 2 (1976), pp. 401–19; Chittolini, *La formazione dello stato regionale
e le istituzioni del contado: secoli XIV e XV* (Turin, 1979), pp. 3–35; Elena Fasano
Guarini, 'Introduzione', in Fasano Guarini (ed.), *Potere e società negli stati regionali
italiani del '500 e '600* (Bologna, 1978), pp. 7–47; Fasano Guarini, 'Gli Stati dell'Italia
centro-settentrionale tra Quattro e Cinquecento: continuità e trasformazioni', *Società
e storia*, 6 (1983), pp. 617–39.

coherent monarchies. It was accepted that the state-building experiences of France, Spain, England and Prussia, however much they diverged, belonged to a common European history of absolutism, comprising the reinforcement of secular rule, the growth of centralised state apparatuses, the formation of enduring administrative elites, and, ultimately, the rise of a feeling of national identity.[7] But it was not nearly so certain whether or how the smaller states of Europe conformed to these patterns. Italian historians of the peninsula's regional states were stimulated in part by a Braudelian interest in the *longue durée* of these states, most of which survived with few changes to their boundaries from the later middle ages down to the Napoleonic period. The success of these smaller states, as measured simply by their endurance, suggested the importance of regional, rather than national factors, in the history of state building. In recent decades, as this scholarship has matured, there has been a great deal of important work on the theory and practice of statecraft in the Italian peninsula in the later middle ages and early modern period.[8] In even the recent work of Italian scholars, there remains an attachment to the regional state as something that functioned as a living system or organism. As Fasano Guarini sees it, geography – albeit a 'geography of power' – is as important as laws and institutions in describing the functioning of the state.[9] It should be noted that in contrast to the 'regional' state of much Italian scholarship, Becker's 'territorial' state was an artificial creation, imposed with violent force by Florence on an unwilling human landscape.

Spurred by these antecedents and the already rich tradition of Florentine studies, the study of Florentine statecraft in Tuscany has in recent years become one of the most exciting areas of Italian Renaissance scholarship, attracting an energetic international group of scholars who are represented by the essays in this volume. The surviving records concerning Florentine government in Tuscany are probably the richest

[7] P. Anderson, *Lineages of the Absolutist State* (London, 1974), noting pp. 143–72 on Italy's 'micro-absolutisms'; C. Tilly (ed.), *The Formation of National States in Western Europe* (Princeton, 1975).

[8] See especially Kirshner (ed.), *Origins*; and the larger Italian collection of essays from the same conference, G. Chittolini, A. Molho and P. Schiera (eds.), *Origini dello Stato: processi di formazione statale in Italia fra medioevo ed età moderna* (Bologna, 1994). The influence of the regional approach is strikingly evident in the more recent writings and collaborative efforts of Charles Tilly. See his *Coercion, Capital, and European States, AD 990–1992*, rev. edn (Oxford, 1992); and C. Tilly and W. P. Blockmans (eds.), *Cities and the Rise of States in Europe, A.D. 1000 to 1800* (Boulder, 1994).

[9] Fasano Guarini, 'Center and Periphery', in Kirshner (ed.), *Origins*, p. 96; and compare her earlier discussions of historical geography in her *Lo Stato mediceo di Cosimo I* (Florence, 1973), *passim*.

for any territorial state in late medieval and early modern Europe, comprising not just collections of laws and statutes, fiscal records and official correspondence, but also private letters and diaries, account books, notarial acts, criminal records and the deliberations of local councils. In exploring this wealth of documentary evidence, these essays develop new hypotheses about the relations of Florence with her subject territories and they offer new perspectives on one of the earliest and most fascinating of Europe's Renaissance states.

The editors are deeply grateful to Giorgio Chittolini, Sergio Gensini, Anthony Molho and Giuliano Pinto for their assistance in planning this volume. The Centro di Studi sulla Civiltà del Tardo Medioevo at San Miniato provided important financial assistance and hosted the two-day conference during which most of the essays were discussed by all of the contributors to this volume. The Department of History of the University of Florence, the Florentine State Archive, Seton Hall University and the Society for Renaissance Studies provided generous institutional support. Gina Paolercio assisted with the preparation of the typescript. We are also indebted to our editor, William Davies, and the Cambridge University Press.

CHAPTER I

THE 'MATERIAL CONSTITUTION' OF THE FLORENTINE DOMINION

ANDREA ZORZI

It was in 1986 that Gian Maria Varanini invited historians, in their study of the Italian territorial states, to look beyond the phase of 'accomplished stability' to a 'prehistory' in which the characteristic practices of these states took shape. Convinced that the modes of governing of the Italian states were not new with the fourteenth and fifteenth centuries, Varanini argued that these political structures originated in the communal period: in the experience of establishing control over the countryside and in the development of a hierarchy among the north Italian cities.[1] Seen from the perspective of this communal prehistory, the formation by Florence of a territorial dominion was not an inevitable process, but a process open to different possible paths for development. If, therefore, a linear understanding of political development is abandoned, I should prefer to speak of the 'material constitution' of the territorial state. This seems a term well suited to describing the early hierarchy of Tuscan cities and the asymmetries among them that historically preceded the creation of a Florentine dominion.

To anticipate this chapter's conclusion, the Florentine process of expansion took place slowly, and in continual interaction with the territorial expansion of rival states. The ordering of the territory did not follow a unitary scheme, nor was there a progressive refinement of public functions; what took shape, rather, was a system characterised from the beginning by a low degree of integration among its components. The creation of institutions was not in itself the aim of policy. The only true end of the territorial order was to preserve the political, military and economic might of Florence.

The territory that Florence had acquired by the 1420s comprised

[1] G. M. Varanini, 'Dal comune allo stato regionale', in *La storia: i grandi problemi dal Medioevo all'Età contemporanea*, II, *Il Medioevo*, pt 2, *Popoli e strutture politiche* (Turin, 1986), pp. 706ff. See also G. Chittolini (ed.) *La crisi degli ordinamenti comunali e le origini dello stato del Rinascimento* (Bologna, 1979).

what was really a sub-regional dominion, a small state of about 11,000 km². This was certainly larger than the Sienese dominion in the open marshlands of southern Tuscany (6000 km²) or the Lucchese contado-state (about 1000 km²). But it was clearly diminutive when compared with the Venetian *Terraferma* (30,000 km²) and the Duchy of Milan (27,000 km²), to consider two Italian states that also began as cities. Moreover, the Florentine dominion was not at all comparable in size with the kingdoms of the south, the Papal state, the Savoy state or even with middling territorial principalities of northern Europe.[2]

Even so, the dimensions achieved by Florence constituted an exceptional result when compared with her starting circumstances more than two centuries earlier. When the Florentine commune began to organise its own contado in the twelfth and thirteenth centuries, there was no indication that the seat of a small diocese, distant from the most important Italian road (the Via Francigena that linked Rome with the north), and deprived of outlets to the sea, would become the capital of a dominion that included the greater share of the Tuscan cities.

If we attempt to chart this expansion over time, surely the thirteenth century was the decisive period in which Florence laid the foundations of her demographic, economic and political hegemony. What took place was a 'primary accumulation' of resources that allowed the Florentine ruling class ultimately to prevail in the difficult military competition that accompanied the redrawing of the Italian political map to the scale of regions rather than cities.[3]

ORDERING THE TERRITORY

In the thirteenth century, the area that Florence would later control was characterised by three fundamental elements: the marginalisation of signorial formations, the density of its urban network, and the important role assumed by certain 'sub-urban' centres, known as *terre* or *borghi*.[4]

---

[2] Compare G. Chittolini, 'Cities, "City-States", and Regional States in North-Central Italy', in C. Tilly and W. P. Blockmans (eds.), *Cities and the Rise of States in Europe, A.D. 1000 to 1800* (Boulder, 1994), pp. 28–43; and E. Fasano Guarini, ' "Etat moderne" et anciens Etats italiens. Eléments d'histoire comparée', *Revue d'histoire moderne et contemporaine*, 45 (1998), pp. 15–41.

[3] Cf. G. Pinto, 'L'economia della Toscana nella seconda metà del Duecento', in Pinto, *Toscana medievale: paesaggi e realtà sociali* (Florence, 1993), pp. 13–24; and S. R. Epstein, 'Town and Country: Economy and Institutions in Late Medieval Italy', *Economic History Review*, 46 (1993), pp. 453–77.

[4] A. Zorzi, 'L'organizzazione del territorio in area fiorentina tra XIII e XIV secolo', in G. Chittolini and D. Willoweit (eds.), *L'organizzazione del territorio in Italia e in Germania: secoli XIII–XIV* (Bologna, 1994), pp. 279–349.

The early marginalisation of the signorial presence in Tuscany, thanks to the weak dynastic efforts of Tuscany's post-Carolingian lordships and the aggressiveness of Tuscany's very dynamic cities, is a phenomenon well known to scholars of the central centuries of the middle ages.[5] Not always, however, has this earlier phenomenon been understood as preliminary to the later process of forming a territorial dominion. Yet the vigour and the determination shown by the Florentine commune, beginning in the first half of the twelfth century, in successfully challenging the signorial powers present within its diocese-contado undoubtedly helped make possible later growth.

From the beginning, Florence found herself competing in a geopolitical space crowded with sturdy, war-hardened cities. More than elsewhere in Italy, Tuscany's cities, rather than its lordships, functioned as hegemonic poles for the organisation of the territory. Around 1300, the area of the Arno basin probably arrived at a level of urbanisation unequalled in Europe, with the result that the urban network functioned as a kind of connective tissue for the region.[6] Each city and town developed its own experiences of urban government and control, and these were projected outward onto the surrounding territory. Thus, Florence was in contact with other cities that were expanding and redefining their dominions, as was the case of Pisa, which imposed a complex network of new boundaries on her contado at the end of the thirteenth century.[7] These examples seem to have been crucial for the important Florentine decision to separate subject cities from their contadi.

A very special part was played in Tuscany by the many towns, known as *terre* or *borghi* to distinguish them from cities (*civitates* or *città*). These centres were really 'quasi-cities', to use a recently coined term.[8] The *terre* were governed by political institutions quite advanced for the time, and they functioned as capital-centres for territories of respectable

[5] See G. Cherubini, 'Qualche considerazione sulle campagne dell'Italia centro-settentrionale tra l'XI e il XV secolo', in Cherubini, *Signori, contadini, borghesi: ricerche sulla società italiana del basso Medioevo* (Florence, 1974), pp. 100ff.; and C. Wickham, 'La signoria rurale in Toscana', in G. Dilcher and C. Violante (eds.), *Strutture e trasformazioni della signoria rurale nei secoli X–XIII* (Bologna, 1996), pp. 343–409.

[6] M. Ginatempo, 'Toscana e Italia centrale', in Ginatempo and L. Sandri, *L'Italia delle città: il popolamento urbano tra Medioevo e Rinascimento (secoli XIII–XVI)* (Florence, 1990), p. 108.

[7] K. Shimizu, *L'amministrazione del contado pisano nel Trecento attraverso un manuale notarile* (Pisa, 1975); F. Leverotti, 'L'organizzazione amministrativa del contado pisano dalla fine del '200 alla dominazione fiorentina: spunti di ricerca', *Bollettino storico pisano*, 61 (1992), pp. 40ff.

[8] G. Chittolini, '"Quasi-città". Borghi e terre in area lombarda nel tardo Medioevo', *Società e storia*, 13 (1990), pp. 3–26.

dimensions: 90 km² at Colle, 107 km² at San Casciano, 131 km² at Prato, 139 km² at San Gimignano, 146 km² at Borgo San Lorenzo, and 160 km² at San Miniato.[9] The importance achieved by certain of these *terre* suggested to Florence that their autonomy should be recognised through the establishment of alliances rather than thoroughgoing subjugation. In the central decades of the fourteenth century, the first phase of the expansion of the dominion was characterised by alliances with intermediate-sized towns such as Prato, Colle, San Gimignano and San Miniato.[10] Indeed, these towns were the first areas to experience the direct ties with Florence that were an important characteristic of the later policy towards subject contadi. In these middling towns, Florentine expansion became the catalyst for a substantial political and institutional resurgence on the local level.[11]

DEMOGRAPHIC STRUCTURES

If we move on to consider the evolution of demographic structures, an intrinsic Florentine superiority emerges with clarity during the thirteenth century. This was when Florence irrevocably surpassed Pisa. The latter city, which counted no fewer than 30,000 inhabitants in 1228, arrived at just above 50,000 in the first decades of the fourteenth century. Florence, on the other hand, with probably about 15,000–20,000 inhabitants at the beginning of the thirteenth century, quintupled in size over the next one hundred years, showing an extraordinary capacity to attract population and resources and to produce wealth. With more than 100,000 inhabitants at the beginning of the fourteenth century, Florence was one of the largest cities of the European West. Tuscany as a whole probably had 1 million or 1,100,000 inhabitants in the fourth decade of the fourteenth century, and Florence alone accounted for one-tenth of them. This was more than twice the population of Pisa or Siena (each at about 40,000–50,000 inhabitants), four times that of Lucca (25,000) and five or more times the populations of Arezzo (20,000), Pistoia (18,000) and Prato (10,000–15,000). Thus, even before setting out on her policy of

---

[9] Zorzi, 'L'organizzazione del territorio in area fiorentina tra XIII e XIV secolo', pp. 284–5.
[10] Cf. A. Zorzi, 'Lo Stato territoriale fiorentino (secoli XIV–XV): aspetti giurisdizionali', *Società e storia*, 13 (1990), pp. 799–825.
[11] See G. Chittolini, 'Ricerche sull'ordinamento territoriale del dominio fiorentino agli inizi del secolo XV', in Chittolini, *La formazione dello stato regionale e le istituzioni del contado. Secoli XIV e XV* (Turin, 1979), pp. 292–352; and Zorzi, 'L'organizzazione del territorio in area fiorentina tra XIII e XIV secolo', pp. 344ff.

territorial expansion, Florence exercised demographic and economic hegemony over the region.[12]

To judge things properly, however, the decisive phase of the formation of the territorial states in Italy took place during the demographic downturn of the fourteenth and fifteenth centuries: between the peak of greatest demographic growth in the first decades of the 1300s and the take-off of a new ascendant curve in the second half of the fifteenth century. This was absolutely the case for Florence. The beginning of expansion beyond the boundaries of her traditional contado occurred in the years immediately after the great famine of 1328–30, which signalled the start of population decline in the region. And the submission pacts of Prato, Colle and San Gimignano were signed just after the devastating epidemic of 1347–8.[13] Recently, Stephan Epstein has shown how during the general demographic decline of Tuscany (which was relatively accentuated compared with other Italian regions), Florence increased her lead over the region's other cities.[14] The comparison with Pisa is striking. Overtaken during the thirteenth century, at the beginning of the fourteenth century Pisa still had half as many inhabitants as Florence. At mid-century, though, Pisa had only one-third as many inhabitants as Florence, one-fifth as many in 1427, and by 1552 the proportion was only one to six.[15] The trend is equally true for other Tuscan centres. The individual rankings of cities in the Tuscan hierarchy remained unchanged, but all remained at a relatively low demographic level. In 1427–30, for instance, when Florence had 37,000 inhabitants, Pisa was reduced to only 7500, Pistoia and Arezzo to 4500, Prato, Volterra and Cortona to 3500, and San Gimignano and San Miniato to 1500.[16] This demographic superiority helps to explain why Florence was able to realise a territorial policy that

---

[12] Cf. G. Pinto, *La Toscana nel tardo Medioevo: ambiente, economia rurale e società* (Florence, 1982), pp. 75ff.; Ginatempo, 'Toscana e Italia centrale', pp. 106ff.; M. Ginatempo, 'L'Italia delle città tra crisi e trasformazione', in Ginatempo and Sandri, *L'Italia delle città*, pp. 224–5.

[13] C. M. de La Roncière, *Prix et salaires à Florence au XIVe siècle (1280–1380)* (Rome, 1982), pp. 626ff.; Pinto, *La Toscana nel tardo Medioevo*, pp. 75ff.

[14] Cf. S. R. Epstein, 'Stato territoriale ed economia regionale nella Toscana del Quattrocento', in R. Fubini (ed.), *La Toscana al tempo di Lorenzo il Magnifico: politica economia cultura arte* (Pisa, 1996), III, pp. 871–4. See also, Epstein, 'Cities, Regions and the Late Medieval Crisis: Sicily and Tuscany Compared', *Past and Present*, 130 (1991), pp. 16ff.; and Epstein, 'Town and Country', pp. 459ff.

[15] Cf. E. Cristiani, *Nobiltà e popolo nel Comune di Pisa: dalle origini del podestariato alla signoria dei Donoratico* (Naples, 1962), pp. 167–72; and Epstein, 'Stato territoriale ed economia regionale nella Toscana del Quattrocento', p. 873.

[16] D. Herlihy and C. Klapisch-Zuber, *Les Toscans et leurs familles: une étude du catasto florentin de 1427* (Paris, 1978), pp. 225ff.

was much more coercive when compared with the Milanese and Venetian experiences. In the Po valley, these ruling powers continued to deal with urban centres of a size and social articulation of absolute importance. About the year 1400 such subject cities as Brescia and Cremona had numbers of inhabitants equal to or greater than Florence.[17]

Still, the demographic decline of these subject centres has too often been read as the consequence of Florentine rule. On the contrary, demographic decline preceded Florentine control, making it more likely that these cities and towns would be ruled by Florence. The definitive submissions of the principal cities coincided with the demographic 'nadir' of the region in the first decades of the fifteenth century.[18] The demographic crisis of the territory contributed in good measure also to the redrawing of territorial boundaries that Florence undertook in those years.

POLITICO-MILITARY COMPETITION

The fierce politico-military competition that redrew the Italian political map between the second half of the thirteenth century and the first half of the fifteenth century had important consequences for the Florentine dominion. It is possible to distinguish three sub-periods of this competition, each with its special characteristics.

A first phase can be traced from the central decades of the thirteenth century to the first decades of the subsequent century. In this period, Florence consolidated and maintained control over her own contado, while external alliances and a vigilant defence policy established the foundations for later political hegemony. In all of the decisive military situations in these years, Florence emerged either undamaged or as the victor. Her growth took place above all at the expense of Siena, which was increasingly confined within a territory deprived of important urban centres. Meanwhile, a usually stable Guelf alliance with Lucca, on the other hand, allowed Florence to extend her hegemony over a number of cities in central and eastern Tuscany. Furthermore, Pisa, dedicated as she was to the defence of important holdings in the Mediterranean, did not challenge Florentine efforts and reconciled herself to the control of a narrow coastal contado.[19]

---

[17] Ginatempo and Sandri, *L'Italia delle città*, pp. 100–1.

[18] Herlihy and Klapisch-Zuber, *Les Toscans et leurs familles*, pp. 165–88, citation at p. 177.

[19] Zorzi, 'L'organizzazione del territorio in area fiorentina tra XIII e XIV secolo', pp. 305ff.

A second period can be defined between the first decades of the
fourteenth century (when Florence began to expand beyond its traditional contado) down to the conclusion of the war against the papacy in
1378. Although the Po valley witnessed the first fourteenth-century
attempts to create larger territorial formations, offshoots of these efforts
appeared also in Tuscany, most notably in Lucca, which for not brief
periods of the Trecento experienced the rule of several lordships.

Not without difficulty and only at great expense to her citizens did
Florence fend off the expansionism of her rivals in this period. Florence
in these years was threatened by the philo-Imperial duchy created by
Castruccio Castracane in western Tuscany, comprising Pisa, Lucca and
Pistoia, and also by the Lucchese lordship of Mastino della Scala. In
addition, there was a costly struggle with Pisa, which, after defeat at
Meloria in 1284 by the Genoese, and the loss of Sardinia in 1326, had
returned somewhat tardily to the Tuscan chessboard. The all-out war
between Pisa and Florence was won by the Florentines in 1364 at the
battle of Cascina. Another threat came from the Duchy of Milan, which
made advances in the region in the 1350s and established firm control
over Sarzana after the conflict with Florence of 1369–70. There was
also a challenge from the papacy, which, with the renewed submission
of Bologna, Perugia and the Romagna, menaced Florence from the
east. Only after two years of a very difficult war did Florence conclude
the victorious peace in 1378 that ended papal pretensions in Tuscany.[20]

The intensification and diffusion of this politico–military competition
was the driving force behind Florentine expansion. Defensive in its
initial intent, Florentine policy aimed to create a protective zone around
the original Florentine contado, while making every effort to preserve
access to commercial routes: outlets to the sea, passes through the
Apennines, and highways to the south.[21]

A third phase in Florence's evolving territorial policy can be distinguished in the period that began in the 1380s with the acquisition of
Arezzo and ended more or less with the battle of Anghiari in 1440.
When Gian Galeazzo Visconti, Duke of Milan, unleashed his offensive
in Tuscany, Florence found herself alone and encircled, with the entire
central Italian chessboard lined up against her. During twelve years of
warfare, from 1390 until 1402, Florence faced the seemingly inexorable
force of the Visconti, who successively brought Lucca, Pisa, Siena,
Perugia and Bologna into their fold. The Milanese strangled the

---

[20] See the general view of M. Luzzati, *Firenze e la Toscana nel Medioevo: seicento anni per
la costruzione di uno Stato* (Turin, 1986), pp. 94ff.
[21] Zorzi, 'Lo Stato territoriale fiorentino', pp. 800–1.

Florentine economy and threatened a final solution that only the sudden and unexpected death of the duke made unrealisable.[22]

The Visconti threat has been studied often, but historians have not sufficiently discerned the connection between the incredible pressure on Florence and the determination of her ruling class to consolidate their dominion in a definitive way. Between 1384 and 1421, in the space of one political generation, Florence annexed Arezzo, Volterra, Pistoia, Pisa, Cortona, Montepulciano, Castrocaro, Livorno, and an infinity of minor centres.[23] The renewed challenge brought by Filippo Maria Visconti from 1423 to 1440 was really just an epilogue to the longer period of struggle that gave life to the famous system of Italian states. Until the arrival of the European monarchies on the Italian scene, there would be a precarious balance of five greater territorial powers: Milan, Venice, Florence, the southern Kingdom and the Papal state.[24]

ECONOMIC RESOURCES

The decisive factor in the formative process of the dominion was the capacity of the Florentines to join their immense economic resources with a military policy and territorial policy. Above all, they were able to sustain this policy over time by mobilising ideology and civic unity in making strategic choices.

Florentine society became the protagonist in an extraordinary accumulation of resources and a progressive concentration of capital. However, the apparently inexhaustible wealth of Florence does not really help to explain the success of a military policy that met the challenges of so many rivals. Explanations that rely on economic factors – as in much of the literature on 'state building' – tend to be overly simplistic.[25] In reality, the survival of the Florentine regime depended on the ability of its stable ruling class of merchants to mobilise the necessary resources and to develop a firm set of territorial policies. Especially striking was the commitment to military expenditures.

The vertiginous ascent of the military budget began in the first half of

[22] G. Brucker, *The Civic World of Early Renaissance Florence* (Princeton, 1977), pp. 102–86.

[23] See Zorzi, 'Lo Stato territoriale fiorentino'.

[24] See A. K. Isaacs, 'Condottieri, stati e territori nell'Italia centrale', in G. Cerboni Baiardi, G. Chittolini and P. Floriani (eds.), *Federico di Montefeltro: lo stato, la cultura, le arti*, 3 vols. (Rome, 1986), I, pp. 23–60; and R. Fubini, *Italia quattrocentesca: politica e diplomazia nell'età di Lorenzo il Magnifico* (Milan, 1994).

[25] See, for example, P. Anderson, *Lineages of the Absolutist State* (London, 1974); or the volume J.-P. Genet and M. Le Mené (eds.), *Genèse de l'état moderne: prélèvement et rédistribution* (Paris, 1987).

the Trecento, when it coincided with the transformation of the army from a citizen militia to a mercenary force.[26] Evidence of the change can be seen in the growth of the public debt. This increased from 47,000 florins in 1303 to 450,000 florins at the end of the della Scala war in 1338 to 600,000 at the end of the conflict with Lucca in 1343.[27] When the debt was consolidated in 1345, the original intent was to put paid to past military expenditures, but the consolidation mechanism was soon converted into a determined strategic policy: that of financing the chronic shortfall of revenues (from indirect taxes in Florence and fiscal levies on the contado) against expenses (principally for defence and interest on the debt) with forced loans. This political decision had the effect of committing a sizeable share of the citizenry's wealth to the destiny of the republic.[28]

Thereafter, the growth of the public debt, known as the Monte Comune, continued to be determined by territorial factors. Already in 1364 (at the end of the war with Pisa), the debt tripled to 1,500,000 florins; in 1395 (with the first truce in the Visconti war) it further doubled to 3 million florins. The figure reached 3,500,000 florins in 1433; and, with the creation of the Dowry Fund (*Monte delle Doti*), the total public debt arrived at 8 million florins by mid-century.[29] In this regard, a comparison between the sums gathered through forced loans and the wealth of the city's population is illuminating. In only ten years, from 1424 to 1433, the Florentines were compelled to loan more than 5 million florins to their government. It was an immense sum when one considers that the total wealth declared by city residents in the catasto of 1427 was roughly 10,170,000 florins.[30]

---

[26] See D. Waley, 'The Army of the Florentine Republic from the Twelfth to the Fourteenth Century', in N. Rubinstein (ed.), *Florentine Studies: Politics and Society in Renaissance Florence* (London, 1968), pp. 70–108.

[27] Cf. B. Barbadoro, *Le finanze della Repubblica fiorentina: imposta diretta e debito pubblico fino all'istituzione del Monte* (Florence, 1929), pp. 507, 616; and C. M. Cipolla, *Il fiorino e il quattrino: la politica monetaria a Firenze nel 1300* (Bologna, 1982), p. 11.

[28] On this point, see A. Molho, 'Fisco ed economia a Firenze alla vigilia del Concilio', in P. Viti (ed.), *Firenze e il Concilio del 1439* (Florence, 1994), I, pp. 59–94; and Molho, 'The State and Public Finance: A Hypothesis Based on the History of Late Medieval Florence', in J. Kirshner (ed.), *The Origins of the State in Italy, 1300–1600* (Chicago, 1996), pp. 97–135.

[29] Cf. M. B. Becker, *Florence in Transition*, I (Baltimore, 1967), p. 74; A. Molho, 'The Florentine Oligarchy and the *Balìe* of the Late Trecento', *Speculum*, 43 (1968), p. 39; Molho, *Florentine Public Finances in the Early Renaissance, 1400–1433* (Cambridge, Mass., 1971), p. 20; Becker, *Florence in Transition*, II (Baltimore, 1968), p. 152.

[30] Cf. Molho, *Florentine Public Finances*, pp. 62–3; and Herlihy and Klapisch-Zuber, *Les Toscans et leurs familles*, p. 664.

The Florentine territory, comprised of the contado and distretto, made a noteworthy contribution to this revenue inflow. The fiscal burden borne by the territory was heavier in both absolute and relative terms, and it was borne in conditions of depopulation, which was in the order of 50–60% with respect to the period prior to the Black Death. The rural countryside suffered especially. From the second half of the fourteenth century, the tax burden was between two and four times greater than for persons dwelling in Florence.[31] Fiscal pressure developed out of military pressure. The sharpest increases in taxes on the dominion took place during the wars of the fourteenth and fifteenth centuries. After the 1430s, however, a substantial stability in the tax load was broken only by the crises of the Pazzi War (1478–80) and the Pisan rebellion (1494–1509).[32]

POLITICO-MILITARY PRIORITIES IN THE CREATION OF THE DOMINION

The Florentine example appears, therefore, as a positive combination of 'concentration of capital, concentration of the means of coercion', the two necessary instruments for the formation of the 'state' under its many historical guises, according to Charles Tilly.[33] The needed commitment of resources – 'to borrow tax, purchase, and wage war effectively without creating bulky, durable national administrations'[34] – was happily commensurate with the relatively small scale of Florence's territory and the economic and demographic weakness of her vanquished regional adversaries. The expansion of Florence was contained with a sub-regional area. When her dominion was at its greatest extent in the second half of the Quattrocento, it still comprised only 12,000 km², an area slightly more than triple the size of the historical contado (about 3900 km² in 1300).

From its original defensive aims, the Florentine war effort was transformed by Visconti aggression into an offensive campaign. The control of castles and fortresses and the control of commercial and military highways became urgent priorities. These priorities in turn

---

[31] M. B. Becker, 'Le trasformazioni della finanza e l'emergere dello stato territoriale a Firenze nel Trecento', in Chittolini (ed.), *La crisi degli ordinamenti comunali*, pp. 178ff.; Epstein, 'Stato territoriale ed economia regionale nella Toscana del Quattrocento', pp. 875–6.

[32] Molho, 'The State and Public Finance', pp. 118ff.

[33] C. Tilly, *Coercion, Capital and European States, AD 990–1992*, rev. edn (Oxford, 1992).

[34] Tilly, *Coercion*, p. 151.

established the approach that the Florentines adopted towards subject areas. As Francesco Guicciardini once noted, Florence first tried to preserve political and military control in her dominion.[35] It was only afterwards that she proceeded to the creation of administrative structures.[36]

TERRITORIAL POLICY IN THE ALBIZZI AND MEDICI PERIODS

Historians have generally seen the late fourteenth and early fifteenth centuries as a period in which Florence constructed more stable and centralised administrative apparatuses for the territory; the later fifteenth century, by way of contrast, is often read as a period that saw the flourishing of 'informal' or 'private' practices of control, such as clientelism and patrimonialism.[37]

There is no doubt that the Albizzi regime was characterised by a decided hegemonic will, and, above all, by a shared understanding of the irreversible need to establish a territory-wide approach to the problems of the dominion.[38] Such an understanding can be seen in political debates, which reveal how these profound transformations were the subject of a sharp contest within the ruling class. The archival

---

[35] See, for example, Francesco Guicciardini, *Dialogo del reggimento di Firenze*, ed. G. M. Anselmi and C. Varotti (Turin, 1994), pp. 54ff., 95ff.

[36] See Zorzi, 'Lo Stato territoriale fiorentino'; and Zorzi, 'Ordine pubblico e amministrazione della giustizia nelle formazioni politiche toscane tra Tre e Quattrocento', in *Italia 1350–1450: tra crisi, trasformazione, sviluppo* (Pistoia, 1993), pp. 419–74.

[37] See, for example, Becker, *Florence in Transition*; Brucker, *Civic World*; N. Rubinstein, *The Government of Florence under the Medici (1434 to 1494)*, 2nd edn (Oxford, 1997); A. Molho, 'Cosimo de' Medici. *Pater patriae* or *padrino?*', *Stanford Italian Review*, 1 (1979), pp. 5–33; Molho, 'Patronage and the State in Early Modern Italy', in A. Mączak (ed.), *Klientelsysteme im Europa der Frühen Neuzeit* (Munich, 1988), pp. 233–42; D. V. Kent, *The Rise of the Medici: Faction in Florence, 1426–1434* (Oxford, 1978); Kent, 'The Dynamic of Power in Cosimo de' Medici's Florence', in F. W. Kent and P. Simons (eds.), *Patronage, Art, and Society in Renaissance Italy* (Canberra, 1987), pp. 63–77; D. V. Kent and F. W. Kent, *Neighbours and Neighbourhood in Renaissance Florence: The District of the Red Lion in the Fifteenth Century* (Locust Valley, 1982); F. W. Kent, 'Il ceto dirigente fiorentino e i vincoli di vicinanza nel Quattrocento', in *I ceti dirigenti nella Toscana del Quattrocento* (Florence, 1987), pp. 63–78; and R. Fubini, 'Dalla rappresentanza sociale alla rappresentanza politica: alcune osservazioni sull'evoluzione politico-costituzionale di Firenze nel Rinascimento', *Rivista storica italiana*, 102 (1990), pp. 279–301.

[38] Cf. R. Fubini, 'Classe dirigente ed esercizio della diplomazia nella Firenze quattrocentesca', in *I ceti dirigenti nella Toscana del Quattrocento*, pp. 117–89; and Fubini, 'La rivendicazione di Firenze della sovranità statale e il contributo delle "Historiae" di Leonardo Bruni', in P. Viti (ed.), *Leonardo Bruni cancelliere della Repubblica di Firenze* (Florence, 1990), pp. 29–62.

series of Florentine *Consulte e pratiche* shows in fact the existence of groups that opposed the prevailing territorial policy. On the one hand, there was the party of the Albizzeschi decidedly in favour of an aggressive territorial approach, while on the other hand there was an opposition (later solidified as the Medici party) that feared the economic and political costs of an expansionism that pushed too far.[39] Military competition was understood as a call to duty, as can be seen in the often-studied texts of 'civic humanism'. Anti-Visconti propaganda was rooted in the reality of Florentine regional superiority.[40]

In step with this ideological elaboration, the Florentine ruling elite took unprecedented measures in responding to the Visconti threat. It is well known by now that the Albizzeschi regime changed the dominion's jurisdictional layout and created a new series of territorial offices.[41] It is also important to remember that the idea to establish a new statute, valid and normative for the entire territory, was behind the 1408–9 project for reforming the Florentine statutes.[42] And there was also a plan (modelled after political expansion in the Lucchese, Pisan and Volterran dioceses) to create an ecclesiastical province in Tuscany that would correspond with the new territorial reality: Florence would be raised to the level of archdiocese, while the subject towns (with the exception of the archdiocese of Pisa) would become suffragan seats.[43] The resistance these plans encountered, and their only partial realisation, stand as testimony to their strongly innovative character.

Similarly, the homogeneous framework for the new territorial policy

---

[39] Cf. Brucker, *Civic World*, pp. 436ff.; E. Conti (ed.), *Le 'consulte' e 'pratiche' della Repubblica fiorentina nel Quattrocento*, I, *1401* (Florence and Pisa, 1981); and R. Ninci (ed.), *Le Consulte e Pratiche della Repubblica fiorentina (1404)* (Rome, 1991).

[40] H. Baron, *The Crisis of the Early Italian Renaissance*, rev. edn (Princeton, 1966). See now J. Hankins, 'The Baron thesis after forty years and some recent studies of Leonardo Bruni', *Journal of the History of Ideas*, 56 (1995), pp. 309–38; and R. Witt, 'The *Crisis* after Forty Years', *American Historical Review*, 101 (1996), pp. 110–18.

[41] Cf. L. Martines, *Lawyers and Statecraft in Renaissance Florence* (Princeton, 1968), pp. 220–45; and A. Zorzi, 'Giusdicenti e operatori di giustizia nello Stato territoriale fiorentino del XV secolo', *Ricerche storiche*, 19 (1989), pp. 517–52.

[42] Chittolini, 'Ricerche sull'ordinamento territoriale del dominio fiorentino', pp. 294–5; Fubini, 'La rivendicazione di Firenze della sovranità statale', pp. 47–57; Fubini, 'Dalla rappresentanza sociale alla rappresentanza politica', pp. 290–1; E. Fasano Guarini, 'Gli statuti delle città soggette a Firenze tra '400 e '500: riforme locali e interventi centrali', in G. Chittolini and D. Willoweit (eds.), *Statuti città territori in Italia e Germania tra medioevo ed età moderna* (Bologna, 1991), pp. 86–95.

[43] Cf. *Statuti città territori* in G. Chittolini, 'Progetti di riordinamento ecclesiastico della Toscana agli inizi del Quattrocento', in S. Bertelli (ed.), *Forme e tecniche del potere nella città (secoli XIV–XVII)* (Perugia, 1980), pp. 275–96; and R. Bizzocchi, *Chiesa e potere nella Toscana del Quattrocento* (Bologna, 1987), pp. 72–74.

can be seen at work in other spheres of government policy in this period. With expansionism having reached its peak, in the 1420s there took place a movement to measure and take charge of the resources of the dominion. In 1421, the Five of the Contado completed a survey of the financial well-being of all of the communities of the dominion.[44] In 1426, the Sea Consuls undertook to study the manufacturing industries of the dominion with the aim of encouraging specialised local production and defending the privileged position of Florentine industry.[45] Beginning the following year, in 1427, the Florentine catasto, a uniform system for declaring landed wealth, was extended to the dominion.[46] When, in 1429, the Defenders of the Laws were asked to draw up a kind of political registry to make clear the criteria for eligibility to offices, they were instructed to begin with the territorial offices, which were considered *di utile* or 'well-paid', and therefore most desirable.[47]

The restructuring of Florentine institutions in the Albizzi period also extended to the redaction and conservation of public documents. It was in these years that the government established the basic framework that still survives in the present-day organisation of the Florentine State Archive.[48] Thus, the collection of privileges and rights known as the *Capitoli* dates from the 1380s.[49] In successive years, the approval of new statutes promoted by Florence in all of her subject jurisdictions became the basis for an archive consisting of copies of these statutes.[50] The office of the *Tratte* was separated from the archive of the *Riformagioni* between 1374 and 1378, while Coluccio Salutati was chancellor; and from the beginning of the 1380s registers for the election of territorial officers were kept separate from those for other offices.[51] In the same way, beginning in the 1380s, the directors (*provveditori e massai*) of the

---

[44] See ASF, Misc. rep., 102.

[45] F. Franceschi, 'Intervento del potere centrale e ruolo delle Arti nel governo dell'economia fiorentina del Trecento e del primo Quattrocento. Linee generali', *Archivio storico italiano*, 151 (1993), pp. 902ff.

[46] See Herlihy and Klapisch-Zuber, *Les Toscans et leurs familles*, pp. 34ff.; E. Conti, *L'imposta diretta a Firenze nel Quattrocento (1427–1494)* (Rome, 1984), pp. 138ff.; and Giuseppe Petralia in Chapter 4 of this volume.

[47] Cf. A. Zorzi, 'The Florentines and Their Public Offices in the Early Fifteenth Century: Competition, Abuses of Power, and Unlawful Acts', in E. Muir and G. Ruggiero (eds.), *History from Crime*, (Baltimore, 1994), pp.113–15.

[48] See D. Marzi, *La cancelleria della Repubblica fiorentina* (Rocca San Casciano, 1910), pp. 106ff., 153ff.; and C. Guasti (ed.) *I Capitoli del comune di Firenze: inventario e regesto*, I (Florence, 1866), pp. xviii–xix.

[49] See ASF, Capitoli. Compare also Guasti (ed.) *I Capitoli*, I, p. xviii.

[50] ASF, SCAS. Compare also Fasano Guarini, 'Gli statuti delle città soggette a Firenze tra '400 e '500', pp. 70ff.

[51] Cf. P. Viti and R. M. Zaccaria (eds.), *Archivio delle Tratte* (Rome, 1989), pp. 89–91.

Camera del comune followed exactingly detailed accounting methods in inscribing government's revenues and expenses in a swelling series of ledgers.[52]

Vice versa, there is no doubt that the innovations of the Albizzi period were not followed with the same intensity under the subsequent Medici regime. Still, it needs to be understood that in this later period the territorial dimension of Florentine government was no longer a novelty but a political given. Diminished political and military competition resulted in attitudes quite different from those that characterised the ideological struggle against the Visconti. A writer like Antonio Ivani, the humanist chancellor of Volterra and Pistoia, could thus abandon the defence of municipal *libertates* in the tradition of medieval *dictatores* and justify instead the decline of communal autonomies, now become irrelevant in a system of territorial states.[53]

Beginning with the 1440s, lessened military risk meant that it was no longer so important to control and measure the economic and fiscal resources of the dominion. Practices for the redaction and preservation of official documents, from fiscal records to judicial ones (which became more elliptical), became less exacting, while correspondence – *carteggi* between individuals, and between individuals and magistracies – grew at an enormous rate.[54]

The enduring balance of power of the Italian states had the effect of blocking further territorial expansion, save in marginal areas and in modest dimensions.[55] Consequently, in the Medici period, there was no restructuring of territorial offices as occurred in the Albizzi period. The blueprint that was produced in the first decades of the fifteenth century resulted in institutions that, as scholars have shown, remained mostly unchanged down to the reforms of the eighteenth century. The few significant modifications that did occur took place in the Grand Ducal period.[56]

---

52 Molho, 'The State and Public Finance', pp. 110ff.
53 See R. Fubini, 'Antonio Ivani da Sarzana: un teorizzatore del declino delle autonomie comunali', in Fubini, *Italia quattrocentesca*, pp. 136–82.
54 See Molho, 'The State and Public Finance', p. 120; A. Zorzi, *L'amministrazione della giustizia penale nella Repubblica fiorentina: aspetti e problemi* (Florence, 1988), pp. 87ff.; Zorzi, 'The Judicial System in Florence in the Fourteenth and Fifteenth Centuries', in T. Dean and K. J. P. Lowe (eds.), *Crime, Society and the Law in Renaissance Italy* (Cambridge, 1994), pp. 47–8, 55–6; V. Arrighi and F. Klein, 'Segretari e archivi segreti in età laurenziana', in Fubini (ed.), *La Toscana al tempo di Lorenzo il Magnifico*, III, pp. 1381–95; and Fubini, *Italia quattrocentesca*, pp. 19–21.
55 Cf. Chittolini, 'Ricerche sull'ordinamento territoriale del dominio fiorentino', pp. 321–4; and Fubini, *Italia quattrocentesca*, pp. 185ff.
56 Cf. E. Fasano Guarini, *Lo Stato mediceo di Cosimo I* (Florence, 1973).

As the threat to Florence of territorial loss diminished, subject cities
found the manoeuvring room to recover some of their lost prerogatives
with respect to their own contadi.[57] And the changed climate permitted
the Medici regime to attempt what the Albizzi leaders had never
allowed themselves, namely, to acquire the consent of the notable
classes of the subject towns. Thus developed a policy that relied in large
part on the mediation of the clients of Florentine leaders, and not only
of Florentines who were Mediceans. Clientelism became notable in the
control of ecclesiastical benefices, selection for public office, assistance
in fiscal and judicial matters, and so forth.[58] Conversely, experience
with effective political management under the Albizzi meant that the
Medici were able skilfully to deploy extraordinary constitutional instruments, such as balìe and plenipotentiary commissions, that conferred
certain advantages in time of war, but were increasingly difficult to
justify in the new political climate.[59]

INTERPRETING THE FLORENTINE TERRITORIAL STATE

That there were differences between the territorial policies of the
Albizzi and Medici regimes is unquestionable. The impression of
centralisation and rationalisation that has been seen in the first period
has led some historians to speak of a true and proper phase of 'state
building',[60] while the Medicean propensity to drain communal institutions of their substance and stuff them with Medici partisans has been
interpreted as a renewed contamination of private and public interests
and as political empire-building.[61]

[57] Chittolini, 'Ricerche sull'ordinamento territoriale del dominio fiorentino',
pp. 313–18.
[58] See W. J. Connell, 'Clientelismo e Stato territoriale. Il potere fiorentino a Pistoia nel
XV secolo', Società e storia, 14 (1991), pp. 523–43; Connell, 'Changing Patterns of
Medicean Patronage. The Florentine Dominion during the Fifteenth Century', in
G. C. Garfagnini (ed.), Lorenzo il Magnifico e il suo mondo (Florence, 1994),
pp. 87–107; P. Salvadori, 'Rapporti personali, rapporti di potere nella corrispondenza di Lorenzo dei Medici', in Garfagnini (ed.), Lorenzo il Magnifico e il suo tempo
(Florence, 1992), pp. 19–35.
[59] On the Medicean balìe, see Fubini, 'Classe dirigente', pp. 166ff.; Fubini, 'Dalla
rappresentanza sociale alla rappresentanza politica', pp. 289ff.; Rubinstein, The
Government of Florence, passim.
[60] See, for example, Brucker, Civic World, pp. 6ff; and, generally, Fubini, Italia
quattrocentesca, pp. 19–37.
[61] See, for example, Kent, The Rise of the Medici; or F. W. Kent, 'Ties of Neighborhood
and Patronage', in Kent and Simons (eds.), Patronage, Art, and Society, pp. 79–98;
Molho, 'Cosimo de' Medici'; and Alison Brown, 'Public and Private Interest:
Lorenzo, the Monte and the Seventeen Reformers', in G. C. Garfagnini (ed.),
Lorenzo de' Medici: studi (Florence, 1992), pp. 103–65.

Of course, this scenario is already sufficient to invalidate any linear or evolutionary explanation of the process of state construction. Precisely because the Renaissance (in accordance with the ever latent Burckhardtian paradigm) is usually seen as the crucible in which 'Western civilisation' was forged,[62] one would have to speak, if at all, of the Medicean period of these Florentine developments as a phase of regression.

But that is not the point. Greater doubts arise from the attempt to measure degrees of state formation according to a yardstick that consists of such modern concepts as 'centralisation', 'rationalisation', and so forth. The cognitive value of these terms seems in fact to be in a state of growing crisis, above all because they impose categorical dichotomies – centralism/pluralism, public/private, centralisation/resistance – on historical situations that were more fluid and polyvalent than these categories allow.[63] Thus, there is a growing understanding of the need to discount 'the passive acceptance of the dualistic paradigms that express the relation between local realities and the external world of institutions and centralised power'.[64]

If, instead, the accent is placed on the relation between ends pursued (which is to say, political and military priorities) and instruments at hand (economic resources and the juridico-institutional tools that can be mobilised), the transition from the Albizzi phase to the Medici phase appears, in fact, to resolve itself in a substantial continuity of governmental practices. Apart from the apparent loosening of control over the *publicum* and the greater informality of their practices, the Medici in fact followed a policy for preserving the dominion, rather than for structuring an administrative state able to (or intended to) counterbalance putative centrifugal tendencies in the pluralism of local territorial experiences. It was a policy, in fact, that had also belonged to the regime that, in the late fourteenth and early fifteenth centuries, had 'constructed' the dominion.

---

[62] See now A. Molho, 'The Italian Renaissance, made in U.S.A.', in Molho and G. Wood (eds.), *Imagined Histories: American Historians Interpret the Past* (Princeton, 1998), pp. 263–94.

[63] On this point, see the considerations of G. Chittolini, 'The "Private", the "Public", and the State', in Kirshner (ed.), *Origins*, pp. 34–61; and L. Mannori, 'Genesi dello Stato e storia giuridica (a proposito di *Origini dello Stato: processi di formazione statale in Italia fra Medioevo ed età moderna)*', *Quaderni fiorentini per la storia del pensiero giuridico moderno*, 24 (1995), pp. 485–505.

[64] A. Torre, 'Società locale e società regionale: complementarità o interdipendenza?', *Società e storia*, 17 (1995), pp. 113–24. See also O. Raggio, 'Visto dalla periferia. Formazioni politiche di antico regime e Stato moderno', in M. Aymard (ed.), *Storia d'Europa*, III, *L'Età moderna* (Turin, 1994), pp. 507ff.

If there is, therefore, an interpretative direction to be given to the plurisecular process of Florentine state formation in the territory, it seems to me that this can be found with the realisation that for Florence the goal was never a matter of 'administering a state', but rather of 'governing a dominion'.

In other terms, the basic policy of the Florentine ruling class seems to have been not so much to achieve a unitary administrative entity, in which so-called 'public' functions served to advance state integration (through the growth of fiscal resources, standing armies, institutional specialisation both in the capital and provinces, and the training of skilled functionaries), but rather to 'rule' politically a territorially variegated dominion in which the administrative and judicial apparatus and the practices of government above all served to preserve the *status quo*. In fact, this involves returning to the judgments that contemporaries and the first historians of the republic – Machiavelli and Guicciardini – passed on the priorities of territorial policy in the dominion.[65] This is especially evident in analysing the jurisdictional regime, the role of territorial officers and the administration of justice.

THE JURISDICTIONAL ORDER

The jurisdictional order conferred on the dominion did not in fact evidence a unitary framework. This was true with respect both to normative documentation, where one finds the above-mentioned fragmentation of the *Capitoli* and the statutes, and also to questions of juridical representation, where doctrine had a hard time assuming a position of homogeneity.[66] The dominion created itself through a series of progressive aggregations and the result was 'a mosaic of smaller arrangements held together by a thick web of negotiated links'.[67] However homogeneous it may have appeared on the institutional level, the single territorial components (cities, towns and rural communes) belonged to it only in consequence of the individual agreements (*capitolazioni*) through which they agreed to submit to Florence. The dominion was therefore deprived of a unitary constitution. The

---

[65] See, for suggestions on this point, E. Fasano Guarini, 'Machiavelli and the crisis of the Italian republics', in G. Bock, Q. Skinner and M. Viroli (eds.), *Machiavelli and Republicanism* (Cambridge, 1990), pp. 19–40; G. Silvano, 'Dal centro alla periferia. Niccolò Machiavelli tra stato cittadino e stato territoriale', *Archivio storico italiano*, 150 (1992), pp. 1105–41; and O. Cavallar, *Francesco Guicciardini giurista: i 'Ricordi degli onorari'* (Milan, 1991), pp. 119–136.

[66] See L. Mannori, *Il Sovrano tutore: pluralismo istituzionale e accentramento amministrativo nel principato dei Medici (secc. XVI–XVIII)* (Milan, 1994).

[67] Mannori, *Il Sovrano tutore*, p. 21.

arrangement would best be characterised as a coherent grouping of bilateral accords between Florence and a large number of single entities. Hence the dominion had a character that was something like a 'league' or 'federation' of communities which found in Florence their only common reference point.[68]

The coherence of the system was derived especially from the elaboration of doctrinal and ideological principles. Ever since Bartolus' distinction between iurisdictio and administratio, there were proposals to legitimise the differing degrees of the lawgiving capability (ius statuendi) of subject communities. Legal doctrine, moreover, recognised that these communities retained a certain libertas, above all to preserve an autonomous corpus of laws.[69] There were at the same time references to the tradition of Justinian concerning the 'origin of law' (origo iuris) in the proemium to the proposed Florentine statutes of 1409, justifying the establishment of legal norms for the dominion.[70] The diffusion of the Bartolan theories supporting the subjugation of 'cities and castles' to stronger powers, and the thesis that conferred iurisdictio on 'cities that recognised no higher power' (civitates superiorem non recognoscens), permitted jurists such as Pietro d'Ancarano, Angelo degli Ubaldi and Niccolò Tedeschi to see Florence as possessing the 'laws of the empire' (iura imperii) and 'supreme jurisdiction', as a consequence of the vicariate that the Florentine priors made sure was confirmed by the Holy Roman Emperors in 1355, 1369 and 1401.[71]

But the legitimation of Florentine territorial sovereignty was accompanied by recognition of the jurisdictional autonomies of the subject communities. The policy of subtracting contadi from their cities was not in fact undertaken with the aim of creating a jurisdictionally homogeneous order, but rather to make every part of the territory directly dependent politically on Florence. It is in this light that we need to see the encouragement given local communities by the Albizzi regime to redact local laws and statutes. This should not be seen simply as the creation of a new balance of power that was opposed to the city,[72] or as

---

68 Mannori, Il Sovrano tutore, pp. 23ff.
69 Mannori, Il Sovrano tutore, pp. 114ff.; and M. Montorzi, Giustizia in Contado: studi sull'esercizio della giurisdizione nel territorio pontederese e pisano in età moderna (Pisa, 1997), pp. 18–24.
70 ASF, Stat. com., 23, 'Codex membranaceus archetypus statutorum populi florentini, ex publica recensione [anni] MCCCC[VIII]', 1r, rub. 'De origine iuris'.
71 See M. Ascheri, 'I giuristi e Firenze, "mater omnis eloquentiae": qualche spunto dal Tre al Quattrocento', in Ascheri, Diritto medievale e moderno: problemi del processo, della cultura e delle fonti giuridiche (Rimini, 1991), pp. 139–45.
72 Chittolini, 'Ricerche sull'ordinamento territoriale del dominio fiorentino', pp. 303–9.

an instance of acculturation to urban norms by rural communities,[73] but rather as an instrument of legitimation. Treaties of submission and statute revisions promoted and approved by the ruling city constituted the result of a bilateral negotiation that, however asymmetrical, favoured the reciprocal recognition of the Florentine ruling class and local political interlocutors. Hence, the development of a polycentric normative system, mediated by bilateral connections: a system made up of normative nodes, each strongly restructured by the centre and tied to it directly, factors which necessarily conferred on the dominion a low degree of integration among the subject territories.

TERRITORIAL OFFICES

Jurisdictional pluralism was not incompatible, moreover, with a homogeneous apparatus of territorial offices. The only level at which we see an appreciable degree of unitary organisation in the dominion is in the institutions created by the ruling city.

One of the peculiarities of the Florentine system, when compared with other contemporary states, consisted in creating a thick network of territorial offices firmly controlled by the ruling class of the capital city. Save for only a few isolated instances – such as at Cortona and Volterra, where the Podestà continued to be elected locally – all of the officers who served as rectors, from the greatest (such as the Captains and Podestà of the subject cities) to the smallest (such as the Podestà of rural and mountain communes), were Florentines.[74]

Seen from Florence, therefore, the dominion appeared to have a well-organised framework with a homogeneous institutional apparatus designed to impose Florentine might on the territory. In the Albizzi period, above all, the officeholding apparatus became the focus of reforms that accentuated the degree of structural uniformity. Thus, in the statutes of 1409 and 1415, 'the territory appears only to the extent that it is the subject of Florentine magistracies'.[75]

However, the apparatus still did not really serve priorities of an administrative nature. Sufficient to demonstrate this is the almost total lack of real government investment in these citizen offices. The salaries of the Florentine rectors were paid entirely by the local communities.[76]

---

[73] Fasano Guarini, 'Gli statuti delle città soggette a Firenze tra '400 e '500', pp. 75–7.

[74] See A. Zorzi, 'Giusdicenti e operatori di giustizia'; Zorzi, 'Gli ufficiali territoriali dello Stato fiorentino (secc. XIV–XV)', in Il corpo degli officiali negli stati italiani del Quattrocento, Annali della Scuola Normale Superiore di Pisa, ser. iv, Quaderni, 1 (Pisa, 1997), pp. 191–212.

[75] Fasano Guarini, 'Gli statuti delle città soggette a Firenze tra '400 e '500', p. 90.

[76] Zorzi, 'Giusdicenti e operatori di giustizia', pp. 519–20.

And it is no accident that these offices were seen by Florentines as 'those by which our citizens get ahead, since they are salaried and prized',[77] as Goro Dati wrote. It was also for this reason that the retinues (*famiglie*) that accompanied the rectors in office were kept small.

Careful analysis reveals that these offices were really of a political nature. In large part, this was a consequence of a transformation of these originally judicial magistracies that occurred at the time of submission to Florence. Offices that in earlier periods had been filled by a specialised personnel recruited from an intercommunal circuit of itinerant functionaries were now filled by citizens of the ruling city who were generally ignorant of the law.[78] On the one hand, the fact that legal training was not requested corresponded to the low level of the jurisdictions they supervised. That explains, too, why many Florentine jurisconsults disdained these offices, preferring the more lucrative possibilities open to them as technical consultants in government affairs and in private legal practice.[79] On the other hand, however, this progressive 'detechnicisation' highlighted the political rather than administrative work of the territorial rectors.

It would be misleading to continue to study the role of the territorial rector as though he were an 'administrator' or a 'bureaucrat'.[80] As the wide range of his powers makes clear, the rector was principally a politician. The responsibility of the rector was centred not on a specific task, but on his ability to coordinate government matters in a large number of areas, including taxation, defence, the judiciary, maintaining peace, and public works. In certain periods, and in certain contexts, certain tasks became more important than others. In the phase of territorial expansion, for example, the rector's role in fiscal matters was especially important. This is clear from certain registers of the *Camera del comune* of Florence which show that territorial officers were asked to participate directly in the collection of taxes and to make amends for the inadequacies of the other local communities.[81]

It has been said in more than one context that territorial officers acted as mediators who were trusted both by Florence and by local communities. In addition to mediating relations between the ruling city and her subjects, they also mediated conflicts within subject communities. What

---

[77] Goro Dati, *L'Istoria di Firenze dal 1380 al 1405*, ed. L. Pratesi (Norcia, 1904), p. 158: 'sono quelli di che i nostri cittadini avanzano e hanno salario e premio'.

[78] Zorzi, 'Ordine pubblico e amministrazione della giustizia', pp. 459–60.

[79] Martines, *Lawyers and Statecraft*.

[80] On this point, see Zorzi, 'Gli ufficiali territoriali dello Stato fiorentino'.

[81] Becker, 'Le trasformazioni della finanza', pp. 178ff.; Zorzi, 'Ordine pubblico e amministrazione della giustizia', pp. 469–73.

is important to underline is that on both levels the goal was to set in
motion a process of reciprocal legitimation among political actors. Such
a process of legitimation was basic to the preservation of the dominion,
and it found its most evident realisation in the work of political
mediation carried out by the territorial officers.

In the mediation between Florence and these communities, a search
for interlocutors took place on two levels that were antithetical only in
appearance. Contacts took place both through institutions and through
networks of patrons and clients. In reality, both methods were
responding to the same political necessity, which was to govern the
dominion. Thus, from the first decades of the fifteenth century, when
Florentine rectors regularly collaborated with the reformers of the lists
of eligible officeholders in subject communes,[82] they were acting both
to identify local leaders as political interlocutors and also to establish a
basis for negotiation that was defined in institutional terms. In a similar
manner, whenever there were conflicts that arose between Florentine
law courts and those of the periphery, rectors could act as mediators by
resorting to their personal ties with local political interlocutors. Moreover, in many cases, Florentine officers transmitted local wishes to the
central political bodies of Florence, relying often on a sort of triangula-
tion involving their personal connections in the capital (not just the
Medici, but also the Capponi, the Rucellai, the Soderini, and so
forth).[83] Thus, many of the practices we call 'informal' or 'private', and
that we label as 'clientelism', were not really alternatives to the
institutional treatment of problems and conflicts. The overriding goal
was simply the preservation of the dominion.

ADMINISTRATION OF JUSTICE

An interpretative scheme that has long prevailed in studies of state
building has seen the building of a judicial apparatus as a turning point
in the territorial affirmation of state sovereignty.[84] But here, too, it is
difficult to accept a linear, evolutionary view of the progressive growth
of public functions. On the contrary, the administration of justice in

---

[82] Fasano Guarini, 'Gli statuti delle città soggette a Firenze tra '400 e '500', pp. 99ff.

[83] Connell, 'Changing Patterns of Medicean patronage'; and Salvadori, 'Rapporti
personali, rapporti di potere'.

[84] Compare, for a general review, R. Lévy and X. Rousseaux, 'Etats, justice pénale et
histoire. Bilan et perspectives', Droit et société, 20 (1992), pp. 249–79; for Italy,
A. Zorzi, 'La justice pénale dans les Etats italiennes (communes et principautés
territoriales) du XIIIe au XVIe siècle', in X. Rousseaux and R. Lévy (eds.), Le pénale
dans tous ses états: justice, états et sociétés en Europe (XIIe–XXe siècles) (Brussels, 1997),
pp. 47–63.

Florentine territory should perhaps be seen not so much as a function of the construction of the state, but as a kind of open political field in which extra-judicial practices for the resolution of conflicts were commonly accepted.[85] Unlike Venice, where territorial control was established in an enduring way through the efficient administration of justice,[86] Florence conferred only a marginal role on judicial administration in forming its territorial dominion, privileging instead other methods for resolving conflict.

Policy for governing the Florentine dominion territory was dictated largely by three concerns: the pacification of local conflicts, mediation among various local powers, and the maintenance of control against external threats. Intervention by the ruling city usually involved a mixture of coercion and mediation. Central to this policy was the recognition of local political practices that were traditionally expressed through conflict between factions. Florence accepted the practices of the feud as 'idiomatic' in her subject territories, with the result that she recognised the leaders of rival factions as political actors, using them to advance her policy of reciprocal legitimation between local and central powers.[87] This was a policy begun in the first phases of expansion. Already in the first decades of the fourteenth century, for example, at the time of the Duke of Athens, numerous peaces were signed publicly in Florence by local factions, for example between the 'house of the men from Pallarino' and 'the house of the men from Querceto' in Castelfiorentino; and between the clans of the Lamberti and the degli Ardovini of Signa, and between the Baldanzi and the Ghiandoni of Montelupo.[88]

Central power was so closely bound with the structures of local political conflict that attempts to ignore established patterns provoked severe reactions. Thus, the Medici policy in the fifteenth century of intentionally ignoring the Pistoiese rivalry between the Cancellieri and Panciatichi factions, whether by favouring new client networks or by

[85] See also A. Zorzi, 'Conflits et pratiques infrajudiciaires dans les formations politiques italiennes du XIIIe au XVe siècle', in B. Garnot (ed.), L'infrajudiciaire du Moyen Age à l'époque contemporaine (Dijon, 1996), pp. 19–36.

[86] See G. Cozzi (ed.), Stato società e giustizia nella Repubblica Veneta (sec. XV–XVIII) 2 vols., (Rome, 1980–85); A. Viggiano, Fra governanti e governati: legittimità del potere e esercizio dell'autorità sovrana nello stato veneto della prima età moderna (Treviso, 1993).

[87] Cf. also A. Zorzi, ' "Ius erat in armis". Faide e conflitti tra pratiche sociali e pratiche di governo', in G. Chittolini, A. Molho and P. Schiera (eds.), Origini dello Stato: processi di formazione statale in Italia fra medioevo ed età moderna (Bologna, 1994), pp. 623–6. About the 'idiomatic' value of feuding, see also Raggio, 'Visto dalla periferia', pp. 515ff.; and A. Torre, 'Feuding, Factions, and Parties: The Redefinition of Politics in the Imperial Fiefs of Langhe in the Seventeenth and Eighteenth Centuries', in E. Muir and G. Ruggiero (eds.), History from Crime (Baltimore, 1994), pp. 135–69.

[88] ASF, Bal., 1, 45v–46v, 52r–53v, 55r, 56r–v, 73r–74r.

offering themselves (as did Lorenzo) as supreme mediators, unleashed a local conflict that targeted Lorenzo's own person as well as his favourites. When the rivalry re-emerged in the traditional guise of a feud after the fall of the Medici regime, the Florentine regime returned to the more traditional, faction-based approach.[89]

Episodes such as this demonstrate the strong interaction between local practices and the policies of the ruling city. It was here that territorial institutions took on real shape. The principle of 'ruling with factions' was not the same as a policy of 'divide and conquer'. It represented instead a strategic choice to base Florentine rule on the existing political and social practices.

The process of interaction between extra-judicial practices and government actions was mediated above all by the territorial officers – peacemakers, mediators between factions, negotiators among the various levels of territorial power. It was owing to their ability to mediate between local wishes and central prerogatives that the dominion was preserved. From the mid-Trecento they received explicit mandates from the Florentine chancery to follow a policy of pacification in subject areas.[90] Direct evidence can be found in the record-books of certain Florentine officers, such as Francesco di Tommaso di Giovanni, who, while Captain at Cortona in 1444, wrote that he had persuaded many families and individuals 'to agree and make peace among themselves'.[91] On the other hand, it was precisely in this area that the ability of the officer to win authority and reputation was tested. It was here that the Florentine could acquire 'honour' – a quality that depended not on administrative expertise but on winning the approval of local notables and on being able to understand the needs of the community.[92] Florentine control depended on the interaction between extra-judicial practices and government policy: consensus, more than coercion, gave authority to Florentine rule.

With the establishment of the dominion, the administration of justice in the territory saw a strong discontinuity with respect to earlier periods of communal autonomy. The administration of justice by professional

---

[89] See Connell, 'Clientelismo e Stato territoriale'; Connell, ' "I fautori delle parti". Citizen Interest and the Treatment of a Subject Town, c. 1500', in C. Lamioni (ed.), *Istituzioni e società in Toscana nell'età moderna*, 2 vols. (Rome, 1994), I, pp. 118–47; and M. Dedola, ' "Tener Pistoia con le parti". Governo fiorentino e fazioni pistoiesi all'inizio del '500', *Ricerche storiche*, 22 (1992), pp. 239–59.

[90] Marzi, *La cancelleria della Repubblica fiorentina*, pp. 623ff.

[91] ASF, CS, II, 16bis, 'Ricordanze di Francesco di Tommaso di Giovanni', 2v–3r.

[92] On this point, see also G. Chittolini, 'L'onore dell'officiale', *Quaderni milanesi*, 17–18 (1989), pp. 3–53.

judges in established and locally recognised courts was not, in fact, a Florentine priority. Here we see clearly a conflict of interest, between Florentine efforts to preserve the dominion and local desires to be protected by the traditional judicial modes of the communal period.

A change in the character of Florentine magistracies, which became political rather than judicial bodies, has already been mentioned. This perhaps was the most evident sign of the extent to which Florentines neglected judicial administration when it was not obviously connected with public safety or with the material interests (usually economic) of Florentine citizens. Not even in civil matters did judicial mechanisms satisfy local needs. Unlike other Italian states – for example in the Venetian territory, where certain subject cities maintained their own tribunals (e.g., the *consolati* of Verona, analogous offices in Brescia, and the *giudici pedanei* of Padua)[93] – Florence did not allow her subject cities to maintain locally controlled tribunals.

Ever smaller was the number of legal professionals at work in the dominion. The jurisdiction of the Podestà of the subject cities was drastically reduced to include only the few miles of countryside immediately outside the walls. When the number of territorial offices was at its peak, at the beginning of the 1420s, the number of legally trained judges assisting Florentine governors was only eighteen, and these were situated only in the larger subject centres. Vicarial jurisdictions, made up mostly of rural areas carved out of the contadi of subject cities, were generally governed by a Florentine rector who was accompanied by a notary but not a lawyer.[94]

There were numerous complaints about the quality of the judicial officers sent out by Florence, and these increased during the Medicean period, when there were fewer foreign threats and the regime was more eager to pursue a policy of consensus in the dominion. Certain cities – Pisa, Arezzo, Pistoia, but also towns like Cortona, Montepulciano and Borgo San Sepolcro – succeeded in obtaining that their Florentine rectors should be accompanied not just by persons generically 'knowledgeable in the law' (*iurisperiti*), but rather by persons who had obtained a specific licence or doctorate in civil law. Thus, these subject centres succeeded in obtaining for themselves a level of legal professionalism that was in some ways comparable with what they had enjoyed in the communal age.[95]

[93] Compare G. Cozzi, *Repubblica di Venezia e Stati italiani: politica e giustizia dal secolo XVI al secolo XVIII* (Turin, 1982), pp. 280, 285.

[94] See Zorzi, 'Giusdicenti e operatori di giustizia', pp. 544–5.

[95] Zorzi, 'Lo Stato territoriale fiorentino', pp. 809–10.

CONCLUSIONS

That which we might call the 'material constitution' of the dominion
can be distinguished in three characteristic Florentine policies:

1 reciprocal legitimation of the ruling and subject communities, as
   evidenced in the individuation of local interlocutors and the work of
   mediation undertaken by territorial officers;
2 recognition of local political practices (bipartite regimes, factionalism
   as a local idiom), and their influence on the policies of the ruling city
   (including reciprocal legitimation and the need to preserve the
   dominion);
3 negotiation among the different territorial power centres (resulting in
   submission pacts, treaties, a proliferation of statutes, and specific
   negotiations on questions of taxation, public safety and military
   defence).

The plurality of asymmetrical relationships gave shape to a politico-
territorial system in which a mosaic of unintegrated clusters was
arranged about Florence as a central pole, each defined by separate
autonomies and privileges. It was a system in which political power was
exercised by powers that were diffused throughout the territory.
   The 'federal' order that structured most of these territorial arrangements was not the product of resistance to Florence. Rather it was the
result of a conscious political decision of the ruling city, made in full
knowledge of the relationships of economic resources, legal and
institutional mechanisms and political priorities. The separation of the
contadi from the subject cities, the redrawing of territorial boundaries,
the creation of a network of rectors, show both the intensity with
which the regime was able to innovate, and the lack of resistance on the
part of local communities.
   In other words, the pluralism that has been assumed as a characteristic
of the states of the Renaissance was not the result of local resistance to
centralisation,[96] but rather the coherent outcome of a policy designed
to preserve political superiority under the particular conditions we have
described. The oft-mentioned absence of a 'coherent state model' was
not the outcome of some putative failure in the process of constructing
an integrated and unitary regime. Florence aimed to create not a 'state

---

[96] On this point, see M. Berengo, 'Il Cinquecento', in *La storiografia italiana negli ultimi
venti anni* (Milan, 1970), pp. 483–518; and G. Chittolini, 'Stati padani, "Stato del
Rinascimento": problemi di ricerca', in G. Tocci (ed.), *Persistenze feudali e autonomie
comunitative in stati padani fra cinque e settecento* (Bologna, 1988), pp. 9–29.

of offices'[97] and public functions, but rather an ensemble of institutions
and practices that would permit it to maintain its territorial superiority.

The magnetic force that Florence had exerted over Tuscany since the
thirteenth century appears to have been both a reason for and the
consequence of a policy of 'dominion' rather than 'integration'.[98] The
Florentine choice was based on a centuries-old tradition that began in
the communal period, in the 'prehistory' of the formation of the
territorial state. For, in effect, the Florentine dominion was not so much
a 'state', but rather a 'great contado'.

---

[97] As in the pattern outlined by F. Chabod, 'Y a-t-il un état de la Renaissance?', in
Chabod, *Scritti sul Rinascimento* (Turin, 1967), pp. 605–23.

[98] E. Fasano Guarini, 'Center and Periphery', in Kirshner (ed.), *Origins*, p. 94, referring
to the work of S. R. Epstein.

CHAPTER 2

THE LANGUAGE OF EMPIRE

ALISON BROWN

The Florentine statutes were based on Roman law and Florence regarded itself proudly as heir to Rome. As Leonardo Bruni boasted in his *Laudatio* of Florence, 'your founder is the Roman people – the lord and conqueror of the entire world' and since their '*imperium* was equal to the entire world . . . therefore to you also, men of Florence, belongs by hereditary right *dominium* over the entire world and possession of your parental legacy'.[1] Dominion (*dominium, dominio*) was the word used by the Florentines to describe their growing state at this time; and, although Bruni tells us that no one, after seeing the city, failed to believe that Florence was capable of acquiring 'the dominion and *imperium* of the whole world', he was careful not to lay claim to *imperium* by hereditary right.[2] For Florence was still legally subject to the German emperor, and to have described its state as an empire would have been tantamount to *laesa maiestas*.[3] Since Bruni was also laying claim to

---

[1] *Laudatio Florentinae Urbis*, ed. H. Baron, *From Petrarch to Leonardo Bruni* (Chicago, 1968), p. 244: 'Vobis autem populus Romanus, orbis terrarum victor dominusque, est auctor . . . cuius imperium, terris adequatum . . . Quamobrem ad vos quoque, viri Florentini, dominium orbis terrarum iure quodam hereditario ceu paternarum rerum possessio pertinet', trans. B. G. Kohl, in Kohl and R. G. Witt (eds.), *The Earthly Republic: Italian Humanists on Government and Society* (Manchester, 1978), pp. 149–50, who misses the contrast here between Roman *imperium* and Florentine *dominium* by translating both as 'dominion'. See also Riccardo Fubini, 'La rivendicazione di Firenze della sovranità statale e il contributo delle *Historiae* di Leonardo Bruni', in P. Viti (ed.), *Leonardo Bruni cancelliere della repubblica di Firenze* (Florence, 1990), pp. 29–62, especially pp. 29, 51–2.

I am grateful to William Connell and Andrea Zorzi for inviting me to contribute a chapter to this volume. I would also like to thank Samuel Cohn for discussing *imperium* with me and for contributing references.

[2] *Laudatio*, pp. 238–9: 'Nam simul atque urbem conspicati sunt . . . illico omnium mentes animique ita mutantur ut . . . potius sufficientem autument ad totius orbis dominium imperiumque adipiscendum.' The words jurisdiction (*dictio*) and territory (*territorium*) are also used to describe the Florentine dominion.

[3] On *imperium* as the plenitude of powers of the emperor, founded in *ratio iuris communis* and on its extension via the formula *rex superiorem non recognoscens in regno suo est*

Florence's republican inheritance from Rome, he was equally careful to stress that the city was founded 'when the _imperium_ of the Roman people was at its peak' – that was before the Caesars and their successors had deprived the Romans of their liberty, hence Florence's own inherited love of freedom and hatred of tyranny.

As this last quotation suggests, _imperium_ had a double meaning, as territory and as power or rule, such as the _merum et mixtum imperium_ of Roman generals that under the principate came to consist of judicial as well as military power.[4] This, by derivation, became the source of the mixed powers exercised by citizens of communes who were sent to govern their subject cities as Vicars, Podestàs and Captains – as well as of their sovereignty over feudal lords. The formula used in 1351 was to forbid the commune and men of Prato to legislate against the 'rule, the lordship, the honour, the jurisdiction, either criminal and civil justice, or the rights which the commune of Florence has or claims for itself in the said land of Prato', whereas when purchasing Monteaguto in 1380, Florence laid claim to 'jurisdiction and sovereignty (_omne imperium_) and the power of the sword and all fidelity and the rights of fidelity'.[5] As Baldus had written, 'there is no doubt that the emperor could concede liberty to the Roman people through his privilege and rescript and also all regalian rights and jurisdiction in public matters . . . and Frederick made such a concession to the Lombards in the Peace of Constance . . . In the same way, therefore, he could confer these [rights] through acquiescence.'[6] It was in this wider sense of _de facto_ power or sovereignty

imperator, see F. Calasso, _I glossatori e la teoria della sovranità_ (Milan, 1951), pp. 124–5. On _laesa maiestas_, see M. Sbriccoli, _Crimen lesae-majestatis_, pp. 202–4; J. Chiffoleau, 'Sur le crime de majesté médiéval', in _Genèse de l'état moderne en Méditerranée_ (Rome, 1993), pp. 183–213.

4 See A. Pagden, _Lords of All the World: Ideologies of Empire in Spain, Britain and France, c.1500–c.1800_ (New Haven, 1995), pp. 14–15, defining _imperium_ as sovereignty as a third meaning of the word (pp. 16–17).

5 E.g. ASF, PR, 38, 190r (27 February 1350/1, 'Circa reductione Terre Prati'): 'nequeunt ordinare seu providere aliquid per quod dominio signorie honori iurisdictioni vel mero et mixto imperio aut iuribus que ipsum comune Florentiae habet seu sibi competunt in dicta terra Prati'; ASF, PR, 71, 97r (11 August 1380, 'Ratificatio et acceptatio et facta de emptione Montisaguti'): 'iurisdictionem et omne imperium et gladii potestatem et omnem fidelitatem et iura fidelitatis'. I owe these references to the generosity of Sam Cohn.

6 Cited by J. Canning, _The Political Thought of Baldus de Ubaldis_ (Cambridge, 1987), p. 118. Cf. G. Rezasco, _Dizionario del linguaggio italiano storico ed amministrativo_ (Florence, 1881), p. 517 (Impero, XIII): 'imperio mero o puro . . . l'impero senza mistura di giurisdizione, la facoltà di giudicare le cause criminali e far sangue'; 'misto e mero imperio . . . l'impero congiunto colla jurisdizione per costringer l'uomo a giudicati civili', citing the 1355 _Statuti del Podestà_: 'ciascuno dei detti giudici . . . possa conoscere e diffinire sopra tutto le cose che appartengono a jurisdizione o misto

that the *balìa* created in 1378 proclaimed that the two communal councils of the People and the Comune had recovered power from the Council of Fifty-Six and now enjoyed 'tota et universalis auctoritas, potestas, arbitrium et imperium populi et comunis Florentiae'.[7]

The different meanings of empire as state, and empire as power or sovereignty, created an ambiguity about the use of the word that could be exploited by the Florentines as they expanded their territory in Tuscany. Inappropriate though Rome's world empire might seem as a paradigm for Florence's modest dominion, it provided the city with a useful conceptual and administrative model for expansion. For it not only glossed the city's ambitions with republican idealism but it replaced the 'rational' language of statute and conciliar legislation with the administrative vocabulary for direct rule: arbitrary orders (*iussa*) and decrees (*decreta*) of special magistracies and tribunals instead of the provisions (*provisiones*) and rescripts (*reformationes*) of the statutes and legislative councils.[8] What follows is an attempt to trace the development of this new vocabulary for the light it throws on the consolidation of Florence's state in the fifteenth century.

The early fourteenth-century *Statutes of the Captain of the People*, like the *Statutes of the Podestà*, referred only to the 'City and District of Florence' (the Captain, like the Podestà, is described as 'Conservator Pacis Civitatis et Districtus Florentiae', not to be chosen from any city or place bordering on 'civitate vel districtu Florentiae'.[9] It was the 1409 statutes that used the word *territorium*. Distinguishing the city itself (*urbs*) from its wider juridical entity (*civitas*), the statutes claimed for the first

---

imperio'; A. Zorzi, *L'amministrazione della giustizia penale nella repubblica fiorentina: aspetti e problemi* (Florence, 1988), pp. 20–7; Zorzi, 'Lo Stato territoriale fiorentino (sec. XIV–XV). Aspetti giurisdizionali', *Società e storia*, 13 (1990): 799–825; G. Chittolini, *La formazione dello stato regionale e le istituzioni del contado* (Turin, 1979), pp. 292–352, esp. 296–300.

[7] Edited by R. C. Trexler, in *Archivio storico italiano*, 143 (1985), p. 459 (whereas the Priors and Standard Bearer of Justice enjoyed 'omnem baliam, auctoritatem, potestatem, officium, et arbitrium ac privilegium et alia quecumque', p. 444). Cf. Fubini, 'La rivendicazione', p. 45, that the councils 'intelligantur esse et sint libera et soluti'. *Impero* also means 'rule' in Rezasco's citation from ASF, SC Delib. ord., 17 (14 February 1475): 'paese ove si esercitò impero sotto qualunque forma di reggimento'; *Dizionario*, VIII, p. 517.

[8] 'Sed nostro vocabulo, tum provisiones, tum reformationes appellantur', Bartolomeo Scala, *De legibus et iudiciis dialogus*, in Scala, *Humanistic and Political Writings*, ed. A. Brown (Tempe, 1997), p. 354; cf. G. Cadoni (ed.), *Provisioni concernenti l'ordinamento della repubblica fiorentina, 1494–1512* (Rome, 1994), listing laws passed with the formula 'provisum et ordinatum fuit'.

[9] *Statuti della Repubblica Florentina*, ed. R. Caggesi, I, *Statuti del Capitano del Popolo*, 1322–5 (Florence, 1910), pp. 5, 6; cf. II, *Statuti del Podestà*, 1325 (Florence, 1921), p. 435, referring to 'mercatoribus et districtualibus Florentiae'.

time that the _urbs_ with its _territorium_ was subject to Florentine laws, and
that the whole territory was subject to 'our jurisdiction, power and
dominion'; moreover, 'the city-state (_civitas_) of Florence, by which
name we understand the whole of this territory to be included, we want
to be governed and ruled by the offices which we will appoint to in the
places themselves'.[10] This 'audacious' legislation, as Fubini described it,
was ahead of its time and was replaced only six years later with the
revised statutes of 1415. Even so, the word _imperium_ was still not used to
describe Florence's dominion. When the word appeared in the 1415
statutes, it was either to attribute Florence's growth in riches and
possessions to 'God as ruler of his empire' (_Deo auctore, eius gubernante
Imperium_), or to refer to the lands of the German emperor, from whom
'anyone in the city, county or district of Florence who presumes to buy
or lay claim in any way to any possessions or rights of the Empire or
which belong to the Empire in Tuscany or in any part of Tuscany will
lose his head and all his possessions will be laid waste'.[11]

It may have been the visit of the emperor Frederick III to Florence in
1453–4 that directly encouraged the Florentines to emulate imperial
protocol and elevate the status of their government. Not only did
ceremonial become more grandiose and 'Roman' after his visit but
Florence's head-of-state, the Standard Bearer of Justice, replaced the
foreign Podestà in processions and in political ceremonies. After the
political crisis of 1458, as a continuation of these changes, the name of
the government was changed to 'the Priors of Liberty' from 'the Priors
of the Guilds', a name that was all right 'when the city was small and it

---

10 The 1408–9 unpublished _Statuta_ (ASF, Stat. com., 23, 1r) are cited by Chittolini, _La
    formazione_, pp. 294 and 327 note 6, and Fubini, 'La rivendicazione', p. 52: 'nostre
    iurisdictioni, potestati dominioque', 'civitatem nostram Florentinam, cuius appella-
    tione ad hoc totum territorium supradictum decernimus comprehendi, per officia de
    quibus et prout in suis locis disponemus, regi volumus et gubernari'; on Bruni's
    contrasting use of _urbs_ and _civitas_, ibid., p. 51. Cf. Fubini, 'Classe dirigente ed esercizio
    della diplomazia nella Firenze quattrocentesca', in _I ceti dirigenti nella Toscana del
    Quattrocento_ (Florence, 1987), pp. 158–70, repr. in Fubini, _Quattrocento fiorentino:
    politica, diplomazia, cultura_ (Pisa, 1996), pp. 61–75.
11 _Statuta Populi et Communis Florentiae_, 3 vols. (Freiburg [but Florence], 1778–81), I,
    Proemium, p. 1: 'a cunabulis suis parvas possidentes opes et angustis finibus contenta,
    Deo auctore eius gubernante Imperium, divitiis opibus<_que_> ut plurimum aucta,
    terminos et agros suos ampliavit' (cf. the 1409 Statutes, ed. Chittolini, p. 294, 'divina
    favente gratia', on the basis of which I have added _que_ above); I, p. 302 (bk III,
    rub. 86): 'De poenis ementis ab Imperatore bona vel iura in Tuscia: Quicunque de
    civitate, comitatu vel districtu Florentiae praesumpserit emere vel quocunque alio
    titulo acquirere ab Imperatore, vel alio, bona sive iura Imperii vel quae ad Imperium
    spectare in Tuscia vel aliqua parte Tusciae capite puniatur et omnia eius bona
    devastentur. . .'.

had a small or non-existent *imperium* and little wealth'; but now that 'all these things had changed and greatly increased', its title too needed to be changed, the title of liberty being entirely consonant – we are told – with its glorious defence of liberty in a great number of wars and attacks.[12] Although the ruler did not replace Florence's patron saint, John the Baptist, as the 'sovereign' to whom subject territories did annual obeisance until the sixteenth century, under the Grand Dukes, these earlier changes in protocol must have affected the territory as much as its capital city.[13]

Though glossed with the name of 'liberty', the reality of the growing powers of the central government became clear in the aftermath of the 1458 crisis. It was the decision to introduce a new 'enlightened' tax assessment in 1458 (*a lume*, like the catasto of 1427, based on openly declared sources of wealth) that created the crisis. The Medici regime was saved only by recourse to a *parlamento* and a *balìa*, which used its special powers to modify the tax proposal. It also created a new Council of One Hundred, the *Cento*, and a short-term magistracy of Thirty Reformers of the Monte to resolve these fiscal problems.[14] It is the latter which interests us here. Although finance was the Thirty Reformers' prime concern, their wider political scope was demonstrated by the concluding decrees in the 'Liber del Posthac, ut dicitur', a small vellum volume elegantly written by their notary, Ser Nastagio Vespucci.[15] These declared that henceforth, *decretum est quod posthac, important magistracies* like the Defenders of the Laws (*Conservatori delle*

---

[12] ASF, Bal., 29, 118v–119r, 30 January 1459, cited by Fubini, 'Classe dirigente', p. 181 (repr. p. 88); Fubini, 'La rivendicazione', p. 61; and A. Brown, 'City and Citizen: Changing Perceptions in the Fifteenth and Sixteenth Centuries', in A. Molho, K. Raaflaub and J. Emlen (eds.), *City-States in Classical Antiquity and Medieval Italy*, (Stuttgart, 1991), pp. 106–7, repr. in A. Brown, *The Medici in Florence: The Exercise and Language of Power* (Florence, 1992), p. 298: 'cum civitas parva esset parvumque aut nullum ei foret imperium exigueque opes . . . his omnibus magnum in modum mutatis et adauctis', 'ab eadem libertate titulum summere non indignum, sed rationi plurimum consentaneum'.

[13] R.C. Trexler, *Public Life in Renaissance Florence* (New York, 1980), pp. 259–60.

[14] See E. Conti, *L'imposta diretta a Firenze nel Quattrocento (1427–1494)* (Rome, 1984), pp. 51–3, and compare p. 42.

[15] ASF, Misc. rep., 110 (I cite the pencilled archival pagination, not the fifteenth-century foliation). Its title derives from the opening words of its first provision, which subsequently recur as a *leitmotiv* to introduce new reforms: 'Quod posthac finito officio provisorum et gubernatorum gabelle salis . . .' (p. 1), cf. p. 17 ('conducens posthac in urbem Florentiae') or p. 24 ('posthac taxandi solvere . . . posthac ad solutionem taxarum', and below). Vespucci was a Notary of the Signoria in 1455 and 1459 and his son Antonio became Notary of the *Tratte* in 1498; D. Marzi, *La cancelleria della repubblica fiorentina* (Rocca San Casciano, 1910), pp. 501, 502, 284–5.

leggi), the *Otto di guardia*, and the Monte officials were to be elected by the new Council of One Hundred. The Reformers were thus the conduit for giving to the *Cento* their 'important place in the system of electoral controls' and the functions of shorter-term *balìe*.[16]

Finance nevertheless dominated their work, as we can see from their involvement with Jewish moneylenders, customs officials and maritime affairs, the *Grascia* and the Tower officers, and the Dowry Fund – as well as from their involvement with taxes, customs duties and import licences into and within the territory.[17] These reforms provided the context in which the word *imperium* was first used administratively. Although not replacing entirely the use of the older word 'territory' or 'county and district',[18] *imperium* first appeared in a measure intended to prevent the removal of silk worms from the contado 'into the Florentine district or outside the Florentine empire'.[19] It then reappeared in several 'decrees' (*decreverunt*) to mitigate the life of hardship and often danger on the confines 'of the jurisdiction and empire of Florence' by granting special privileges and tax concessions to several frontier communes.[20]

There were also scattered allusions to the Florentine dominion as an empire in the public letters, or *Missive*, written by the chancellor Bartolomeo Scala. When in 1467, for example, he thanked the Duke of Milan for his gift of lions (Florence's heraldic symbol), he referred to them as the insignia of empire; or when he wrote to Francesco Gonzaga as Cardinal legate of Bologna, he declared that the cities under Florence's rule (*ditione*) were free from 'all tributes except for those

---

[16] ASF, Misc. rep., 110, pp. 47, 50; N. Rubinstein, *The Government of Florence under the Medici, 1434–1494*, 2nd edn (Oxford, 1997), p. 129 and note 4; the decrees were initiated by the Thirty on 12 and 20 September 1459, predating the ratification of the *Cento* on 6 November 1459.

[17] ASF, Misc. rep., 110, pp. 8–12, 27 October 1458–2 January 1459; pp. 12–23, 25 January 1459; pp. 33–5, 15 June 1459 (cf. A. Brown, 'The Guelf Party in Fifteenth-century Florence', in Brown, *Medici in Florence*, p. 119 note 59); pp. 39–43, 28 June–22 August 1459; pp. 49–50, 20 September 1459; pp. 6–8, 21–3, 27 October 1458–25 January 1459 (cf. Conti, *L'imposta diretta*, pp. 51–3).

[18] *Ibid.*, p. 28, 14 June 1459: 'vel ultra seu habuerunt uxorem de territorio florentino . . . vel comprehensi fuerint in oneribus civitatis comitatus licet districtus Florentie'.

[19] *Ibid.*, p. 25, 14 June 1459: 'in futurum minime liceat immo prohibitum sit . . . extrahere nec extrahi facere de comitatu Florentiae bigactos seu firugellos qui in eo fient comitatu vel ibi orientur aut sericum causa conducendi illos in districtu Florentiae seu extra imperium Florentinum'.

[20] *Ibid.*, pp. 30–3, 15 June 1459: 'in confinibus dictionis et imperii Florentini . . . Ideo decreverunt', repeating this formula for the other decrees; they relate to the communes of Montecarelli, Cavrenno, Bruscoli, Piancaldoli and Pietramala, three of these being prorogated in 1479 according to a marginal note.

subject to our direct sovereignty' (*a nobis imperaruntur*).[21] But it is once again in the context of another commission with extraordinary powers that we find more consistent use of the word. The commission of Seventeen Reformers of the Monte and Gabelles was appointed in 1481–2 and again in 1490–1, on each occasion at a time of financial crisis, like the Thirty Reformers, and with equally extensive and wide-ranging powers. Fiscal legislation had important political implications, both in terms of concessions made to private citizens like Lorenzo de' Medici, and in terms of Florence's territory.[22] When the Reformers used the word empire, it was, on one occasion, to remove the 'black money' that was circulating throughout Florence 'and its empire', just as in 1491 the Seventeen used it when reducing gabelles on merchandise and cattle leaving 'the Florentine empire'.[23] On another occasion, it was to punish those who attempted to avoid paying taxes on contracts. Notaries who failed to report contracts rogated within the city or 'outside the city of Florence and its empire, within or beyond a hundred miles radius', were deprived of offices for two years: 'nor can they accompany or exercise any office with any rector, office, or official of the Florentine empire'. Those who had contracts rogated 'outside the Florentine empire' by 'foreign, non-matriculated notaries who are not subject to the Florentine jurisdiction', or by notary-priests 'in the Florentine empire or outside the empire', were fined and their contracts were invalidated. Subjects of 'the Florentine empire' were made liable for taxes on contracts they made with non-subjects or those otherwise exempt.[24] The novelty of this legislation against the notaries is suggested

---

[21] ASF, Miss. I canc., 45, 175v–176r, 28 November 1467: 'Quod autem id animal insigne est, quo hoc quocunque imperii habemus partum est'; Miss. I canc., 46, 100r, 2 February 1473: 'Ii enim ex quo sub ditione nostra sunt et reguntur a nobis semper immunes extiterunt liberique penitus ab omnibus tributis preterquam ab his qui (*ex que?*) a nobis imperaruntur.'

[22] On the Seventeen, see A. Brown, 'Lorenzo, the Monte and the Seventeen Reformers. Public and Private Interest', in Brown, *Medici in Florence*, pp. 151–211, esp. pp. 154–9.

[23] ASF, Cento, 3, 77v, 16 June 1491.

[24] ASF, Misc. rep., 109, 18r, 13 October 1481: 'considerato la ciptà di Firenze et suo imperio essere ripieno di moneta nera . . . nella città di Firenze o suoi sobborgi et circustanze et fuori d'essa città et suo circustanze in alchuno luogo dello imperio di quella'; and 55r–57r, 30 January 1482: 'fuori della città di Firenze et suo imperio infra le cento miglia et oltre alle cento miglia . . . Né possa etiandio andare né exercitare alcuno officio con alcuno rettore, ufficio o uficiale dello imperio fiorentino' (55r); 'fuori dello imperio fiorentino a notai forestieri non matricolati né sottoposti alla iurisdictione fiorentina o a notai preti . . . nello imperio fiorentino come fuor d'esso imperio' (55v); 'Item providono et deliberorono che qualunche sottoposto allo 'mperio fiorentino per sé o per altri non sottoposto a esso imperio o privilegiato' (57r).

by the fact that it was 'maliciously condemned', *malignamente damnato*, by some notaries for the way in which it could be interpreted. This decision, they 'insolently told many worthy and wise citizens . . . would lead to the closure of the *Mercanzia* and merchants and workers would be deprived of the means of trading and doing business'. When the unpopular January legislation was modified in June 1482 because of this criticism, we find that the word *imperium* was replaced with *iurisdictio* as if to suggest a return to more traditional ways of doing things.[25]

It is not, of course, always clear why the word *imperium* was used or what its connotations were. In the earliest instance I cited of its administrative use for 'territory' or 'state', we may surmise that as silk was a relatively new industry for Florence, new vocabulary may have been thought appropriate to glorify the enterprise. Or was it maybe used as an attempt to justify strict export controls in the name of empire? The 'name of empire' carried other resonances, however, as we know from citizen debates at this time. At the time of the political crisis in July 1458, for instance, one citizen quoted Sallust to make his point that it was not by force of arms that the Roman republic defended itself and indeed expanded, but by 'industry at home, just rule (*imperium*) abroad and an open mind in decision-making'.[26] It was perhaps this sense of 'just rule' that the Thirty Reformers wished to convey when promising tax concessions to some communes on the frontier of 'the empire of Florence' in the following year. The moral role of the Roman empire was of course a *locus communis* of the humanists. So it may be no coincidence that at the time of the 1458–9 reforms Benedetto Accolti was chancellor of Florence. As a professional humanist, he developed a high-flown classical style of writing in which he invoked the Roman world empire as a model of virtue. He also introduced extensive reforms to record the Signoria's letters abroad as well as its correspondence with its subject dominions.[27]

---

[25] The Reformers' legislation of 4 July 1482 that refers back to the 30 January legislation on the taxes on contracts replaces the word *imperio* with *iurisdictione*, ASF, Misc. rep., 109, 70v.

[26] ASF, CP, 55, 25v, Donato Cocchi, 2 July 1458: 'et cum iuxta Sallustii sententiam, "domi industria, foris iustum imperium et animus in consulendo liber", maxime respublica tueatur atque etiam augeat', quoting *Bellum Catilinae*, 52.22–3. Cf. the *Epistola consolatoria de' Caldi, Freddi e Tiepidi & una frottola insieme*, where the same words are quoted, in Cambridge University Library, 2427 [4529] Pet.G.7.10[10] [Lorenzo Morgiani, 1496], cited in A. Brown, 'Partiti, correnti, o coalizioni: un contributo al dibattito', in A. Fontes, J.-L. Fournel and M. Plaisance (eds.), *Savonarole: enjeux, débats, questions* (Paris, 1997), p. 73.

[27] See R. Black, *Benedetto Accolti and the Florentine Renaissance* (Cambridge, 1985), esp.

But the language of empire also implied the right to exercise full sovereignty over the state, with the power to issue decrees based on the will and command of the emperor. These were the words used by the Signoria when describing its embassy to the emperor Rupert, Duke of Bavaria, in 1401, that 'we paid the money which he ordered (*precepit*) as a census . . . Not only this, but whatever he should order (*iusserit*) it is our duty to obey, since he is our natural lord.'[28] Therefore, when the Florentines started to use this language of command as well as the word empire itself, it surely suggested an attempt to take over these imperial prerogatives. As we have seen, the Seventeen Reformers used the word empire in contexts closely related to sovereign rights, such as coinage and notaries. The attempt to extend this language more widely in the fields of administration and law took place in the second half of the fifteenth century, largely during the long offices of the chancellor Bartolomeo Scala and the government legislator Giovanni Guidi.

I have described elsewhere how Scala assumed another sovereign prerogative in writing sealed letters on vellum, which the Duke of Milan had been told only the pope and emperor could do. He also assumed the right to rogate mandates in the form of letters patent without the attestations of imperial notaries, who until then were deemed necessary to authenticate communal documents on behalf of the emperor as Florence's overlord. According to medieval formula, notaries as the representatives of the delegated authority of the emperor were 'asked' (*rogati sunt*) to prepare a mandate in legal form. Now, however, the government (either the Signoria and Colleges or the Councils, both of which represented the Florentine people), instead of 'asking for' (*rogantes*) a mandate from the notaries, ordered it (*iusserunt*) from the chancellor, who, like the Roman *rogator*, 'asks' (instead of being asked) if he is acting in accordance with their will and pleasure (*Interrogat enim scriba: velint iubeantne illud quid agitur?* – according to the Roman republican formula cited by Livy).[29] Although as First Chancellor Scala was not responsible for writing letters within the territory

pp. 145 ('Sic Romani . . . cum eorum industria terrarum orbem subegerunt. Et tam diu apud illos libertas et imperium fuerunt quam diu vitiis virtus prevaluit et dominata est') and 151–4.

[28] Letter dated 27 September 1401, cited in E. Conti (ed.), *Le 'Consulte' e 'Pratiche' della repubblica fiorentina nel Quattrocento* (Florence, 1981), p. 246 (note): 'facimus ei pecunias quas precepit pro census absolutione . . . Non enim hoc solum, sed quicquid iusserit nostrum est, cum sit nobis naturalis dominus, obedire'.

[29] See A. Brown, *Bartolomeo Scala, 1430–1497, Chancellor of Florence* (Princeton, 1979), pp. 168–78, cf. pp. 144–5, note 28 (Italian edn, Florence, 1992, pp. 117–20, 107); Brown, *The Medici in Florence*, pp. 324–5. See also R. Black, 'The Political Thought of Florentine Chancellors', *The Historical Journal*, 29 (1986), pp. 1002–3.

(this was made the responsibility of the Second Chancellor in 1437),[30] his reforms did eventually lead to the replacement in the chancery of imperially qualified notaries by secretaries like Machiavelli, who had no notarial qualifications but were nevertheless able to exercise executive authority in the territory.

More directly relevant to the administration of the territory were the judicial reforms that similarly replaced the statute-based or 'rational' decisions of the courts of the Podestà and the Captain of the People with executive law based on the will and command of eight citizens, the *Otto di guardia*. In the course of the fifteenth century, as has often been described, this magistracy with *balìa* exercised summary justice in matters of state.[31] Moreover, it increasingly extended its authority throughout the territory, sending orders to Florentine Podestàs and Captains, assuming authority over the Jews and intervening in judicial cases by means of pre-emptory orders or bulletins.[32] So, for example, we find the *Otto* appointing Pagolo Riccialbani their commissary in August 1480 with full powers to punish criminals 'in the Florentine empire', and in 1497 exiling Bernardo Accolti from 'the Florentine territory, jurisdiction and empire' for five years.[33] In this way, it came to take over another imperial prerogative – that of prosecuting cases of *laesa maiestas* or treason – on the assumption that the Florentine

---

[30] Marzi, *La cancelleria*, pp. 196–7. The division was made during Bruni's office.

[31] G. Antonelli, 'La magistratura degli Otto di Guardia a Firenze', *Archivio storico italiano*, 112 (1954), pp. 3–39, esp. p. 16: 'giudicare e condannare a loro pienissimo arbitrio chinque avesse tentato o compiuto reato alcuno "contro lo stato della città e buon governo di quella o in vergogna o vilipendio d'essa"'. See also Zorzi, *L'amministrazione della giustizia*, pp. 42–5, 67–72, 83–9; Brown, *Scala*, pp. 336–7; and Brown, *Medici in Florence*, p. 152. The Statutes of the *Otto*, copied in OGBR, 224, state they have full powers 'ex mero imperio et gladii potestate'.

[32] See especially Zorzi, *L'amministrazione della giustizia* pp. 44, 71–2. The expansion of its authority is evident from the registers of the *Otto di guardia*: ASF, OGBR, vols. 55–108 (1480–97).

[33] ASF, OGBR, 56, 36v, 9 August 1480: 'con pienissima auctorità, in modo che possa perseguhitare pigliare condamnare & punire qualunque delinquente in qualunque luogho si fussi nell' imperio fiorentino'; *ibid.*, 108, 25r, 19 September 1497: 'ad eundum standum & permanendum extra territorium iurisdictionem & imperium florentinum'. Compare ASF, Zecca, 66, 12v–13r, 18 November 1485, exiling a counterfeiter from the 'Florentinum imperium et ultra per xxx miliaria' and SC Delib. ord., 96, 102r–v, 2 December 1494, exiling Piero de' Medici 100 miles 'confinibus districtus et imperii florentini'. On the role of the commissary (created at the same time as territorial vicars), see W. J. Connell, 'Il commissario e lo stato territoriale fiorentino', *Ricerche storiche*, 18 (1988), pp. 591–617, esp. pp. 599–60, arguing that the use of the word by the Signoria in the 1360s probably reflected its role as territorial *princeps* during the Pisan War.

government (or in one instance its leading citizen Lorenzo de' Medici)
enjoyed the majesty of state.[34]

We know that these administrative and juridical developments were
breaking new ground from the fact that both Scala's reforms and the
jurisdiction of the Otto were challenged. Scala's reforms were considered invalid when first introduced, and it was later argued that the Otto
di guardia did not have the authority to prosecute the crime of laesa
maiestas, both because of its own status and because by definition the
crime could be committed only against the emperor or the republic –
not against one of its citizens nor against its state.[35]

One event perfectly illustrates the growing powers of Florence over
its territory and the use of the language of empire to justify them, the
revolt of Volterra in 1472. As Riccardo Fubini recently argued, the
revolt had less to do with the alum monopoly than with power-politics
in Florence that were mirrored in Volterra. The take-over of the alum
monopoly by the Volterrans was initially dealt with by powers granted
to the Otto di guardia, which exiled the leading trouble-makers to
Florence. After Lorenzo de' Medici was asked by Volterra to arbitrate
between the city and the alum company in January but before he had
delivered his verdict, two members of the pro-Medici faction in
Volterra were murdered; subsequently other members of the faction
were exiled by the Florentine Captain in the city on the advice of the
Ten of War in Florence. Faced with this loss of authority, Lorenzo and
a special balìa of Twenty invoked the military help of the Duke of
Urbino to crush the revolt and inflict – in response to the continued
resistance of the peasants – the ensuing sack of the city. For his victory,
Federigo was rewarded in a public ceremony, in which he was
fulsomely praised for his valour and bestowed with Florentine citizenship, a house in Florence and a silver helmet. By contrast, Volterra was
subjected to 'Draconian' punishment: the city was made part of the
contado instead of the district of Florence; some fifty citizens were
exiled or imprisoned, others lost their homes to make way for a
mammoth prison, the Maschio, which towered over the city as a
symbol of Volterra's new subject status; and as a final sign of its

---

[34] On imperial prerogatives, see W. Ullman, 'The development of the medieval idea of
sovereignty', English Historical Review, 64 (1949), pp. 1–33; F. Calasso, I glossatori e la
teoria della sovranità (Milan, 1957); and on laesa maiestas, see note 3 above. See also
Lorenzo de' Medici, Lettere, V, ed. M. Mallett (Florence, 1989), pp. 226–8; and
A. Brown, 'Lorenzo, the Monte, and the Seventeen Reformers', in Brown, Medici in
Florence, pp. 152–3.

[35] See O. Cavallar, 'Il tiranno, i dubia del giudice ed i consilia dei giuristi', Archivio storico
italiano, 155 (1997), pp. 265–346, which I am very grateful to the author for letting
me read in typescript.

subjection the alum mines themselves were transferred to Florence as a regalian right of the conquering city.[36]

As an exercise in sovereignty, the revolt is instructive from several points of view: the young Lorenzo's role as an arbiter with full powers to mediate between conflicting groups; the appointment of a war *balìa* of Twenty, whose chancellor, Scala, was unusually given full control of its communal seal; and the employment of an outstanding *condottiere* to crush it.[37] Two years later, these events were recorded in an epic poem, the *Volaterrais*, by the humanist Naldo Naldi. Naldi was a Medici eulogist who had hoped for a position in the chancery as Scala's assistant before becoming a university teacher; and although dedicated to Federigo of Urbino, the poem clearly served as a justification of Lorenzo de' Medici's first assay in territorial control.[38] Reflecting the revolt's exceptional features, the poem adopted exceptional language to describe it, the language of empire.

Thus after praising Florence's expanding *imperium* and hopes of a Golden Age under Lorenzo, the *Volaterrais* describes in detail the events which led up to the revolt, Lorenzo's appointment as arbiter, his unwillingness to embark on war before addressing in the Duomo all those accused of *laesa maiestas* towards the Florentine people and senate, and their misrepresentation of the amnesty promised them in return for obeying Florentine orders (*iussa*).[39] The next book uses the device of a council of the gods to predict the growing expansion of the Florentine *imperium* under the Medici. What does Volterra think it is doing, Venus

---

[36] R. Fubini, 'Lorenzo de' Medici e Volterra', repr. in Fubini, *Quattrocento fiorentino*, pp. 123–39; E. Fiumi, *L'impresa di Lorenzo de' Medici contro Volterra (1472)* (Florence, 1948), and on the 'draconiane misure', pp. 151–6. The subsequent restoration of certain rights 'non implicava pertanto il ritorno al comune dei diritti che vi si riferivano . . . così la sovranità del sottosuolo era passato nell'ambito della giurisdizione fiorentina' (p. 156).

[37] On the seal, Brown, *Bartolomeo Scala*, p. 151 (Ital. trans. p. 101).

[38] See Naldo Naldi, *Bucolica, Volaterrais, Hastiludium, Carmina Varia*, ed. W. L. Grant (Florence, 1974), pp. 61–115; Brown, 'The humanist portrait', in *Medici in Florence*, pp. 23, 33. On the 'glorificazione propagandistica del capitano anche in sede letteraria e iconografica', see Fubini in Medici, *Lettere*, I (Florence, 1977), p. 553. Scala's oration, which is reported by Naldi, is in Scala, *Humanistic and Political Writings*, ed. Brown, pp. 205–11.

[39] Naldi, *Volaterrais*, ed. Grant, p. 62, lines 33–9, 'Florentia late / proferat imperium et populis dominetur abactis/ protinus et multos quos possidet illa per annos / proroget ulterius fines . . . nec dubiis ea signa dedit Laurentius heros / adventasse dies quibus aurea saecula condat'; p. 73, lines 412–14, 'nostra quicunque fuissent / hactenus urbe gravi detenti crimine, laesam / ob maiestatem populi laesumque Senatum'. Compare also p. 89, lines 475–6, 'cum tanto Florentis nomine laesa / maiestas populi fuerit'; and pp. 74–75, lines 475–6, 'modo quae sint iussa facessat / ac Volaterranus veniam petat'.

asks, as she looks down on Martian Florence from the clouds: surely no people in the world could dare to scorn the orders of the Tuscan senate or fight shy of the *imperium* of Florence under arms? Don't worry, Jupiter replies, the home of the Medici will survive with the Tuscan cities, still their head as it was before, when the divine Cosimo took the bridle.[40] And so it turns out. The *balìa* of Twenty uses its 'supreme power' to appoint Federigo of Urbino as Captain, and together they ensure Florence's victory, which Naldi celebrates by quoting Scala's lengthy oration, delivered 'by order of the magistracy' to ringing applause.[41]

The *Volterrais* was of course a literary production, but its intention was clearly propagandistic in justifying the harsh action taken against Volterra in terms of Florence's growing imperialism. Yet, as Naldi's poem reminds us, the language of empire had resonances that evoked Rome's literary and moral legacy as well as its political hegemony. It was Lorenzo Valla who had emphasised the role of language as the mark of empire, 'for the Roman empire is there wherever the Roman language rules'.[42] Although humanist poets like Naldo Naldi or

---

[40] *Ibid.*, pp. 76–7, lines 21–9, 'quo, cum Tyrrhenos Medices Laurentius acri / usque gubernaret, veluti facit, arte Quirites, / debeat inde suos in longum extendere fines / rite Fluentinus, priscos imitatus honores / stirpis, et egregius Romani nominis heres, / nullus ut extremis populus sit partibus orbis, / si modo fata sinant, Tyrrheni iussa Senatus // temnere qui cupiat, Sullanae gentis et ipsum/ audeat imperium qui detrectare sub armis'; pp. 77–9, lines 60–3, 'Medicum domus una manebit / urbibus usque caput Tuscis, velut ante fuisset! /ex quo divinus moderandi frena Leonis suscepit Cosmus Patriae pater optimus olim'; and lines 106–8, 'crescat et imperium populi Florentis in oras / extremas, Medices cum nunc Laurentius heros / temperet Etruscos propria virtute Quirites'.

[41] *Ibid.*, p. 99, lines 303–5, 'ut Florentini Sullana in moenia patres / vigintique viri, quibus est data cura suprema / ne detrimenti caperet res publica quicquam'; p. 102, lines 1–3, 'At summus noster summo mandante Senatu / inde magistratus curat Federicus in urbem / Sullanam veniat'; p. 103, lines 39, 41 'Scala magistratus iussu . . . sic est de summis Federici laudibus orsus'; the speech is described on pp. 103–14, lines 42–447, ending 'Dixerat; at, postquam finem dedit ore loquendi / Scala, magistratus gradibus quem summus ab altis / iusserat egregias Federici edicere laudes, / insequitur plaususque virum clangorque tubarum' (p. 114, lines 448–451).

[42] Lorenzo Valla, first preface to *De linguae latinae elegantia libri sex*, edited in M. Regoliosi, *Nel cantiere del Valla. Elaborazione e montaggio delle 'Elegantie'*: 'ibi namque romanum imperium est ubicunque romana lingue dominatur'. On nostalgia for Rome, see D. De Rosa, *Coluccio Salutati il cancelliere e il pensatore politico* (Florence, 1980), pp. 98–9: 'Si trattava piuttosto di un'aspirazione indefinita, di un sentimento nutrito di reminiscenze storiche, della consapevolezza dei vincoli razziali e culturali che univano e distinguevano i popoli della penisola nel ricordo della comune eredità di Roma'; and on Florence as *parva Roma*, pp. 88–90. See also C. T. Davis, *Dante and the Idea of Rome* (Oxford, 1957), pp. 193–4; R. G. Witt, *Hercules at the Crossroads* (Durham, NC, 1983), pp. 168–9.

Ugolino Verino had been writing jingoistic verse encouraging the Medici to restore a Golden Age since the time of Cosimo,[43] it was the circle of writers around Lorenzo in the 1470s and 1480s that developed the idea of cultural imperialism. Lorenzo de' Medici himself made it explicit in the preface to his *Comento sopra alcuni de' suoi sonetti*, where he said that the successful development of Florentine Italian, 'until now in its adolescence', depends on the growth and prosperity 'of the Florentine empire, which we should not only hope for but put every effort into helping to achieve through the good citizens'.[44] It was elaborated in the *Raccolta Aragonese*, a collection of Tuscan verse sent to Alfonso of Aragon in 1476, and in the series of translations by Cristoforo Landino, which he undertook – as he wrote in the preface to his translation of Pliny's *Natural History* – in order to transform the Latin Pliny into a 'Tuscan and from being a Roman a Florentine, so that being written in a language common to all Italy and quite familiar to many foreigners, his work will be of benefit to many people'.[45] However, it was Landino's preface to his *Commentary on Dante* that made the political implications of this cultural campaign most explicit. Printed in 1481 in a edition that was illustrated with engravings influenced by Botticelli and presented in a public *presentazione*, Landino claimed to have restored Dante to his *patria* after a long exile: 'not a Romagnol, nor a Lombard . . . but a pure Florentine', a celebration of

---

[43] See E. H. Gombrich, 'Renaissance and Golden Age' in Gombrich, *Norm and Form* (London, 1971), pp. 29–34, quoting Avogadro's eulogy to Cosimo: 'Si numi vincunt, hercle est fas vincere nobis': 'If money can conquer, by jingo we shall' (p. 33); A. Brown, 'The Humanist Portrait of Cosimo de' Medici', in Brown, *The Medici in Florence*, esp. pp. 22–3.

[44] '. . . perché insino a ora si può dire essere l'adolescenzia di questa lingua . . . aggiugnendosi qualche prospero successo e augumento al fiorentino imperio: come si debbe non solamente sperare, ma con tutto l'ingegno e forze per li buoni cittadini aiutare', in Lorenzo de' Medici, *Comento dei miei sonetti*, ed. T. Zanato (Florence, 1991), p. 149, cited in W. Welliver, *L'impero fiorentino* (Florence, 1956). Compare J. W. Cook, *The Autobiography of Lorenzo de' Medici the Magnificent: A Commentary on my Sonnets* (Binghamton, 1995), p. 51, who translates 'on behalf of the good citizens'. For the early date of the preface, see M. Martelli, 'La cultura letteraria nell'età di Lorenzo', in G. C. Garfagnini (ed.), *Lorenzo il Magnifico e il suo tempo* (Florence, 1992), pp. 49–50; and compare Zanato, pp. 123–4.

[45] Cristoforo Landino, *Scritti critici e teorici*, ed. R. Cardini (Rome, 1974), I, p. 83: 'dare opera che Plinio di latino diventi toscano e di romano fiorentino, acciò che essendo scritto in lingua commune a tuta Italia e a molte esterne nazioni assai familiare, l'opera sua giovi a molti'; and compare C. Dionisotti, *Geografia e storia della letteratura italiana* (Turin, 1967), pp. 123–8. Landino also translated the *Formulario di epistole vulgare* for Ercole d'Este in 1485 and the *Sforziade*, Giovanni Simonetta's Latin history of the life of Francesco Sforza, for Lodovico Sforza in 1485–89, *ibid.*, pp. 177–91. On the latter, see C. Dionisotti, 'Leonardo uomo di lettere', *Italia medievale e umanistica*, 5 (1962), p. 210.

Florence's success, when 'the forces of our empire were exhausted thanks to the wars waged against us by Alfonso of Aragon . . . who was very keen to propagate his empire' and also by Venice, which now wanted to extend its 'empire' in Lombardy to deprive Francesco Sforza of his newly acquired 'empire'.[46]

We know that the language of empire took root from the use Savonarola made of it and from his influence on his followers. The losses of Pisa and Montepulciano in 1494–5 made the subject of empire a sensitive one. Urging the citizens to love the common good, Savonarola carefully explained in his *Treatise on the Constitution and Government of Florence* that this was 'one of the reasons for the expansion of the Roman empire, that they loved the common good of the city very much . . . and therefore God, to reward this virtue . . . caused the common good of their city to grow and extended their empire over the whole earth'. And so, he went on, 'God will increase [Florence's] empire, as he did that of the Romans. Because the Romans exercised strict and severe justice, He gave them imperial power over the whole world.'[47] His message was not lost on one of his audience, Piero Parenti, who reported that in his sermons Savonarola urged the Florentines to be patient and took great comfort from the fact that 'we will soon have Pisa back and that we will increase our *imperio*, etc.'.[48] So empire was a reward for good behaviour, a carrot Savonarola must have known the Florentines would find irresistible.

Empire, as we have seen, had many connotations, and it was possible for Savonarola – as for the Florentines – to combine its moral role with its territorial expansionism and claims to sovereignty and world rule. If it is difficult to distinguish its levels of meaning in the fifteenth century, we can at least see change between the fifteenth and the early sixteenth centuries. The inhibitions that had deterred Florentines from calling their own territory an empire had been dispelled and Florence's state

[46] *Scritti*, ed. Cardini, I, pp. 102, 109: 'né romagnuolo essere né lombardo . . . ma mero fiorentino'; 'Erano molto attrite le forze del nostro imperio per la guerra immer-itamente fattaci da Alfonso aragonese . . . molto cupido di propagare lo 'mperio . . . ed ecco nuova guerra raccendersi non solo dal già detto re ma dallo excellentissimo imperio veneto', going on to refer to 'la novità dell'imperio' of Francesco Sforza; and on this whole campaign, G. Tanturli, 'La Firenze Laurenziana davanti alla propria storia letteraria', in Garfagnini (ed.), *Lorenzo il Magnifico e il suo tempo*, pp. 1–38, at p. 9: 'un completo disegno della cultura fiorentina'.

[47] *Trattato circa el reggimento e governo della città di Firenze* (Florence, 1498), III, ch. 2, translated in R. N. Watkins, *Humanism amd Liberty: Writings on Freedom in Fifteenth Century Florence* (Cambridge, Mass., 1978), pp. 254–5.

[48] Piero Parenti, *Storia fiorentina*, ed. A. Matucci, I (Florence, 1994), p. 196: 'con la pazienza ci governassimo, che si confortava molto riavremo presto Pisa e amplieremo il nostro imperio etc.'.

was now <u>unequivocally called an empire.</u>[49] However, foreign invasions and the loss of territory suffered by Florence after 1494 left their mark on its view of empire. <u>Both Machiavelli and Guicciardini now agreed that Rome's method of acquiring its empire was not feasible as a model.</u>[50] When discussing in his *Dialogue on the Government of Florence* whether Florence should try to 'extend its dominion', Guicciardini had del Nero reply that if it was a question of remaining small and free or thinking 'of creating *imperio*', he knows what he would say, but since the Florentines were already among 'those who have dominion', he could not criticise seizing the opportunity for expansion if it were offered. Nevertheless <u>such empires were condemned by Guicciardini, and by his alter-ego del Nero, as illegitimate because based on force</u>, and we know that he also thought that a republic was a <u>much worse overlord than a prin</u>ce, because 'a republic oppresses all its subjects and allows only its citizens a share in power'.[51] His comment marked the transition from Florence's republican empire to the principate, for which, as we can see, the ground was already prepared.

[49] Machiavelli, *Il Principe*, ch.12, in *Il Principe e Discorsi*, ed. S. Bertelli (Milan, 1973), p. 55, referring to the Venetians' and Florentines' use of arms to increase 'l'imperio loro'; *Discorsi*, I, 39, *ibid.*, p. 222: 'Avendo la città di Firenze, dopo il 94, perso parte dello imperio suo.' See also II, 21, p. 341: 'la città di Pistoia venne volontariamente sotto lo imperio fiorentino'; and Machiavelli, *Istorie fiorentine*, ed. F. Gaeta (Milan, 1962), p. 463, on Cosimo de' Medici's regret that he had not 'accresciuto lo imperio fiorentino d'uno acquisto onorevole'. See *Il Principe*, ch. 1, p. 15, on *imperio* as rule.

[50] Machiavelli, *Discorsi*, II,4, 'Le repubbliche hanno tenuti tre modi circa lo ampliare', ed. Bertelli, pp. 290–1: 'Vedesi ancora che quel modo di fare sudditi è stato sempre debole . . . Conoscesi pertanto essere vero modo quello che tennono i Romani . . . e dopo Roma non è stato alcuno che gli abbi imitati . . . dumila anni fa la potenza de' Toscani fusse grande, al presente non ce n'è quasi memoria'. Compare Francesco Guicciardini, *Dialogo del reggimento di Firenze*, ed. R. Palmarocchi (Bari, 1931), pp. 148–51, trans. A. Brown (Cambridge, 1994), pp. 143–7; and Guicciardini, *Ricordi*, C.110, ed. R. Spongano (Florence, 1951), p. 121, trans. Brown (Cambridge, 1994), p. 173.

[51] *Dialogo del reggimento*, p. 159, trans. Brown, p. 154: 'o voltare lo animo al fare imperio . . . perché noi siamo di quegli che abbiamo dominio', cf. p. 163, trans. pp. 158–9; *Ricordi*, C.48 and 107, ed. Spongano, pp. 57, 118, trans. Brown, pp. 172–3: 'Non si può tenere stati secondo conscienza, perché . . . tutti sono violenti . . . e da questa regola non eccettuo lo imperadore e manco e preti'; 'la republica deprime tutti e sudditi e non fa parte alcuna della sua grandezza se non a' suoi cittadini'.

CHAPTER 3

CONSTITUTIONAL AMBITIONS, LEGAL REALITIES AND THE FLORENTINE STATE

JANE BLACK

In 1409 Leonardo Bruni wrote in a letter to Niccolò Niccoli that a state was a society of people united in jurisdiction and living under the same laws (*civitas autem est congregatio hominum iure sociatorum et eisdem legibus viventium*).[1] As Riccardo Fubini has pointed out, Bruni was articulating the pride which the Florentines must have felt at the beginning of the fifteenth century as they witnessed the spectacular expansion of their dominion over neighbouring cities; they believed they were participating in the foundation of a new territorial entity.[2] Bruni's notion that the acceptance of a single body of laws constituted an essential element of statehood was reflected in the new set of statutes compiled in 1415. In a conscious imitation of Justinian's example, the Florentines aimed to publish a coherent collection of laws that would be binding both on their own citizens and on their subject territories.[3]

The Florentines had been preoccupied for some time with the mass of confused and contradictory legislation that had been issued over the years. The statutes of 1409, the work of Giovanni da Montegranaro, were an attempt to bring some order to this near chaos. The 1415 version, drawn up under the auspices of Paulus de Castro and Bartolomeo Volpi and better known thanks to its eighteenth-century edition, was revolutionary, both in terms of its organisation and in terms of its

---

[1] Leonardo Bruni, *Epistolarum libri VIII*, ed. L. Mehus (Florence, 1741), I, p. 78.

[2] R. Fubini, 'La rivendicazione di Firenze della sovranità statale e il contributo delle "Historiae" di Leonardo Bruni', in P. Viti (ed.), *Leonardo Bruni Cancelliere della Repubblica di Firenze* (Florence, 1990), pp. 29–62.

[3] 'Urbem nostram florentinam cum toto eius territorio, legibus nostris regi, et gubernari decernimus . . .', in *Statuta populi et communis Florentiae publica auctoritate collecta et praeposta anno saluti MCCCCXV* (Freiburg [Florence], 1763), III, p. 479. Fubini discusses the relationship between the notion of territorial sovereignty in the statutes and in the works of Bruni, and the use of Justinian's *prooemium*, *Deo Auctore*, by the Florentine government at the inception of the new statutes in the 1390s and 1409; Fubini, 'La rivendicazione di Firenze', pp. 47ff.

purpose, which was to provide a legal code for the new territorial state that had emerged.[4] The Florentines were by then conscious of the need to bring a sense of unity to their disparate conquests and acquisitions.

Yet, instead of increasing uniformity within Florentine dominions, there continued to be a proliferation of local legislation.[5] Ever smaller communities were able to boast their own books of statutes and collections of laws. Issued in response to particular needs, or drawn up in the wake of previous autonomous collections or of local customs, these laws often contradicted the Florentine statutes. They were issued haphazardly over the years by often less than competent local officials, frequently containing, as a result, internal inconsistencies and generally without consideration for the statutes of neighbouring communities.[6] The upshot was, by the sixteenth century, that morass of statutes so vividly outlined by Elena Fasano Guarini in her study of the government of Cosimo I.[7] Nor did the process stop there. Local as well as central government under the Duchy and Grand Duchy carried on making new laws, so adding to the confusion. What needs to be clarified is why the Florentines, in spite of their desire for coherence, encouraged this maddening proliferation of laws. How much control did Florence exercise over local statutes? And, in relation to all of this local legislation, what was the role of the 1415 statutes?[8]

---

[4] The motives behind the revisions are discussed by G. Chittolini, *La formazione dello stato regionale e le istituzioni del contado* (Turin, 1979), pp. 294–5; L. Martines, *Lawyers and Statecraft in Renaissance Florence* (Princeton, 1968), pp. 184–7; L. I. Stern, *The Criminal Law System of Medieval and Renaissance Florence* (Baltimore, 1994), pp. 107–8; E. Fasano Guarini, 'Gli statuti delle città soggette a Firenze tra '400 e '500: riforme locali e interventi centrali', in G. Chittolini and D. Willoweit (eds.), *Statuti, città, territori in Italia e Germania tra medioevo ed età moderna* (Bologna, 1989), pp. 86–8.

[5] On this phenomenon in general, see G. Chittolini, 'Statuti e autonomie urbane. Introduzione', in Chittolini and Willoweit (eds.), *Statuti*, pp. 7–45, and the ample bibliography he cites. On Florence in particular, see E. Fasano Guarini, 'Gli statuti', pp. 69ff.

[6] For example, the statutes of the villages of Rincine and Fornace of 1446. They were drawn up at the same time as those of the neighbouring S. Leolino but were very different. U. Santarelli (ed.), *Statuto dei comuni di Rincine e Fornace 1446* (Florence, 1969), p. 21.

[7] E. Fasano Guarini, *Lo stato mediceo di Cosimo I* (Florence, 1973), pp. 54ff.

[8] Florence's motives in encouraging so much statute-making were examined by E. Fasano Guarini, 'Città soggette e contadi nel dominio fiorentino tra quattro e cinquecento: il caso Pisano', in M. Mirri (ed.), *Ricerche di storia moderna*, vol. I, (Pisa, 1976), pp. 6ff. The separation of the former contadi from their dominant cities once they became part of the Florentine dominion, emphasised by Fasano Guarini, is taken up by L. Mannori, *Il sovrano tutore: pluralismo istituzionale e accentramento amministrativo nel principato dei Medici* (Milan, 1994), ch. 2. In general, Mannori sees more continuity in the relationship between subject cities and their contadi than does Fasano Guarini. On the control exerted by Florence over local legislation, see Fasano Guarini, 'Gli

What the Florentines had to accept was that local statute making was a recognised right and an established fact. The beginnings of local legislation coincided with the origins of the communes themselves. As the earliest towns and cities formed themselves into communes, sworn contracts, accepted customs and thence written laws came spontaneously into being.[9] As the study of Roman law was revived, communal legislation found its justification in Book I of the *Digest* with the law *Omnes populi* (D. 1.1.9.): 'All people who are governed by laws and customs (*legibus et moribus*) use partly their own particular law and partly that common to all men'.[10] This passage was regarded as the foundation stone of the law-making process and of local legislative rights and was tirelessly quoted by glossators and commentators. It provided the justification, not only for local statutes, but for the fact that such statutes might contradict or add to some aspect of Roman law or *ius commune*. By their very nature, indeed, local statutes differed from Roman law: there would have been no point issuing legislation which merely reiterated *ius commune*; or as the jurists put it: 'if a statute decrees the same thing as *ius commune*, it is not called a statute'.[11] Moreover, statute law had to come first; it was only when local law did not suffice that *ius commune* would be observed: in the words of Bartolomeus Socinus (d. 1507): 'It is a legal maxim that in any city local statutes should be followed before all else, in accordance with the law *Omnes populi* . . . Common law should only be used when these are inadequate'.[12] The commentators were unanimous, for example, that where a will or

statuti', pp. 81ff., who stresses the effectiveness of the Florentine system of controls; Mannori, *Il sovrano tutore*, pp. 102ff, in contrast shows the survival of genuine local autonomy. The role of the Florentine statutes of 1415 in relation to Pisa is discussed by R. Celli, *Studi sui sistemi normativi delle democrazie comunali: Pisa, Siena* (Florence, 1976), pp. 138ff., who argues that the independence of the Pisans from the statutes of Florence was a notable exception to the norm, whereas Fasano Guarini emphasises the efficacy of the 1415 statutes as a means of centralisation, and Mannori argues that the statutes enjoyed limited applicability in the Florentine state.

9 M. Sbriccoli, *L'interpretazione dello statuto* (Milan, 1969), pp. 29ff. and U. Gualazzini, *Considerazioni in tema di legislazione statuaria medievale* (Milan, 1958), pp. 2ff.

10 'Omnes populi qui legibus et moribus reguntur partim suo proprio partim communi omnium hominum iure utuntur'. See C. Storti Storchi, 'Appunti in tema di "potestas condendi statuta"', in Chittolini and Willoweit (eds.), *Statuti*, pp. 319ff, for an introduction to the importance of this law in local statute making.

11 For example, Paulus de Castro, *In secundam Infortiati partem* (Venice, 1548), Ad legem falcidiam l. Lex falcida (D. 35.2.1), para 2: 'si statutum disponit id quod ius commune, non dicitur statutum'.

12 *Consilia* (Venice, 1580), IV, 91, incip. 'Quoniam in hac consultatione', para. 19: 'Est enim una maxima in iure quod in qualibet civitate ante omnia statuta eius servanda sunt, iuxta legem Omnes populi . . . Eis autem deficientibus servari debent iura communia.' Or, in the words of Baldus, 'Omnes populi possunt facere sibi statuta, et

contract stipulated that something was to be done in accordance with established law, and the simple word 'law' (*ius*) was used, it was understood that *ius* meant local statute. As Jason de Maino (d. 1519) explained in his commentary on *lex Omnes populi*: 'when the word "ius" is used on its own it is understood to mean statute law'.[13]

The question of how the legislative rights of subject communes squared with those of their *signori* or the dominant city was tackled by jurists, starting in the fourteenth century. It was, as so often, Bartolus (d. 1357) who provided the *locus classicus* for commentators and legal practitioners until the eighteenth century. In his long commentary on the *lex Omnes populi*, he set out the main lines of judicial practice.[14] In answer to the central question, whether every community can pass its own laws without the authority of a superior, Bartolus replied, in a statement intensively examined by jurists and modern scholars, that its freedom to do so depended on how much jurisdiction those people enjoyed.[15] A community without any independent jurisdiction could not draw up its own statutes without the authority of its superior whereas a people enjoying full jurisdiction needed no outside approval. Those enjoying limited jurisdiction might make statutes in matters where they had jurisdiction, but in other areas, could do so only with the authority of the superior.[16]

This logical framework reflected and encouraged the process whereby *signori* and dominant cities inspected, pruned and confirmed the statutes of subject towns.[17] This was certainly established procedure in Florence's dominion; local laws had to be approved by Florentine officials.[18] Given that proviso, the communities taken over by Florence continued to live by their established statutes and to make new ones as of right. Thus, local statutes proliferated in the fifteenth century and beyond, causing infinite difficulties in the administration of justice. Such problems were the focus of reams of surviving comment and

ubi cessat statutum, habet locum ius civile': *In primam Digesti Veteris partem commentaria* (Venice, 1577), De ius. et Iur., l. Omnes populi (D.1.1.9), para. 1.

[13] *In primam partem Digesti Veteris commentaria* (Venice,1598), De ius. et iur., l. Omnes populi (D.1.1.9), Repetitio para. 23: ' "iuris" appellatione simpliciter facta, intelligitur de iure statuario'.

[14] *In primam Digesti Veteris partem* (Venice, 1585), De ius. et iur., l. Omnes populi (D.1.1.9).

[15] Recent accounts of Bartolus' theory are again to be found in Storti Storchi, 'Appunti', pp. 322ff., and Mannori, *Il sovrano tutore*, pp. 98ff.

[16] *In primam Digesti Veteris partem* (Venice, 1585), De ius. et iur., l. Omnes populi (D.1.1.9), paras. 3–5.

[17] Storti Storchi, 'Appunti', pp. 323ff.

[18] Approval was given by the Florentine priors and colleges until 1380 when the process was taken over by four specially appointed *approvatori*: Fasano Guarini, 'Gli statuti', p. 97.

analysis by the jurists of the period and must have been a source of income for countless practising lawyers as they tried to untangle the property and commercial affairs of their clients.

The jurists had had to deal with the complexities arising from the proliferation of local statutes from as early as the mid-fourteenth century, and so the Florentines would have been aware of the pitfalls as they extended their supremacy in succeeding decades. Nevertheless, there appear to have been compelling reasons for allowing, and indeed encouraging, local statute making. In the first place, it was a necessity of government: local authorities had to make provision for the day-to-day exigencies that cropped up. Then, too, statute making was a fundamental right, recognised by all jurists, as laid down in the *lex Omnes populi* and similar laws: it was an ancient tradition and a quintessential aspect of communal life. In addition, there were political reasons. For example, the Florentines tended to want to sever the links between the cities that they took over and the lands that had previously been subject to those cities. One way of establishing direct dependence on Florence was to encourage even the smallest communities to draw up their own statutes, so forsaking the laws of their old rulers. Fasano Guarini has shown this process at work in the contado of Pisa after 1406, and once again, with renewed vigour, after its reconquest in 1509. Places such as Peccioli, Palaia, Cascina and Ripafratta, which before 1406 had never had their own statutes, were told to draft laws which would then be used by the Podestà appointed by Florence.[19]

However, this was not perhaps the main political reason behind Florence's active encouragement of statute making in its subject territories. Since it was the right of *omnes populi* to live by their own laws, there could be no better way for a superior to enforce its political will over subject communities than through their own statutes. As a result, many local statutes originate as directives from Florence. For example, the Pisan statutes of 1476 contain a provision for the speeding up of judicial procedures. The Florentine Signoria and its colleges had, according to the *prooemium*, directed their attention to certain amendments of the Pisan statutes and it was as a result of this that the present statute was issued, 'in accordance with the letter and following the instructions of the Florentine authorities'.[20] In the back of collections of local statutes there often appear laws passed in Florence that had

---

[19] 'Città soggette', pp. 6ff.

[20] *Statuti pisani inediti dal XIV ed XVI secoli*, ed. A. Era (Sassari, 1932), pp. 83ff: 'secundum jussum et litteras dictorum Dominorum'. Fasano Guarini quotes a Pistoiese example: 'Gli statuti', p. 114.

relevance for that particular community, for example regarding payment of taxes. Even where the evidence is not quite so explicit, the usual practice in subject towns such as Arezzo and Pistoia was for the Captain (*Capitano*), who was a Florentine, to attend meetings of the General Council (*Consiglio generale*), ensuring that any laws passed would be acceptable to Florence.[21] Thus, the statutes of subject towns came to reflect Florentine domination as well as long-recognised local rights. Later, under Cosimo I, central government regularly issued decrees enforceable throughout the state. Still, even then, Cosimo continued the practice of using local statutes as an important method of legislating. In fact the government became at that time even more assiduous in ordering local officials to pass laws on specific matters; such laws were only in the formal sense local statutes.[22] Their importance for the ducal authorities is reflected in the law of 1546, which reiterates the obligation of judges (*rettori*) to abide by local statutes and stipulates that every community which had statutes should make a copy of them 'di buonissima lettera' to be submitted to the *Cancelleria delle Riformagioni* and deposited in the archive for safe-keeping.[23]

Again, the key to this system of legislation was the practice of approval and confirmation by the Florentine authorities. From the moment a city capitulated, the Florentines claimed the right to approve or annul its past and future legislation.[24] It was Bartolus who had laid down the general principle: a subject town required approval for its statutes exactly in so far as it lacked jurisdiction: where a community had never possessed or had given up jurisdiction, it required permission to draw up statutes. His formula was neat, logical and immensely valuable to a city such as Florence that was attempting to govern its subject communities largely through established communal institutions.

It perhaps comes as a surprise, therefore, to realise that it was precisely this aspect of Bartolus' scheme that other jurists rejected. The question of whether or not a subject town needed approval before its legislation became valid was much discussed by the lawyers.[25] It was Bartolus' own pupil, Raynerius de Forlivio (Ranieri Arsendi, d. 1358), who led the opposition to the scheme, refusing to accept that only a

---

[21] Fasano Guarini, 'Gli statuti', pp. 112ff.

[22] D. Marrara, *Studi giuridici sulla Toscana Medicea* (Milan, 1965), p. 47.

[23] Law of 27 July 1546, *Legislazione Toscana*, ed. L.Cantini, I (Florence, 1800), pp. 313ff.

[24] Martines, *Lawyers and Statecraft*, p. 419; Fasano Guarini, 'Gli statuti', pp. 81 and 97.

[25] Storti Storchi has given an account of the debate, with copious bibliography, focusing on the Pavian school of jurists ('Appunti', pp. 322ff.). Mannori too has looked at the debate among jurists on the issue of approval with evidence particularly from the eighteenth century (*Il sovrano tutore*, pp. 108–17).

people with jurisdiction might draw up statutes. <u>Baldus (d. 1400)</u>, lecturing later in the fourteenth century, <u>vacillated.</u>[26] But in his comment on the *lex Omnes populi*, in response to the question whether local statutes ever required the authority of the superior, he concluded: <u>'if the statute neither prejudices the jurisdiction of the superior</u> . . . <u>nor concerns those matters reserved to the superior, then it is valid</u> because it is allowed by this law (*Omnes populi*) and other similar ones'.[27] In a *consilium* involving a dispute over the statutes of Trevi, a town under the domination of Perugia, he declared that 'communities <u>can make statutes concerning their own affairs</u> and do not require any particular confirmation', listing eight separate arguments for this conclusion.[28]

Where Florence in particular is concerned, the opinions of <u>Paulus de Castro (d. 1441)</u> are of special significance since it was he, as someone familiar with the legal problems encountered by the Florentines in establishing their territorial state, whom they chose to help draw up their new statutes of 1415. We have to take note, therefore, when he follows Baldus in upholding the rights of subject towns to live by their own statutes without the approval of the ruling city. He made his views clear in his commentary on the *lex Omnes populi*: 'Every community has the right to make its own statutes through this law; from this many things follow. . . [amongst which is that] the <u>authority of the superior is</u> <u>not required, since [such statutes] are authorised through Roman law</u> (*iure scripto*), <u>so long as they do not have the effect of prejudicing</u> the rights of the superior.'[29] He elaborated on this opinion in the 1420s in a *consilium* concerning the statutes of Pistoia and his discussion illustrates the <u>limitations surrounding the Florentine prerogative of approval.</u>[30] In this dispute, <u>local Pistoiese statutes</u>, both earlier ones and those issued in

---

[26] Storti Storchi, 'Appunti', pp. 337ff.

[27] *In primam Digesti Veteris partem commentaria* (Venice, 1577), De ius. et iur., l. Omnes populi (D.1.1.9), paras. 4 and 15–17: He asks, 'numquid in tali statuto requiratur auctoritas superioris', and concludes: 'Aut quis statuit super aliis non reservatis, et tunc valet statutum, quia est concessum fieri per hanc legem et similes'. The debate between Bartolus and Baldus is outlined by Sbriccoli, *L'interpretazione*, pp. 32ff.

[28] *Consilia* (Venice, 1575), IV, 324, incip. 'Quod dicti statuentes', para. 2: 'Communitates possunt statuere super re peculiari ipsarum, nec egent talia statuta alia singulari confirmatione'.

[29] *In primam Digesti Veteris partem* (Lyons, 1548), De ius. et iur. l. Omnes populi (D.1.1.9.), paras. 4–5: 'Collige ergo ex ista lege quod quilibet populus . . . habet facultatem condendi propria statuta per hanc legem. Ex hoc sequuntur plura . . . Tertio quod non requiritur authoritas superioris postquam habent a iure scripto, dum tamen non tendant in superioris praeiudicium'.

[30] *Consilia* (Venice, 1581), II, 256, incip. 'Videtur manifeste'.

1417, upheld a woman's claims to family property. But were Pistoiese statutes valid? According to Paulus, if Florentine rights of approval were to be upheld, the earlier Pistoiese statutes were not valid because they had been expressly annulled in 1401 as part of the process of submission. Even though they were adhered to in practice in the subsequent period, they lacked the requisite approval and were then superseded by the new statutes of 1417. These statutes were themselves approved for three years only and after that the approval had not been reissued. Paulus was in fact demonstrating that, if the Pistoiese really did have to obtain Florentine approval as laid down in the 1401 *capitoli*, then they would be left with no statutes at all. But as we have seen, he did not believe approval had any force in these circumstances, arguing that, 'from the facts which have been revealed, it is clear that the intention of the people of Pistoia is to govern themselves according to their own statutes and not according to the statutes of Florence'.[31] The sole purpose of the process of approval, according to Paulus, was to ascertain whether local statutes contained anything prejudicial to Florentine rights: since the Pistoiese statutes concerned only local matters, approval was not required. The Florentine law which laid down that statutes had to be approved could penalise the officials who ought to have sought the approval but could not have the effect of invalidating the statutes themselves. For Paulus it was the intentions of the citizens of Pistoia which mattered; their statutes remained in force – with or without the confirmation of the Florentine *approvatori*.

This trenchant opinion of Paulus' was not idiosyncratic: Baldus and others had preceded him as we have seen, and there were important jurists in the succeeding decades who supported his position. Jason de Maino was perhaps the best known and, though not much connected with Florence, he did teach in the *studio* for a short time.[32] In his commentary on the *lex Omnes populi*, he refers to Baldus 'where he says that in statutes or constitutions of the people the consent of the prince is not required . . . since the authority of their own magistrate is sufficient together with the general permission which they have through this law [*Omnes populi*]'. He sums up unambiguously: 'take note then that, since people of all kinds have the power to found statutes, I hold that the law does not require any other confirmation of the superior'.[33] These jurists

---

[31] *Ibid.*, para. 3: 'Breviter licet praedicta multum videantur urgere contra amitam in tantum ut vix possit dari ad congruum responsum, attamen quia ex his quae proponuntur in facto apparet quod intentio populi Pistoriensis est regere se secundum statuta sua, non secundum statuta Florentiae'.

[32] A. F. Verde, *Lo studio fiorentino 1473–1503* (Florence, 1973–94), II, p. 334 (a. 1488).

[33] *In primam Digesti Veteris partem commentaria* (Venice, 1598), De ius. et iur., l. Omnes

were content to accept much of what Bartolus had to say on this subject, but not that confirmation or approval was required for subject cities to make or live by their own statutes.

Lawyers and judges practising day to day in the courts of the Florentine dominions in the fifteenth century, therefore, were being advised that local legislation was valid whether or not it had passed the scrutiny of the *approvatori degli statuti*. The question that immediately arises is why the lawyers were seemingly at odds with the Florentine government on this issue. We can follow the logic of their arguments: it is difficult to get round the *lex Omnes populi,* which does state, without ifs or buts, that communities have the right to live by their own laws. Then again, jurists, including those connected with Florence, found that the approval of a superior in itself had various limitations that called into question the status of such confirmation. According to Franciscus de Accoltis (Francesco Accolti, d. 1488), a superior, through approval, confirms only just, not unjust, statutes.[34] This opens the door to endless cavilling. Then again, some confirmations were more potent than others. According to Accolti, approval of a specific provision is stronger than confirmation in general.[35] Going back to Paulus, approval can only work where statutes are already valid: 'a superior intends only to complete the incomplete, not validate the invalid'.[36] Nor did confirmation have the effect of keeping in being statutes that a subject city wished to abolish: 'Even though approved by the superior, statutes can be revoked by those who made them', said Paulus, adding that 'confirmation is understood to last as long as the statutes themselves, and

---

populi (D.1.1.9), Repetitio, paras. 34–5: 'nunc addo Baldum . . .ubi tenet quod in statuto vel in constitutione populi non requiritur consensus principis . . . quia sufficit auctoritas proprii magistratus et licentia generalis quam habent per istam legem . . . Item adverte, cum quilibet populus habeat facultatem faciendi statuta, teneo quod de iure non requiritur alia confirmatio superioris'. Storti Storchi includes Jason in her survey and she mentions Abbas Panormitanus (Niccolò dei Tedeschi) and Alexander Tartagni ('Appunti', pp. 340ff.).

34 *Commentaria in primam et secundam partem Digesti Novi* (Lyons, 1533), De adquirenda [vel amittenda] possessione, l. Quod Servus (D.41.2.24), para. 4: 'si superior confirmat omnia privilegia quae competunt verbi gratia uni civitati vel uni ecclesiae, videtur confirmare illa quae sunt iusta non iniusta. Et idem in statutis quae generaliter confirmantur'.

35 *Ibid.*: 'Est enim fortior specialis approbatio quam generalis.'

36 *Commentaria in secundam Infortiati partem* (Lyons, 1548), De legatis et fideicom. l. 121, Si quando (D.30.109): 'Item scias quod quaedam sunt de sua natura imperfecta nisi confirmentur, ut electiones quae indigent confirmatione superioris, et statuta facta per subditos, tunc si superior confirmat generaliter omnia statuta vel electiones, talis confirmatio non compreendit nisi valida statuta, vel electiones, quia superior intendit perficere imperfecta non autem validare invalida'.

for as long as those who made them continue so to decree'.[37] As Jason subsequently put it: 'a statute approved by the authority of a superior may nevertheless be revoked by the statute makers alone and without the permission of the superior'.[38]

But perhaps the most devastating criticism of the system of approval came from Paulus himself, in the above-mentioned *consilium* concerning the Pistoiese statutes. He was particularly scathing when, as he put it, 'such confirmation of the same statutes is required many times, as indeed it is in the city of Pistoia, where it is demanded every three years, even if they contain nothing new. For it cannot be claimed then that approval is required for any other motive than financial gain, either for the commune of Florence or for the chancery'.[39] We know that there was a special tax paid by subject communities for securing Florentine confirmation of their statutes.[40] The tax, in Paulus' opinion, undermined the force of approval: financial gain could not provide a basis in law for validating local legislation.

But jurists must have been aware of the difficulties of governing a territorial state. The Florentines needed a system of confirmation if they were to have oversight of the legislation passed in subject cities and be in a position to implement their policies. Such objectives, indeed, found theoretical justification in Bartolus' analysis. And yet, for their part, the lawyers had to apply the law in court and it was impossible in practice to ensure that every piece of legislation passed in the Florentine territories had received approval. Confirmation could be a time-

---

[37] *In secundam Codicis partem* (Lyons, 1548), De testamentis l. Omnium testamentorum (C.6.23.19), para. 6: 'statuta licet confirmata per superiorem possint revocari per statuentes etiam sine auctoritate superioris quia confirmatio intelligitur quousque durant statuta et statuentes persistant in eadem dispositione de quo per eum in lex omnes populi'.

[38] *Commentaria in secundam partem Digesti Veteris* (Venice, 1598), De legatis, l. 26, Non Amplius, verb. Si certum (D.30.26), para 12: 'Statutum confirmatum auctoritate superioris potest tamen per solos statuentes revocari absque licentia superioris'. See also Jason, *Commentaria in secundam partem Codicis* (Venice, 1598), De Testamentis, l. Omnium testamentorum (C.6.23.19), para. 10: 'Item in quantum Bartolus ibi dicit et est notabile verbum, quod statuentes qui non habent facultatem statuendi et statutum sit confirmatum a superiore, si volunt illud revocare et redire ad ius commune, quod possunt sine consensu principis . . . Ad hoc bene facit quia res de facili revertitur ad naturam suam'.

[39] Para. 6: 'Et potissime quando talis approbatio super eisdem statutis requireretur pluries, ut etiam in civitate Pistorii, ubi requiritur in singulis trienniis, etiam si non essent in aliquo innovata. Nam non potest dici quod tunc requiritur nisi pro lucro aut communis Florentiae aut cancellariae'.

[40] Fasano Guarini, 'Gli statuti', p. 122; Mannori, *Il sovrano tutore*, p. 109; see also L. Mannori, *L'amministrazione del territorio nella Toscana Granducale* (Florence, 1988), p. 13.

consuming procedure that took place sporadically, whereas passing the measures needed for everyday government was, especially in the larger towns, a ceaseless activity. And, as Paulus said, 'statutes and laws (*reformationes*) are binding as soon as they can plausibly have had time to come to public notice'.[41] There was inevitably, as Paulus found at Pistoia, a backlog of legislation that had not been officially sanctioned by Florence.[42] The Florentine territorial state was too loose a structure for a rigid system of approval to work. And so it may have been with day-to-day issues of law enforcement in mind that the jurists rejected the Florentine ideal that no local legislation in the subject territories should be valid without authorisation.

In Florentine territory then, as elsewhere, all communities were permitted to draw up their own statutes, which, it is important to stress, always took precedence. Florence attempted to keep this process in check by means of its *approvatori*, but lawyers considered local statutes valid even without formal approval. Faced with the kind of fragmentation that these principles encouraged, the Florentines attempted, in the 1415 statutes, to set out some sort of unified framework for the whole territory. The first rubric of the fifth book (*De legibus*), beginning *Urbem nostram*, lays down the principle that 'our city of Florence and all its territory is to be ruled and governed by our laws', but adds the proviso 'that the particular statutes and laws of the locality should always be observed'.[43] It was recognised that Florentine statutes would always come second to local laws. However, one might be tempted to ask whether they could, even then, be enforced outside the city itself. Did the Florentines succeed to any extent in having their statutes implemented in the subject territories?

Paulus de Castro himself seemed to be in no doubt about the role of the Florentine statutes, and here he followed the principle laid down in the law *Urbem nostram*. In his *consilium* concerning an unnamed community formerly subject to Pisa that had been encouraged to draw up its own statutes for the first time, Paulus declared that:

the Pisan statutes are not to be followed in this *podesteria*, now that it is

---

[41] *Consilia* (Venice, 1580), I, 51, incip. 'Visis et ponderatis', para. 2: 'Sed statuta et reformationes ligant adhuc citius si transivit tantum tempus quod versimile sit ea devenisse in notitiam'.

[42] Mannori has pointed out that subject communities were chronically lax in fulfilling their obligation to have statutes confirmed (*Il sovrano tutore*, p. 109).

[43] *Statuta*, III, p. 479: 'salvis semper specialibus statutis et iuribus locorum . . . et . . . consuetudinis cuiusque dictorum locorum'. This passage has been looked at again by Celli, *Studi sui sistemi normativi*, p. 141; Fasano Guarini, 'Gli statuti', pp. 87ff. and Mannori, *Il sovrano tutore*, pp. 104ff.

subject no longer to Pisa but to Florence, even if in former times the Pisan statutes, as those of the superior city, were used there. The statutes of the city of Florence, rather, should be used where the *podesteria* has none of its own and nothing else has been laid down for that area . . . although, now that the *podesteria* has statutes of its own confirmed by Florence, the statutes of Florence should not be used.[44]

This principle left to the Florentine statutes the role of filling the gaps in local statutes. This in itself was a revolutionary idea. It had long been accepted that urban statutes encompassed the contado,[45] but it was a different matter to expect that Florence's own laws should be embraced by their subjects in the expanded territorial state even as a back-up for local legislation. Just as it was not easy to make use of the concept of approval to undermine local rights, so it was difficult to overturn entrenched tradition in order to impose Florentine law locally. For one of the cornerstones of statute law, as we have seen, was that it assumed the existence of Roman law as its system of reference, not the statutes of another city.

This problem led to a lively debate at the time.[46] Certain subject cities in the Florentine dominion had in their statutes specific provisions for direct recourse to *ius commune*, thus bypassing the statutes of Florence. This was so in Pisa, which became the focus of a discussion between the lawyers beginning with Ludovicus Romanus (Ludovico Pontano, d. 1439). His argument was that, where the Pisan submission of 1406 stated that *ius commune* was the next point of reference after local statutes, the authors were referring to Florentine law, which would thus be imposed on the people of Pisa as a means of backing up their statutes.[47] But Ludovicus was the target of much outraged dissent

---

[44] *Consilia* (Venice, 1580), I, 129, incip. 'Statuta Pisana', para. 1: 'Statuta Pisana non sunt hodie servanda in dicta potestaria, postquam non est dictae civitati hodie subdita, sed civitati Florentiae etiam si aliquando fuerint ibi servata tanquam statuta civitatis superioris . . . sed potius essent servanda statuta civitatis Florentiae in defectum statutorum dictae potestariae si super illa non esset aliter dispositum . . . Sed nec illa sunt servanda postquam dicta potestaria habet propria statuta confirmata a communi Florentiae'.

[45] See, for example, Paulus, *In primam Digesti Veteris partem*, De ius. et. iur. l. Omnes populi (D.1.1.9.), para. 7: 'Item an statutum civitatis debet servari in terris comitatus? Glossator tenet quod sic . . . quod est verum in defectum proprium statutorum'.

[46] See note 7 above for recent discussion.

[47] *Consilia* (Frankfurt, 1577), 218, incip. 'Presens casus', para. 6: 'Tertio obiicitur de quadam Florentina reformatione cuius est dispositio ut Pisana civitas suis constitutionibus gubernetur, ubi autem casus aligua earum constitutionum decisus non esset recurratur ad ius commune. Ad hoc autem . . . responderi potest quod et hoc stante, quod in casibus a iure municipali Pisanorum non decisis ad ius commune recurrendum sit, nihilominus verissimum erit quod et hic casus de quo in puncto

in the fifteenth and early sixteenth centuries. Bartolomeus and Marianus
Socinus, as well as Philippus Decius, were among a group of fifteenth-
century lawyers who would not accept that the term *ius commune* could
stand for the Florentine statutes. Bartolomeus Socinus (d. 1507), who
taught for many years in the Florentine Studio, rejected this idea totally,
concluding that, regardless of what was decreed by Florence in the law
Urbem nostram, 'where cases remain unresolved, recourse should be had
to Roman law (*ius commune*); the authority of the Florentine statutes
does not extend, when in doubt, to the city of Pisa'.[48] Communal
statutes did not extend *extra territorium*, says Socinus, and, 'although the
city of Pisa is not outside [Florentine] territory, that is still the basic
reason why, in that city, Pisan and not Florentine statutes should be
followed'.[49] Writing in the earlier part of the sixteenth century,
Philippus Decius (d. 1535), who had also taught in Florence, supported
Bartolomeus' conclusion: 'Socinus argued the case against Romanus
with a multitude of proofs . . . and his opinion has usually been
practised and followed in Florence.'[50]

> quaeritur secundum Florentina statuta terminabitur, cum per illa terminatus reper-
> iatur cum hic sit ius commune, scilicet, ut loca inferiora superioribus constitutionibus
> et consequenter Florentini dominii gubernentur atque regantur'. See Celli, *Studi*,
> pp. 138ff.; Fasano Guarini, 'Gli statuti', p. 83; Mannori, *Il sovrano tutore*, p. 111.
> [48] *Consilium* 271 para. 7: 'in non decisis recurri debet ad ius commune; et sic statuta
> Florentina non extendunt vires suas, in dubio, ad civitatem Pisanam'. The *consilium*
> was published in II of the *Consilia* of Marianus Socinus (Venice, 1571). See also *ibid.*,
> paras. 2–3: 'Primo ex illa ratione quia ex quo in hac materia si nulla sunt statuta in
> civitate Pisarum, quae civitati Florentiae est subiecta, constitutionibus civitatis
> Florentinae regi debet . . . Confirmatur etiam per primum capitulum statutorum
> civitatis Florentiae in quinto libro in quo disponitur quod loca subdita si non habent
> in aliquo casu statuta particularia, regantur statutis civitatis Florentiae quod statutum,
> cum sit clarum, non videtur esse opus alia interpretatione . . . Sed ad hoc
> respondetur quod statutum est in civitate Pisarum concessum a civitate Florentiae
> per quod disponitur quod in casibus in quibus non reperitur dispositum a statutis
> civitatis Pisarum recurratur ad ius commune . . . Sed contra hoc iterum posset instare
> pars adversa quod imo ius commune civitatis Pisarum dicuntur statuta civitatis
> Florentiae quae dicuntur ius commune immediatum quo ad urbem Florentinam et
> omnes subditos . . . ergo recurrendum est ad statuta Florentina ut causa decidatur
> secundum ius commune et ita in statuto Pisano per istam rationem consuluit
> Ludovicus Romanus . . . Sed in veritate usque nunc dicta interpretatio visa fuit
> falsa'.
> [49] *Ibid.*, para. 7: 'Et licet Civitas Pisana non sit extra territorium, tamen est eadem ratio
> ex quo in ea leges servari debent et statuta Pisana et non Florentina'.
> [50] *Consilia* (Venice, 1608), II, 469, incip. 'Visa inquisitione', paras. 11–12: 'Et licet hoc
> statutum non debeat servari hic Pisis, ubi civitas habet propria statuta . . . tamen
> secundum statuta Pisana disponitur quod deficientibus statutis Pisanis recurratur ad
> ius commune et secundum [Ludovicum] Romanum . . . verbum illud "ius
> commune" intelligitur pro iure civitatis superioris dominantis et sic esset recur-
> rendum ad statuta Florentina. Sed breviter respondetur quod illa interpretatio

Pisa has been the focus of more discussion than any other city in the Florentine dominion because of the initial debate sparked off by Ludovicus; but it was certainly not unique in having an acknowledged right to refer directly to *ius commune*. Arezzo and Volterra had the same privilege,[51] as did Pistoia, Cortona, Fucecchio[52] and Barga.[53] Even the 1415 statutes themselves contain hints that the proper point of departure after local statutes was Roman law. The Podestà of Arezzo, it was decreed, was to administer the law 'according to the statutes and ordinances of the city of Arezzo, and in default of those statutes, according to *ius commune*'.[54] This formula, as repeated in the statutes with regard to Pisa, was applied to other, even quite small, subject communities.[55] Amongst the local statutes themselves there seems to be no fixed pattern. Some, such as the 1360 statutes of Montopoli, say nothing about where to turn when circumstances are not provided for;[56] others, such as those of Prato, specify that the statutes of Florence are to be used where neither current nor past local statutes have anything to say, and failing those, Roman law;[57] yet others are vague: the 1446 statutes of Rincine and Fornace, for example, decree that one has to make analogies with other similar statutes in the same book and, if there are no similar ones, Florentine statutes or common law should be used.[58] The 1536 statutes of Arezzo follow the same rule as those of

Romani non est vera quia verbum illud "ius commune" de iure communi Romanorum intelligitur . . . Illa verba non possunt intelligi quod ad statutum Florentinum recurratur et hoc contra Romanum pluribus rationibus comprobat Socinus . . . et ista opinio saepius practicata et observata fuit Florentiae'. Cf. *ibid.*, 429, incip. 'Licet in causis', paras. 5–6, and see Celli, *Studi*, p. 140; Fasano Guarini, 'Gli statuti', pp. 83ff.

[51] Fasano Guarini, 'Gli statuti', p. 84.

[52] Mannori, *Il sovrano tutore*, p. 118.

[53] See note 60 below.

[54] *Statuta*, III, 'De officio potestatis Aretii' (Rub. XX), p. 538: 'secundum statuta et ordinamenta civitatis Aretii et ubi dicta statuta non disponerent secundum ius commune'.

[55] For Pisa, *ibid.*, p. 518; for the Alpes Florentinorum, *ibid.*, p. 598.

[56] E.g. the statutes of Montopoli, ed. B. Casini (Florence, 1968).

[57] E.g. the statutes of Prato, preserved in Florence at the Centro di Studi per la Storia del Pensiero Giuridico Moderno, Università degli studi di Firenze, ms. D.1.295, 191r: 'in casibus in quibus statuta praesentia non loquerentur, recurratur et recurri debeat ad antiquiora statuta terre Prati approbata per commune Florentiae et illa servare debeant. Et in casibus in quibus non loquuntur nec presentia nec antiquiora, recurratur ad statuta Communis Florentiae. Et in casibus in quibus non loquuntur, recurratur ad ius commune Romanorum tam in civilibus quam in criminalibus causis'.

[58] *Statuto dei comune di Rincine e Fornace 1446*, ed. U. Santarelli (Florence, 1969), 'De procedere di simile ad simile' (Rub. LXII): 'se proceda et termini siconda gl'ordini di Firenze ò di ragione comune'.

Pisa: 'And in matters not covered by these statutes recourse should be had and reference made to the *ius civile* which is called Roman law'.[59]

The debate over whether the Florentine statutes could stand as *ius commune* in its dominion, with or without certain exceptions, clearly fascinated contemporary jurists. But since by tradition *ius commune* could be ignored at will by 'omnes populi', even the attempt to make an analogy between Florentine statutes and *ius commune* was not the same as claiming that the Florentines could impose their own laws on a subject community. The point is highlighted by Marianus Socinus (d. 1556) in a case concerning the town of Barga. It involved the classic situation where local statutes had not foreseen the particular circumstances surrounding a woman's dowry and so the question arose of whether to turn to Book Two of the Florentine statutes. Marianus goes through all the standard arguments that put the Florentine statutes in the role of *ius comune*; but he is not convinced.[60] What persuades him in the end that a Florentine law could be used is that this was what local custom decreed in this instance: 'for the people of Barga have made it clear by their actual practice that, whatever might happen in other cases, in this particular set of circumstances they wanted to turn to the statutes of Florence'.[61] Marianus, in other words, is not persuaded by Florentine claims to supremacy; in matters of law, it is the wishes of the people themselves that count. It is worth remembering that this was the point which persuaded Paulus that, even without Florentine approval, the local statutes in Pistoia were valid: 'for it is clear that the intention of the people of Pistoia is to govern themselves according to their own statutes and not according to the statutes of Florence'.[62]

Not that it was solely a question of local rights: statutes often differed to such an extent from place to place that it would be impossible to have recourse from one to another, as envisaged in the law *Urbem nostram*. Even Paulus, author of the 1415 statutes, found it difficult to make use of Florentine statutes to fill the gaps in the case, referred to above, arising in the *podesteria* in the territory of Pisa. How could one make use of Florentine law, which assumed that the children should inherit the whole of their mother's dowry, when local legislation

---

[59] *Liber statutorum Arretii* (Arretij per Calixtum Simeonis, MDXXXVI), NN: 'Et in quibus dicta statuta ut supra non providerent ad ius civile quod Romanorum appellatur recurratur et recurri debeat'.

[60] *Consilia* (Venice, 1580), I, 1, para. 32: 'et ego pro nunc non firmo'.

[61] *Ibid.*, para. 32: 'nam homines Bargae ita observantes circa hoc videntur voluisse quod revertatur ad statuta Florentina, quicquid in aliis casibus sit determinatum'.

[62] *Consilia* (Venice, 1581), II, 256, para. 3: 'ex his quae proponuntur in facto apparet quod intentio populi Pistoriensis est regere se secundum statuta sua, non secundum statuta Florentiae'.

decreed that one half should be retained by the husband and the other was being claimed by his wife's family? Nor, in this instance, would *ius commune* help; and so Paulus was forced to fall back on local custom to resolve the dispute.[63] The trouble with turning to the Florentine statutes to back up local law was that the two systems might be so different that they could not be integrated.

Whatever the Florentine statutes decreed, in other words, it was not easy to ensure that Florentine law would become the law of second reference in the subject territories. *Ius commune* meant Roman law,[64] and it was difficult to insist that Florentine statutes should be the next point of referral when it was the universally accepted tradition that Roman law provided the background for all statutes: 'statutes should be interpreted according to *ius commune*'.[65] This was the first point Paulus himself made in his comment on the *lex Omnes populi*: 'where their own laws are insufficient, people abide by the common law of the Romans'.[66] In practice, the jurists followed this scheme: when they wanted to elaborate on a point of law raised in a local statute they referred to *ius commune*. The Florentines may have made token gestures in the direction of uniformity between their laws and local statutes;[67] and yet, as Paulus recognised with reference to the statutes of that unnamed *podesteria* in the Pisan contado, 'it does not matter that the confirmation of these statutes was issued on the understanding that they did not contradict the statutes of Florence . . . because I maintain that, when the *approvatori* made this qualification, it was understood to mean in matters that would have the effect of injuring the city of Florence, not in things that only affect this *podesteria*'.[68]

What then was the status of the Florentine statutes of 1415 in their

---

[63] *Consilia* (Venice, 1571), I, 129, incip. 'Statuta Pisana'.

[64] 'Verbum illud "ius commune" de iure communi Romanorum intelligitur'; Decius, *Consilia*, II, 469, incip. 'Visa inquisitione', para. 12.

[65] Jason, *In primam Digesti Veteris partem commentaria* (Venice, 1598), De ius. et iur., l. Omnes populi (D.1.1.9), Repetitio para. 63: 'statuta debeant intelligi secundum ius commune'. Sbriccoli, *L'interpretazione*, pp.112ff., 354, 438ff., 460ff. See also F. Calasso, *Il concetto di 'Diritto comune'* (Modena, 1934), pp. 38ff.

[66] Para. 3: 'in defectum proprii iuris viverent iure Romanorum communi'.

[67] A typical provision, in this instance with reference to Arezzo, was that the Captain and Podestà should observe local statutes provided they contained nothing 'contra honorem aut iurisdictionem seu praeminentiam vel iura communis Florentiae' (*Statuta*, III, p. 539).

[68] *Consilia*, I, 129, incip. 'Statuta Pisana', para. 1: 'Nec obstat quod confirmatio dictorum statutorum facta est, dummodo non contrarientur statutis communis Florentiae . . . quia dico quod dicta reservatio approbatorum intelligitur facta quo ad illa quae tenderent in praeiudicium communis Florentiae, non quo ad ea quae ipsos tantum de dicta potestaria tangunt'.

dominions? Whatever the law *Urbem nostram* decreed, and whether or not local statutes themselves referred back to Florentine law or to *ius commune*, one has to bear in mind both the practical difficulties and the weight of a legal tradition which militated against the ideal of a universal Florentine code that would fill the gaps in local legislation throughout the dominion. Of the statutes that made up the 1415 collection, those that dealt with the new organs of government imposed by Florence in its subject territories and which reiterated the various *capitoli* of submission were not to be ignored. To do so would 'have the effect of injuring the city of Florence', as Paulus put it. But the parts that incorporated the local statutes of the city of Florence were of a different status. It would not, perhaps, be quite fair to say that nothing more than lip service was paid to these parts of the 1415 statutes in the subject territories; but it seems that at best they were regarded as though of marginal value.

Local statutes were paramount and, with the active encouragement of the Florentine government, legislative pluralism remained a cardinal feature of the state. As a consequence Florentine law reached a point of chaos that was graphically described by Pompeo Neri in his *Discourse* on the reform of legislation published in 1747.[69] He estimated that, for the Florentine territories alone, there were more than five hundred separate books of local statutes. Over and above these there were the additions and revisions made in the course of many years ('così si è proceduto col metodo di aggiungere Legge sopra Legge') leading to 'infinite variations and contradictions' with the *Statuto generale* of Florence.[70] According to Leonardo Bruni, a state was an extended territory where 'the people live by the same laws and under one statute-making body' (*iisdem legibus unoque statutis consilio vivant*),[71] but the Florentines were far from satisfying this definition: indeed, their state may have achieved political pre-eminence but it never established legislative sovereignty.

[69] *Discorso primo tenuto nell' adunanza dei deputati alla compilazione di un nuovo codice delle leggi municipali della Toscana*, in J. B. Neri Badia, *Decisiones et responsa juris* (Florence, 1776), II, pp. 498–515.

[70] *Ibid.*, p. 502.

[71] Ed. Mehus, I, p.78.

CHAPTER 4

FISCALITY, POLITICS AND DOMINION IN FLORENTINE TUSCANY AT THE END OF THE MIDDLE AGES

GIUSEPPE PETRALIA

I

Between the later middle ages and the early modern period Florentine citizens managed money, pen and ink for princes and sovereigns in all of Europe. But this clear fame in finance has not stopped modern historians from passing severe judgment on these same men when it came to the fiscal administration of their own state. The most recent historiography has emphasised the inability of the Florentines to separate reasons of state from personal, family and factional interests. Its hypotheses are rooted in an alleged Florentine abandonment during the fifteenth century of the mainstream of simplification and rationalisation of the fiscal system. After the return of Cosimo *il Vecchio* to Florence in 1434, it is asserted, major fiscal confusion and less rigour in the administration of state finances were consonant with the rising political fortunes of the Medici family. This recent understanding was arrived at in the study of Florentine domestic politics, through reconstructing the vital ties between the public debt, short-term credit, and the political connections of the governing families of Florence. The interpretation has also been extended 'outward', as it were, to involve the history of the Tuscan regional state. Medicean hegemony, it is said, interrupted relevant processes that had started during the decisive period of territorial expansion, namely the administrative integration of the Florentine dominion, the erosion of the power of the local intermediaries between the central fisc and its taxpayers, and the reinforcement of direct taxes on subjects. Evidence of a turning point, it is argued, can be found in a qualitative change in the written fiscal sources, since from the mid-1430s there ceased to be detailed inventories of the accounts of the principal fiscal offices of the city and territory in the records of the Treasury of the Commune (*Camera del comune*). Fiscal policy would thus seem to confirm the validity of a historical distinction that has often been made between first and second 'phases' of the development of the Florentine

territorial state. In the first stage, a clear political plan for institutional
centralisation, developed between the final submission of San Miniato in
1370 and the acquisition of Arezzo in 1384, was followed with force and
discipline into the first decades of the fifteenth century. This 'virtuous'
path would subsequently be abandoned, however, as clientelism and the
'privatisation' of the regime took off under the Medici. The result of this
second phase would be a territorial regime that lacked coherence and
uniformity throughout the early modern period.[1]

The legacy of old debates overshadows all of these evaluations. The
theme of the 'regional state', which in the last thirty years has renewed
the entire historiographical panorama of late medieval Italy, has also
reinvigorated Anglo-American scholarship on Florence, which had
traditionally been motivated almost exclusively by the desire to understand competition and the social life of citizens within the city walls.
But a new mix of historiographical interests does not mean that scholars
will necessarily avoid reviving the numerous older discussions about the
degree of the 'political modernity' of Renaissance Florence that for
many years animated discussions of civic humanism, the political and
familial behaviour of urban elites, and the transformation of institutions.
The separation of private and public, the juxtaposition of the interests of
family and state, the distinctions between personal entourage and
institutions of political control, and the degrees of simplification and
centralisation in the exercise of power over men and territory are all

---

[1] I will limit the essential bibliography to the principal works of the last decades on
fiscality and the state: L. F. Marks, 'The Financial Oligarchy in Florence under
Lorenzo', in E. F. Jacob (ed.), *Italian Renaissance Studies: A Tribute to the late Cecilia M.
Ady* (London, 1960), pp. 123–47; M. Becker, 'Problemi della finanza pubblica
fiorentina della seconda metà del Trecento e dei primi del Quattrocento', *Archivio
storico italiano*, 123 (1965), pp. 433–66; A. Molho, *Florentine Public Finances in the Early
Renaissance* (Cambridge, Mass., 1971); E. Conti, *L'imposta diretta a Firenze nel
Quattrocento (1427–1494)* (Rome, 1984); A. Molho, 'L'amministrazione del debito
pubblico a Firenze nel quindicesimo secolo', in *I ceti dirigenti nella Toscana del
Quattrocento* (Florence, 1987), pp. 191–207; A. Brown, 'Public and private interest:
Lorenzo, the Monte and the Seventeen Reformers', in G. C. Garfagnini (ed.),
Lorenzo de'Medici. Studi (Florence, 1992), pp. 103–65; A. Molho, 'The State and
Public Finance: A Hypothesis Based on the History of Late Medieval Florence', in
J. Kirshner (ed.), *The Origins of the State in Italy, 1300–1600* (Chicago, 1996),
pp. 97–135. More generally on the territorial state see: M. Becker, *Florence in
Transition*, 2 vols. (Baltimore, 1967–8); G. Chittolini, 'Ricerche sull'ordinamento
territoriale del dominio fiorentino agli inzi del secolo XV', in Chittolini, *La formazione
dello stato regionale e le istituzioni del contado* (Turin, 1979), pp. 292–352; A. Zorzi, 'Lo
stato territoriale fiorentino (secoli XIV–XV): aspetti giurisdizionali', *Società e storia*, 50
(1990), pp. 799–825; A. Zorzi, 'L'organizzazione del territorio in area fiorentina tra
XIII e XIV secolo', in G. Chittolini and D. Willoweit (eds.), *L'organizzazione del
territorio in Italia e in Germania: secoli XIII–XIV* (Bologna, 1994), pp. 799–825.

reasonable analytical categories to use in histories of modernisation which go back as far as the later middle ages. Such histories either tend to show the evolution of western political structures towards their present forms, or they make continual comparisons between modern political ideas and the structures of the past. It is a limitation of both approaches, however, that the historian easily risks losing sight of the logic that was proper to the past in its own day. In sketching, in this chapter, the essential lines of a reading of the connection between fiscality and territorial control in the fifteenth century, I shall seek to show the advantage of abandoning many of the modernising models still present in our discussions of Florentine rule in fifteenth-century Tuscany.

II

The introduction and then the revocation of the catasto tax within the Florentine dominion between 1427 and 1431 are often considered the two principal moments of a watershed distinguishing the fiscal policy and governmental practice of the Albizzi and Medici regimes. Such an interpretation, however, has developed out of a marked preference among historians to imagine the catasto's strategic potential for region-wide fiscal control, rather than to investigate its actual motivations. It will be helpful, therefore, to consider the great Florentine catasto in the context of contemporary fiscal practice. Of course, the method of declaring wealth under the catasto was not tried for the first time in 1427. Fairly accurate ways of describing household property for fiscal exactions had already been developed and applied in the contadi of Florence and Pisa by about 1406. Commissioners in Pistoia and Arezzo had already developed 'catasti' for these areas between 1415 and 1425. A permanent and updated catasto of landed urban and rural property (typical of early fourteenth-century tax registers) had existed, moreover, for some time at Cortona, even before its acquiescence to Florence in 1411.[2]

---

[2] E. Conti, *I catasti agrari della repubblica fiorentina e il catasto particellare toscano (secc. XIV–XIX)* (Rome, 1966), pp. 73–4; G. Petralia, 'Imposizione diretta e dominio territoriale nella repubblica fiorentina del Quattrocento', in *Società, istituzioni, spiritualità: studi in onore di Cinzio Violante*, 2 vols. (Spoleto, 1994), II, pp. 643–4; L. Gai, 'Centro e periferia: Pistoia nell'orbita fiorentina durante il '500', in *Pistoia: una città nello stato mediceo* (Pistoia, 1980), pp. 9–147, at p. 13 and note 45; ASF, SC Delib. spec., 17, 28v–30v; 18, 68v–70r; P. Benigni, L. Carbone and C. Saviotti (eds.), *Archivio di Stato di Arezzo: fonti per la storia del sistema fiscale urbano (1384–1533)* (Rome, 1985), p. 83; P. Benigni, 'Fonti per lo studio dell'imposizione diretta in Arezzo tra il XIV e il XV secolo: problemi di ordinamento e di utilizzazione', in *Studi in onore di Leopoldo Sandri*, 3 vols. (Rome, 1983), I, pp. 109–11; G. Mancini, *Cortona nel Medio Evo* (Florence, 1897), p. 286.

Yet, despite these earlier examples, the census of 1427 undoubtedly constituted a substantial and traumatic innovation. But what was threatening about it was not its particular method, but rather the fact that it was imposed by Florence without negotiations in a context of severe fiscal pressure. Even in subject communities that had already imposed direct taxes on their inhabitants based on precise declarations of individual property, the contemporaneity and universality of the catasto's implementation by Florentine officers sparked hostility and resistance. The enactment of the catasto of 1427 was not only the first but also the last occurrence of such a sudden, sweeping, unilateral, and therefore 'illegitimate' act of fiscal aggression in the history of the Florentine regional state in Tuscany. It revealed discontent with the existing balance of power between the citizens of the subject towns and their contadi; in many instances, it violated written agreements; and, most importantly, it limited the local prerogatives of urban and rural populations.

Florence had acted unilaterally and in violation of agreements before, albeit not in fiscal matters, when it diminished the rank and power of its subject cities by stripping them of juridical and administrative rights in their contadi: at Arezzo in 1384, Pistoia in 1401, Volterra in 1429 (when the city refused the imposition of the catasto), and 1472, and Pisa immediately after its conquest in 1406. These episodes undoubtedly assisted the centralisation of power, even if only partially and temporarily. What is important for our purposes, however, is that these measures were always taken as punitive actions, 'legitimated' by the disintegration of earlier ties between Florence and the urban aristocracies in the subject towns. (At Pisa, such ties did not even exist.) When Florence confronted acute problems of security in these subject cities, autonomy was offered to the communities in their contadi, both as a reward to the contadi for a closer and more direct bond with Florence and as more or less 'legitimate' punishment of the cities.

The circumstances that prompted Florence to hazard the unilateral institution of a territory-wide catasto were entirely different, since the catasto did not involve the punishment of perceived 'wrongs' committed by particular subjects, but rather constituted a kind of universal doom. It would be difficult to exaggerate the failure of the catasto, which has to be understood as the regime's mistaken and rash response to a desperate military and financial crisis.[3] The catasto radically

---

[3] In the first instance, the catasto was deliberated for Florentine citizens only; then it was extended to other territorial bodies, those in the contado, the district, ecclesiastics and foreigners. This was to prevent the hiding of citizens' properties under other names. Florentine citizens possessed two-thirds of the state's private wealth.

diminished fiscal revenues. Even the loyalty of the least troubled communities (such as Colle Valdelsa and San Gimignano) was put at risk. And by 1431 the Florentines themselves were convinced that the catasto should be abandoned as a fiscal instrument and used simply as an excellent archival resource – as is easily understood by the many historians who have so used it since![4]

Yet the abandonment of the universal catasto by Florence did not diminish significantly the central power's ability to gather information about the resources of the territory and its subjects. Thus, under the Medici, just as before 1427, in the presence of grave problems in calculating the yields generated by a tax distribution that had become entirely inefficient, and of the many special concessions that were made to individual taxpayers, Florence continued to draw up fiscal censuses (even in the form of 'catasti') of the property and men of a community or of an entire area, on the basis of which it established, without too much scandal, a new tax that was reasonable for a community and even for a single household to pay. In the distretto, to be sure, it was simpler and more remunerative to demand extraordinary taxes to back up exceptional military undertakings – as had been the case in the first decades of the century – rather than to enforce a tax from the centre based on a general fiscal census. But there is little evidence that in themselves the tax methods used after the abandonment of the catasto were somehow defective or less efficacious.

In comparison with their predecessors, the Medici had the advantage of not finding themselves in a predicament in which political control of the entire dominion was at risk because of financial crisis. The major change between the first and second halves of the fifteenth century was not caused by radical differences between the political behaviour of the Albizzi and the Medici. Instead, the decisive factor was that Florence faced no military emergency of the dimensions of the period from 1424 to 1432, when Florentines paid out between 500,000 and 700,000 florins a year in forced loans (*prestanze*), whereas ordinary peacetime public revenues rarely reached 300,000 florins.[5] The catasto of 1427 was thus an unsuccessful wartime innovation, rather than the culmination of a rational plan for territorial government.

It also seems best to play down the importance of the abandonment by the Treasury, during the mid-1430s, of the practice of compiling a detailed inventory of the income and expenditures of the chief fiscal

[4] Petralia, 'Imposizione diretta', pp. 647–50.
[5] Conti, *L'imposta diretta*, pp. 18–20; Molho, *Florentine Public Finances*, pp. 61–2.

magistracies. These inventories (*campioni*) were necessitated by the complexity of the transition from a fiscal system founded on a single city and its contado to a system that encompassed other subject areas. The transition, moreover, took place during decades of continuous and complicated fiscal evolution. Thus, there were entanglements within the same fiscal year between current taxes and taxes in arrears, and between the ordinary and extraordinary taxes on persons in the contado and the distretto, which came predominantly to the Treasury (*Camera del comune*). Funds from forced loans, both old and new, which had gone principally to the Officers of the Monte to offset the public debt, needed to be accounted for, as did the gabelles on the city and the contado registered with the Monte and the gabelles that came in from the distretto that were instead assigned to the Treasury. This complex situation had changed, however, by the mid-1400s, when the Medici party was in charge. One factor was that more revenues went directly to the Monte instead of the Treasury.[6] In addition, the less frequent imposition of extraordinary taxes made it easier in the later period to keep track of the government's revenues. Finally, since territorial expansion was already winding down by the 1420s, the commune's fiscal officers found it much easier in later years to achieve a simplified and more manageable summary of the republic's revenues and expenses.

III

Historians have been hunting for fiscal innovations when perhaps what were essential to the system were its continuities. Nevertheless it would also be a mistake to argue that the patchwork nature of the later Tuscan fiscal system resulted from the mere survival of institutions that antedated the territorial state. I believe instead that it needs to be emphasised how, in expanding and reinforcing their dominion over Tuscany, the Florentines confronted many local instances of a fiscal system that was already structured according to a relatively uniform typology. Persons residing in the contadi were taxed by gabelles, direct

---

[6] This was so much the case that from the middle of the century, the registers of the Monte contained summaries of a large portion of the Commune's assets and expenses; see A. Molho, *Marriage Alliance in Late Medieval Florence* (Cambridge, Mass., 1994), pp. 59–60. Since the early fifteenth century, the ordinary direct tax on communities in the district was collected and registered directly in the Monte registers; see *ibid.*, note 27 and J. Brown, *In the Shadow of Florence: Provincial Society in Renaissance Pescia* (Oxford, 1982), appendix 5, pp. 216–18.

taxes, and the monopoly and forced distribution of salt. Persons in the city were taxed by gabelles and forced loans.[7] In truth, there was little left to invent. Given the deep similarities among local systems from the past, the territorial system did not therefore derive its varied aspects from the continuity of special old fiscal practices, but instead from the different and sometimes partial ways in which these were instituted within the new regional framework, even in the very years of supposed 'centralisation'. The coexistence within the Florentine state of numerous localities with long traditions of liberty alongside others with histories of stricter subordination has offered some justification to those historians who lament the absence of a uniform fiscal system in Florentine Tuscany. But the very same historical phenomenon has also been cited by other scholars who argue that Florence instead imposed an exceptional degree of centralisation and uniformity in the area of legal jurisdiction: Arezzo, Pistoia and Pisa did indeed lose control of their contadi. But whether 'centralisation' is fiscal or jurisdictional, both historical interpretations resort to a form of abstract reasoning that describes a putative Florentine 'public order' that lies outside the actual relations of power, loyalty and conflict that existed among Florentine citizens and the persons, families and communities of the subject territories. Factors such as these – and not a centralising 'project' (failed or successful) – were what created the fiscal diversity of the Florentine dominion.

The final configuration of Florentine fiscal policy in the dominion was largely determined by three important historical cases: those of Arezzo, Pisa and Pistoia. The submission of Arezzo in 1384 and Pisa in 1406 led to the almost complete surrender of those cities' revenues to Florence, establishing the right of the Florentines to acquire the proceeds of tolls, gabelles on exchange and consumption, and the salt monopoly, and their right to assess and levy direct taxes. Only at Arezzo and Pisa was the jurisdictional separation of the cities from their former contadi accompanied by a break in their fiscal ties.[8] These extreme solutions resulted from the exceptional circumstances under which Florence extended its dominion over the two cities. In both instances, it was necessary for Florence to make a clean break with the pre-existing political power of the local urban aristocracies. In Pisa, this was essential because it had not been possible to negotiate a peaceful

---

[7] P. Cammarosano, 'Il sistema fiscale delle città toscane', in S. Gensini (ed.), *La Toscana nel secolo XIV. Caratteri di una civiltà regionale* (Pisa, 1988), pp. 201–14.

[8] C. Guasti (ed.), *I Capitoli del Comune di Firenze. Inventario e regesto*, I (Florence, 1866), pp. 371–87; P. Silva, 'Pisa sotto Firenze dal 1406 al 1433', *Studi storici*, 18 (1909), pp. 133–83.

surrender.[9] At Arezzo, the political class had dissolved into confusion by the middle of the Trecento. The leading class of Arezzo had never been able to control all of its territory, which now was formed largely into separate civil and criminal districts. The Florentines purchased the signorial rights to Arezzo and imposed them on a semi-deserted city, to which they recalled all possible citizens to swear allegiance to Florence. When the leading Aretines re-entered the city, they voluntarily offered their submission, which Florence accepted. Although Pisa would remain an occupied city, presided over by a military garrison throughout the fifteenth century, at Arezzo the restoration of normal relations and of a political dialogue with the urban patriciate was relatively rapid. Thus, beginning in 1427, when Leonardo Bruni assumed office as chancellor of Florence, the Florentine Chancery was entrusted for nearly forty consecutive years to a man from Arezzo. A similarly close tie to the Florentine government would have been inconceivable for almost anyone from a Pisan family, whether it was an old or new family, throughout the fifteenth century.[10] With respect to its surrounding territory, Arezzo was allowed to conserve a small part of its contado (the *cortine*) which had over 5000 inhabitants and was more populous than the contadi of Volterra or Cortona. The citizens reacquired their fiscal jurisdictions, a certain liberty in the distribution of direct taxes and the right to collect their own gabelles.[11]

The complete 'sequestering' by Florence of the subject town's treasury was perhaps even more important than juridical separation from its contado. The absorption of an urban treasury was a manifestation of extreme force, showing that peaceful political relations between Florence and the leaders of a subject town were unattainable. Although Florence separated the contadi from its large subject cities, complete fiscal degradation was applied in a definitive way only in the case of the state of Pisa. This was clearly a product of the irreducible hostility that existed between Florentines and the city they called 'the principle member of our commune' (*principalis oculus nostri Communis*). The only

---

[9] G. Petralia, '"Crisi" ed emigrazione dei ceti eminenti a Pisa durante il primo dominio fiorentino. L'orizzonte cittadino e la ricerca di spazi esterni (1406–1460)', in *I ceti dirigenti nella Toscana del Quattrocento* (Florence, 1987), pp. 291–452.

[10] Guasti (ed.), *I Capitoli del Comune*, I, pp. 397–408; R. Black, 'Cosimo de' Medici and Arezzo', in F. Ames-Lewis (ed.), *Cosimo 'il Vecchio' de' Medici, 1389–1464* (Oxford, 1992), pp. 34–5; G. Petralia, 'Pisa laurenziana: una città e un territorio per conservazione dello "stato"', in R. Fubini (ed.), *La Toscana al tempo di Lorenzo il Magnifico: Politica Economia Cultura*, 3 vols. (Pisa, 1996), III, pp. 955–80.

[11] See above, note 2, and below, note 20.

fiscal treasury (*camera*) of its own that Florence established entirely in the territory was that of Pisa, into whose coffers flowed about two-thirds to three-quarters of the income from the distretto as it was constituted immediately after the conquest (and without taking into account the Florentine contado).[12] The profundity of the political fracture and the importance of economic competition made irreconcilable and necessary the 'punishment' that the Florentines inflicted on the Pisans.

In the rest of the dominion and in the history of the fourteenth- and fifteenth-century regional state, the combination of the two measures – the juridical break with the contado and the sequestering of a community's assets – was used only as a forceful but temporary political weapon. It was used twice against Volterra, in 1429 and in 1472 – on both occasions Florence took over Volterra's contado and its assets[13] – and once in Pistoia, in 1401. Here, where an ancient entanglement of political ties between the local aristocratic families and Florence had provided from the early fourteenth century a peaceful political and military tutelage, the double punishment appeared necessary for the unthinkable approach of the Pistoiese towards the Visconti from Milan, following a violent clash of internal factions. But if, on the one hand, Florentine rectors seated in the Pistoiese territory remained at their posts, on the other hand the treasury was restored to the city almost immediately.[14] The minor financial importance in relation to that of the Pisan case, but also the force of the old political dialectic between the Florentines and the Pistoiese, influenced a compromise within a few months. In exchange for the annual tribute, Pistoia recovered its rights over the gabelles traditionally levied on the contado, and the direct powers of assessing and collecting the ordinary direct tax. From 1401 an ambiguity thus remained, in which the authority of the city over its territory appeared clearly weakened because of the presence of the Florentine rectors, but the republic had no longer any right *a priori* to contest the interests of the Pistoiese within their contado or to involve itself without precise reasons in local politics. The prevalent direct and indirect taxes imposed by the city became a source of recurrent tensions, of unrest and spontaneous revolt, which, from time to time, was quelled

---

[12] See below, note 26.

[13] L. Fabbri, 'Autonomismo comunale ed egemonia fiorentina a Volterra tra '300 e '400', *Rassegna volterrana*, 70 (1994), pp. 97–110; L. A. Cecina, *Notizie storiche della città di Volterra* (Pisa, 1758); A. F. Giachi, *Saggio di ricerche storiche sopra lo stato antico e moderno di Volterra* (Florence, 1883), p. 115.

[14] Chittolini, 'Ricerche', p. 329.

by Florence's use of arbitrary justice and pacification, without ever being able to cut its roots.[15]

IV

The geography of territorial fiscality was thus closely dependent on the original network of the relations between the Florentine aristocracy and the local elites. The quality of these relations endured for the long term, once they had been interwoven within the political orbit, even before it had been instituted in Florence, from which the variety of solutions arose. The mesh of institutional and personal forms of power therefore remained a constant feature of the fiscal system. Often the same Florentines and their banks financed the current payments of the communities within the republic, and the continuous tax debts. Florentine credit in the finances of other communes was a real and personal bond, which at the end of the thirteenth century – before any institutional subordination – contributed to leading middle-sized and minor centres into the orbit of political protection exercised by their larger neighbours. On the other hand, once the political context has been fixed, articulation between the fiscal system of the republic and the fiscal systems of its subject members – given its physiological affinity – was not a question that could produce many variables. After the conquest of Pisa in 1406, ten years were enough to establish the final geography that took shape during the territorial expansion of Florentine power.

Beyond their acquisition of the salt monopoly, the payment of the salaries of their rectors, and (in many cases) the major gabelles at the passes and gates for a large number of cities and territories, comprising, in 1427, more than half the inhabitants and taxable property in the distretto, a large portion of the financial obligations owed to Florence involved the ordinary annual tribute, which had been established in the agreements of submission to Florence. The tribute was paid by all of the minor cities (Castiglione Fiorentino, Montepulciano, Colle, San Gimignano, Volterra). Independent of the conditions of their entry into the regional state, these towns were able to gain from Florence a relationship that repeated earlier models of territorial integration within the dominion. The absence in these agreements of almost any right of Florence to the revenues of its new localities was in these cases the sign that their status had not declined to the rank of residents of the

---

[15] *Ibid.*, p. 343; Petralia, 'Imposizione diretta', p. 645.

Florentine contado (*comitatini*). Each city with its own contado, each land with its own curia, guaranteed the conservation of the desired perpetual loyalty of a 'popular Guelf state', by the concession to the dominant commune, and to its governors or rectors, of legal jurisdiction and military power.[16] The tribute, as with the extraordinary tax requested in times of war (which was especially frequent in the early fifteenth century), was in compensation for the expenses of guard duty and protection. In some cases, the ordinary annual tax accompanied the tax of the 'lances' (for defence), which were established in the period of permanent war that began in the 1380s. The cities and the subordinate lands under this fiscal regime constituted the central nucleus of the 'taxed communities of the distretto' ('comuni taxati del distretto' or 'distrettuali taxati'), as expressed in the financial registers of the fifteenth-century republic. (And they helped generate the distinction, which became clearer in the sixteenth-century state, between a contado – belonging to Florence – and the rest of the state, that is, the distretto.)[17]

Considering the above, it is entirely natural that even Pistoia rejoined this group, notwithstanding its juridical separation from its contado. But the condition of 'distrettuali taxati' was in fact extended in the fiscal and financial practices of Florentine governments also to other communities and areas, where this was done as though the communities had been offered a kind of 'elevation' to the status of the Florentine contado. The reason was that the starting points for these places were those of communities that had once belonged to the contadi of other cities, so it was possible to prepare a new context of non-conflictual political relations. The results on the level of fiscal status tended thus to be very analogous to those of 'subjects with liberty'. The fixed tribute was the price Florence paid for renouncing the exercise of its normal right as a city to impose taxes and gabelles in a contado. It was the same for the communities in the Aretine territory. Between 1384 and 1386, these became subject to the local Florentine Podestà, and then they were placed under the jurisdiction of the previously established Vicars of Anghiari and Monte San Savino. The Florentine Treasury retained for itself the tolls (gabelles) at city gates and passes, while the local communities were allowed to cancel the various direct taxes charged by

---

[16] Guasti (ed.), *I Capitoli del Comune*, I, pp. 56–65, 112–15, 257–67, 295–307; Fabbri, 'Autonomismo comunale'.

[17] For these observations and to distinguish between items relevant to taxes in the contado and the distretto, I have looked again at ASF, CCP, registers 15–37, which were the basis of Molho's classic study, *Florentine Public Finances*.

Arezzo and to preserve, in exchange for the payment of an ordinary tax, the local gabelles on contracts and consumption.[18]

Gradually, by the beginning of the fifteenth century, a similar arrangement began to characterise relations with many older territorial acquisitions (which in the preceding century had been tightly controlled by means of the estimo and other taxes). The provinces of the Valdinievole (Pescia, Montecatini) and the Lower Valdarno, which remained under the ecclesiastical domain of Lucca, had preferred the wider margin of autonomy guaranteed in their agreements of political submission to Florence during the first half of the fourteenth century.[19] The financial summaries in the 1420s already used rubrics labelling various 'taxed communes' also for tax payments from Arezzo and other communities of the contado. Even in this zone, the direct levy was calculated as a fixed annual tribute, while the gabelle was conceded as a tax farm to the Aretines – even if assigned to the Florentine treasurer's general assets in Arezzo. In the same way, all gabelles and tolls on exchanges and consumption levied in the city and contado of Cortona (acquired in 1411 along with its fiscal returns) were rapidly turned over as tax farms to the local commune in exchange for a tax of 4000 florins payable in monthly instalments.[20]

With the exception of the salt tax and tolls at passes and city gates, Florence granted initial exemptions that were relatively open and lengthy in duration (naturally with the exception of Pisa). For this reason, it was possible to arrive at a relative simplification of the number of taxes and of the procedures for taxation, even for communities in areas not classified as 'the taxed members of the district'. Through the termination of tax exemption, Florence attempted to transform the return of at least a part of the principal gabelles into an annual fixed levy based on the estimo surveys of individuals and communities. By such a path, Florence could construct particular customs and 'modes of taxation' that in various ways replaced the current taxes, whether in the former contado of Pisa or within Florence's own contado (San Miniato and Prato above all).[21]

Until the beginning of the fifteenth century, and probably as early as 1409, the Florentines (and the concerned communities) also found it convenient to unify the gabelles on consumption, largely on wine and meat, into a single direct tax based on the estimo, especially within their own contado.[22] A few years later, the manifold and varied exemptions

[18] Guasti (ed.), *I Capitoli del Comune*, I, pp. 127–64.

[19] Brown, *In the Shadow of Florence*; Chittolini, 'Ricerche', pp. 300–21.

[20] ASF, SA, 6, Statuti 1385–1453, 21r; CCP, 28, 295r; 29, 339r, 264v–365r.

[21] See Guasti (ed.), *I Capitoli del Comune*, I, 239; and note 23 below.

[22] ASF, CCP, 23, 207r.

that had been given to many communities as the conquest of Pisa was progressing expired. These had been granted under a variety of conditions that obviously favoured those who had given assistance more or less spontaneously to the new Florentine 'lords' (and often to Gino Capponi in person) before the fall of Pisa. The new census of property and persons drawn up in 1416, which from the perspective of the methods and means of direct taxation anticipated the catasto of 1427, signalled a return to practices that already formed a part of Pisan governmental practices, not only in establishing coefficients but also in the form of its levy. Persons from Pisa's contado continued the old practice of paying an ordinary tax based on the operating estimo, considered to be substituted by the gabelles on grain and the 'thirds' (the so-called 'interzata'), and they were allowed to manage locally the wine and grain gabelles. These were calculated by periodic approximations of the consumption of each community and were sold as tax farms.[23]

V

If again we approach the inventories (campioni) of the income and payments of the Florentine Treasury, analysed in the classic and pioneering work of Anthony Molho, already by the opening years of the fifteenth century we notice the same structure of payments from the dominion that will later become a part of the summary balances noted in the second and later part of the century. The income from the territory flowed into Florentine coffers under a few distinct categories: from the estimo of the contado of Florence; from the contado of Pisa; from the various 'taxed members' of the district; from the income of the general treasurer of Pisa; from the treasurer of Arezzo; from the salt gabelles, the pass and gate tolls, the gabelles on contracts. (These last were collected in the territory and sent directly to the corresponding Florentine offices, not to the treasuries in Pisa, Arezzo or Cortona.) In registering only the income from the central treasuries of the salt gabelles and the gabelles on passes, gates and contracts, the campioni of the beginning of the century did not therefore distinguish, through these taxes, the tax yield of the city of Florence that derived from its contado and other places in the district where a general treasurer did not reside. Even those very detailed books in fact allowed the calculation of income from the principal gabelles collected in the

[23] ASF, CCP, 28, 303r; ASPi, Comune, B, 24, 30r–40v; ASPi, Gabella dei Contratti, 280, 142v, 28 April 1453; 348v, 8 January 1481.

territory only for the treasurer of Pisa. From the general treasurer's income records of Arezzo, the administrators frequently noted only the final withdrawal (*ritratto*), that is, the amount that had been spared and remitted to Florence after satisfying the expenses of the Six of Arezzo (the Florentine office with military jurisdiction and surveillance of the city and its contado, as well as over various fortifications in other places in the dominion).[24] The same thing tended to happen in Cortona, where the treasury spent practically all its income on provisions and castle guards. On the other hand, and already from 1406, thus for at least a decade, the tax of the lances and the ordinary tax on persons in the district were only registered in the books held by the Monte.[25]

Even if the structure and the forms of taxation in the territory had a sort of genetic tendency towards stability and continuity, the level of fiscal income from the district and the contado still presents notable oscillations over the short term. In the first place, direct taxes appear connected to the curve of Florentine financial needs and followed this trend with a slight delay. The principal instrument for increasing fiscal pressure (other than attempting 'to squeeze' the communities more tightly) was always to impose for one, two or three years an 'extra-ordinary' direct tax, which in the Florentine and Pisan contadi were paid in florins and soldi on the lira assessments determined by the estimo. For those from the distretto it was distributed more or less proportionally to the annual tax on each member. It will be useful to give a concrete example. As is clear also from the work of Molho, in 1409 the gross income from the territory reached one of its highest points.[26] We can in fact estimate it between 200,000 and 210,000 florins (to which it would be necessary to add the sums collected in the territory, which are 'hidden' in the accounts of the central offices of the gabelles on salt, gates and contracts). Those from the contado of Florence paid as much as 80,000 florins, half from the ordinary direct tax (the estimo plus the gabelles on wine and meat) and half from various extraordinary direct taxes. Around 30,000 florins were the 'taxes' paid by those in the district, also half from the ordinary tax (the real taxes and those from the *lance*) and half from extraordinary levies. Moreover, one must add slightly less than 30,000 florins collected from old and current payments on the wheat and 'thirds' in the Pisan contado. A little less than 90,000 florins was the income of the treasurer

---

[24] ASF, CCP, 26, 284r, 357r–358r.

[25] Brown, *In the Shadow of Florence*, pp. 216–18; ASF, MC, 1090.

[26] Molho, *Florentine Public Finances*. His summary tables, however, do not distinguish between the contado and the distretto, and he gives only the net income going to the central Treasury after payment of the local expenses of the particular treasurers.

in Pisa, and about 10,000 florins was the gross income of the treasurer in
Arezzo (based on estimates I have made from other years).[27]

Except for the tax on lances, the extraordinary taxes on the territory
did not become regular ones, notwithstanding that during the first half
of the fifteenth century they were suspended rarely and for brief
periods. As is made explicit in the 'justifications' of the provisions
directed towards the communities, these taxes appeared only because of
high military expenses. War increased the expense of hiring troops
under contract (*condotta*), creating a deficit which immediately resulted
in imposing forced loans on Florentine citizens and, in the second
round, adding to the forced loans income from extraordinary taxes
imposed on those from the contado and the distretto. In 1409, the
expenses from the *condotta* shot up to 460,000 florins as opposed to a
little less than 190,000 florins the year before. Suddenly, the forced loans
rose from 116,000 to 360,000 florins.[28] Approximately 40,000 florins of
extraordinary income from the contado and 10,000 to 15,000 from the
distretto came from various taxes previously deliberated. In December
1409, Florence decided therefore to demand new sums for the following
year.[29] But in 1420, a year of peace,when the deficit of a little more
than 22,000 florins was easily covered by less than 36,000 florins of
forced loans collected from Florentine citizens, only around 3,500 of
25,000 florins paid by those from the contado came from extraordinary
direct taxes (all from arrears) and only 800 of 14,000 florins from those
in the distretto.[30] In 1424, the year of the rekindling of the anti-Visconti
war and the defeat at Zagonara, no extraordinary tax was currently
charged. Again, the Florentine contado paid exactly 25,000 florins and
the distretto less than 10,000, while 560,000 was collected as the
emergency from forced loans.[31]

This time, either by choice or because Florentine oligarchs were
unable to press the territory at the levels of the beginning of the
century, the emergency did not result in a corresponding increase in the
fiscal yield from the territory. Thus, there began a most profound
financial crisis. It led to taxing citizens, under the bland name of
'catasto', through estimo declarations (which had already been in
operation in the contado) and to demanding the same terms for those in

---

[27] ASF, CCP, 23, 20r–47r, 178r–180r, 190r–v, 201r, 204r–205v, 207r–208r, 284r,
306–308r, 375r–376v; MC, 1091, 39v–40r, 49v–57r.
[28] Molho, *Florentine Public Finances*, p. 62.
[29] ASF, SC Delib. spec., 14, 180r–181r.
[30] Molho, *Florentine Public Finances*, p. 62; ASF, CCP, 28, 128v, 146r, 152r–v, 164r–v,
290r, 301r.
[31] ASF, CCP, 29, 313r–318v.

the distretto as existed in the Florentine contado. (But the distinction was maintained between payments made as forced loans on Florentine citizens and direct taxes 'to be lost' on all the others.) The illusory plan for hounding out the hidden wealth in the pockets of Florentines was extended to the distretto, perhaps together with the conviction of being able indeed to make the levy more acceptable by basing it on the proportional estimated taxable wealth of each contributor. But in 1430 the net income from the contado and the distretto of 92,000 florins from the previous year (the figure that had lasted for the past decade) fell to 62,000. In the next three years, the catasto impeded the collection of the forced loans from citizens that had sustained the war effect in the first place.[32] No less disastrous was the political fallout: the revolt and punishment of Volterra; the insurrection of peasants in the Pisan contado 'out of caprice, not fear of the enemy', as soon as it had been announced that Niccolò Piccinino had entered the Lunigiana in 1431; plots in Arezzo and the unquiet of *distrettuali* in the southern part of the state; the sudden restitution of the contado and its income to Volterra; the rapid renunciation of the universal catasto.[33]

VI

Behind the oscillations of the tax yields and the variability and number of extraordinary taxes deliberated in war years, it is possible to detect several structural and permanent characteristics of Florence's territorial fiscality. The most evident one is the long-term stability of the level of ordinary direct taxes imposed on the distretto. It is enough to compare the levels of income illustrated above with those of 1400 – before the conquest of Pisa – and with those of 1457 and 1470 (one of the years in which the reform of the Monte occasioned the registration directly into the acts of the republican councils of an estimated balance). In 1400 the yield from ordinary taxes on the inhabitants of the distretto was a little more than 15,000 florins; in 1409 and 1420 it was no more than 20,000, but including 3000 florins from the contado of Pisa; in 1424, 10,000 without Pisa; in 1457, a little more than 15,000; in 1470, 20,000, but including 2000–3000 florins from the Jewish banks, which had been given authorisation to lend.[34] Thus, the oscillations did not

[32] Molho, *Florentine Public Finances*, p. 62; Conti, *L'imposta diretta*, p. 322.
[33] Petralia, 'Imposizione diretta'; for the citation of the spontaneous character of revolt by Pisans in the contado, see Chittolini, 'Ricerche', p. 335.
[34] For 1400, see ASF, CCP, 15, 297r, 308r, 376r; for the accounts of the following years, see notes 27, 30 and 31 above; BRF, ms. 1848, 197v; Conti, *L'imposta diretta*, pp. 24–25, 27.

vary widely from a level of 15,000 florins, and these variations can be explained by brief periods of military action and in part by economics. It was not an age when levels and forms of taxation could easily be budged from what had been customary.

The tendency towards stability, however, hides an erosive effect on the tax base played by several crucial areas of the distretto. Such was the long-term tendency in the contadi of Pistoia and Pisa. In 1474, the Florentine commissioners, sent to settle the enormous differences between the Pistoiese and their contadini in fiscal matters, recognised that in the territory the patrimony of the inhabitants of the Pistoiese contado had dropped by a little less than half, while their ordinary tax had remained unchanged for forty years. This is a confirmation that after the halfway 'punishment' of 1401, the city had recovered and had maintained with its own treasury a large part of its privileges over its contado. Also on this occasion, the Florentines, who were pressured to leave unchanged the total tax on Pistoia for the Monte, diligently avoided issuing new lower taxes on those in the contado, which would have generated 'plenty of confusion between this community and the contado', but equally sought a compromise to keep them quiet. The technical solution was simple and elegant (even if it was not final), and in some way prefigured the methods of the sixteenth-century *Decima*: it sanctioned the principle that when exchanging property, the property must, from that moment on, continue to be taxed in the community where it had been registered in the last estimo.[35]

It was not only to manoeuvre cleverly within the ambiguous circumstances of Pistoia that the Florentines tried to maintain the level of taxes on each member within the distretto, without regard for changing resources. For the entire century, the same happened in the contado of Pisa. In this zone, too, the taxable wealth of the 'communes' appeared as a net reduction between the first Florentine estimo of 1416 and that of Lorenzo the Magnificent in 1491; nevertheless for more than half a century the tax remained fixed at 4000 florins a year.[36] The stability of the levy and its yield had been maintained at earlier rates notwithstanding an increased population of immigrants (we do not know how many) who were attracted by repeated twenty-year exemptions from taxes and fees (not only as a means for repopulation

---

[35] ASPt, Com., Raccolte, 6, 299r–v, 294r–298v; Petralia, 'Imposizione diretta', pp. 650–1.

[36] ASF, PR, 105, 303v–306v, 27 January 1416; 107, 19r–21r, 15 April 1417; 126, 375v, 13 January 1436; Cento, 3, 112v–113r , 27 July 1491. See also M. Luzzati, 'Estimi e catasti del contado di Pisa nel Quattrocento', in *Ricerche di storia moderna*, I (Pisa, 1976), pp. 95–6.

but also for social control in a contado whose honeymoon with Florence had been broken in a few years following its subjection, and where tax exemptions were given to the Florentine peasants who had wanted to move to Pisan territory and *vice versa*).[37] As was explained in a Laurentian deliberation of 1491, to seek taxes in any way from the exempted foreigners meant 'chasing them from the country'. Thus, the Florentines registered only those whose twenty-year privileges had expired or were near expiration, in order naturally to increase in proportion the total tax.[38]

A hypothetically objective tax system would have been incompatible with the political equilibrium of the entire dominion. To have equalised the levy throughout Pistoiese territory according to changes in the distribution of resources would have rekindled antagonism with Pistoia. In the case of Pisa, it would have contradicted the painstaking politics of new loyalties and clientelism that encouraged foreign settlement and the growth of a Florentine economic presence. In general, given the erosion of the property holdings of the rural tax payers in the distretto, it was anything but a disadvantage – in order to hold steady the level of the ordinary direct tax – to negotiate from time to time with 'the powerful of the contado' the modes of distribution and the criteria for dividing the portions of the tax. In 'privileged' zones such as the Valdinievole, the Casentino or the Florentine Mountains local wealth probably increased over the course of the fifteenth century, and therefore the fiscal weight perhaps diminished in real terms.[39] But this happened in local contexts that for a long time had enjoyed or had regained political stability. Florence had no interest in sacrificing these places on the altar of territorial equalisation of fiscal pressure. Both the politics of domination and financial need determined conservative fiscal practices. If this was the real situation, only quite praiseworthy prejudices from the Enlightenment could have made us think that the objective and permanent interests of the Florentines lay in promoting and maintaining updated estimi and universal catasti and that impediments to measures such as these resulted simply from the resistance of their subjects.

---

[37] Petralia, '"Crisi" ed emigrazione', pp. 317–20.

[38] ASF, Cento, 3, 112v–113r.

[39] S. R. Epstein, 'Stato territoriale ed economia regionale nella Toscana del Quattrocento', in Fubini (ed.), *La Toscana al tempo di Lorenzo il Magnifico*, pp. 868–90; S. K. Cohn, 'Insurrezioni contadine e demografia: il mito della povertà nelle montagne toscane (1348–1460)', *Studi storici*, 36, n. 4 (1994), pp. 1022–49.

VII

The space for financial manoeuvre in the fiscal system of the territory thus tended to be always restricted more or less to the gabelles. However, even here, they were destined to clash with the practical ceiling on taxes imposed by the weakness of the economic environment. Recent comparative studies on the lifting of the crisis of the Trecento in various regions of Italy offer a decisive refutation of the irenic vision of the construction of the regional state in Tuscany that seems to have passed, insensibly, from institutional to economic history. The real question concerns taxation from more than one point of view. Because Florence wished to maintain unaltered its fiscality or at least to remodel it always to its own advantage, the structure of the gabelles and its internal trade borders seem to have been one of the reasons for the limited performance of the Tuscan economy.[40] Behind this argument, there lurks the more general theme of the effectiveness and success of the Florentine government within its territory. I will here restrict my argument to the area of Pisa, which remains fundamental for judging the quality and the problems posed for the new power of the Florentines in Tuscany, even if we do not want to take account of the dispersion of the mercantile aristocracy and the politics of the city in the face of its irreconcilable break with Florence. None of the urban centres under Florentine rule surpassed 5000 inhabitants at the opening of the fifteenth century, while Pisa counted probably between 10,000 and 12,000.[41] Without the conquest of the Pisan state, we would certainly have less reason, after almost six centuries, to be now discussing the Florentine 'regional state'.

The balance sheets tell just how important Florence's take-over of Pisan assets was at the beginning of the fifteenth century for the financial structure of republican Florence. Well at the head with its 90,000 florins in the income accounts of the territory in 1409, the Pisan Treasury appears as indeed a novelty in the history of Florentine fiscal resources. It was not the direct taxes that made the sums held in the Florentine Treasury at Pisa so large. The payments from its contado, which were in any case remitted directly to the Florentine Treasury, added only between 3000 and 4000 florins. From 1408 to 1413 the taxes imposed

---

[40] Epstein, 'Stato territoriale'; S. R. Epstein, 'Town and country: economy and institutions in late medieval Italy', *Economic History Review*, 46 (1993), pp. 453–77.

[41] D. Herlihy and C. Klapisch, *Les Toscans et leurs familles: une étude du catasto florentin de 1427* (Paris, 1978); G. Petralia, 'Un documento per la storia della popolazione di Pisa tardomedioevale: il libro dei debitori delle taglie dell'anno 1402', *Bollettino storico pisano*, 60 (1991), pp. 257–66.

on the citizens were extremely high: 48,000 florins a year. But their yield never passed much more than 12,000 florins. In 1416, Niccolò da Uzzano, seeing what could be garnered, finally decided that it made no sense to demand from the Pisans more than 6000 florins. From that time on, the ordinary tax on the Pisans was reduced to the payments of the salaries of the Captain and Podestà. Nonetheless, for the entire century, it produced indebtedness, exemptions, suspensions of the office of the Podestà, tentative transformations of the burdens of salaries on indirect taxes (gabelles on consumption in order to tax in some way the ever increasing numbers of exempted immigrants, within a context of continuous and unarrestable demographic crisis).[42]

The major part of the 90,000 florins collected by the Florentines in Pisa shortly after the conquest came thus from the gabelles, above all from those of the gate and the sea and from internal ones (even if they comprised the income from sales of the gabelles on wine and meat in the city and contado, on contracts, and other taxes on local consumption). With the flight of the mercantile aristocracy and the city's bankers, urban production, trade and exchange remained the only source of wealth at the disposition of the Florentines. In the first months of occupation, the local expenses of the presiding military, fortification and other burdens incurred by the conquest left the Florentine Treasury with only a small part of the Pisan money. But already by 1409 the expenses had declined to half of the income. In 1420, the expenses on provisions and castle guards from the Pisan Treasury had now been reduced ordinarily to 5000 or 6000 florins (which became integrated with the payments from the principal funds of the Florentine Treasury). At that date, however, the global gross income was halved, reduced to 45,000 florins. The periodic and troublesome interventions in the system of Pisan gabelles to increase the tax yield (alternating increases in tariffs with diminutions in an attempt to attract commerce and resources) did not succeed in reversing the trend. In 1457, the balance of the Pisan Treasury – the expenses of protection having been assumed totally by Pisa – was 18,000 florins. In 1469, the gross income was at little more than 33,000 florins, in the face of expenses for provisions and castle guards of 14,000 florins. The following year the Monte officers valued it at 30,000 florins. The fragmentary series of records that survive from the Pisan Treasury at the end of the fifteenth century show a substantial stability around these levels, until it was broken within less than four months in 1492, when in the previous year the extreme

[42] ASF, CCP, 21, 181r–183r; 22, 181r–83r; 23, 178r–80r; 24, 198r–200r; Silva, 'Pisa sotto Firenze', pp. 144–55, 287–8, 539; Petralia, 'Pisa laurenziana', pp. 972–3.

remedy of a monetary revaluation of 25 per cent on the payments in silver had been made to check a statewide contraction in the yield from the gabelles. It is difficult to avoid the conclusion that Florence killed the hen – the only one at its disposal – that laid golden eggs.[43] Despite what the Florentines wanted to think, a better demographic and economic trend in the second half of the fifteenth century showed itself in other places in the dominion of less importance and centrality, where for reasons of political history, their grasp remained or was becoming less tight.

The ties and limits of fifteenth-century Florentine fiscality on its territory was thus not determined by its incapacity to follow a more or less simplistic action of administrative or proto-bureaucratic renovation of the state. At the beginning of the fifteenth century as at the end, the fiscal system was the product and instrument of political relations whose forms were determined by internal relations within the Florentine oligarchy and those between the Florentine oligarchy and its territorial subjects. There is no case for doubting the efficiency of the Florentines in managing the system, as far as it would have been possible in the case of the financial structures of other states. One would expect no less from an elite of bankers and merchants. The ties and limits were instead objective and closely tied in a single and inextricable knot: on the one hand the context formed by political relations; on the other, that traced by the trend of regional economics, which in its turn was hardly independent of the political relations.

VIII

It is to the politics of the Florentine territorial state that we must finally turn our attention. For the entire fifteenth century, Florence looked upon Venice as a genuine 'sister republic' – albeit often a rival – from which she could always gain useful lessons. For their part, the Venetians responded to this attention from Florence with an interest, depending on the diplomatic circumstances, that was generally benevolent but also rather critical. For many reasons it will be convenient for us, too, to make several brief comparative observations on the two republics.

---

[43] ASF, CCP, 21, 181r–183r, 186r–189v, 192r–v, 384r–385r; 22, 181r–183r, 192r–197v, 384r–386v; 23, 178r–180r, 182r–188v, 190r–194v, 384r–386r; 28, 178r–182r, 186r–189v; BRF, ms. 1848, 197v; ASPi, Comune B, 41–2, 'Libri dell'entrata e dell'uscita del Camerlengo generale', 17 October 1468–16 October 1469; Conti, *L'imposta diretta*, p. 25; ASPi, Comune B, 52, 19 April–8 August 1492; R. Goldthwaite and G. Mandich, *Studi sulla moneta fiorentina (secoli XIII–XV)* (Florence, 1994), pp. 21–2.

We must, however, go beyond the restatement of the hoary news that Venice distinguished itself by its cautious empiricism, by its attachment to tradition, and by a respect for the autonomy of local communities that preserved intact the ties of subject cities and their contadi. It is true that the Venetians never dreamed of making themselves immediately responsible for rural territories or of risking the establishment of a city-based fiscal treasury. Nor did they ever meddle much in the local management of direct taxation of cities and the countryside. They cared so little about the estimi of the Terraferma that they did not even know how they worked.[44] In all of these matters the Florentines could, if necessary, act not only as the teachers but as the bosses. Even some years before the catasto of 1427, the magistracy known as the Five of the Contado tried to establish ceilings on local public spending commune by commune throughout the Florentine dominion. All of this has justified the observation that Venice in the fifteenth century, when compared with Florence, adhered more strictly to the traditional logic of the dominance of the city over its contado.

From another perspective, however, just the opposite may be affirmed. For, although Venice left each city with its contado, Florence is found on many occasions to have applied solutions typical of a city/contado scheme – but in a manner that was indeed much more pervasive. Thus far, I have suggested that the traditional historians' division between a period of Albizzi state-building and a period of Medicean clientelism obscures important continuities. The fact that the history of the construction of the dominion should derive from a reading according to the categories of continuity in the rules of political action, and the pragmatism of decisions, does not annul the undeniable self-reliance in handling the territorial orders that was manifested across the fourteenth and fifteenth centuries, nor the conspicuous capacity to take on direct forms of government even if almost always on the basis of well 'justified' and immediate political decisions. But these were qualities that perhaps should not be interpreted as resulting from an original and forceful innovatory impulse, or from an especially robust system of territorial control.

[44] J. S. Grubb, 'Patriciate and estimo in the Vicentine Quattrocento', in G. Borelli, P. Lanaro, and F. Vecchiato (eds.), Il sistema fiscale veneto: Problemi ed aspetti, XV–XVII secolo (Verona, 1982), pp. 147–73; M. Knapton, 'Il fisco nello stato veneziano di Terraferma tra '300 e '500: la politica delle entrate', in Borelli et al. (eds.), Il sistema fiscale veneto, pp. 15–47; M. Knapton, 'City Wealth and State Wealth in Northeast Italy, 14th–17th centuries', in N. Bulst and J.-Ph. Genet (eds.), La ville, la bourgeoisie et la genèse de l'état moderne (Paris, 1988); G. M. Varanini, Comuni cittadini e stato regionale: ricerche sulla Terraferma veneta nel Quattrocento (Verona, 1992), in particular pp. 73–123, 197–277.

The comparison between Florence and Venice shows that the categories of centralisation, innovation and force – intended as the capacity to intervene in the affairs of the territory without the mediation of other urban elites – are not adequate for understanding the nature and the state of health of a regional power in fifteenth-century Italy. The fiscal aspects of the two republics are on this score a crucial test. It seems difficult to sustain the argument that the Venetian system was weaker and more inefficient than the Florentine, when the fact was that Venice simply could afford the luxury of leaving its subjects alone. The Venetians limited themselves to settling a general treasury in each subject city. In the five larger members of the dominion the Venetian treasuries collected an ordinary direct tax (the tax of the lances), and the major gabelles. A Weberian perspective, which might lead us to judge the quality of a state by measuring the extent to which it imposed its monopoly over fiscal matters, actually carries us a little off course. On the one hand, Venice did afford all of its subjects their own autonomous fiscal sphere, but, on the other hand, it installed its own treasury in all of these subject cities. The amount of subjects' wealth that could be taxed was so high that the Venetian fisc did not have to ask for more, and indeed it could not ask for more. Florence, on the other hand, had to bring itself to the point, in some cases, of absorbing a local treasury within its own, and in other situations, of renouncing installing its own treasurer in a subject community.

It is obvious that the Florentines did not act according to free or arbitrary choice. There were aspects of the system that were imposed by the logic of things and others that were necessitated by political tradition. From the fiscal treasuries of the *Terraferma* alone the Venetians collected a figure equal to that of Florence's entire budget during the second half of the fifteenth century. And, more significant, while a fifth of the Venetian income from the *Terraferma* was made up of direct taxes, for the same period in Florence – where even the years of the conquest of Pisa had seen a percentage only a little superior to it – that percentage was 50 per cent. And this occurred notwithstanding that from the first to the second half of the fifteenth century, Florence ceased to demand extraordinary taxes and was forced to content itself with maintaining the ordinary direct tax at a fixed level, so naturally moving its interests predominantly to indirect taxation. One sees here, in comparison with the other large republican Italian city that formed a regional state, the limited extent to which the Florentine republic assumed the characteristics of a city exercising lordship (*signoria*) over other cities. The Florentine treasurers (*camarlinghi*) in Pisa and Arezzo collected together what the Treasury of Treviso alone accumulated every year.[45] The catasto of 1427 illustrates, no less from the structure of its fiscal income, the deformity of Florence's political body in the fifteenth century. The dominion possessed an extraordinarily large head in relation to its other members, with more than half of its inhabitants and more than three quarters of its wealth concentrated in the capital city and its own contado.

The logic of things corresponded with the logic of men. The most tight connection between the geography of territorial fiscality and the map of the relations between the Florentine aristocracy and the leading local classes, the threat of taking away a city's contado as a constant threat of political punishment – these are the signs of the difficulty for Florence in constituting a new form of sovereignty over the territory, or in redefining in the consciousness and practices of the governors and the governed the political role of the dominant power in terms of the 'prince' (even for the author of The Prince).[46] The binary logic of the city/contado relationship constituted the idiom of regional politics and was ingrained in the attitudes of Florentines as much as in those of men from the subject communities. The actions of the governing classes of Florence in the dominion must appear here in good measure as 'neo-communal' rather than 'modernising'. To judge from the evidence available, it appears to me that neo-communal practices still prevailed even in the period of Lorenzo the Magnificent. But this was not the case in the dominions of the Italian princes, nor even in the lands ruled by the Venetian republic. In a region of Italy such as Tuscany, which experienced the widest extension of the power of the urban communes over the countryside, it should not be surprising to find that this structured binary relationship, developed so early and so forcefully, should have persisted through time into the fifteenth century. And, just as the dichotomy of city and contado prevented until the early fifteenth century the creation of a large territorial lordship as in Lombardy and the Veneto, so, too, it made it impossible throughout the fifteenth century for Florence to adopt the more pacific strategy of co-ordination among existing territorial entities that characterised the administration of the Milanese and Venetian states. Indeed, the Venetians, because they had no contado of their own, found it all the more easy to function as substitutes for the Trecento lords who formerly controlled the Terraferma.

If these, then, were the historical rules and the state of play in

---

[45] Varanini, Comuni cittadini, p. 78.
[46] See E. Fasano Guarini, 'Machiavelli and the crisis of the Italian republics', in G. Bock, Q. Skinner and M. Viroli (eds.), Machiavelli and Republicanism (Cambridge, 1990), pp. 17–40.

Tuscany in the later middle ages, it should also be clear why the structures and the tensions to which they gave rise have so often led historical judgment down the slope that leads to discussion of the modernity of the Florentines (a modernity exalted or corrupted by the Medici, according to one's tastes). As Giorgio Chittolini emphasised twenty years ago, this historiography is always on the verge of falling into the rhetoric of the 'modern state'.[47] Much depends, as is obvious, on the persons who are doing the observing, persons who often – like myself – feel towards that rhetoric, at least in the present, a fierce ideological sympathy. But this is a sympathy which, in the case of Florence, we are right to leave behind. The political form of fifteenth-century Florentine Tuscany appears more modern only because it was more ancient.

[47] Chittolini, 'Ricerche', p. 325. For a recent discussion of this risk, see G. Petralia, ' "Stato" e "moderno" in Italia e nel Rinascimento', Storica, 3 (1997), pp. 7–48.

CHAPTER 5

MARKET STRUCTURES

STEPHAN R. EPSTEIN

I

In recent years, the debate on the nature and outcome of the late medieval 'crisis' has taken a new lease on life. According to the more recent interpretation, the demographic and political 'crises' acted as a catalyst for structural changes that pushed the late medieval economy onto a higher path of growth, rather than ushering in a long phase of contraction, as has long been argued by historians of a 'neo-Malthusian' persuasion.[1]

This revisionist case rests on two propositions. In the first place, the consequences of the demographic slump following the Black Death are seen in a more optimistic light. On the supply side, the demographic crisis reduced population pressure on basic agricultural resources and made it possible to make more efficient use of land and labour; on the demand side, the sharp tightening of labour markets caused a redistribution of income from landlords and employers to the peasantry and urban wage earners, who spent much of their increased disposable income on cheap manufactures and on foodstuffs with higher added value. This claim has a long intellectual pedigree and has gained a broad acceptance among scholars.[2]

The second proposition is that the rise in the late middle ages of

---

[1] The terms of the debate are set out in detail in S. R. Epstein, *An Island for Itself: Economic Development and Social Change in Late Medieval Sicily* (Cambridge, 1993), chs. 1–3. For a general 'revisionist' model, see S. R. Epstein, *Freedom and Growth: The Political Economy of Markets in Renaissance Europe* (London, 2000).

[2] The case for late medieval economic expansion was first put by A. R. Bridbury, *Economic Growth: England in the Later Middle Ages* (London, 1962). Although the book has been faulted in its details, many of its more wide-ranging claims have withstood the test of time.

more centralised states, and the consolidation of parcellised sovereignty
that it entailed, reduced the institutional costs of trade in commodities
and information both by lowering feudal and urban tariffs, and by
aiding the development of more efficient and integrated trading networks. Centralisation lowered consumer prices and stimulated
economic integration and specialisation within states; but strong political resistance by lords and towns meant that most administrative
reorganisation and integration took place within pre-existing regional
or county boundaries, rather than within broader but more recently
established national ones. As a result, the late medieval crisis stimulated
regional more than national market integration. Hence also, in the
Italian context which concerns us here, the fact that political
centralisation only got as far as establishing regional states meant that the
boundaries of the new economic regions were more likely to coincide
with the political frontiers of the new territorial states.[3]

This second strand in the revisionist argument must still be convin-
cingly tested. Its methodological assumptions have come under fire for
confusing the concept of the economic-functional 'region', as defined
by economic geographers, with that of the institutional 'region', as
defined by political and legal historians. According to the critics, an
'economic region' is shaped by purely commercial forces, among which
transactions costs rank highest, whereas the frontiers of an 'institutional
region' are the result of largely random historical and political events;
there is therefore no reason to believe that the boundaries of the two
will coincide except by chance.[4] But while there is undoubtedly some
value to the argument that economic and political boundaries do not
always coincide, the criticism also implies that transactions costs are
wholly impervious to the political context of exchange, and therefore
that the bundle of laws and social norms that underpin transactions and
which naturally vary across states make little difference to economic
performance. In this chapter I reject such a fundamentalist claim. I

---

[3] See P. Malanima, 'La formazione di una regione economica: la Toscana nei secoli
xiii–xv', *Società e storia*, 6 (1983), pp. 229–69; M. Tangheroni, 'Il sistema economico
della Toscana nel Trecento', in S. Gensini (ed.), *La Toscana nel secolo XIV: caratteri di
una civiltà regionale* (Pisa, 1988), pp. 41–66; S. R. Epstein, 'Cities, Regions and the
Late Medieval Crisis: Sicily and Tuscany Compared', *Past and Present*, 130 (1991),
pp. 3–50; Epstein, 'Town and Country in Late Medieval Italy: Economic and
Institutional Aspects', *Economic History Review*, 2nd ser. 46 (1993), pp. 453–77.

[4] See *Lo sviluppo economico regionale in prospettiva storica. Atti dell'incontro interdsiciplinare,
Milano 18–19 maggio 1995*, Dipartimento di Storia della Società e delle Istituzioni,
Facoltà di Scienze Politiche, University of Milan, Quaderni 2 (Milan, 1996), in
particular P. Malanima, 'Teoria economica regionale e storia: il caso della Toscana
(XIII–XVI secolo)', pp. 133–48.

presume that the fiscal, jurisdictional and provisioning policies of states *did* influence the processes of location, integration and specialisation at a regional level, and put this claim to the test. The broad question which I address is not, 'Did political structures make *any* difference?', but rather, *'How, and to what extent,* did they make a difference?'[5]

The following interpretation of the late medieval 'crisis' makes two general assumptions. First, the rise of more centralised states lowered the costs of trade *within* politically bounded regions proportionally more than *between* institutionally independent regions.[6] Second, institutional differences between states influenced the degree to which economic integration and diversification could be pursued within a region. Clearly the most significant institutions in this respect would be ones which affected market structures directly, both through taxation over trade (by means of tariffs and systems of urban food provision) and through legislation upholding the market power of special interest groups. This explains this chapter's focus on internal developments in the toll system, in the network of markets and fairs and in the system of grain provisioning, and why a more systematic comparison between Florence and other late medieval territorial states will be taken up in a future essay.[7]

II

Before the War of the Eight Saints and Arezzo's submission in 1384, the Florentine government followed the typical two-pronged economic strategy of most contemporary city-states: in the contado, it encouraged the development of an efficient road system,[8] controlled the number

---

[5] On the other hand, as P. Krugman argues in *Geography and Trade* (Louvain and Cambridge, Mass., 1991), historical contingency also plays a role in the development of industrial districts featuring economies of agglomeration.

[6] Even where political centralisation occurred in territories with 'national' dimensions, like France, Spain and the Burgundian States, the composite nature of these states meant that most of the jurisdictional and fiscal barriers between different 'regions' remained in place, exerting similar effects to the barriers that separated smaller regional or territorial states. It follows that the main effect of late medieval centralisation on the larger monarchies was arguably to promote integration within, rather than between, individual 'regional' constituents of the 'national' whole. This fact would explain why the first integrated *national* market only emerged in the late seventeenth century in England, followed by its larger continental neighbours at least a century later.

[7] The only general study along these lines is still R. Poehlmann, *Die Wirtschaftspolitik der Florentiner Renaissance und das Princip der Verkehrsfreiheit* (Leipzig, 1878).

[8] C. M. de La Roncière, *Florence centre économique régional au XIVe siècle*, 5 vols. (Aix-en-Provence, 1976), III, pp. 871–906.

and functions of marketplaces, strove to enforce the use of the city's own weights and measures,[9] and extended its control over rural surpluses at times of dearth; further afield, it agreed reciprocal tariff reductions and exemptions with neighbouring communes so as to ensure food supplies and sustain its commercial interests.[10] After 1384, having embarked irreversibly upon territorial expansion, Florence attempted to extend the arrangements devised for the contado to its newly acquired district (distretto), with a particular focus on restricting the subjects' rights to set commercial tolls and excises independently.[11] As a result of these efforts the Florentine fisc, the Camera del comune, became directly responsible for the gabelles of Arezzo, Cortona and Pisa;[12] only Pistoia, whose fiscal independence had been established in some early fourteenth-century tariff agreements with Florence, managed to evade the latter's control.[13]

For several decades after 1384 Florence seemed to view commercial sovereignty principally as a means to maximise its tax revenue.[14] However, a request in late 1422 to the newly appointed Sea Consuls to enquire about the state of Tuscan trade and manufacture[15] indicates a more sophisticated understanding of the opportunities provided by territorial expansion. Although Florence continued to exploit its sub-jects' tax base along the bipolar lines which traditionally regulated town–country relations, it also began to show improved awareness of

---

[9] *Ibid.*, III, pp. 951–64, 995, 1003–6; IV, p. 337 nn. 41–2; G. Guidi, *Il governo della città-repubblica di Firenze del primo Quattrocento*, 3 vols. (Florence, 1981), III, p. 161 n. 16. By contrast, I have found only one provision during the republican period whose purpose was to unify regional measures along Florentine lines: ASF, PR, 119, 278v–279v, 27 November 1428.

[10] La Roncière, *Florence*, III, pp. 887–90.

[11] ASF, PR, 75, 28v–29v, 17 April 1386: the Signoria and the *Regolatori delle entrate* assert full jurisdiction over 'quibuscumque gabellis et pedagiis civitatis comitatus Aretii tam ordinariis quam extraordinariis et tam usitatis quam non usitatis', with the right to modify existing gabelles and to introduce new ones.

[12] See ASF, PR, 110, 96r–97v, 30 September 1420, for various changes to the gabelles of Cortona, which included a 25 per cent increase in the main gate tolls.

[13] See D. Herlihy, *Medieval and Renaissance Pistoia: The Social History of an Italian Town, 1200–1430* (New Haven, 1967), p. 160; W. J. Connell, 'Clientelismo e Stato territoriale. Il potere fiorentino a Pistoia nel XV secolo', *Società e storia*, 14 (1991), p. 529; ASF, DAC, 373, 276r–278v, 1401; ASF, PR, 91, 21v–22v, 1402.

[14] The only studies of indirect taxation refer to the period before 1380. See C. M. de La Roncière, 'Indirect Taxes or "Gabelles" at Florence in the Fourteenth Century. The Evolution of Tariffs and Problems of Collection', in N. Rubinstein (ed.), *Florentine Studies: Politics and Society in Renaissance Florence* (Evanston, 1968), pp. 140–91; D. Herlihy, 'Direct and Indirect Taxation in Tuscan Urban Finance, c.1200–1400', in *Finances et comptabilités urbaines du XIIIe au XVI siècles* (Brussels, 1964), pp. 385–405.

[15] ASF, PR, 112, 245v–246v.

the longer term needs of regional trade by making more allowance for local diversity and specialisation. The psychological and political roots of this change of heart can probably be traced back to the conquest of Pisa of 1406,[16] which provided Florence with a long-sought-after outlet to the sea through which it could channel foreign grain supplies, and which had handed it control over one of the main trade routes between the western Mediterranean and the northern Italian plains.[17]

Florence reacted to the centrifugal effects of the Pisan acquisition on its trading system by modifying both its internal tariff system and its macro-economic policies of supply. In the first place, the Signoria attempted to regulate commercial flows by establishing a dense network of toll officials throughout its territory. A preliminary analysis of the toll receipts registered by the Florentine *Camera* suggests that the turning point in the taxation of overland trade occurred during the second half of the 1420s, when the average share of the main transit toll (*gabella dei passeggeri*) from the distretto rose from 5–10 per cent to 13–15 per cent of total receipts.

Nonetheless, the beneficial effects of fiscal consolidation were not immediately apparent. On the institutional side, it took the Florentines the better part of a century to determine the final location of their customs houses;[18] in economic terms, the customs reforms produced a decline in total trade duties, but had a negligible impact on regional market integration.[19] By contrast, the topographical distribution of customs houses raises some interesting questions about policy *attitude* (Fig. 5.1). Most check-points ran along the main frontiers, starting from Volterra in the south-east and running east through San Gimignano,

---

[16] S. R. Epstein, 'Stato territoriale ed economia regionale nella Toscana del Quattro-cento', in R. Fubini (ed.), *La Toscana al tempo di Lorenzo il Magnifico: Politica Economia Cultura Arte*, 3 vols. (Pisa, 1996), III, pp. 881–4.

[17] For an earlier attempt along these lines to tax Pisan traders who took a more northerly route through the Valdinievole and the lower Valdarno to avoid paying Florentine transit dues, see ASF, PR, 58, 199v, 1371.

[18] Major customs reforms are recorded in ASF, DAC, 372, 494r–v, 1438–9; ASF, PR, 147, 101v–103v, and DAC, 372, 635r–v, 1456; DAC, 375, *passim*, 1474; DAC, 375, 230r–v, 1503. For customs posts that are absent from the lists of 1503, see DAC, 373, 67r–v, 1473 (Castel del Bosco); DAC, 319, 109v, 1511 (Pietramala). In July 1490, the *Balìa* of the Seventeen Reformers proposed to review the entire system of tolls, ports and customs (A. Brown, 'Public and Private Interest: Lorenzo, the Monte and the Seventeen Reformers', in G. C. Garfagnini (ed.), *Lorenzo de' Medici. Studi* (Florence, 1992), pp. 108, 111, 115–16); but the proposal was never recorded in the registers of the *Dogana* which list all subsequent reforms. Changes to the tariff system seem to have had no effect on how the customs were organised; see DAC, 373, 110r–124v, 1471–2; PR, 193, 74r–77v, 1502.

[19] See below, pp. 114–17.

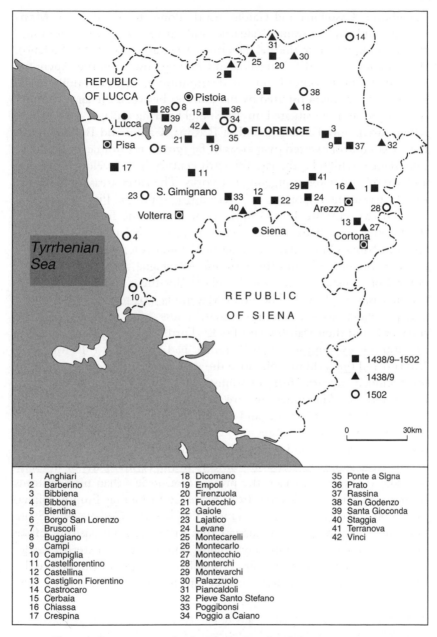

Fig. 5.1 Customs posts in the Florentine dominion, *c.* 1430–1500

Legend within map:

■ 1438/9–1502
▲ 1438/9
○ 1502

0   30km

1 Anghiari	18 Dicomano	35 Ponte a Signa
2 Barberino	19 Empoli	36 Prato
3 Bibbiena	20 Firenzuola	37 Rassina
4 Bibbona	21 Fucecchio	38 San Godenzo
5 Bientina	22 Gaiole	39 Santa Gioconda
6 Borgo San Lorenzo	23 Lajatico	40 Staggia
7 Bruscoli	24 Levane	41 Terranova
8 Buggiano	25 Montecarelli	42 Vinci
9 Campi	26 Montecarlo	
10 Campiglia	27 Montecchio	
11 Castelfiorentino	28 Monterchi	
12 Castellina	29 Montevarchi	
13 Castiglion Fiorentino	30 Palazzuolo	
14 Castrocaro	31 Piancaldoli	
15 Cerbaia	32 Pieve Santo Stefano	
16 Chiassa	33 Poggibonsi	
17 Crespina	34 Poggio a Caiano	

Poggibonsi, Castellina and Gaiole, south along the Valdarno to Montevarchi and San Giovanni Valdarno and on to Castiglion Fiorentino, then moving north up the Val Tiberina (Anghiari, Pieve Santo Stefano), the Casentino and the Mugello, and ending just over the Apennine watershed. On the other hand, the distribution in terms of numbers was more erratic, as demonstrated by the contrast between the large number of customs houses situated in the neighbouring villages of Levane, Montevarchi and Terranova and of Rassina, Campi and Bibbiena, and the weak control exerted over areas of far greater economic and military importance, which by the late fifteenth century had developed thriving and partially tolerated smuggling networks. The latter areas included the mainly pasturing region of the Maremma, south of Pisa, which was assigned two customs houses only at the end of the fifteenth century; the frontier zone between Pisa and Lucca, which had a single official based in Santa Gioconda; the wealthy Valdinievole, with one customs point in Buggiano;[20] and the Pistoiese Montagna, also under the sole control of a customs official in Pistoia.[21] But these apparent anomalies can be easily explained. The Pisan Maremma was too underpopulated and peripheral to warrant more than a few officials overseeing the shepherds and their transhumant flocks. Furthermore, the large number of customs exemptions that Florence had granted to Pistoia, San Miniato and the Valdinievole since the mid-fourteenth century more or less excluded any strict form of control over the western hills leading to Lucca and the Apennines; in any case, the conquest in 1441 of the Lucchese port of Motrone and of the village of Montecarlo which dominated the eastern routes into Lucca allowed Florence to control much of the western and north-western trade.[22]

The large number of customs officers in the central parts of the state is harder to explain. In fact, the presence of no less than nine customs houses along the road leading from Florence to Pisa (at Empoli, Signa, Fucecchio, Poggio a Caiano, Vinci, Verghereto, Cerbaia and Santa Gioconda) would appear to suggest that the Florentine customs office was more concerned with controlling internal than external trade. Although the customs posts were probably a carry-over from before the Pisan conquest, the fact that Florence did not abolish them after 1406

---

[20] The correspondence and judicial acts of the sixteenth-century customs officials are rife with 'abuses' committed in this area; see DAC, 319 and 322, *passim*.

[21] The Pistoiese official is missing from the list of 1456, but is referred to in a list drawn up in 1466 (ASF, MC, II, 1354).

[22] See M. Bratchel, *Lucca 1430–1494: The Reconstruction of an Italian City-Republic* (Oxford, 1995), pp. 214, 235, for a discussion of the subsequent conquest by Florence of the village of Pietrasanta on the road to Genoa, Milan and Lombardy.

indicates a significant degree of anxiety over free trade. This sense of insecurity emerges quite starkly by comparison with conditions in the Duchy of Milan. Not only was the density of customs officials far higher in Tuscany than in Lombardy,[23] but Florence insisted on administering the system directly rather than by means of tax-farming as was generally the case in the state of Milan. The difference is particularly noteworthy because the Duchy of Milan was surrounded by easily accessible, wealthy and highly commercialised territories, making it far more susceptible to smuggling than Tuscany.[24]

The second major change in economic and fiscal strategy induced by territorial expansion took place in the region's supply policies. The latter were an extension of practices developed in the course of the late thirteenth and fourteenth centuries, but also included some significant innovations. Fifteenth-century policy featured a curious mixture of authoritarian and short-term control over trade[25] typical of the communal past, and of more liberal attempts to stimulate the transit trade principally by lowering aggregate tariffs on merchandise. On the one hand, Florence responded to occasional shortages in food staples like wine, olive oil and meat with temporary combinations of export bans and import bounties.[26] On the other hand, the city followed a policy of fiscal moderation which took account of neighbouring states' actions with respect to locally scarce goods like iron,[27] or of foreign merchan-

---

[23] In addition to its own paid officials, the Florentine customs made use of the state's network of castellans, Captains and Podestà; see ASF, DAC, 319, 67r–v, 109r–v, 110r–v.

[24] F. Saba, 'Le forme dello scambio. I mercati rurali', in G.Taborelli (ed.), *Commercio in Lombardia*, 2 vols. (Milan, 1982), I, pp. 176–85; M. A. Romani, 'L'annona e il mercato dei grani. Un commercio a libertà vigilata', in *ibid.*, II, pp. 103–17; C. M. Belfanti, 'Una geografia impositiva. Dazi, gabelle e contrabbandi fra Cinque e Settecento', in *ibid.*, II pp. 121–33.

[25] Such as the one-off tax on the pilgrims to Rome. See ASF, PR, 119, 90r–91v, 223v–225v, 21 June 1428, revoked 15 October 1428; and PR, 161,107r–108v, 1470.

[26] For wine, see ASF, PR, 129, 246r–247v, 1439; PR, 157, 147r–v, 1466; PR, 201, 48v–49v, 1511. For olive oil, see PR, 118, 49v–51v, 1427; PR, 127, 296r–v, 1437; PR, 133, 118v–119v and 183r–v, 1442; PR, 137, 129v–130, 1446; PR, 205, 59r–v, 1522. The reduced pressure on food supply caused by declining population is discussed by G. Pinto, 'Commercio del grano e politica annonaria nella Toscana del Quattrocento: la corrispondenza dell'Ufficio fiorentino dell'Abbondanza negli anni 1411–1412', in *Studi di storia economica toscana nel Medioevo e nel Rinascimento in memoria di Federigo Melis* (Pisa, 1987), pp. 257–83. By contrast, a strategic measure aimed at increasing the supply of olive oil in the contado was characteristically restrictive; see PR, 147, 65v–66v, 18 June 1456.

[27] For tariff reductions see ASF, PR, 122, 284r–v, 1431; PR, 123, 135v–136, 1432; PR, 132, 211r–212v, 1441; PR, 136, 38v–39v, 1445 (the latter included changes to tolls levied in Cortona, Arezzo and Montecchio so as to increase iron imports from

dise which could be sent over other routes if local tariffs were too high.[28] Rather than simply relying on the tried and tested policy of bilateral trade agreements,[29] Florence reduced customs dues unilaterally, both in Porto Pisano and inland, when it feared that its tariffs might cause merchants to go elsewhere[30] and as part of a broader strategy to promote trade between the western Mediterranean and northern Europe.[31]

It is therefore clear that territorial expansion led to an important change in attitude by Florentine elites towards foreign trade. Whereas foreign trade under the commune had been treated as a function of Florence's industrial and commercial requirements, by the early fifteenth century it was being promoted for its own sake as a source of tax revenue. The conquest of Arezzo and Borgo San Sepolcro to the southwest, and the acquisition of Porto Pisano and of the territories bordering Lucca to the east and north-east, conveyed to the Florentine elites a greater awareness of their region's strategic position between south-central Italy and the western Mediterranean on the one hand, and the Lombard plain and the German lands north of the Alps on the other. Territorial expansion and military competition also forced the Florentine state to increase its financial requirements, and the politically uncontentious transit and re-export trades became a prime target for raising income. On the other hand, Florence faced the constant danger of killing the goose with the golden eggs, by over-taxing trade which

Perugia, the Marche and Abruzzo). Volterra's submission was followed by an increase in its gate tolls in 1475; see PR, 166, 65r–66v.

[28] This concern applied also to transhumance. After the reorganisation of the *Dogana del bestiame* in 1428 (ASF, PR, 119, 91r–v), the Signoria set out to attract transhumant flocks to the Florentine Maremma (PR, 122, 207v–208v, 1431; PR, 123, 240v–241v, 1432; PR, 126, 241v–242v, 1435; PR, 144, 82v–83v, 1454; PR, 1465,11r–12v, 1465).

[29] Agreements of this kind, which had been typical of the communal age, were, however, never wholly abandoned. See ASF, PR, 79, 95v–98v, 31 May 1390, for an agreement with the lord of Ravenna; PR, 157, 103v–104v, 27 June 1466, for renewal of a commercial treaty of 1370 with Bologna.

[30] See ASF, PR, 119, 187r–188v (1428); PR, 170, 15r–v (1479); PR, 180, 95r–96v, 1489; PR, 200, 129r–v, 1510.

[31] See ASF, PR, 120,17v–18v, 1429 (on trade with England and Flanders); PR, 128, 3r–v, 1437 (for Lombardy and Venice); PR, 131, 167v–168v, 1440 (Lombardy); PR, 171, 18r–v, 1480 (Lombardy for four years). Florence was less concerned about trade relations with central Italy; an example in PR, 179, 87r–88v, 1489 (trade with Siena, Città di Castello, Faenza and Bologna). In 1529, it decided to confirm a 33 per cent reduction of customs dues in Pisa and Livorno in view of the rise in the tax returns that the reduction had caused; PR, 207, 74r–v. See G. Pistarino, 'I porti di Milano,Venezia, Genova, Pisa', in G. Taborelli (ed.), *Commercio in Lombardia*, 2 vols. (Milan, 1986), II, pp. 86–92, on trade between Tuscany and Milan.

could be <u>diverted to more competitive routes</u> through other ports and
regions. This competitive threat seems to have induced an unusual
<u>degree of fiscal caution: paradoxically, it is probably the state's rising</u>
<u>fiscal obligations that explain Florence's unaccustomed moderation in</u>
<u>the use of the trade boycotts, reprisals and punitive tariffs</u> which had
been its stock in trade in its days as an independent city-state.[32]

III

Let us now turn to the effects of territorial integration on domestic
trade. The hypothesis that the rise of more integrated territorial states
caused domestic transactions costs to decline seems to be contradicted
by the increases in Florentine gate tolls documented by La Roncière for
the years between 1350 and 1400,[33] and by their continued albeit more
moderate rise over the course of the following century. In fact, these
<u>increases</u> – whose <u>impact was in any case mitigated</u> by substantial rates
<u>of inflation</u> – were <u>unusual by the standards prevailing elsewhere in the</u>
<u>state.</u> A preliminary examination of gate tolls in the subject communes
suggests that <u>charges were generally quite stable</u> during the fifteenth
century, implying that they <u>actually declined in real terms.</u>[34] Furthermore, <u>several tariffs on trade between Florence and subject communities</u>
were either <u>reduced</u> in nominal terms or <u>abolished altogether,</u> as

[32] See E. Conti (ed.), *Le 'consulte' e 'pratiche' della Repubblica fiorentina nel Quattrocento*, I,
1401 (Florence and Pisa, 1981), p. 134, 2 May 1401 (right of reprisal granted to
merchants of Volterra and Pistoia against other Pistoiese); ASF, PR, 99, 82r–v, 1410
(punitive tariffs of 50 per cent *ad valorem* on Genoese and Savonese merchandise);
PR, 127, 281v–282v, 1436 (trade ban with lands under the control of the Duke of
Milan). In 1504, Lucca suffered Florentine reprisals, possibly because it had given aid
to the Pisan rebels (PR, 195, 1r–2v). In 1428, Florence came to a tariff agreement
with Siena, making it easier for the Sienese to trade in, and bring livestock into,
Florentine territory (PR, 119, 223v–225v). For the use of commercial reprisals by
fourteenth-century Florence, see A. Astorri, 'La Mercanzia fiorentina nella prima
metà del XIV secolo: funzione economica e ruolo istituzionale', doctoral thesis,
Dipartimento di storia, Università degli studi di Firenze, 1993, pp. 70–2; W. M.
Bowsky, *A Medieval Italian Commune: Siena under the Nine, 1287–1355* (Berkeley and
Los Angeles, 1981), ch. 5; also Epstein, *An Island*, pp. 284–7.

[33] See n. 14 above.

[34] This decline may have been an effect of the loss of fiscal autonomy previously
referred to, which had allowed a relative increase in direct taxation. After 1402,
Florence forbade Pistoia from increasing the salt tax and the gate tolls to the
detriment of the contado (Herlihy, *Pistoia*, p. 159 note 22, citing G. C. Gigliotti
(ed.), *Cronache di Ser Luca Dominici*, II, *Cronaca seconda* (Pistoia, 1937), p. 85).
Machiavelli was probably reflecting on a Tuscan practice when he stated, regarding
the acquisition of 'new' states by older ones, that one should not 'alter either their
laws or their trade dues' (*dazi*) (*The Prince*, ch. 3).

occurred for example in the former feudal jurisdictions of the Casentino valley;[35] although most of these reductions applied to trade flowing towards the ruling city,[36] at least in the case of Pistoia tariffs were reduced equally on both sides.[37]

This cursory examination of Florentine legislation gives some support to the claim that the development of an integrated customs system reduced the general tariff level. Given how unreliable the evidence on tariffs is, however, we must look elsewhere for a more rigorous assessment of the claim. One means of assessment is to exploit the fact that tariff reductions improve opportunities for arbitrage between markets and therefore lead to a convergence of prices over time. This hypothesis was tested on price series for the most frequently traded commodity, grain, sold in Florence and Arezzo between 1400 and 1564. Over this period the difference in price between the two cities included the cost of transporting a unit of grain between Arezzo and Florence and differences in toll rates; Florentine prices were generally higher because Florence was a net importer and had higher consumer taxes than Arezzo, which was also a net exporter (often to Florence itself). Figure 5.2 displays the results of our test, which shows that the average price differential between the two cities fell by about 10 per cent (from a factor of 1.13 to a factor of 1.03) between the mid-fifteenth and the mid-sixteenth centuries, as political integration brought about a decline in domestic transaction costs.

On the other hand, territorial expansion was also associated with policies that seem superficially to run entirely counter to any commercial benefits arising from integration. At the same time that it was busily lowering internal barriers to trade, the Florentine Signoria was also regaling subject communities with significant jurisdictional privileges whose main economic purpose was to exonerate the recipients from control by the Florentine guilds, to reduce or abolish entirely most tariffs on trade, and to authorise trade in otherwise restricted goods. The apparent result of this was to *increase* jurisdictional fragmentation and to undermine both the letter and the spirit of political integration. How

---

[35] See ASF, PR, 64, 283v–284v, 1377.

[36] See Epstein, 'Stato territoriale', p. 881. A further case of discrimination occurred in 1465, when Florence raised the duty on livestock moving from its contado to the district. Arezzo and Cortona complained that this would damage their fairs and asked to exempt the livestock sold there (ASF, PR, 157, 246–247v; DAC, 373, 555r–557v, 1467). Subsequently, the Signoria decided to reduce the tariff on plough oxen, but not cattle 'for trade' (*per mercatantia*), from 2 florins to 12 *soldi* in the *distretto* (PR, 166, 64v–65v, 1475).

[37] Connell, 'Clientelismo', p. 529.

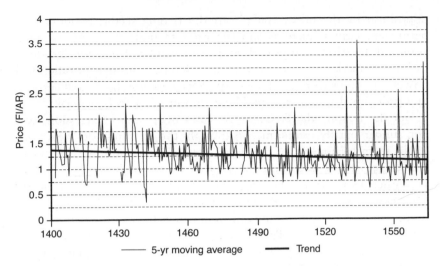

Fig. 5.2 Convergence of grain prices, Florence and Arezzo, 1400–1564

can this seeming contradiction be explained? To what extent did this policy of jurisdictional fragmentation neutralise the economic benefits of integration?

Although the ubiquity and political and constitutional implications of pre-modern privileges or 'freedoms' are a well-studied feature of the *ancien régime*, their economic implications have been ignored or consigned to the historical rubbish heap of the 'deadweight costs' of pre-modern states. In as much as this oversight follows from the idea that pre-modern 'freedoms' were an anachronism, which delayed but did not deflect the course of political and economic integration and progress, it is based on a fundamental misunderstanding of pre-modern markets. For it is a fact that, between the fourteenth and the eighteenth centuries and across most of Europe, jurisdictionally 'free' enclaves – comprising individual and associated communities endowed with some degree of legal and fiscal autonomy, mainly from neighbouring cities – acted as a fundamental source of economic *competition* against the overweening commercial and manufacturing monopolies of the more powerful towns.[38] In the manufacturing sector, jurisdictional autonomy nearly always underpinned the rise of rural 'proto-industries' against

---

[38] See S. R. Epstein, 'Freedom and Growth. The European Miracle?', in E. V. Barker (ed.), *LSE on Freedom* (London, 1995), pp. 165–81.

opposition by the urban crafts.[39] In the trading sector, temporary or permanent tariff reductions and the right to trade freely in restricted commodities stimulated growth and specialisation. Paradoxically, then, so long as market power was directly exercised through jurisdictional power – in other words, so long as markets were not 'free' – concessions of jurisdictional autonomy could be economically very beneficial.[40]

But the reason why Renaissance states made these concessions was not fundamentally economic. Although the granting of 'freedoms' might seem to undermine the state's sovereignty in the short term, in the longer run it was more likely to extend its jurisdiction and to strengthen its political legitimacy. This ambiguity emerges very clearly from Florentine practices. Economic franchises, particularly tariff reductions, were used systematically during territorial expansion between the 1370s and the 1440s.[41] The opening concessions were made in the context of a community's formal capitulation. They generally granted exemption from most forms of indirect taxation and reduced the level of the compulsory salt tax; only Florence's gate tolls were never tampered with. Exemptions usually lasted five to ten years and could be renegotiated;[42] but since from Florence's point of view they were essentially a means for enforcing jurisdictional sovereignty, they could also be rescinded as political and financial circumstances changed.[43] Not surprisingly, the best terms were invariably granted to frontier communities that possessed the greatest strategic bargaining power – as the insurrections of 1402–5 discussed in this volume by Samuel Cohn demonstrate. Valleys like the Casentino, the Alpi fiorentine and the Valdinievole, whose commercial privileges went back as far as the

---

[39] See S. R. Epstein, 'Manifatture tessili e strutture politico-istituzionali nella Lombardia tardo-medievale. Ipotesi di ricerca', *Studi di storia medioevale e diplomatica*,14 (1993), pp. 55–89. European examples of this pattern are to be found in the essays collected in S. C. Ogilvie and M. Cerman, (eds.), *European Proto-industrialization* (Cambridge, 1996).

[40] Clearly, the benefits of jurisdictional exemptions only applied if the beneficiaries were not granted rights to tax trade in their own stead. The latter outcome may have occurred, for example, as a result of the way the Spanish Habsburgs sold off their demesne lands in the sixteenth and early seventeenth centuries; see H. Nader, *Liberty in Absolutist Spain: The Habsburg Sale of Towns, 1516–1700* (Baltimore, 1990).

[41] See E. Fasano Guarini, 'Città soggette e contadi nel dominio fiorentino tra Quattro e Cinquecento: il caso pisano', in M. Mirri (ed.), *Ricerche di storia moderna*, I (Pisa, 1976), pp. 17–18.

[42] In a few cases in the later fifteenth century, concessions were extended for periods of up to twenty-five years; see ASF, PR, 159, 194v–195v (1468, for Poppi and Fronzoli).

[43] A sixteenth-century survey revealed that most of the previous tariff exemptions were no longer in use (ASF, DAC, 838, *passim*).

1350s[44] and were renewed virtually automatically, became zones of permanent fiscal and corporate exemption. Smaller or less well-organised communities closer to Florence found it nearly impossible to renew their concessions.

Jurisdictional privileges were thus a powerful instrument of centralisation. In strictly institutional terms, late medieval states employed fiscal concessions to claim sovereignty over taxation and market jurisdictions – in short, to extend jurisdictional integration. In economic terms, jurisdictional 'freedoms' enabled recipients to challenge the monopolies of politically powerful towns. If nothing else, a tariff exemption or reduction improved the living standards of the recipients, who could buy for less and sell for more. However, if the recipient was of sufficient demographic standing and the franchise lasted long enough, economic privileges could act as *de facto* tariff barriers that protected local producers from encroaching urban guilds. In sum, *ancien régime* 'freedoms' could become the institutional precondition for premodern 'special economic zones'.

This paradox can be illustrated with one of the more striking institutional and economic developments in the late medieval economy, namely the great increase in the number of periodic fairs across western and east-central Europe at a time of sharp demographic decline. Although new fairs responded to a real economic need for more integrated and complex systems of distribution, they were strongly resisted by existing trading centres, for the most part politically and economically well-established towns, which feared competition over trade and a loss of revenue from tolls. To become established, new fairs therefore required special political exemption. In as much as these concessions could be used to challenge the jurisdictional claims of towns and extend territorial and national states' remit, the latter were willing to grant them.[45]

Developments in Tuscany fit well into the European mould (Table 5.1). Between 1350 and 1560 a minimum of thirty-eight seasonal fairs were either newly established or granted privileges giving them a new lease on life. At fifteen of these, participants were granted immunity (*securitas*) from arrest for debt, which included tax arrears owed to Florence – a not insignificant concession, considering that tax arrears were virtually universal and fairs, like markets, were patrolled by state officials. At least seventeen fairs were exempted from all major tolls. We

[44] See C. Guasti (ed.), *I capitoli del comune di Firenze. Inventario e regesto*, I (Florence, 1866), pp. 75–6 (Valdinievole), 89–90 (Alpi fiorentine).

[45] See S. R. Epstein, 'Regional Fairs, Institutional Innovation and Economic Growth in Late Medieval Europe', *Economic History Review*, 47 (1994), pp. 459–82.

Table 5.1. *Markets and fairs in the Florentine dominion, c. 1300–1560*

	Markets					Fairs				
	FN	R	S	FR	total	FN	R	S	FR	total
pre-1350	10	6	–	2	18	2	3	–	1	6
1350–74	3	6	4	3	16	3	3	–	3	2
1375–99	11	3	–	4	18	–	–	1	1	11
1400–24	5	1	1	–	7	1	4	2	4	17
1425–49	2	5	8	–	15	1	8	5	3	17
1450–74	2	4	9	4	19	–	9	4	4	11
1475–99	–	1	12	1	14	1	5	3	2	1
1500–24	7	2	4	–	13	–	1	–	–	2
1525–60	4	11	1	–	15	–	2	–	–	
total	44	39	39	14	135	8	35	15	18	76
total 1350–1524	34	33	39	12	118	6	32	15	17	70

FN: first notation
R: renewal or modification
S: immunity (*securitas*) for debtors
FR: toll franchise

find a similar pattern with respect to weekly markets. No less than thirty-four new weekly markets were established between the mid-fourteenth century and the advent of Duke Cosimo. Twelve of these (and twenty-six others whose origins are unknown) obtained *securitas*. At least twelve markets were exempted from major tolls.

Between 1350 and 1380, a period which according to La Roncière witnessed a sharp contraction of rural trade, no less than three new fairs and six new markets were established. The sharp drop in the number of concessions (to four new markets and three new fairs) suggests that the true economic depression began immediately thereafter and lasted about half a century. After 1435 the number of foundations picked up again as the population began to recover and military activities experienced a lull. Most of these new events, which were distributed quite regularly across the Florentine contado and the northern valleys of the Casentino, the Mugello and the Valdinievole, survived well into the early modern period.[46] Weekly markets were mainly situated along Florence's principal trade routes, at a distance of 6–8 km between each other and of 12–18 km from the major towns (Fig. 5.3). Most fairs – which seem to have specialised mainly in livestock and to a lesser extent in cereals – were held in larger towns like Florence, Arezzo, San Gimignano, Prato

[46] See A. M. Pult Quaglia, *'Per provvedere ai popoli': il sistema annonario nella Toscana dei Medici* (Florence, 1990), pp. 261–4; ASF, DAC 373, 236r–257v and *passim*; DAC, 838, 141r–155v.

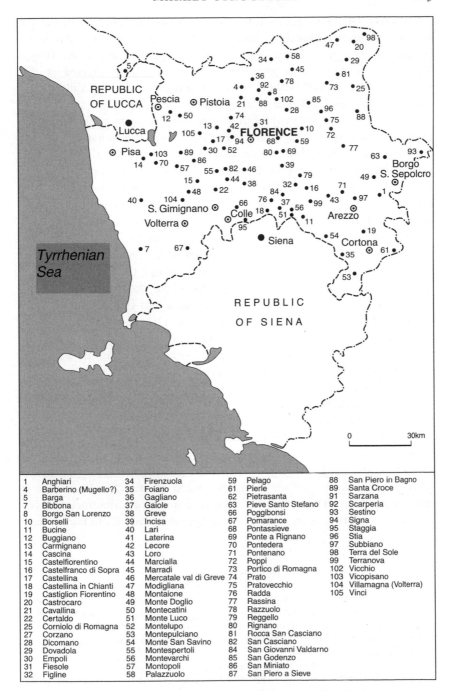

1	Anghiari	34	Firenzuola	59	Pelago	88	San Piero in Bagno
4	Barberino (Mugello?)	35	Foiano	61	Pierle	89	Santa Croce
5	Barga	36	Gagliano	62	Pietrasanta	91	Sarzana
7	Bibbona	37	Gaiole	63	Pieve Santo Stefano	92	Scarperia
8	Borgo San Lorenzo	38	Greve	66	Poggibonsi	93	Sestino
10	Borselli	39	Incisa	67	Pomarance	94	Signa
11	Bucine	40	Lari	68	Pontassieve	95	Staggia
12	Buggiano	41	Laterina	69	Ponte a Rignano	96	Stia
13	Carmignano	42	Lecore	70	Pontedera	97	Subbiano
14	Cascina	43	Loro	71	Pontenano	98	Terra del Sole
15	Castelfiorentino	44	Marcialla	72	Poppi	99	Terranova
16	Castelfranco di Sopra	45	Marradi	73	Portico di Romagna	102	Vicchio
17	Castellina	46	Mercatale val di Greve	74	Prato	103	Vicopisano
18	Castellina in Chianti	47	Modigliana	75	Pratovecchio	104	Villamagna (Volterra)
19	Castiglion Fiorentino	48	Montaione	76	Radda	105	Vinci
20	Castrocaro	49	Monte Doglio	77	Rassina		
21	Cavallina	50	Montecatini	78	Razzuolo		
22	Certaldo	51	Monte Luco	79	Reggello		
25	Corniolo di Romagna	52	Montelupo	80	Rignano		
27	Corzano	53	Montepulciano	81	Rocca San Casciano		
28	Dicomano	54	Monte San Savino	82	San Casciano		
29	Dovadola	55	Montespertoli	84	San Giovanni Valdarno		
30	Empoli	56	Montevarchi	85	San Godenzo		
31	Fiesole	57	Montopoli	86	San Miniato		
32	Figline	58	Palazzuolo	87	San Piero a Sieve		

Fig. 5.3 Markets in the Florentine dominion, *c.* 1300–1560

and Pistoia (I have found no references to a fair in Volterra), in smaller semi-autonomous boroughs such as Monte San Savino, Anghiari, Borgo San Sepolcro, Poppi, Pieve Santo Stefano, Pontassieve, Borgo San Lorenzo, Firenzuola and Pescia, and in centres located at the strategic northern and southern frontiers of the state such as Villamagna, Greve, Montevarchi, Bibbiena and Pratovecchio (Fig. 5.4).

The first impulse for establishing a new trading point came invariably from the communities themselves; Florence took the initiative only for the fortified town of Firenzuola, established to oversee the Apennine pass leading to Imola and the Romagna. But it was then up to Florence to decide whether to accept a community's request; inevitably, the city's concern to stimulate cross-border trade with its neighbours had an important influence on the outcome. Negotiations along these lines resulted in a string of fairs being established along the southern borders with Siena and with the smaller communes of the Marche and Umbria, whose main purpose seems to have been to attract the supplies of grain and livestock which the Florentines believed they were unable to produce themselves.[47] Once more, this fiscal and trading policy contrasts sharply with policies pursued in the Duchy of Milan, which produced grain and livestock surpluses and consequently aimed to restrict exports by banning all markets within 5 km of its frontiers. Interestingly, although both regimes professed to follow proto-mercantilist policies aimed at ensuring constant levels of food supply, they acted within very different economic constraints that compelled them to pursue the same aim by opposite means.[48]

Florentine strategy was also affected by political concerns.[49] It was on mainly political rather than economic grounds that the city refused to confirm a new market in Colle because the inhabitants had established it without seeking Florentine consent, going so far as to exempt it unilaterally from all tolls;[50] that it abolished at a stroke all concessions of immunities from debt and forced the recipients to buy them back;[51] and

---

[47] The purpose of these trade points was explicitly stated in a request of 1441 for immunity at the ancient market of Greve on the frontier with Siena (ASF, PR, 132, 290r–291v). For similar concerns during the communal period, see de la Roncière, *Florence*, III, pp. 957, 995 and G. Pinto, *Il Libro del Biadaiolo: carestia e annona a Firenze dalla metà del '200 al 1348* (Florence, 1978), pp. 107–8. For Florentine beliefs about the 'sterility' of their lands see Epstein, 'Stato territoriale', p. 888.

[48] See above, note 24.

[49] La Roncière, *Florence*, III, pp. 1015–19.

[50] ASS, Colle, Delib., 140, 137v–140v, no. 7, 22 June 1410. The reference was kindly provided by Oretta Muzzi.

[51] ASF, PR, 126, 359r–v, 1435, which refers to a general revocation in 1427.

REPUBLIC
OF LUCCA
Pescia
Pistoia
• 34
• 47
• 8
• 74
• 31
FLORENCE
• 88
• 75
• 72
Lucca
103
• 13
• 68
6 •
• 63
Pisa
• 89
• 30 • 52
23
• 57
• 82
55
49 •
Borgo
S. Sepolcro
104 •
• 56
• 1
90
S. Gimignano
Colle
• 37
Arezzo • 3
100
Volterra
• 19
Siena
Cortona
27 • 61
Tyrrhenian
Sea
• 101
53 •
REPUBLIC
OF SIENA
0   km   30

1	Anghiari	52	Montelupo	90	Sant'Ermo (?) ('Santerno')
3	Arezzo (Cortine)	53	Montepulciano	100	Vada
6	Bibbiena	55	Montespertoli	101	Valiano
8	Borgo San Lorenzo	57	Montopoli	103	Vicopisano
13	Carmignano	61	Pierle	104	Villamagna (Volterra)
19	Castiglion Fiorentino	63	Pieve Santo Stefano		
23	Chiusi della Verna	68	Pontassieve		
30	Empoli	72	Poppi		
31	Fiesole	74	Prato		
34	Firenzuola	75	Pratovecchio		
37	Gaiole	82	San Casciano		
47	Modigliana	88	San Piero in Bagno		
49	Monte Doglio	89	Santa Croce		

Fig. 5.4 Fairs in the Florentine dominion, *c.* 1300–1560

that it occasionally upheld *pro legibus suis* the claims of rural communities in the *distretto*, which formally fell under the sovereignty of subject towns and which wished to set up a market against the neighbouring town's hostility.[52] On the other hand, given that concessions of rural marketing rights were a direct challenge to the towns' jurisdiction, the latter's sensitivities could not be entirely ignored. Although few jurisdictional conflicts of this kind have been recorded,[53] the fact that the *contadi* of Pistoia, Volterra, Arezzo and Pisa were virtually free from rival markets and fairs (Figs. 5.3, 5.4) does suggest that their resistance against rural competition was quite successful. That the only new fairs *not* established in cities arose in communities which for one reason or another lay outside urban jurisdiction points to a similar conclusion.[54]

IV

There has been a long tendency for historians to view the regulatory systems of urban food supply established during the late medieval and early modern period as a necessary response by town authorities to the fundamental economic constraints posed by low agricultural productivity and high transport costs. In this view, a perverse combination of agricultural, mechanical and organisational backwardness made it impossible to overcome local scarcity through the regular importation of food from areas with surpluses. Left to its own devices, a free market in grain would have provoked wild and unpredictable fluctuations in price, causing sharp swings in consumption, deteriorating consumer health and serious social instability.[55] Between the late thirteenth and

[52] See L. Martines, *Lawyers and Statecraft in Renaissance Florence* (Princeton, 1968), p. 225 for Pistoia.

[53] The best documented of these conflicts is that which opposed Arezzo to its banlieu, known as the *cortine*, over the latter's insistence in establishing a fair; the most plausible explanation for the survival of the evidence is that Arezzo, unusually, lost its case. See R. Black, 'Piero de' Medici and Arezzo', in A. Beyer and B. Boucher (eds.), *Piero de' Medici 'il Gottoso' (1416–1489): Art in the Service of the Medici* (Stuttgart, 1993), pp. 24–8; Black, 'Lorenzo and Arezzo', in M. Mallett and N. Mann (eds.), *Lorenzo the Magnificent: Culture and Politics* (London, 1996), p. 228; ASF, PR, 182, 85v–86v, 24 February 1492; PR, 187, 131v–132v, 19 February 1497.

[54] Examples of trade monopolies in A. Gherardi (ed.), *I capitoli del comune di Firenze: inventario e regesto*, II (Florence, 1893), pp. 432–3 (1385), 470–1 (1395).

[55] This interpretation was first set out by C. M. Cipolla, 'The Economic Policies of Governments, V: The Italian and Iberian Peninsulas', in M. M. Postan and E. E. Rich (eds.), *The Cambridge Economic History of Europe*, III, *Economic Organization and Policies in the Middle Ages* (Cambridge, 1963), pp. 399–407. For recent surveys of communal and Renaissance supply policies see G. Pinto, 'Appunti sulla politica annonaria in Italia fra XIII e XV secolo', in *Aspetti della vita economica medievale. Atti del convegno nel X anniversario della morte di Federigo Melis* (Florence, 1985),

the sixteenth centuries, urban authorities responded to the threats posed by such extreme price volatility by establishing a complex array of price controls and barriers to domestic and international trade that became one of the most characteristic features of pre-modern Europe. Consequently, modern commentators dismiss as anachronistic the arguments of the eighteenth-century political economists, who reversed the lines of causation and identified the provisioning legislation as the principal *cause* of low agricultural productivity and commercial inefficiency.[56]

The prevailing technological model of pre-modern market regulation presumes that European towns followed similar food policies across space and time. To assess this claim one needs to distinguish between two quite different kinds of regulation that are frequently confused under the same heading. The first and best-studied form of regulation, which included a combination of price controls and subsidies and aimed to smooth price volatility, was concerned with urban consumer *demand*. This type of welfare support was virtually universal and could be found under slightly different guises in nearly every pre-modern European town. However, eighteenth-century polemicists were mainly concerned with the second form of regulation, which relied on a mixture of export bans and import bounties passed by individual towns and states to smooth variation in the level of wholesale *supply*. Significantly, this second type of regulation displayed far greater regional variation than the first. Although there is little doubt that the prevailing European approach to the grain trade was defensive and protectionist, with most states and towns maintaining strict, albeit slowly weakening, controls over exports, some countries followed an opposite course of action. The best known example of a liberal trade regime was enacted in post-Revolutionary England; a less famous instance of free domestic trade and virtually free foreign trade, which pre-dated England by nearly three centuries, was

---

pp. 624–43; L. Palermo, *Mercati del grano a Roma tra Medioevo e Rinascimento*, I, *Il mercato distrettuale del grano in età comunale* (Rome, 1990), chapter 1. The negative welfare effects of price volatility are discussed by A. Sen, *Poverty and Famines* (Oxford, 1981).

56 For a clear exposition of this model see K. G. Persson, 'The Seven Lean Years, Elasticity Traps, and Intervention in Grain Markets in Pre-Industrial Europe', *Economic History Review*, 49 (1996), pp. 692–714. See also (for a somewhat different argument) R. W. Fogel, 'Second Thoughts on the European Escape from Hunger: Famines, Chronic Malnutrition, and Mortality Rates', in S. Osmani (ed.), *Nutrition and Poverty* (Oxford, 1992), pp. 243–86.

established by the small kingdom of Sicily in the 1390s and was maintained for the entire early modern period.[57]

In both instances, the liberalisation of trade *preceded* a strong rise in agricultural productivity and grain exports. It is therefore not the case that free trade policies were adopted because the two countries were already endowed with abundant food surpluses which could be exported: Sicily in particular established free trade at a time of severe political, social and economic instability and distress. Conversely, one can easily find examples of countries that applied trade restrictions even though they produced regular food surpluses. One such case was ducal and Spanish Lombardy, which had both a highly productive agricultural system and an efficient distribution network; another was fifteenth-century Florence, which never abandoned its autarchic convictions despite the fact that it did not face any major subsistence crisis before the 1490s.[58] All four examples cast serious doubt on the existence of a strict line of causation linking commercial protectionism to available food supply. They suggest that agricultural productivity, or more precisely, domestic food supply, was not the main factor behind the choice of grain policy.

Institutional conditions affecting market structure arguably played a more important role. From the late middle ages, the supply policies pursued by towns and states came into increasing tension with one another. Towns became increasingly embedded in regional and supra-regional systems of production and distribution that were largely outside their control, and to which states for political and fiscal reasons tried to lay claim. For a long time, however, most towns continued to claim privileged access to food supplies from their hinterland backed up by rights of jurisdiction. As long as each town within a given supply area acted independently of its competitors, it tended to respond to an unanticipated decline in food supply with legislation that reinforced its rural monopsony by excluding rival towns from its hinterland. This pattern of behaviour, which was followed by most pre-modern European towns, was entirely rational as long as there was a reasonable

---

[57] For England see R. B. Outhwaite, 'Dearth and Government Intervention in English Grain Markets, 1590–1700', *Economic History Review*, 34 (1981), pp. 389–406; A. B. Appleby, *Famine in Tudor and Stuart England* (Stanford, 1978). For Sicily see Epstein, *An Island*, pp. 136–48; I. Fazio, *La politica del grano: annona e controllo del territorio in Sicilia nel Settecento* (Milan, 1993).

[58] Thus the list in Pinto, 'Appunti', pp. 633–4, of Italian regions that exported grain and of the city-states 'that under normal circumstances were self-sufficient and in good years were in a position to export part of the harvest', includes both areas that practised restrictive trade policies and areas with a more liberal approach.

expectation that all towns within a given supply area would act in the same way.

Unfortunately, this system of reciprocal trade vetoes pushed the towns into a kind of 'prisoner's dilemma'[59] whose unintended consequences were the opposite of the towns' intentions. In effect, the tariff and non-tariff barriers to trade erected by individual towns to defend their supply area and smooth price volatility raised the cost of grain for urban consumers and increased the costs of collecting commercial information. Higher information costs in turn caused delays in grain shipments and forced urban administrators to build up excessive reserves, thereby increasing prices further; once imports had lowered prices again, excess urban stocks had to be sold under cost, thus depressing prices further. Consequently, the net result of barriers to trade was to increase price volatility sharply, rather than decrease it as the trade controls were designed to do.[60]

Heightened volatility and increased competition between towns for scarce resources had potentially destabilising effects. However, because no individual town was in a position to withdraw from this system by unilaterally abolishing all barriers to trade, the prisoner's dilemma could survive in balance for centuries. The balance could only be broken by an outside force − a sovereign prince or an autocratic parliament − that could credibly commit towns to cooperate in a free trade area by punishing any infringement of the rules. Given the inherent instability of an uncoordinated system of grain supply, it would appear to have been in the interest both of the territorial ruler and of urban consumers to establish greater cooperation between towns. In principle, political centralisation should have enabled more coordinated and efficient markets to develop, as the central authority, backed by popular support, enforced the rules of free trade. In practice, however, powerful vested interests meant that the effects of centralisation were far less clear cut.

This model of pre-modern grain markets and of the effects of political centralisation provides two testable hypotheses. In the first place, one

---

[59] In game theory, a 'prisoner's dilemma' arises when the dominant (most valuable) strategy for two players is to act 'egoistically', e.g. not to collaborate, but the outcome of the game is inferior to one in which they collaborated. The players would therefore prefer to collaborate, but transaction costs prevent them from reaching this preferred outcome.

[60] See Persson, 'Seven Lean Years', pp. 699–701, for a statistical demonstration (which the author finds puzzling) that the towns of Pisa, Siena and Cologne regularly built up excess stocks between August and December. As has been suggested, such a build-up would tend to occur because of poor information about competitors' actions and about the level of stocks in exporting regions.

would expect that Florentine expansion would cause a measurable increase in market integration and a significant reduction in price volatility, as previously independent supply policies came under Florentine aegis; second, one might expect specific acts of legislation to have had a measurable impact on both price integration and volatility. I have tested these hypotheses on the basis of price series for grain reconstructed for Florence, Arezzo, Bibbiena, Borgo San Sepolcro, Cortona, Pisa, Pistoia and Volterra; I have used data for late fifteenth-century Bologna to estimate the 'pull' of the Florentine grain market beyond the state's boundaries.[61] These price series have been employed to measure market integration, which indicates the intensity of real or potential exchange between towns; price volatility, which reflects the relative efficiency of distribution; trends in relative prices, which express changes in transaction costs over time; and structural breaks or turning points caused by legislative or other exogenous sources of change.[62] Finally, the statistical evidence has been compared with evidence from government legislation.

The structural analysis identified three distinct phases of market integration, lasting from 1393 to 1461, from 1462 to 1561, and from 1562 to 1671, with the turning points occurring after major legislative reforms in 1461 and the early 1560s. The administrative records give no indication of significant organisational reforms before 1461. Up to the mid-fifteenth century, Florentine policy towards the contado followed the well-practised admixture of paternalism and authoritarianism established during the early fourteenth century,[63] which combined rural export bans and forcible supplies at fixed prices to the city,[64] the forced distribution of grain imports and excess stocks among the peasantry,[65] and loans to stimulate agricultural recovery.[66] In the district, Florence abolished the protectionist legislation which had formerly put it at the

---

[61] The price series extend more or less completely over the following periods: Florence 1320–1567; Arezzo 1385–1732; Bibbiena 1470–98; Bologna 1459–1505; Borgo San Sepolcro 1500–32, 1536–46, 1553–1631; Cortona 1440–1561; Pisa 1454–1537, 1548–1818 (the two Pisan series were kindly provided by Paolo Malanima); Pistoia 1372–84, 1400–1573; Volterra 1378–1426, 1445–1552.

[62] These were estimated with the STAMP 5.0 (Structural Time Series Analyser, Modeller and Predictor) programme developed by S. J. Koopman, A. C. Harvey, J. A. Doornik and N. Shephard.

[63] de la Roncière, *Florence*, II, pp. 551–61. For Florentine policy before the Black Death see Pinto, *Libro del Biadaiolo*, 'Introduzione'.

[64] See ASF, PR, 40, 73r–75v, 1353; PR, 77, 150v–151v, 1388.

[65] ASF, PR, 41, 134v and PR, 42, 51v–52v, 1355 (to Florentines); PR, 72, 172r–v, 1383 (to rural communities). See also note 63 above.

[66] ASF, PR, 74, 100v–101v, 1385 (3000 florins to Arezzo); PR, 92, 228r–229v, 1403 (400 florins to Civitella in 1397).

mercy of trade bans by its urban neighbours, and which had been an important cause of the traumatic subsistence crises of the 1330s.[67] After 1406, Pisa's tolls and customs were modified in such a way that it became cheaper to export grain from Pisa's hinterland to Florence than to supply Pisa itself.[68] Excepting this last measure, however, there is little to suggest that Florentine elites had a strategy of commercial integration: they were happy to get rid of the worst carbuncles of communal legislation but never operated any deeper. Despite providing short-term crisis aid to smaller towns such as Volterra, Cortona and Castiglion Fiorentino,[69] the use of forcible purveyances[70] and of

[67] For the effects of early trade bans on Florentine supplies see Pinto, *Libro del Biadaiolo*, pp. 84–5, 350–4. ASF, PR, 40, 149r–v, 18 September 1353, referred to a consignment of foreign grain to Florence via Arezzo that the latter requisitioned. For later developments see Herlihy, *Pistoia*, p. 160; E. Fiumi, 'Sui rapporti economici tra città e contado nell'età comunale', *Archivio storico italiano*, 114 (1956), pp. 49 and n. 104, 50 n. 106; and *Statuta populi et communis Florentie publica auctoritate collecta castigata et praeposita, anno salutis MCCCXV*, 3 vols. (Freiburg [Florence], 1777–83), bk IV, rub. 174, p. 279. Significantly, the main provider of public assistance and food relief in Arezzo, the Fraternita dei Laici, began to record its grain sales on the town market soon after the city's submission in 1385, probably to give Florence an indication of local food stocks. Nonetheless, before the 1460s, larger towns like Arezzo and Pistoia stayed outside Florence's main supply orbit, while smaller communities, such as Pescia and Volterra, bore the brunt of Florentine pressure. For requisitions of grain in Pescia see J. C. Brown, *In the Shadow of Florence: Provincial Society in Renaissance Pescia* (New York, 1982), p. 139. For Volterra see Fiumi, 'Sui rapporti', p. 49 and n.104; and below, p. 114.

[68] In 1414, Florence gave itself pre emptive rights over food exports from the Pisan hinterland (ASF, PR, 113, 280v–281v); in 1418, it abolished tolls on victuals (*grascie*) taken to Florence from the *dominium* (PR, 108,158r–v); in 1456, it removed its gate tolls on cereals for a year (PR, 147, 165v–166v). Thanks to its early pacts with Florence, Pistoia probably had the most favourable trading arrangements of all subject towns (Herlihy, *Pistoia*, pp. 158–60, suggested that Florence and Pistoia had similar tariffs on two-way trade). Relations with Pisa were as always more ambiguous. See Epstein, 'Stato territoriale', p. 881 n. 45, for a discussion of the discriminatory tariffs applied to Pisa in the new gabelles for 1408. These were partially mitigated in 1418 – by which time the Pisan economy and population had, however, virtually collapsed – when Pisa's entry tolls on victuals were made equal to those in Florence (PR, 108, 156v–158v). Only in 1440 was Pisa allowed to import grain toll-free from its hinterland (PR, 131, 100r–v, 184r–v). Concern for Arezzo was even thinner on the ground. In 1461, Florence specified that the toll franchise granted to Arezzo's new fair did not apply to victuals brought in from the countryside (PR, 151, 380v–381v); and it took until 1465 to modify the town's gabelles on grain, which were three times as high on imports as on exports (PR, 156, 85v–86v).

[69] ASF, PR, 164, 113r–v, (1473, Volterra); PR, 126, 230v–231v 1435 (Cortona); PR, 138, 25r–v, 1447; and PR, 153, 194r–v, 1462 (Castiglion Fiorentino).

[70] See ASF, PR, 126, 424v–425v, 1436: it is unclear whether this provision was ever enacted. See also PR, 144, 58r–59v, 1454, for a forced distribution of Florentine grain in its contado, in Pisa and in the Pisan contado. Black, 'Lorenzo and Arezzo',

compulsory pricing across the state[71] indicates that fifteenth-century Florentines basically perceived the *dominium* in the light of a subject contado. The only major departures from the communal past were the development of a chain of fairs and markets to entice food supply across the borders, discussed previously, and the creation in 1413 of a system of export rights (*tratte*) from Pisa's former contado.[72] Neither these, nor other institutional reforms like the creation in 1448 of the new *Dogana dei traffichi* to oversee the customs system,[73] had any discernible effect on the pattern of grain prices in the region.

The statistical analysis of market integration confirms that Florentine legislation achieved very limited results (Figs. 5.5a and b and Table 5.2a–c).[74] Until the early 1460s Florence had stronger trading links with the small town of Volterra, whose agricultural hinterland was neither large nor particularly fertile, than with the closer and far more productive territory of Pistoia, apparently because the latter was still capable of restricting Florentine access to its hinterland. Market integration with other subject towns also indicates that the intensity of the grain trade with Florence before 1461 stood in an inverse relation to the former's size and power. Thus Arezzo traded less with Florence than did Volterra, even though Arezzo's contado was much more productive,[75] and Florence traded more with Cortona than with Pistoia, even though Cortona lay three times further away. The influence of political factors on the grain trade is further confirmed by the sharp drop in the coefficient of integration between Florence and Arezzo and between Florence and Pistoia after 1406, when Florence probably reoriented demand for grain towards the weaker Pisa.[76]

---

p. 231 refers to an order to Arezzo to send grain in aid of San Sepolcro during the dearth of 1477.

[71] ASF, PR, 155, 224v–225v, 1465.

[72] ASF, PR, 102, 113v–114v. The authority of the Florentine *Abbondanza* over exports from Pisa was confirmed in 1442 (PR, 133, 23v–26v). During the fifteenth century the Florentine Signoria authorised export licences in 1422–4, 1427–8, 1442, 1444, 1447, 1465, 1471, 1475 and 1493; further grain exports from Pisa are recorded for 1473, 1478, 1481–2, 1491 and 1495. Florence banned exports in 1412, 1435, 1441, 1464, 1466 and 1468; it authorised overseas grain imports on twenty-three occasions, and elected officials to the *Abbondanza* in thirty-one years.

[73] B. Dini, *Arezzo intorno al 1400: produzioni e mercato* (Arezzo, 1984), pp. 23–6.

[74] Except for Florence, there are no complete series of grain prices for the period before Arezzo's submission in 1385; it is therefore impossible to compare market integration after territorial expansion with the situation before.

[75] See Machiavelli, *Discorsi*, II, 23, for a starkly formulated statement along these lines.

[76] As indicated by the changes to Pisa's customs tariffs, referred to in Epstein, 'Stato territoriale', p. 881 n. 45, and note 67 above. Unfortunately, there are no price series available for Pisa in this period that could confirm the hypothesis conclusively.

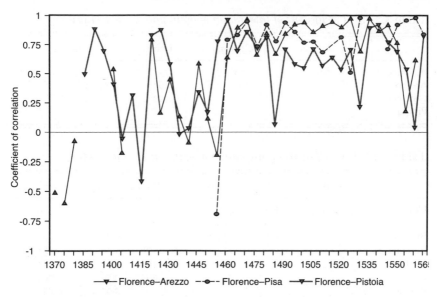

Fig. 5.5 (a) Price correlations for grain, 1370–1569 (Arezzo, Pisa, Pistoia and Florence)

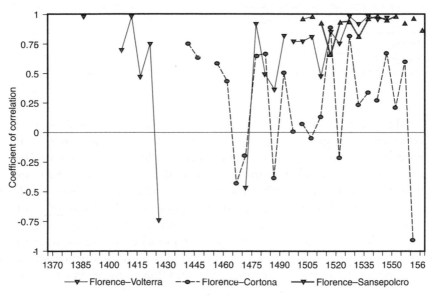

Fig. 5.5 (b) Price correlations for grain, 1370–1569 (Volterra, Cortona, Sansepolcro and Florence)

Table 5.2 (a). *Coefficients of integration of grain prices, 1385–1461*

	Arezzo	Cortona	Pistoia	Volterra
Florence	.646	.511	.555	.747
Arezzo		.428	.393	.442
Cortona			.130	.331
Pistoia				.668

Table 5.2 (b). *Coefficients of integration of grain prices, 1462–1560*

	Arezzo	Bibbiena	Bologna	Cortona	Pisa	Pistoia	Sansepolcro	Volterra
Florence	.859	.827	.898	.474	.922	.932	.953	.926
Arezzo		.566	.709	.430	.821	.828	.771	.653
Bibbiena			.758	.133	.825	.799	n.d.	.062
Bologna				.134	.871	.778	.976	.681
Cortona					.398	.461	.272	.417
Pisa						.895	.889	.709
Pistoia							.897	.857
Sansepolcro								.933

Table 5.2 (c). *Coefficients of integration of grain prices, 1561–1671*

	Sansepolcro	Pisa
Arezzo	.706	.698
Sansepolcro		.767

The effects of grain market legislation during the second phase of commercial integration from 1462 to the early 1560s continued to be insignificant. Of far greater import was a collection of customs laws passed in 1461 which became known as the *Legge dei passeggeri*, and which was concerned with regulating the trading system as a whole. The *Legge* listed in detail the roads and passes which all domestic and foreign traders were obliged to use[77] and was clearly intended both to sustain Florence's position at the hub of regional trade and to make the latter easier to tax. However, a more significant consequence was to establish a clear hierarchy of road usage, and thus to focus repairs on the

---

[77] The law (*legge*), ASF, DAC, 373, 34r–38v, is discussed briefly in Dini, *Arezzo*, pp. 24–6; and Dini, 'Le vie di comunicazione del territorio fiorentino alla metà del Quattrocento', in *Mercati e consumi: organizzazione e qualificazione del commercio in Italia dal XII al XX secolo* (Bologna, 1986), p. 289.

main commercial arteries which a century of demographic decline, social upheaval and near permanent warfare had brought close to collapse. The reorganisation and improvement of the road system caused regional price integration to surge in the space of a few years from 50–70 to 65–95 per cent (Figs. 5.5a, b). Interestingly, the greater transparency in transport costs brought about by the road reform seems to have provoked the increasing disintegration of the distant town of Cortona; the incomplete prices series at our disposal suggest that after the *Legge*, and possibly already some time before, Florence traded less intensively with subject Cortona to its south than with the city of Bologna across the Apennines.[78]

It was previously observed that the decentralised and competitive system of grain supply established by independent city-states undermined its declared objective of stabilising prices. Under these circumstances, one would expect to observe high volatility where towns pursued separate and uncoordinated supply policies, and a corresponding decline in volatility if coordination between towns increased or if urban protectionism declined. This prediction is borne out by the Tuscan evidence. Government records indicate that urban grain policy after 1461 continued much as it had before. In Florence as elsewhere, the provisioning offices of urban *Abbondanza* were manned only when shortages arose and were disbanded just as soon as they passed.[79] Despite occasional sales of grain by Florence to subject communities,[80] at times from the military stocks that were to be found in the larger subject cities,[81] each town acted by and large independently from the others until the early 1560s.[82] The implication is that price volatility would be largely unaffected by the reform of 1461. In fact, volatility after 1461 increased sharply, from an average price variation of 30–35 per cent around the five-year mean in the early fifteenth century to a staggering

---

[78] It is also likely that by the mid-fifteenth century Cortona was coming increasingly within Rome's orbit. See E. Fasano Guarini, 'Center and Periphery' in J. Kirshner (ed.), *The Origins of the State in Italy, 1300–1600* (Chicago, 1996), p. 94 n. 63.

[79] A decision in 1442 to turn the *Abbondanza* into a permanent office was never enacted; ASF, PR, 133, 23v–26v.

[80] See ASF, PR, 126, 100v–102v, 1435, and PR, 131, 43r–44v, 1440 (for Volterra); PR, 135, 41r–42v, 1444 (referring to Montopoli in 1433); PR, 159, 193r–195v, 1468 (for Firenzuola); and PR,172, 26r–27v, 1481 (for Montepulciano).

[81] See ASF, PR, 129, 174r–175v, 1438 and PR, 155,173v–174v, for Arezzo. The decision, taken in 1442, to provide fixed stocks of grain in all the main cities including Florence and Castiglion Fiorentino was apparently never applied (PR, 133, 23v–26v).

[82] See Pult Quaglia, *'Per provvedere ai popoli'*, p. 70.

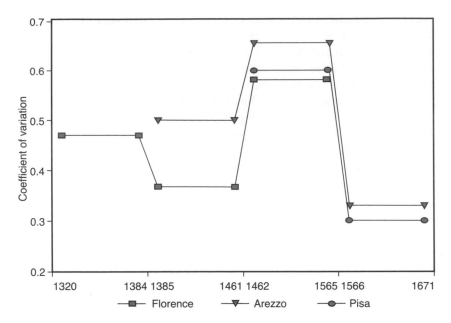

Fig. 5.6 Coefficients of variation for grain prices, 1320–1671
(Florence, Arezzo, Pisa)

40–45 per cent variation after 1461 (Fig. 5.6). The increase, which confirms our hypothesis, resulted from the intensifying friction between the rapidly rising demand for grain (caused by the demographic recovery and greater domestic competition brought about by the *Legge dei passeggeri*) and an unchanged, uncoordinated and protectionist system of urban supply.

In conclusion, although political integration had negligible effects on urban supply policies, its consequences for Tuscan consumers were mostly negative, for two reasons. In the first place, the lack of coordination between towns exacerbated price volatility, with the direct effects being felt by wage earners who bought most of their bread on the market and for whom the expense made up a large proportion of their budget. Secondly, although regional prices during the fifteenth and early sixteenth centuries tended to converge in response to lower transport costs and domestic tariffs (Fig. 5.2), consumers in the main importing city, Florence, benefited more than consumers in exporting towns like Arezzo and Pistoia, where relative prices tended to rise; the effects on towns with a better balance between demand and supply of grain were probably neutral.

It would nonetheless be misleading to lay the entire blame for this unfortunate outcome on the Florentines. Under the circumstances, it is unlikely that, even if it had so wished, the Florentine republic could have found a permanent solution to the stalemate caused by competing urban monopolies. Its elites were too heavily committed to the existing distribution system for them to introduce a reform that could be credibly enforced. Credibility required a strong political will that could cut through the maze of interests vested in the status quo, and the reformers had to be perceived not to be gaining from the change. Although there is no evidence that Florentines ever countenanced a reform on this scale, it is true to say that no urban oligarchy, however powerful and determined, would have been in a position to push one through.[83]

For reasons that must still be explained, the will and the opportunity for reform arose in the early 1560s in the aftermath of the long and costly war against Siena. Duke Cosimo I's decision to establish a permanent *regional* supply office (*Abbondanza*) to supervise and coordinate the importation and distribution of grain between all the ancient urban magistracies of the Florentine territorial state[84] marked the start of the third and possibly most important phase of market integration. The impact of the abolition of traditional urban vetoes on price volatility – which measures the efficiency of the distribution system – was, as predicted, clear and immediate: the average level of volatility dropped sharply (Fig. 5.6) and, for the first time in the available records, its trend turned decisively downwards. Nearly two centuries after Florence set out to establish a territorial state and a regional market under its control, political and commercial integration had become synchronised.

v

The initial hypothesis that late medieval political centralisation gave rise to greater market integration has been broadly confirmed. Florentine expansion produced several institutional changes with important economic effects: first, it led to a consolidation of the domestic tariff system and helped lower the level of total charges; second, it enabled weaker rural communities to establish markets and fairs against urban

---

[83] I discuss the political constraints on state-building by Italian city-states and the resulting market failures more generally in S. R. Epstein, 'The Rise and Fall of Italian City-States', in M. H. Hansen (ed.), *City-State Cultures in World History* (Copenhagen, 2000).

[84] Pult Quaglia, '*Per provvedere ai popoli*', pp. 47–62. The recently annexed Sienese state maintained an independent administration.

opposition; third, it enabled the rationalisation of the regional road network. All these reforms lowered transaction costs, which reduced the net cost of goods and improved opportunities for specialisation. Most consumers stood to gain; but some benefited more than others. The main losers (in relative terms) from market integration were the formerly independent communes, which saw their toll revenues eroded by the Florentine rulers and which in some cases could be faced with higher relative (but lower absolute) food prices.

The devil lies in the detail, however, and this somewhat Panglossian conclusion must be qualified in several important ways. First and most importantly, there is little evidence that the economic benefits from integration were ever perceived as such by the Florence regime. The only evidence of any strategic economic concerns can be found in the way new fairs were established along the eastern and southeastern frontiers in order to stimulate the cross-border trade in livestock and grain. This must in any case be set against the heavy-handed control over domestic trade reflected in the distribution of customs posts near Florence itself, and against other evidence of the political manipulation of markets for the Florentines' benefit.

Indeed, to pose the question of political motivation in strictly economic terms assumes a separation between 'politics' and the 'market' that is basically anachronistic. Regional market integration was the unintended consequence of three fundamental concerns, none of which could be considered economic in the modern sense of the term. In the first place, the city wished to extend – for political besides economic reasons – to the distretto the privileged jurisdictional status it had established over its contado. The economic side to this concern emerges most clearly from the nature of the grain trade prior to the tariff and road reforms of 1461, which demonstrates a clear preference by Florence for trade with more distant and poorly supplied, but politically weaker subject towns. The use of the tools of political hegemony for economic purposes is also apparent during the first years of Pisan rule, when the subject city's tolls were manipulated shamelessly for the capital's benefit. The political aspect of jurisdictional hegemony is instead best revealed by the decision to challenge Pistoia's territorial rights by authorising a rural market in the latter's contado.

Faced with the rapidly escalating military costs associated with the status of a regional power, Florence was equally concerned with expanding its tax base effectively and durably. Both ways of achieving this entailed far-reaching reform. The more forthright and also most contentious route was to extend direct taxation to the whole distretto. This option was followed most notoriously with the catasto of 1427 but, as Petralia demonstrates in this volume, it resulted for several reasons in a dismal failure. The secondary route, which involved bringing much of the district's indirect taxation of trade under Florentine remit, was paradoxically far more successful, possibly because it excited fewer worries among the subject cities' elites.

Florence's third concern, which followed on from the policy of enhancing revenue from indirect taxation, was to take account of, and respond flexibly to, fiscal competition by neighbouring states. An aspect of inter-state competition which was probably of greater concern to smaller states than to large ones, inter-state fiscal competition had a moderating influence on Florentine internal policy; like the development of indirect taxation, this aspect of fiscal policy also deserves to be studied further.

A somewhat different qualification to our conclusion regarding the economic benefits of political integration concerns the question of what was *not* achieved by early Florentine state building. The most obvious limitation in Florentine policy, which has already been mentioned, is the fact that the city's elites could conceive economic relations with their subjects only along traditional dualistic lines. Paradoxically, this made it harder to modify inefficient institutions like the individual urban food agencies (*Abbondanze*), because they appeared to *protect* their subjects from Florentine encroachment. The problem at root was identified by David Hume long ago: 'The conquerors, in such a [republican] government, are all legislators, and will be sure to contrive matters, by restrictions on trade, and by taxes, so as to draw some private, as well as public advantage from their conquests.' This was so much an accepted fact of political life that a genuinely positive reform by the Florentine elites was not fundamentally credible; the effect of such mostly justified cynicism was that no amount of inefficiencies in the existing arrangements could have convinced Tuscan subjects to give them up.[85]

Lastly, we must raise the question whether Florentine policy differed in any significant way from contemporary practice in other states. Although the brief comparisons with Sicilian and Lombard policy have given some indication of possible differences, the latter's implications have to be more fully worked out. Our initial suggestion that the different market structures established in that period defined later patterns of regional economic growth will have to await further exploration elsewhere.

[85] D. Hume, 'That politics may be reduced to a science', in Hume, *Selected Essays* (Oxford, 1993), p. 17.

CHAPTER 6

STATE-BUILDING, CHURCH REFORM, AND THE POLITICS OF LEGITIMACY IN FLORENCE, 1375–1460

DAVID S. PETERSON

Viewed over the span of a long fifteenth century, the histories of Florence, the papacy and the Florentine church align themselves into three distinct phases. First, the period of the papal schism corresponded to that of Florence's most rapid and extensive territorial expansion, and allowed the city's rulers to take the initiative in elaborating fiscal institutions, and a juridical apparatus, that circumscribed the operation of ecclesiastical institutions within their territory. The process reached its culmination in the codification of the city's *Statuta* (1415–18), and with the creation of its 'catasto' or tax inventory (1427). At the same time, such 'state-building' measures were complemented, and limited, by the policies of a governing *reggimento* which, shaken by the city's failed war of the 'Eight Saints' (1375–78) and the Ciompi revolt (1378) that framed the rupture of the papacy into schism (1378–1414), was also in the process of its own oligarchic consolidation. Rather than simply refurbish its old Guelf credentials, the regime deployed strategies aimed at appropriating directly the legitimating power of religion attaching to local ecclesiastical institutions.

Second, over the period from the resolution of the schism at the Council of Constance (1414–18) to the Medicean *parlamento of 1458*, and Pope Pius II's promulgation of the anti-conciliar bull *Execrabilis* (1460), while republican-minded Florentine oligarchs came to terms with the emergence of Roman-financed Medici power, popes from Martin V (1417–31) onwards moved to suppress the conciliar movement, to build a territorial base in Italy and to reassert ecclesiastical prerogatives throughout the peninsula. These pressures, combined with the legacies of the schism, and of Florentine territorial expansion, propelled the Florentine clergy through a cycle of experiments with corporate self-government, papally sponsored and observantine reform and, finally, the episcopal reforms of Archbishop Antoninus (1446–59). By imposing his hierarchical authority over clerical government, and religious discipline on the laity, Antoninus was able to reclaim the church's stewardship of legitimating sacred power, and to underscore the illegitimacy of Medici rule. At the same time, he advanced to a role as advocate and mediator for the clergy of the entire Florentine territory between the Florentine state and the papacy.

Finally, over the last third of the century, Medicean and papal 3 interests moved fitfully towards a convergence that was eventually epitomised by the Medicean pontificates of Leo X (1513–21) and Clement VII (1523–34). However, they also laid the foundations for the sharp Savonarolan reaction against the increasingly manifest Medicean subversion of the Florentine republic, and the papacy's retreat from church reform. This chapter surveys the high points of the first two phases, particularly Florentine initiatives towards the church during the schism, then, more briefly, the phases of ecclesiastical recovery culminating in the archiepiscopate of Antoninus, with a view to their legacies at the end of the century.

Historians have lately moved beyond the secular vision of Renaissance politics instilled by classicising humanist historians, and the Rome-centred view of the Italian church bequeathed by curial biographers, to examine the variegated ecclesiastical structures of the Italian peninsula, and the complexities of religious life in its many regions.[1] Accordingly, the church has emerged in new guises as a problem in fifteenth-century Italian politics: first, because of the challenges that its immunities and jurisdictions posed to emerging territorial states early in the century; then, because of the papacy's subsequent role in diplomacy, and as the dispenser of benefices, in the consolidation of power by Italy's regional political elites.[2] It is by now axiomatic that the history of Italian and European religious life in this period (or any other) cannot

---

[1] Distinctive stimuli were provided by D. Weinstein, *Savonarola and Florence: Prophecy and Patriotism in the Renaissance* (Princeton, NJ, 1970); G. Miccoli, 'La storia religiosa', in *Storia d'Italia*, II, *Dalla caduta dell'impero romano al secolo xviii*, 2 vols. (Turin, 1974), I, pp. 431–1085; D. Hay, *The Church in Italy in the Fifteenth Century* (Cambridge, 1977); and R. C. Trexler, *Public Life in Renaissance Florence* (New York, 1980). Among the most important responses have been the conferences by A. Erba *et al.* (eds.), *Pievi e parrocchie in Italia nel Basso Medioevo (sec. XIII–XV)*, 2 vols., (Rome, 1984); G. De Sandre Gasparini *et. al.* (eds.), *Vescovi e diocesi in Italia dal XIV alla metà del XVI secolo*, 2 vols. (Rome, 1990); and the anthologies by A. Vauchez (ed.), *Storia dell'Italia religiosa*, I, *L'antichità e il medioevo* (Bari, 1993); and M. Rosa (ed.), *Clero e società nell'Italia moderna* (Bari, 1992).

[2] On the former point, see G. Chittolini's synthesis, 'Stati regionali e istituzioni ecclesiastiche nell'Italia centrosettentrionale del Quattrocento', in G. Chittolini and G. Miccoli (eds.), *Storia d'Italia: annali*, IX, *La Chiesa e il potere politico dal Medioevo all'età contemporanea* (Turin, 1986). On the latter, see A. Prosperi's seminal '*Dominus beneficiorum*: il conferimento dei benefici ecclesiastici tra prassi curiale e ragioni politiche negli stati italiani tra '400 e '500', in P. Prodi and P. Johanek (eds.), *Strutture ecclesiastiche in Italia e Germania prima della Riforma* (Bologna, 1984), pp. 51–86. For Florence, see R. Bizzocchi, *Chiesa e potere nella Toscana del Quattrocento* (Bologna, 1987).

merely be subsumed within that of the institutional church, anymore than can the history of politics and institutions in Florence (or else-where) be approached independently of the social worlds in which they evolved. The social and political interests bearing upon it heavily conditioned the church's religious credibility, and its ability to conform to, let alone direct, the changing religious aspirations of the laity. Thus reform, the church's central dilemma in this period, required by turns seeking support from, but also challenging, these interests. Conversely, the extent to which either the church's prerogatives might safely be challenged by temporal states, or its authority might usefully be deployed to enforce social order, depended heavily on the esteem it enjoyed among the laity. The approaches of Florence's rulers were informed by their awareness that, despite many paradoxes and short-comings, the church's fiscal and juridical prerogatives derived not from wealth and power alone but, most fundamentally, from its status as a sacred institution. This, in turn, required that it be perceived as autonomous of (and superior to) the profaning influence of secular politics and lay interference.[3] Because Florence's rulers were concerned not simply to develop the apparatus of a sovereign territorial state, but also to legitimise it, their strategies toward the church therefore featured a careful balancing of policies that aimed to survey, delimit and circumscribe the fiscal and juridical prerogatives of the church in their territory, while leaving it also that degree of autonomy necessary to make it viable as a sacred legitimating agency. This, of course, entailed running the risk that its authority might eventually be mobilised to challenge the legitimacy of the state and of its leaders.

Ecclesiastical institutions in early Quattrocento Tuscany were at once capillary in their penetration of urban space, and pervasive in articu-lating the rural landscape. Yet, they were marked also by profound inequities and deep divisions among the clergy, and aligned only imperfectly with the complex and shifting matrix of lay religious sentiments. While the dense concentrations of medieval parishes in the heart of Tuscan cities underscored the inter-penetration of lay and religious spheres that was a staple of northern Italian social life, the juxtaposition of Florence's baptistery and cathedral complex at the northern end of the city's centre, away from the Palace of the Signoria to its south, offered a deliberate urbanistic representation of an ideal distinction of civil from ecclesiastical authority that ran back for

---

[3] For a fuller statement, see D. S. Peterson, 'Religion, Politics, and the Church in Fifteenth-Century Florence', in D. Weinstein and V. R. Hotchkiss (eds.), *Girolamo Savonarola: Piety, Prophecy and Politics in Renaissance Florence* (Dallas, 1994), pp. 75–83.

centuries. Processions such as those of the *Bianchi* penitents of 1399 connected town and country, and gave expression to a common hunger for peace, for the miraculous and for Christian *renovatio* that ran across social classes, and linked individual salvation to the welfare of the community. Yet they underscored as well the failures of civil and ecclesiastical authorities to bring about peace and union, and highlighted Florence's otherwise richly variegated religious environment. This presents itself by turns as patrician and voluntarist in the texts of humanists like Coluccio Salutati; casuistic and disciplinary in the tracts and sermons of mendicants like Giovanni Dominici and Bernardino of Siena; public, urban and civic in its rituals, but intensely private and spiritualising in its devotional literature; penitential and charitable in the acts of its benefactors, whose largess was nevertheless also calculating and contractual.[4]

Florentines experienced the sacred at a number of levels. Tabernacles of the Virgin and Child guarded the thoroughfares of the city, and Florence's acquisition of Pisa in 1406 brought a fresh infusion of relics into the city's lively traffic. Goro Dati regarded Florence's hospitals as sanctifying the city, nunneries offered spiritual protection to the city's key arteries, gates and bridges, and St Bernardino reminded his audiences that churches were not only the sites of the clergy's miraculous

---

[4] On the *Bianchi*, see D. Bornstein, *The Bianchi of 1399: Popular Devotion in Late Medieval Italy* (Ithaca, 1993). Leading explorations of the humanists' religious thought include E. Garin, 'Problemi di religione e filosofia nella cultura fiorentina del quattrocento', *Bibliothèque d'humanisme*, 14 (1952), pp. 70–82; C. Trinkaus, *In Our Image and Likeness: Humanity and Divinity in Italian Humanist Thought*, 2 vols. (Chicago, 1970); and R. Witt, *Hercules at the Crossroads: The Life, Works, and Thought of Coluccio Salutati* (Durham, NC, 1983). Recent surveys of Florentine religious sentiment include T. Verdon and J. Henderson (eds.), *Christianity and the Renaissance: Image and Religious Imagination in the Quattrocento* (Syracuse, 1990); and A. Benvenuti Papi, F. Cardini and E. Giannarelli (eds.), *Le radici cristiane di Firenze* (Florence, 1994). The civic setting was emphasised by M. Becker, 'Aspects of Lay Piety in Early Renaissance Florence', in C. Trinkaus and H. Oberman (eds.), *The Pursuit of Holiness in Late Medieval and Renaissance Religion* (Leiden, 1974), pp. 177–99; and G. Brucker, *Renaissance Florence* (New York, 1969), pp. 172–212. Florentine devotional reading was analysed by C. Bec, *Les livres des florentins (1413–1608)* (Florence, 1984); and K. Gill, 'Women and the Production of Religious Literature', in E. A. Matter and J. Coakley (eds.), *Creative Women in Medieval and Early Modern Italy* (Philadelphia, 1994), pp. 64–104. Recent studies of penance and charity include J. Banker, *Death in the Community: Memorialization and Confraternities in an Italian Commune in the Late Middle Ages* (Athens, GA, 1988); A. Benvenuti Papi *'In Castro Poenitentiae': santità e società femminile nell'Italia medievale* (Rome, 1990); C. M. de La Roncière, *Tra preghiera e rivolta: le folle toscane nel XIV secolo* (Rome, 1993); and J. Henderson, *Piety and Charity in Late Medieval Florence* (Oxford, 1994). Testamental benefactions have been profiled by S. K. Cohn, Jr., *The Cult of Remembrance and the Black Death: Six Renaissance Cities in Central Italy* (Baltimore, 1992).

sacramental performances, but the homes of angels as well.[5] These, along with the city's monasteries, were also the *loci* of familial, parochial and civic pride, as well as flash points of violence in times of revolt, and key venues for conspiracy at any time.

The Florentine diocese alone embraced eighty-three urban and suburban parishes within the baptismal parish (*pieve*) of San Giovanni, and sixty large rural *pievi* comprehending twenty-five collegiate churches, twenty-eight oratories and 614 parish churches. Another 104 *compagnie*, or confraternities, 114 hospitals and 118 monasteries, hermitages, and friaries were spread throughout the city and diocese. Including the six other dioceses of Fiesole, Pistoia, Arezzo, Volterra, Pisa and Cortona, and portions of Lucca, Florence's territory embraced over 270 *pievi*, ninety collegiate churches, 660 chapels and oratories, 290 monasteries, 275 hospitals and 196 religious *compagnie*. The landed endowments of the church grew to a quarter and more of some parts of the countryside over the fifteenth century, even as ecclesiastics shifted investments to urban properties; and as much as 5 per cent of the population were in some form of orders.[6] The most heavily endowed institutions were a striking mix of the oldest and newest. Although hospitals, confraternities and the mendicant orders had risen to prominence in the last two centuries, they had supplemented rather than supplanted traditional objects of Florentine devotion and benefaction. Among the forty Florentine institutions with capitalisation above 5000 florins were the bishopric, eight hospitals and a confraternity, three colleges of secular clergy, nine nunneries (six regular, three mendicant) seventeen monasteries for men (thirteen regular, four mendicant) and the seat of the Templars. These represented significant agglomerations of wealth, but they were scarcely preponderant in a community, 192 of whose citizens were worth more than 5000 florins, twenty-eight more than 20,000 florins, and four more than 50,000 florins.[7]

Nor was the ecclesiastical establishment monolithic. In the early

---

[5] Goro Dati, *Istoria di Firenze dal 1380 al 1405*, ed. L. Pratesi, (Norcia, 1904), pp. 118–19; S. Bernardino, *Le prediche volgari*, ed. C. Cannarozzi, 2 vols. (Pistoia, 1934), I, p. 212.

[6] For the Florentine diocese, ASF, Catasto, 184, 185, 194, 195; for population, D. Herlihy and C. Klapisch-Zuber, *Les Toscans et leurs familles: un étude du catasto florentin de 1427* (Paris, 1978), pp. 158–9; on the church's endowments in the countryside, E. Conti, *La formazione della struttura agraria moderna nel contado fiorentino* (Rome, 1965).

[7] L. Martines, *The Social World of the Florentine Humanists 1390–1460* (Princeton, 1963) pp. 365–78. I owe the observation to Richard Goldthwaite. The endowment of the archbishopric (21,142 florins) was exceeded only by that of the hospital of Santa Maria Nuova (42,507 florins), ASF, Catasto, 195, 1r and 271v.

fourteenth century, responding to communal challenges, Florentine bishops had distilled the precepts of canon law into synodal constitutions that set forth the clergy's immunities from lay taxation and the jurisdiction of secular courts, as well as their own hierarchical authority over the clergy, their controlling *dominium* over church property, and their right to supervise the religious and moral life of the laity in matters ranging from dress and sexual comportment to the sensitive ethical and economic issues of contracts, testaments and usury.[8] But already bishops' temporal jurisdictions in the Florentine contado and throughout Tuscany had been superseded by communal authorities, male monastic orders had become largely self-governing, and at the Council of Vienne (1311) bishops had unsuccessfully protested the doctrine of papal *plenitudo potestatis*, whereby the mendicant orders and inquisitors had substantially undercut their diocesan authority.[9] The elaboration of the systems of papal provision to benefices and commendation to abbeys, and the creation of a European network of tax collectories by the Avignon popes, only exacerbated the fragmentation of local ecclesiastical institutions that was the price of centralising papal policies. These in turn were thrown into disarray, and opened up for discussion, by the schism.

By the early fifteenth century, lawyers lamented the lack of business at Florence's episcopal curia.[10] Visiting the diocese in 1422, Archbishop Amerigo Corsini found his patrician cathedral canons riven by the high-handed leadership of their provost, Amerigo de' Medici. The twenty-one tiny parishes in the city centre were ringed by a dozen Romanesque and early Gothic collegiate churches, vestiges of Florentine leadership in the eleventh-century reform movement, but now the hubs of a network of multiple benefice-holding that assured that their canons officiated in the other parishes of the city, but also that many *pievi* in the countryside were held *in absentia*. From here to the city walls, nineteen of the city's twenty-eight largest and most populous parishes were attached to monasteries and friaries; nearly half the urban populace was ministered to by clergy nominated by nuns. In the countryside, only a dozen of the sixty *pievi*, located in the wealthier regions of the Mugello

---

[8] Many are published in R. Trexler (ed.), *Synodal Law in Florence and Fiesole, 1306–1518* (Vatican City, 1971). That of Bishop Acciaiuoli (1346) became authoritative: J. D. Mansi (ed.), *Sacrorum Conciliorum Nova et Amplissima Collectio* (Venice, 1784), XXVI, cols. 23–74.

[9] G. Dameron, *Episcopal Power and Florentine Society, 1000–1320* (Cambridge, Mass., 1991); and, for a survey of Tuscany, D. Osheim, *An Italian Lordship: The Bishopric of Lucca in the Late Middle Ages* (Berkeley, 1977), pp. 116–27.

[10] According to Francesco di Lorenzo Machiavelli, 'al veschovado niente si fa', ASF, Catasto, 17, 603v. Thanks to Robert Black for this notice.

and Valdarno, had retained their medieval collegiate organisation. Further north toward the Apennines, moreover, and south towards the war-ravaged Sienese border, many rural parishes verged on extinction. While Florentines undertook the great ecclesiastical building projects that would shape Italy's artistic Renaissance, and lined their churches with chapels that tied their fortunes to the clergy's sacramental offices on the eve of the Reformation, upwards of a third of rural parishes lay near ruin or had been abandoned. Nor were conditions any more florid in neighbouring dioceses.

More than half the clergy were religious and, except for nuns in regular orders, largely beyond episcopal control. While urban nunneries continued to prosper, despite reduced membership, and 'flagship' male institutions like the monasteries at Vallombrosa and Camaldoli still flourished in the countryside, demography and papal commendation had reduced numerous other rural institutions to as few as two or three poor members. Rising benefactions and recruitment in the Carthusian and Augustinian orders reflected patrician support of contemplative and, perhaps, Petrarchan religious strains. But efforts to reform the mendicants had split them during the schism, and while the Dominicans struggled to recruit new members, the Franciscans were plagued by outright flight and sinking public esteem. Meanwhile, the rising demand among the laity for more personal forms of religious devotion, evident in the continuing growth of *laudesi* and, especially, *disciplinati* confraternities, continued to outstrip episcopal resources for spiritual and administrative leadership.[11]

Some of these characteristics were the results of schism, plague and warfare that had affected other regions of Italy and Europe. The event that set the Florentine case apart was the war of the 'Eight Saints', fought by the city against Pope Gregory XI in 1375–8. Since the formation of the Guelf entente in 1267, a generally collaborative relationship between Florentine bankers and the papacy had yielded light clerical taxation and the gift of numerous benefices to Florentine patricians. But in the early 1370s, a *reggimento* whose many 'new citizens' identified their political interests more strictly with the advance of sovereign communal authority, and who were less beholden to papal favour than their Guelf predecessors and colleagues, saw in the French pope's machinations to return to Rome a presage of papal territorial expansion at Florentine expense. Provoked also by Gregory's revival of

---

[11] Based on the Catasto and Archivio Arcivescovile di Firenze, Visite Pastorali, 001.1 (1383), 001.2 (1393), 002.0 (1422) and 004.1 (1514). There is a wealth of materials on the histories of the religious orders and Florentine houses in the registers of ASF, Dipl., and Corp. rel. sopp.

the inquisition, and aggressive intervention in local church affairs, they passed a round of legislation that curbed rights of ecclesiastical sanctuary, and brought the clergy before communal courts in property disputes involving laymen. The break with Gregory in July 1375 was accompanied by measures that barred Florentines from accepting the bishoprics of Florence and Fiesole, permitted citizens to appeal from ecclesiastical to communal courts, and transferred jurisdiction over contract and usury cases to officers of Florence's funded public debt, the Monte Comune.[12]

Gregory's interdict of 31 March 1376 was greeted with proud defiance by Florence's citizens. 'We can see the *corpus Christi* in our hearts, and God knows we are neither Saracens nor pagans', declared one chronicler.[13] Leading religious such as the Augustinian Luigi Marsili and the Vallombrosan Giovanni dalle Celle seconded Chancellor Salutati's justification of the war as a defense of Tuscan *libertas* against papal temporal aggression. Already the commune had begun to levy sizable forced loans on the clergy. But in September 1376, perhaps influenced by the theories of Marsilius of Padua, the *reggimento*, led by Salvestro de' Medici, proceeded to a much more radical measure: financing the war by the direct expropriation of ecclesiastical property for sale to laymen. There ensued the most extensive liquidation of ecclesiastical landholdings anywhere in Europe before the Reformation. The most heavily hit were the secular clergy: more than three-quarters of the episcopal estates were sold off to 585 purchasers, and the collegiate churches of the city were stripped almost entirely of their lands. Hundreds of *pievi* and parishes suffered comparably deep appropriations and broadly based sales, as did monastic institutions, and even hospitals and orphanages throughout the Florentine territory. Only the nunneries went largely unscathed.[14]

---

[12] M. Becker, 'Church and State in Florence on the Eve of the Renaissance (1343–1382)', *Speculum*, 37 (1962), pp. 509–27; G. Brucker, *Florentine Politics and Society 1343–1378* (Princeton, 1962), pp. 131–44, 265–335; R. C. Trexler, *The Spiritual Power: Republican Florence under the Interdict* (Leiden, 1974). On Gregory's revival of the inquisition, see ASF, Dipl., S. Croce, 18 February 1371; on his intervention in the local church, see ASV, RV, 265, 81v–82r (5 November 1373). Florentine legislation is in ASF, PR, 60, 148r–149v (8 January 1372/3); PR, 62, 76r–77v (22 June 1374); and PR, 63, 69r–72v, 73r–75v (7 and 12 July 1375).

[13] 'Ma noi il veggiamo (the *corpus christi*) col cuore, e Iddio il sa, che noi non siamo saracini nè pagani' (11 May 1376), in A. Gherardi (ed.), 'Diario d'anonimo fiorentino dall' anno 1358 al 1389', in *Cronache dei secoli XIII e XIV: documenti di storia Italiana* (Florence, 1876), p. 308. Gregory's (first) condemnation is in ASF, Dipl., Atti Pubblici, 31 March 1376.

[14] Salvestro's proposal is in ASF, CP, 14, 86r (24 September 1376). The enabling legislation is PR, 64, 137r–140r, 153r–154v, 154v–157r, 191r–192r (25 September,

Flagellants now took to the streets, and the purchases had to be forced, as public sentiment turned sharply against the war.[15] Extending the conflict with the pope to an assault on the local church proved to be a political blunder that shifted public attention from Gregory's temporal pretensions to the sacramental powers of the local clergy, and from the defence of Florentine *libertas* to the aggrandisement of the secular state and its profanation of the city's own sacred patrimony. A year later, when the commune abandoned its pretence of observing the interdict, it had not only to compel the clergy to celebrate the mass, but to coerce the laity to attend.[16]

Popular opposition, as well as military reverses, thus forced the city to sue for peace in 1378. Florence agreed to pay Gregory's successor, Pope Urban VI (1378–89), an indemnity of 250,000 florins, to restore the clergy's property, and to annul its legislation 'against ecclesiastical liberty'.[17] The government issued a generic abrogation that excluded, however, all ordinances touching the Monte, and thus preserved its claims against episcopal jurisdictions in matters of contract and usury.[18] Though Urban counted heavily on the indemnities, he received little, and Gregory XII's (1406–15) demands were among the reasons Florence abandoned him just before the Council of Pisa in 1409; the newly elected Alexander V (1409–10) obliged the city by cancelling the 'iniquitous' treaty entirely.[19] The restitution of clerical property took much longer. Under citizen (and clerical) pressure, a system of drawings was devised whereby the clergy would gradually be restored their property, and citizens the sums of their purchases.[20] Meanwhile, the clergy were compensated with 5 per cent interest-bearing shares in the Monte. But the process did not get well under way until the restoration of the Guelf regime in 1382, and was soon suspended when communal

13 October and 5 November 1376). I have gauged the depth of appropriations by contrasting the figures for sales in ASF, MC, 1558, with assessments of taxable property in the catasto.

[15] ASF, CP, 14, 97r (25 October 1376); PR, 64, 153v (13 October 1376).

[16] ASF, PR, 65, 173r–176r (22 October 1377).

[17] ASF, Dipl., Atti Pubblici, 28 July 1378.

[18] ASF, Bal., 16, 7r (1 September 1378).

[19] Urban's demands are in ASV, RV, 310, 165v–166v (6 February 1382); Gregory's are in RV, 377, 114v–115v (7 September 1407). An early example of Florentine excuses is ASF, Miss. I canc., 18, 41r–42r (23 July 1379). The city acknowledged an outstanding debt of 192,000 florins in ASF, SCLC, 4, 103r–104v (9 July 1409). Alexander's absolution is in ASV, RV, 339, 96r–101v (22 May 1409).

[20] The abbot of Vallombrosa led the clergy. ASF, CP, 18, 18v (4 October 1379). One of the first measures establishing the restitution process refers to the advice of 'multorum officiorum et sapientum civium mercatorum et artificium'; ASF, PR, 69, 61v–64r (9 June 1380), 61v.

war expenses rose in the 1390s. Not until the 1420s were the restitutions near completion, making possible the compilation of the catasto. Even then, dozens of disputes were brought to the priors for adjudication, and hundreds more to the Monte officials, the last in 1451.[21]

Before the war, Florence had depended on the papacy as guarantor of its central financial agency, the Monte. Afterwards, popes counted on Florentine indemnity payments, and local clerical finances were tied through the Monte, like those of citizens, to the fiscal and juridical institutions of the Florentine state.[22] The protracted restitution process precipitated a financial and political crisis among the clergy of Florence and neighbouring dioceses that climaxed in the 1420s, but was not fully resolved until the archiepiscopate of Antoninus in the mid-fifteenth century. Laymen, meanwhile, were left with the difficult choice either of holding on to ecclesiastical properties they had acquired against their religious consciences, or of making early restitution at a financial loss. These factors conditioned the surge of lay benefactions to ecclesiastics in the late Tre- and early Quattrocento that in turn shaped the artistic Renaissance in Florence's churches.

The end of the war in 1378 coincided with the outbreak of schism in the church, and the Ciompi revolt in Florence. Chancellor Salutati expressed the view of many when he declared the former to be divine retribution imposed on the papacy for its attack on Florentine *libertas*, the latter a chastisement for Florence's assault on its own church.[23] The shaken Guelf rulers who returned to power in 1382 associated it with social revolution. To restore order, they revived the inquisition to combat a resurgence of the Fraticelli. But executions in 1384 and 1389 provoked public revulsion and divisions among the clergy, and the malfeasance of the inquisitors brought the institution into disrepute among Florence's councillors, and even in Rome.[24] Thereafter, though the commune brooked no interference from the episcopal curia in arresting clerics involved in violent crimes or potentially seditious activity, and passed numerous measures against the threat of subversive *societates*, it intervened only sporadically in the affairs of religious

---

21 E.g. ASF, SC Delib. spec., 16; MC, 1559.

22 M. Becker, *Florence in Transition*, 2 vols. (Baltimore, 1967–8), II, pp. 151–201; and R. C. Trexler, 'Florence, by the Grace of the Lord Pope . . .', *Studies in Medieval and Renaissance History*, 9 (1972), pp. 115–215.

23 Salutati to Ubaldino Buonamici (3 October 1383), in F. Novati (ed.), *Epistolario di Coluccio Salutati*, 4 vols. (Rome, 1891–1901), II, pp. 122–3.

24 ASF, PR, 71,175r–176r (13 December 1382). Public reactions are recorded in A. Molho and F. Sznura (eds.), *Alle bocche della piazza: diario di Anonimo Fiorentino (1382–1401)* (Florence, 1981), pp. 53–4. On inquisitorial corruption, see ASV, RV, 315, 82v–83r (13 June 1396).

confraternities, and that more often to monitor their membership than to suppress their devotions.[25]

More persistently, Florence's rulers articulated a series of political strategies to resacralise the city, and to legitimate their shaky regime, by orchestrating, and identifying with, key strains of the city's religious life. The completion of the cathedral and the decoration of Orsanmichele were but the most visible of numerous Florentine projects that conjoined art and power in the display of wealth and piety, carried out by opere that linked the city's priors, guildsmen (or, increasingly, parishioners) and ecclesiastics in projects to build, repair or decorate the city's leading churches and monasteries. 'Indeed', acknowledged Bruni in his Laudatio, 'in all of Florence nothing is more richly appointed, more ornate in style, more magnificent than these churches.'[26]

In like manner, the reggimento expanded and elaborated the city's calendar of religious holidays.[27] It celebrated its own restoration in 1382, and the 'presens felix et guelfus status civitatis', by instituting the feast-day of St Sebastian, signalled its Angevin (and Clementine) sympathies in 1388 by instituting the festa of the French Franciscan St Louis, commemorated victories over Mantua (1397) and Pisa (1406) by creating the feste of St Augustine and St Victor, and in 1409 promoted a special celebration of (what was hoped to be) the resolution of the schism at the Florentine-sponsored Council of Pisa.[28] The festa of Florence's patron saint, John the Baptist (San Giovanni), was expanded from a civic ritual into a celebration of Florentine territorial dominium and, in 1393, at a crucial point in the oligarchy's consolidation, the priors' procession to the baptistery was placed squarely at its centre.[29] The following year, the statutes of the merchant's court, the Mercanzia, were revised, and henceforth the councils approved a steady stream of

---

[25] Processions of Corpus Christi companies were suspended 'ad removendum divisiones inter cives', ASF, PR, 80, 69r–70r (7 August 1391). The basic laws monitoring confraternities were PR, 109, 160v–162v (19 October 1419); PR, 110, 5rv (23 March 1419/20), and PR, 111, 71r–72r (7 July 1421). An Albizzi proposal to send troops into churches to break up societates failed; ASF, CP, 46, 187r (12 August 1426). The 1429 lex contra scandalosos instead required loyalty oaths of the city's councillors; C. Guasti (ed.), Commissioni di Rinaldo degli Albizzi per il Comune di Firenze dal MCCCXCIX al MCCCCXXXIII, 3 vols. (Florence, 1867–73), III, pp. 169–71.

[26] Leonardo Bruni, Panegyric to the City of Florence, trans. B. Kohl, in B. Kohl and R. Witt (eds.), The Earthly Republic: Italian Humanists on Government and Society (Philadelphia, 1978), p. 139.

[27] ASF, PR, 78, 71r–72v, 113v–114r (21 May and 22 June 1389).

[28] PR, 69, 240r–241r (20 January 1385/6); PR, 77, 124r–125r (2 August 1388); PR, 86, 189r–190v (2 October 1397); PR, 95, 214r–215r (17 December 1406); PR, 97, 201r (4 February 1408/9).

[29] PR, 82, 156v–157v (30 July 1393).

new oblations by the *sei consiglieri* and the consuls of the guilds to the leading churches, monasteries and friaries of the city.[30] Regular subventions to bring the miraculous image of the Virgin of Impruneta into the city identified officialdom with a popular religious devotion in economic and demographic hard times. With the reunification of the papacy under Martin V, the city shifted its support to the clergy's sacramental procession of *Corpus Domini*.[31]

The pattern of distributing oblations to favoured institutions was replicated in the apportionment of gabelle exemptions, fiscal subventions, and assistance in the pursuit of testamentary revenues to churches, monasteries and, especially, hospitals. In most cases, they were put under the special protection of the *Mercanzia* or the Monte officials.[32] Such gestures at once authorised the city's rulers to identify with institutions representing key strains of acceptable religious sentiment, while they also established fiscal control over them. A comparable process was at work in the sphere of Florentine sumptuary legislation. The commune superseded the episcopal curia in the regulation of such life-cycle sacraments as baptisms, marriages and funerals, as well as women's dress codes and gaming restrictions. With the creation of communal brothels and the Officers of the *Onestà* in the early fifteenth century, it passed from occasional legislative condemnations of prostitution and sodomy to the institutionalised supervision of male sexual behaviour and, soon after, the protection of nunneries.[33] Thus the legitimation of the regime, the disciplining of society and the sanctification of the city were all elements in a single process of political consolidation.[34]

---

[30] They begin with Ognissanti, PR, 83, 141v–142v (5 October 1394). A nearly complete list, to 1415, is in *Statuta Populi et Communis Florentie . . . MCCCCXV*, 3 vols. (Freiburg [Florence], 1778–83), III, Tractatus III, pp. 287–370.

[31] ASF, PR, 115, 129r–v (14 August 1425).

[32] For example, PR, 80, 121v–122r (6 October 1391), for S. Spirito and the *Mercanzia*; and PR, 82, 264r–265v (23 December 1393), for S. Maria degli Angeli and the Monte.

[33] On the sacraments, see the measures in *Statuta*, II, Liber IV, pp. 366–90. On women's dress see, for example, PR, 77, 39r–40v (22 May 1388). And on gaming, see PR, 79, 48r–49r (13 April 1390). Prostitution has been studied by M. S. Mazzi, *Prostitute e lenoni nella Firenze del Quattrocento* (Milan, 1991); the *Onestà* by M. Rocke, *Forbidden Friendships: Homosexuality and Male Culture in Renaissance Florence* (New York, 1996). The officers were assigned supervision of the nunneries in PR, 111, 45r–v (19 June 1421).

[34] Recent discussions of these issues are by P. Schiera, 'Legitimacy, Discipline, and Institutions: Three Necessary Conditions for the Birth of the Modern State', in J. Kirshner (ed.), *The Origins of the State in Italy, 1300–1600* (Chicago, 1996), pp. 11–33; and H. Schilling, 'Chiese confessionali e disciplinamento sociale. Un bilancio provvisorio della ricerca storica', in P. Prodi (ed.), *Disciplina dell'anima,*

Hosting the Council of Pisa in 1409 was an opportunity to link the sanctification of the republic to the broader effort to reunite a church whose own sanctity, and legitimacy, had been located by conciliarists in the community of the faithful. The schism had provided a respite from papal aggression that the 'Eight Saints' had not, and Cardinal Piero Corsini's *svolta* from the Roman Pope Urban VI to the French Pope Clement VII, though it earned him official chastisement, was not unrepresentative of Florentine patrician sympathies.[35] By 1408, however, the menaces of Milan and Naples, the unreliability of Gregory XII, the French withdrawal of obedience from Avignon's Benedict XIII, and the arguments of conciliarists such as Francesco Zabarella and Lorenzo Ridolfi, had convinced Florence's rulers that 'it would be for the honour of God, and the salvation of our liberty' to host the Council, and that 'nothing would bring our republic greater merit before God, and fame among men'.[36] Neither the articulation of the legitimating ideology of Florentine republicanism, nor Florence's great ecclesiastical building projects of the early Quattrocento, can be appreciated independently of the regime's efforts in these years to embrace the sacred, and to frame the religious life of Florence's citizenry.

The purchase of Pisa in 1406 was the next great step in the expansion of the Florentine territory after the acquisition of Arezzo in 1384. A steady stream of letters and embassies went out from the Florentine chancery to the Roman curia in support of loyal Florentine candidates for bishoprics, abbacies, and positions in Rome, to defend local institutions from Roman and foreign exploitation, to secure popular (and acceptable) preachers for the Lenten season, and for myriad lesser favours. The mountainous diocese of Arezzo, filled with monasteries, and bordering the Papal state and Sienese territory, was an object of particular Florentine concern. It was the first major addition to the territory, and episcopal power there had long been united to the power of local comital families. Salutati explained at length to Pope Boniface IX (1389–1404) Arezzo's importance as 'a singular fortress and citadel of

---

disciplina del corpo, disciplina della società tra medioevo ed età moderna (Bologna, 1994), pp. 125–60.

35 Salutati scolded Corsini in ASF, Miss. I canc., 18, 110r–112r (3 February 1379/80). But compare the francophile comments in CP, 21, 96r–97r (20 October 1382).

36 Filippo Corsini argued 'quod sit honor dei, et salus nostre libertatis', CP, 39, 110v (20 December 1408), and Antonio di Alessandro Alessandri declared 'quod nullus res . . . possit tractari a nostra republica maioris meriti apud deum, fame apud homines', ibid., 6r (7 February 1407/8). See also A. Landi, *Il papa deposto (Pisa, 1409): l'idea conciliare nel grande schisma* (Turin, 1985), pp. 113–61, and A. Williams Lewin, '*Cum Status Ecclesie Noster Sit*: Florence and the Council of Pisa', *Church History*, 62 (1993), pp. 178–89.

our state', and when Boniface nevertheless attempted to install a foreign bishop, Antonio d'Ascoli, Salutati firmly invited him to step down, and the Captain of Arezzo was deputed to block his accession.[37]

However, as it developed its own system of vicariates and other institutions for territorial administration, the Florentine government became less concerned to use bishoprics as agencies of direct territorial control, and more interested in circumscribing their administrative prerogatives to prevent the mobilisation of religious authority for seditious ends. In this respect, its policies were more 'statist' than those of its peers, Milan and Venice, who regulated (and depended upon) the bishoprics within their territories much more closely as elements of territorial administration. The *reggimento* wanted prelacies to be held by Florentines as an assertion of the city's pre-eminence, just as it expected oblations from subject communities on the Feast of San Giovanni. Where ecclesiastical institutions retained temporal jurisdictions that might obstruct the state's authority, as at Camaldoli, *accomandigie* were negotiated whereby these prerogatives were yielded in exchange for Florentine 'protection'.[38] Where, again in the Aretino, castles were needed instead of monasteries, the monasteries were simply moved.[39] By the 1420s, it was the absenteeism of Arezzo's Bishop Francesco da Montepulciano (1413–26) that exasperated Florentines, while in Ghibelline Pisa Florentine power had been imposed so aggressively that the Signoria urged Bishop Giuliano Ricci (1418–61) to curb his own curial severities.[40]

The law prohibiting Florentines access to the episcopal *dignitas* was reinvoked until the *reggimento* had consolidated its power in the 1390s.[41] Thereafter, as it did for other vacancies in the territory, the government regularly forwarded to Rome the names of acceptable candidates, recommending them for their piety and learning, the distinction of their families, and their fidelity to the *status florentinus*. To avoid factional squabbling, however, the *reggimento* preferred to leave final selections to Rome. Thus, when Pope Boniface IX deposed the Florentine Bishop Onofrio Visdomini (1390–1401) for malfeasance, there was fury in the

---

[37] 'Civitas Aretina cunctis respectibus arx est, singulareque presidium nostri status', ASF, Miss. I canc., 26, 21v (17 November 1403); and Miss. I canc., 22, 112r (28 November 1390), to Antonio, and CP, 28, 110v (26 November 1390), deputing the Captain.

[38] ASF, SCAS, 442, Moggiano (1382).

[39] ASF, Miss. I canc., 24,158r (20 September 1395); SC Delib. spec., 7, 78r–79v (27 June 1397).

[40] For Arezzo, ASF, Miss. I canc., 32, 1r–v and 69v (29 October and 24 April (*sic*), 1429); for Pisa, *ibid.*, 180v (10 February 1429/30).

[41] E.g., ASF, Miss. I canc., 20, 66r–v (22 October 1385).

councils, and appeals to the pope (and his mother), but in the end Florence's rulers concurred with Antonio Alessandri that 'it is an ecclesiastical matter', and let it stand.[42] Pope John XXIII raised the uninspiring Amerigo Corsini (1411–35) to the see to bring one of Florence's leading francophile families firmly into his Pisan fold. But popes resisted awarding Florence's leading dignity to scions of the city's most powerful families. Thus Ubertino degli Albizzi (1426–34) and Donato de' Medici (1434–74) both ended their episcopal careers parked in neighbouring Pistoia. Because the Fiesolan curia was actually located in Florence it was filled by rather credible reformers like Jacopo Altoviti (1390–1408) and Benozzo Federighi (1421–50), who compensated (somewhat) for their colleagues across Piazza San Giovanni.

Florentines were concerned also to defend the prerogatives of regional monastic institutions, particularly of home-grown orders such as Vallombrosa and Camaldoli. Old legislation against lay spoliation and usurpation (de accedendo) continued to be enforced.[43] But from Boniface IX (1389–1404) onwards, the greater problem was to defend local institutions from fiscally truncated Roman popes, who exploited their powers of commendation to collect common service payments on bishoprics and abbeys, thus creating considerable absenteeism and rapid turnovers.[44] In 1394, the councils created a commission to assure that the revenues of benefices held by foreigners went to the institutions themselves. A decade later, responding to Bishop Jacopo Palladini's prolonged absence in Rome (he failed even to return for the crucial 1402 San Giovanni procession), they directed the Monte officials to begin sequestering the incomes of episcopal properties. Two years later, the same Monte officials were charged to impound the revenues of appointees who failed to officiate within five years, and the priors were empowered to tax the patrimonies of unattached clergy.[45] Gregory XII's manipulation of cardinals and benefices on the eve of the Council of Pisa sparked proposals that Florence assume direct supervision of appointments in the territory. But the issue was dropped, in part to

---

[42] 'Quod quia res est ecclesiasticalis episcopatus (sic), non videtur eis ad se pertinere', ASF, CP, 34, 170r (23 March 1401/2).

[43] The old laws are in R. Caggese (ed.), Statuti della repubblica fiorentina, 2 vols. (Florence, 1921), II, Statuto del Podestà del anno 1325, Liber II, cap. 9, 10, pp. 98–9, and Liber III, cap. 5, pp. 146–7. Reinvocations are in ASF, PR, 74, 244r–245r (22 January 1385/6); and PR, 101, 5r–6v (26 March 1412).

[44] Boniface was quite frank with Baldassare Cossa, ASV, RV, 320, 92rv (22 January 1403).

[45] ASF, PR, 83, 212v–214r (10 December 1394); PR, 93, 71v–72v (18 July 1404); PR, 95, 57v–58r, 63r (8 and 15 June 1406).

facilitate negotiations for the council, but also for fear that political control of appointments would inflame partisan competition.[46]

No sooner was Alexander V elected at Pisa than the Florentines began lobbying the new pope for a scheme to redraw diocesan boundaries to bring them into line with territorial administrative units.[47] But they readily dropped the plan in order to accept instead a papal licence to impose a 100,000 florin direct tax on the clergy. Already, though the restitution of church property appropriated during the war of the 'Eight Saints' was far from complete, Florence had quietly begun taxing the clergy of the territory in the 1390s, and Gregory XII had split with them a clerical levy of 30,000 florins in 1407. John XXIII (1410–15), in turn, allowed Florence to levy a forced loan (*prestanza*) of 10 per cent on the revenues of benefices and 15 per cent on clerical patrimonial income, and himself imposed an 80,000 florin levy for payment to Florence's Ten of War (*Dieci di balìa*). During the Council of Constance, Florence continued to collect back-taxes from the clergy, and to appropriate the revenues of vacant benefices.[48]

Though these levies were a small part of their budget, the Florentines justified them as essential to meeting military expenses from which the clergy also benefited.[49] They fell hard on clerics who, even if their estates had been restored, could not easily raise the necessary cash payments. The government also moved to check the fraudulent donations of property that laymen made to ecclesiastics to avoid taxation. The juridical status of hospitals, in particular, which often claimed exempt status while avoiding ecclesiastical supervision, continued to be a knotty problem.[50] In 1407, a small contract gabelle was laid on all lay benefactions to ecclesiastics which attached taxability to such property, providing the foundation for further bureaucratic initiatives that delimited ecclesiastical from lay property, and monitored its movement as a check on the shrinkage of the state's tax base.[51] Meanwhile, communal

---

[46] Protests are in ASF, CP, 39, 49v–58v (May–June 1408), and Miss. I canc., 28, 65r (24 February 1407/8).

[47] G. Chittolini, 'Progetti di riordinamento ecclesiastico della Toscana agli inizi del Quattrocento', in S. Bertelli (ed.), *Forme e techniche del potere nella città (secc. xiv–xvii)*, (Perugia, 1979–80), pp. 275–96.

[48] For taxation under Boniface IX, see ASF, PR, 95, 80v–81r (21 June 1406); under Gregory XII, ASV, RV, 336, 82v–83v (8 August 1407); under Alexander V, ASF, PR, 98, 92r–93r (16 November 1409), and MC, 3412. John XXIII's concessions are in PR, 101, 407r (23 March 1412/13), and ASV, RV, 345, 247r–248r (25 July 1413).

[49] Giovanni Ristori was given a full list of arguments to use before Pope Alexander V in Miss. I canc., 28,136v–138v (16 October 1409).

[50] See Lapo da Castiglionchio's 58 *questiones* in BAV, Ross., 1038, 370r–383v.

[51] ASF, PR, 96, 68r–69r (17 July 1407).

officials were increasingly active in regulating usury and Jewish money-lenders.[52]

All of these measures were brought together in a major recodification of the Florentine *Statuta*, issued in 1415–18. These statutes integrated recent legislation circumscribing the financial operations of ecclesiastical institutions in the Florentine territory, with measures from the city's communal period curtailing the operation of ecclesiastical courts, all framed now within a unified corpus of territorial law.[53] Naturally, they attracted the attention of Pope Martin V who, recently elected at Constance and returned to Rome, was determined to reassert the church's prerogatives throughout Italy. In May 1427, to facilitate negotiations for papal permission to levy a tax on the clergy, the councils passed a provision promising to annul all Florentine laws that might violate ecclesiastical liberty. This juridical placebo had been served up to popes before, though in this case the councils actually itemised five laws that they were willing to strike, and three, touching election to the bishopric, access to benefices and the right to monitor ecclesiastical benefactions, that they absolutely would not.[54] Equally important, two days later they passed the law creating the catasto, a complete inventory of all wealth in the Florentine territory meant to be used for future taxes on the laity, but which also included inventories of clerical wealth.[55] Having nearly completed the restitution of clerical property appropriated during the war of the 'Eight Saints', the government now put in place a bureaucratic instrument that could (and would) be used to monitor the flow of property from laymen to ecclesiastics, as well as to carry out future levies on the clergy themselves.

Passed in apparent deference to renewed papal authority, these measures in fact consummated a series of state-building initiatives taken by Florence over the course of the schism to assert its territorial sovereignty. They delimited and circumscribed the temporal immunities

---

[52] U. Cassuto, *Gli ebrei a Firenze nell'età del Rinascimento* (Florence, 1918), pp. 13–42.

[53] R. Fubini analyses their compilation in 'Classe dirigente ed esercizio della diplomazia nella Firenze quattrocentesca. Rappresentanza esterna e identità cittadina nella crisi della tradizione comunale', in *I ceti dirigenti nella Toscana del Quattrocento* (Florence, 1987), pp. 158–63. E. Fasano Guarini underscores their novelty in 'Gli statuti delle città soggette a Firenze tra '400 e '500: riforme locali e interventi centrali', in G. Chittolini and D. Willoweit (eds.), *Statuti, città, territori in Italia e Germania tra Medioevo ed Età moderna* (Bologna, 1991), pp. 86–95.

[54] ASF, PR, 117, 39r–40r (19 May 1427) cancelled *Statuta*, I, bk II, rub. 18, 'De declinante', rubs. 21 and 22, on interdicts, and rub. 24, 'De compromisso', pp. 123–8. But it retained *Statuta*, I, Liber III, rubs. 46 and 47, pp. 262–4, and *Statuta*, II, 'De extimis', rub. 40, p. 356.

[55] ASF, PR, 117, 38v–45r (21 May 1427).

enjoyed in judicial and fiscal matters by ecclesiastics, even as the church's distinctive religious authority was at the same time being recognised and, so far as possible, appropriated by the Florentine *reggimento*. Future negotiations with Rome were thus carried out on the basis of Florentine institutional strength.[56] Still, though the bureaucratic development of the Florentine state in this period was laicising, it was far from secularising. For the concurrent efforts to legitimise that state included strategies to resanctify the community and to embrace the sacred authority of the very institution whose temporal prerogatives were being curtailed.

These developments provided much of the context in which, from the end of the schism to the archiepiscopate of Antoninus, the clergy made a series of efforts to recover control of their own affairs, and to restore the religious credibility of the Florentine church itself. By the end of the schism, combined (and often collaborative) papal and Florentine fiscal exploitation of the Florentine church had brought to a head the crisis in diocesan government that had been steadily deepening since the war of the 'Eight Saints'. Frustrated by decades of weak episcopal leadership, in the aftermath of the Council of Constance, with the example of a conciliar resolution to the papal schism before them, Florence's secular clergy undertook their own unique experiment in diocesan conciliar government by forming a self-governing corporation that challenged the hierarchical authority of Archbishop Corsini. (Martin V elevated the diocese over Pistoia and Fiesole in 1419.) Featuring a representative assembly and a collective executive, it was a unique fusion of conciliar principles drawn from canonists like Francesco Zabarella with Florentine republican ideals celebrated by the humanist Leonardo Bruni. But in the struggles with Archbishop Corsini that ensued, the clergy split along urban and rural lines, and all parties appealed to Rome for mediation. Local conflict, rather than papal intrusiveness, eventually led Martin V to impose a resolution favourable to Corsini.[57]

Shortly afterwards Martin's successor, Pope Eugenius IV (1431–47), found a refuge in Florence the same year, 1434, that Cosimo de' Medici

---

[56] R. Bizzocchi argues instead that they represented a capitulation to papal power in *Chiesa e potere*, pp. 82–8.

[57] The constitution is published in Trexler (ed.), *Synodal Law*, pp. 347–71. I have analysed its theoretical foundations in 'Conciliarism, Republicanism, and Corporatism: the 1415–1420 Constitution of the Florentine Clergy', *Renaissance Quarterly*, 42 (1989), pp. 183–226, its electoral operations and membership in 'Electoral Politics and the Florentine Clergy: A Meeting of the *Maius Concilium* in 1424', *Renaissance Studies*, 5 (1991), pp. 359–97, and the narrative of the corporation's relations with Archbishop Corsini in 'Florence's *universitas cleri* in the Early Fifteenth Century', *Renaissance Studies*, 2 (1988), pp. 185–96.

returned from exile. Contemporaries did not fail to note the coincidence. The Florentines soon hosted another church council (1439) at which the pope, briefly reconciling the Greek and Latin churches, was able to assert his monarchic leadership of the Western church in the face of the renewed conciliar challenge at the Council of Basel (1431–49). But they charged him heavily for the favour by imposing another onerous cycle of 25,000, 80,000 and 60,000 florin levies on the Florentine clergy.[58] Though their banking ties to the papacy provided the Medici with the wealth that was a fundament of their power, and with influence at the centre of papal administration, this period saw not a collusive softening of Florentine policies towards the clergy, but a sharp renewal of papal– Florentine conflicts over ecclesiastical jurisdictions and fiscal immunities. Eugenius began his stay protesting the interference of the *Mercanzia* in clerical fiscal affairs, but ended it having tied clerical and papal finances more tightly to the Monte, and appealing for a loan of Florence's catasto registers to carry out his own clerical levies.[59]

Meantime, Eugenius sought to resanctify and legitimise the papacy itself by using the Florentine church as model of papally sponsored reform. But Florentine resistance, and the pope's own reliance on foreign commissioners to govern the church, frustrated his efforts. By the end of his pontificate it was clear that only local leadership could bring about credible reform of the local church. In this period civic and corporate building projects were giving way to more private forms of ecclesiastical patronage, evident in the growing number of family chapels filling Florence's cathedral, collegiate and monastic churches. The Medici had pursued a more coherent strategy of cultivating clients within the Florentine church than their Albizzi predecessors. They patronised baptismal parishes, helped supervise hospitals, and found in the creation of charitable confraternities and the observant wings of religious orders new opportunities to extend their influence and prestige, indeed to challenge the state as patrons of the church in their own pursuit of social and political legitimacy.[60] But their progress was

---

[58] ASF, PR, 123, 94v–96r (27 May 1432); PR, 128, 265r–267r (27 February 1438); ASV, RV, 367, 164v–165r (26 January 1444). I survey Florentine taxation in this period in 'Archbishop Antoninus: Florence and the Church in the Earlier Fifteenth Century', Ph.D. thesis, Cornell University (1985), pp. 162–245.

[59] ASV, RV, 374, 10v–12r (4 December 1435); RV, 367, 164v (28 January 1444); and J. Kirshner, 'Papa Eugenio IV e il Monte Comune. Documenti su investimento e speculazione nel debito pubblico di Firenze', *Archivio storico italiano*, 127 (1969), pp. 339–82.

[60] R. Gaston, 'Liturgy and Patronage in San Lorenzo, Florence, 1350–1650', in F. W. Kent and P. Simons (eds.), *Patronage, Art and Society in Renaissance Italy* (Oxford, 1987), pp. 111–33, and N. Rubinstein 'Lay Patronage and Observant Reform in

checked when, in 1445, Eugenius bypassed Donato de' Medici's aggressive campaign for the archbishopric, and instead reached down the social ladder to appoint Antonino Pierozzi (1389–1459), a notary's son, protégé of the Observant Dominican reformer Giovanni Dominici, and committed papal hierocrat renowned for his acuity as a moral casuist. The pope aimed to counter his conciliar critics at Basel, and Medici influence in Florence, by harnessing disciplinary impulses emanating from the lower orders of Florentine society, through the episcopate, to the papacy.[61]

More than his patrician predecessors, Antoninus epitomised the impulse of his social peers to use religious institutions to impose controls, and discipline, on the social orders above as well as below them. His rise as a political force derived from his success in reforming the clergy, which in turn depended upon intervening between Florence and Rome to defend the prerogatives of a Florentine territorial church. In 1447, for example, the Florentine government yielded to him and repealed the law of 1404 sequestering the incomes of foreign benefice holders.[62] And when, in 1451, the councils imposed a 25 per cent tax on all transfers of lay property subject to Florentine taxation, *supportantes*, to tax-exempt corporations or persons, *non supportantes*, including ecclesiastics, Antoninus intervened to force repeal of the measure. In the aftermath, however, he formed a commission with the priors to monitor the flow of lay property to ecclesiastics.[63] While shielding the clergy from Florentine taxation and fiscal supervision, he collaborated with Florentine officials to assure that the expanding ecclesiastical patrimony would not be a haven for tax fraud by the laity.

Fulfilling many of the material goals that had spurred the clergy to experiment with corporate self-government in the 1420s, Antoninus was able in turn to impose his hierarchical authority over them. He was the first Florentine archbishop since the war of the 'Eight Saints' to issue a full set of constitutions for clergy and laymen, and whose court was sufficiently active to give them effect. Touring the diocese, he stripped recalcitrant clerics of their benefices, while uniting impoverished rural

Fifteenth-Century Florence', in Verdon and Henderson (eds.), *Christianity and the Renaissance*, pp. 63–82.

61 See my 'An Episcopal Election in Quattrocento Florence', in J. R. Sweeney and S. Chodorow (eds.), *Popes, Teachers, and Canon Law in the Middle Ages* (Ithaca, 1989), pp. 300–25.

62 The deliberations are in ASF, CP, 52, 19v (14 July 1447). The law's repeal is recorded in PR, 138, 112v–113r (8 August 1447).

63 ASF, PR, 142, 216r–217r (9 September 1451). Antoninus' protest, and the law's repeal, are recorded in SC Delib. ord., 74, 23v (5 September 1452). The new commission was formed in Bal., 27, 93r–95r (27 February 1453).

parishes to form viable livings for priests. His visitations and synods extended to neighbouring dioceses, and he intervened in the reform of monasteries throughout the Florentine territory.[64] Antoninus' reform of the clergy prepared the laity to accept increased episcopal discipline of their religious lives as well. He curbed the growth of public religious festivals, wrote a widely circulated confessional manual for laypeople, and reviewed the statutes of confraternities that were a vital link between ecclesiastical institutions and the penitential and charitable exercises of the laity.[65]

Through his reforms, Antoninus reasserted the church's control of the sacred in Florentine life. This in turn brought him moral capital that he eventually turned to political use, forcing the Medici to choose between power and political legitimacy. Antoninus walked a fine line between the city's factions, challenging Florentine legislation while writing devotional manuals for Medici women. But in 1458, when the Medici moved to consolidate their power by abolishing secret balloting in the city's councils, he intervened, out of a Dominican sense of legalism, but on grounds of pastoral care, to forbid such a violation of the councillors' oaths. The sanctity of oaths of office, and secret balloting, were principles that had been reaffirmed repeatedly in recent Florentine political history.[66] The Medici were obliged to abandon quiet subversion and resort instead to an open coup, convoking a public assembly (parlamento), supervised by mercenaries, in which they set forth the terms of their future control of the government. Unable to

---

[64] Antoninus' constitutions are published in R. Trexler (ed.), 'The Episcopal Constitutions of Antoninus of Florence', *Quellen und Forschungen aus italienischen Archiven und Bibliotheken*, 59 (1979), pp. 244–72. His visitations are published in S. Orlandi, *S. Antonino: studi bibliografici*, 2 vols. (Florence, 1959–60), I, pp. 136–78. Additional documents are in R. Morçay, *Saint Antonin Archevêque de Florence (1389–1459)* (Paris, 1914), pp. 432–95. For clerical complaints of Antoninus' severities see, for example, ASV, RV, 455, 210r–v (12 December 1455).

[65] G. Brucker illustrates the operation of his court in *Giovanni and Lusanna: Love and Marriage in Renaissance Florence* (Berkeley and Los Angeles, 1986). On his preaching, see P. F. Howard, *Beyond the Written Word: Preaching and Theology in the Florence of Archbishop Antoninus, 1427–1459* (Florence, 1995). I survey Antoninus' reform of the clergy in Peterson, 'Archbishop Antoninus', pp. 548–606.

[66] The edict, and a portion of the councillors' deliberations, are published in Morçay, *Saint Antonin*, pp. 429–30, 493–94. N. Rubinstein underscores the importance of these events in *The Government of Florence under the Medici (1434–1494)*, 2nd edn (Oxford, 1997), pp. 99–153. I offer fuller details on Antoninus' activity in Peterson, 'Archbishop Antoninus', pp. 85–144. On the importance of oaths, see now P. Prodi, *Il sacramento del potere: il giuramento politico nella storia costituzionale dell'Occidente* (Bologna, 1992), pp. 161–282. Florentine precedents are in ASF, PR, 104, 94v–95v (21 February 1414/15); CP, 50, 160r–161r (22 May 1434); PR, 140, 71r–73r (29 April 1449); and note 25, above.

block the Medici reach for power, Antoninus nevertheless underscored its illegitimacy, and highlighted its profanity.

It is tempting to see in the processes narrated here anticipations of the social disciplining, and even confessionalisation, that have been described for Europe in the sixteenth to the eighteenth centuries. But the period 1458–60, of the Medicean *parlamento*, the death of Antoninus, and Pius II's final condemnation of conciliar doctrines, was a point of rupture in the histories of Florence, the papacy and the Florentine church. To the extent that, under the Medici, church and power may have embraced in the last third of the fifteenth century, it was at the cost of the religious credibility of the former, the legitimacy of the latter. Antoninus' reforms were not carried on by his successors. Rather, they served as a foil, both to the late fifteenth-century emaciation of Florence's republican institutions, and to the papacy's retreat from church reform, visible to Florentines not as the products of slow decline, but measurable in recent memory. As Lorenzo de' Medici tied his family's fortunes ever more tightly to Rome, Florence witnessed increasingly ostentatious displays of religious pageantry, but also a growing polarisation between private religious sensibility and social norms.[67] At the end of the century, Savonarola, attempting to revive Florentine republican and religious traditions, cited Antoninus as a model of clerical intervention in communal politics.[68] When the Medici, restored to Florence in 1512, attempted to appropriate Antoninus' pious reputation by sponsoring his canonisation, the process instead became a forum for renewed activity among the Savonarolans.[69] In these years, Machiavelli was led to ruminate on the possibility of exercising political power stripped of its legitimating trappings. A few decades later, Catholics would respond to the Protestant challenge by re-embracing at Trent the model of episcopal reform and religious discipline exemplified by Antoninus.

---

[67] On the alliance between Lorenzo and Pope Innocent VIII, see M. Bullard, *Lorenzo il Magnifico: Image and Anxiety, Politics and Finance* (Florence, 1994), pp. 134–53; on religious sensibilities, S. Strocchia *Death and Ritual in Renaissance Florence* (Baltimore, 1992), pp. 188–217.

[68] Weinstein, *Savonarola and Florence*, p. 247.

[69] L. Polizzotto, 'The Making of a Saint: The Canonization of S. Antonino, 1516–23', *Journal of Medieval and Renaissance Studies*, 22 (1992), pp. 353–81.

CHAPTER 7

THE HUMANIST CITIZEN AS
PROVINCIAL GOVERNOR

WILLIAM J. CONNELL

I

Giannozzo Manetti was angry. By rights the case should have appeared months earlier in his court in the Mugello: the Eight of Security (*Otto di guardia*) in Florence should never have been involved. On 11 December 1452, Manetti was pronouncing judgment in a number of criminal cases in the Palace of the Vicar at Scarperia, about 30 km to the north of Florence.[1] Scarperia was a fortified town of perhaps 220 inhabitants and capital of the Vicariate of the Mugello, a hilly and strategically important area of the Florentine dominion.[2] Manetti, the well-known humanist, was then serving as governor, or 'Vicar' as the office was called. For six months, from 1 August 1452 to 1 February 1453, he was responsible for administering both civil and criminal justice in the Mugello. He was accompanied to his post by a retinue, known as a *famiglia*, which included a knight, a notary, four pages, fifteen retainers and five horses; and he received a salary of 2000 lire.[3]

The case that so upset Manetti began with an incident which took place in September of that year in the popolo of S. Maria di Peretola, a rural parish of about 420 inhabitants, which lay in the plain just 4 km north of Florence in the southernmost part of the Vicariate.[4] According to the sentence pronounced in Manetti's court, Silvester Iohannis Bartoli, otherwise known as 'del Massaio', 'did throw a rock at Domina

---

[1] This account is based on two of Manetti's sentences, which are preserved in ASF, GA, 106, 202r–203v. I should like to thank Arthur Field and the late Paul Oskar Kristeller for their comments on a draft of this chapter.

[2] There were 223 inhabitants in 1427–30: C. Klapisch-Zuber, *Una carta del popolamento toscano negli anni 1427–1430* (Milan, 1983), p. 37.

[3] ASF, Tratte, 984, 19v. See also G. C. Romby (ed.), *Nel vicariato di Scarperia, prima e dopo Lorenzo il Magnifico* (Brescia,1992).

[4] There were 424 inhabitants in 1427–30. See Klapisch-Zuber, *Una carta*, p. 34.

144

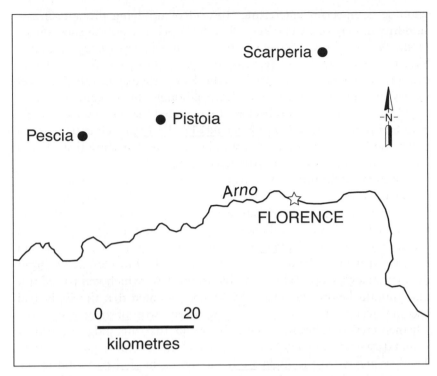

Fig. 7.1 Giannozzo Manetti's three governorships

Maria, the wife of Chiarus Bettini, bruising her left arm'. Silvester then followed Domina Maria into her home carrying a wooden pole with which he struck her on the head, inflicting a bruise and swelling. He further kicked her about the kidneys, although no blood was shed. Manetti's sentence did not state Silvester's motive for attacking Maria, and it is not clear from the record what previous relations there may have been between them, but Manetti found that Silvester had done these things 'knowingly and with the intent of doing harm' and 'against Maria's will and to her great harm and prejudice'. Silvester's nickname, which was reported once as 'del Massaio' but another time as 'Massaio', suggests that he may have been a prosperous peasant, or possibly that he or his father was estate agent (*massaio*) for an absentee landlord.[5]

Chiarus, Maria's husband, learned of the attack in October, and his

---

[5] Silvester was called 'del Massaio' in the sentence against him, and simply 'Massaio' in the sentence against Chiarus (see note 1, above).

response is especially interesting. Instead of notifying the appropriate authority in Peretola, an officer called the 'Rector' who was subordinate to the Vicar of the Mugello, Chiarus immediately (*statim*) reported Silvester to the Eight of Security in nearby Florence. Why Chiarus denounced Silvester to the Eight, who had particular jurisdiction over crimes of state, is not entirely clear, although the December record stated that Chiarus did this because he reasoned that Silvester would be punished more harshly (*acrius puniretur*) by the Eight. Chiarus possibly understood that trial in Florence would be more damaging than trial in a small and relatively distant provincial centre.

The Eight of Security was a magistracy originally established in 1378, in the wake of the revolt of the Ciompi, with full powers to protect Florence against internal and external threats to her security. With time, the Eight extended its jurisdiction to include crimes involving Jews and a wide range of moral offences.[6] The Eight became so powerful and intrusive that on 25 January 1452 a law was passed in Florence to limit the magistracy's scope. The preamble to this law, which was passed just nine months before the attack on Maria, lamented that the Eight had become accustomed to intervene 'in every sort of matter or case, whether civil or criminal', with the result that 'no judge or officer would dare enter into any business in which he saw the Eight involved'. The law prevented the Eight from interfering in civil cases and in the work of the foreign judges who administered justice in Florence, although their jurisdiction over crimes of state, cases that involved Jews and moral crimes was confirmed.[7]

Chiarus' denunciation of Silvester to the Eight was therefore somewhat extraordinary, for although the crime against Maria was morally offensive, it was not technically a moral offence, and it should thus have been tried in the Mugello. Nonetheless the Eight accepted the charge. Their retainers were sent out to Peretola in the middle of the night to arrest Silvester, whom they found at home. He was brought to Florence and tried by the Eight, who imprisoned him and imposed a fine.

The case might have ended there, were it not that Giannozzo Manetti believed the Eight had infringed on his jurisdiction as Vicar. So, after Silvester was released from prison and returned home to

---

[6] On the Eight of Security, see G. Antonelli, 'La magistratura degli Otto di Guardia a Firenze', *Archivio storico italiano*, 112 (1954), pp. 3–39; L. Martines, *Lawyers and Statecraft in Renaissance Florence* (Princeton, 1968), *passim*; A. Zorzi, *L'amministrazione della giustizia penale nella Repubblica Fiorentina: aspetti e problemi* (Florence, 1988).

[7] The law of 25 January 1451/12 was discussed by Antonelli, 'La magistratura', p. 19; and Zorzi, *L'amministrazione*, p. 67.

Peretola, both he and his accuser Chiarus were made to appear in the Vicar's court in Scarperia for the trial that resulted in Manetti's sentence of 12 December. On Silvester, for his attack on Maria, Manetti imposed a standard fine of 25 lire.[8] Chiarus was fined too, in the amount of 10 lire, on the grounds that the denunciation to the Eight had been made 'to the disgrace and dishonour of [the Vicar's] office' and 'contrary to the form of the law, statutes and ordinances of the commune of Florence and the Vicariate of the Mugello'.

It is easy to imagine that both Silvester and Chiarus felt wronged by Manetti's proceeding, since the one was twice sentenced for the same crime and the other had after all denounced the crime to the Florentine authorities. As for the Eight, they seem to have grasped the significance of Manetti's challenge to their competency, which they now moved swiftly to secure.

On 30 December 1452, only eighteen days after Manetti's sentence, a new law was passed in Florence that concerned crimes against women and female servants. It granted the Eight of Security the same powers as governors and judges throughout the dominion in treating this class of crimes.[9] The sweeping character of the new law indicated the importance of the issue at stake in the conflict between Manetti and the Eight: this was nothing less than the character of the Florentine territorial state. For, by extending their power over such crimes as Silvester's, in communities like Peretola, the Eight were pursuing a centralising policy at the expense of the dominion's established jurisdictions. Theirs was the policy of empire. In resisting the Eight, Manetti was treating the dominion as a group of historically independent communities that had entered into a series of associations or partnerships with Florence. Harking back to the communal period, his was the policy of tradition.

II

In the mid-fifteenth century there were eighty-two provincial governorships in the Florentine territory which were filled by officers who were called 'Captains', 'Podestà' or 'Vicars'.[10] Territorial office brought, as the Florentines said, both 'honour and gain' (*onore et utile*): salaries

---

[8] On 11 December 1452 Manetti delivered three other sentences in which persons charged with beating another person, but without shedding blood, were fined 25 lire; ASF, GA, 106, 202r–210r.

[9] Antonelli, 'La magistratura', pp. 20–1, discussed the law. Zorzi, *L'amministrazione*, p. 67, gave its date of passage as 30 December 1452.

[10] Martines, *Lawyers*, p. 221.

and <u>income from fees were substantial</u>, as was the attraction of assuming a <u>position of authority for six months</u>. Thus certain manuscripts of Gregorio Dati's *History of Florence* (c. 1410) likened serving in office to <u>holding a 'lordship' (*signoria*)</u>.[11] It is true that some Florentines declined office because of illness or commercial affairs, and the humanist Niccolò Niccoli avoided these offices on principle, declaring territorial service to be work for 'vultures'.[12] But Niccoli delighted in flouting convention – and the <u>conventional view was that these offices conferred great advantages on their holders</u>.

In some respects these offices were administrative survivals from the age of independent communes, when a socially elevated class of itinerant officeholders administered justice during regular terms of brief duration throughout Italy. The ceremonies and procedures followed by Florentine officers were established in an earlier period of communal independence. And the ruling city's officers swore oaths before local councils promising to uphold their statutes and ordinances. But on the other hand, <u>governors in the Florentine dominion were almost exclusively Florentine citizens,</u> and most of them were <u>chosen and paid</u> by the Florentine government. As a consequence they were expected to <u>look after Florentine interests</u> in addition to those of the communities they served. There was <u>thus a historical ambiguity built into</u> these offices, in that they were responsible in a traditional way to local subjects but also in very material ways to the Florentine republic.[13] These responsibilities sometimes diverged and, as in the case of Manetti's prosecution of Silvester, the governors on occasion chose to defend local rights against encroachment from Florence. Perhaps the best known such episode involved Bonaccorso Pitti, who in 1399 was serving as

---

[11] Goro Dati, *Istoria di Firenze dal 1380 al 1405*, ed. L. Pratesi (Norcia, 1902), p. 159 n. 1: 'questi sono signori di quelle terre mentre che durano sei mesi di tali ufici'.

[12] Vespasiano da Bisticci, *Le vite*, ed. A. Greco, 2 vols. (Florence, 1970–6), II, p. 230: 'più volte fu tratto d'alcuna podesteria, et tutte le rifiutò dicendo che le voleva lasciare agli avoltoi, ch'era pasto da loro. Chiamava avoltoi quegli vanno in bireria a consumare i poveri uomini'. (Cf. Vespasiano, *Renaissance Princes, Popes and Prelates*, trans. W. George and E. Waters, ed. M. P. Gilmore (New York, 1963), p. 397, which mistranslated 'bireria' as 'alehouses'.) At his death, Niccoli's confessor '[t]rovava la sua conscientia molto netta et purgata di non . . . avere voluto mai ignuno magistrato, dove avessi a dare sententie contro a persona'; Vespasiano, *Le vite*, II, p. 241. For a sense of the desperation with which ordinary Florentines instead hoped for election to office, whether within the dominion or abroad, see the analysis of the novella of Bianco Alfani by L. Martines, *An Italian Renaissance Sextet: Six Tales in Historical Context* (New York, 1994), pp. 95–137.

[13] Compare G. Chittolini, 'L'onore dell "officiale"', in S. Bertelli, N. Rubinstein and C. H. Smyth (eds.), *Florence and Milan: Comparisons and Relations* (Florence, 1989), I, pp. 101–33, which discusses this transformation as it took place in the Milanese state.

Captain of Pistoia. Pitti had captured a thief who was to be tried locally, and he refused to accede to repeated requests from the Florentine Signoria to send the thief to Florence. He argued that to do so would be to infringe the 'rights' (*franchigie*) of the Pistoiese and to violate the 'oaths' (*sa[c]ramenti*) he had taken on entering office.[14] Still, notwithstanding the examples of Pitti and Manetti, it seems clear that other governors were generally more heedful of instructions from Florence.

Giannozzo Manetti served three terms as a provincial governor – first as Vicar of the Valdinievole in Pescia in 1440,[15] then as Captain of Pistoia in 1446–7,[16] and, finally, as we have seen, as Vicar of the Mugello in Scarperia in 1452–3 – and he seems to have taken positive pride in his officeholding. His exemplary behaviour as governor features prominently in the three fifteenth-century biographies of Manetti, two of which were written by Vespasiano da Bisticci and one by Naldo Naldi.[17]

The hagiographic quality of these biographies is nowadays mildly irritating, but Manetti's accomplishments were considerable. Scion of a wealthy merchant family, he was proficient in Latin, Greek and Hebrew letters. As Arthur Field pointed out, Manetti made substantial forays into natural philosophy and metaphysics, subjects less commonly explored by humanists like Leonardo Bruni.[18] A brilliant orator and a skilled diplomat, he served many times as Florence's ambassador to foreign princes and republics. Contemporaries thought he stood for an impressive combination of extensive learning and devoted public service.[19] Even Manetti's provincial postings did not hinder his humanistic studies, since they afforded time for writing. 'So that I should not

---

[14] Bonaccorso Pitti, *Ricordi*, in V. Branca (ed.), *Mercanti scrittori* (Milan, 1986), pp. 414–15.

[15] The term in Pescia was from 2 April to 2 October 1440; ASF, Tratte, 984, 25v.

[16] The term in Pistoia lasted from 1 October 1446 to 31 March 1447; ASF, Tratte, 984, 7v, although he left several weeks early.

[17] Vespasiano's two biographies of Manetti, the *Vita di meser Giannozo Manetti, fiorentino* and the lengthier *Comentario della vita di Messer Giannozzo Manetti*, were both published in Vespasiano, *Le vite*, I, pp. 485–538 and II, pp. 513–627, hereafter respectively cited as *Vita* and *Comentario*. A critical edition of the *Comentario* once promised in G. Cagni, *Vespasiano da Bisticci e il suo epistolario* (Rome, 1969), p. 87 n. 1, has never been published. Vespasiano wrote the *Comentario* to be used as the basis for a Latin biography that Alamanno Rinuccini was supposed to write (see Vespasiano, *Comentario*, II, p. 515), but this was done instead by Naldo Naldi, whose *Vita Jannotii Manetti*, published in L. A. Muratori (ed.), *Rerum Scriptores Italicarum*, XX (Milan, 1731), cols. 521–608, was largely dependent on the *Comentario*.

[18] A. Field, *The Origins of the Platonic Academy of Florence* (Princeton, 1988), pp. 64–71.

[19] E. Garin, *Portraits from the Quattrocento*, trans. V. and E. Velen (New York, 1972), p. 58.

be thought by learned men to have slept during all the time of my governorship, I have chosen to leave something to be remembered by rather than remain silent', was how he put it in the Preface to his _Lives of Socrates and Seneca,_ which was composed in its first redaction at Pescia between July and October 1440.[20] The _Pistoiese History_ was written mostly at Pistoia in 1446–7.[21] And at Scarperia, in 1452–1453, Manetti completed the most famous of his writings, the treatise _On the Dignity and Excellence of Man._[22]

According to Manetti's biographers, he displayed exceptional integrity in these governorships and won the hearts of his subjects. We are told that he went to great lengths to administer justice carefully in the cases that came before him, to review local finances and to arbitrate private disputes. Typical of these accounts is what we learn of his posting to Pescia in 1440. When he arrived there, Manetti found heaped in the piazza piles of firewood and straw, the customary gifts that were made upon the Vicar's formal assumption of office (_presentatio_). To the Pesciatines' surprise, Manetti told them to take back their wood and straw, 'that he had brought with him money enough to buy these things'.[23] The next day, calling together the members of his retinue, Manetti instructed them that they were to do nothing without his being informed of it, and furthermore they were by no means to accept gifts from the inhabitants.[24] When one of his subordinates, a notary who had served with other governors, failed to report to Manetti certain of his actions, the notary was fired.[25] Although Manetti was sometimes constrained to accept gifts in office, he always made in return

---

[20] Giannozzo Manetti, _Vita Socratis et Senecae,_ ed. A. De Petris (Rome, 1979), pp. 5, 110: 'Ne igitur hoc toto prefecture mee tempore forte a doctis hominibus dormitasse existimarer, aliquid memorie mandare quam silere malui'.

[21] Giannozzo Manetti, _Historia Pistoriensis,_ published with the title _Chronicon Pistoriense,_ in L. A. Muratori (ed.), _Rerum Italicarum Scriptores,_ XIX (Milan, 1731), cols. 987–1076. Muratori's version notwithstanding, _Historia Pistoriensis_ is the proper title. Two fifteenth-century manuscript versions have been consulted: BAV, Fondo latino-palatino, 932; and Paris, Bibliothèque Nationale, Fonds latin, 18405. The completed history was received by the Pistoiese Council on 31 July 1447: ASPt, Com., Provv. e rif., 40, 58r.

[22] Giannozzo Manetti, _De dignitate et excellentia hominis,_ ed. E. R. Leonard (Padua, 1975). For the circumstances of its composition see C. Trinkaus, _In Our Image and Likeness: Humanity and Divinity in Italian Humanist Thought,_ 2 vols. (Chicago, 1970), I, pp. 231, 413–14; and P. O. Kristeller, 'Frater Antonius Bargensis and His Treatise on the Dignity of Man', in Kristeller, _Studies in Renaissance Thought and Letters,_ 4 vols. (Rome, 1956–96), II, pp. 531–60.

[23] Vespasiano, _Comentario,_ II, p. 530; Naldi, _Vita,_ cols. 539–540.

[24] Vespasiano, _Vita,_ I, pp. 495–6; _Comentario,_ II, p. 530; Naldi, _Vita,_ col. 540.

[25] Vespasiano, _Comentario, II, p. 531._

a gift of equal value.[26] With 'invincible patience' he resolved the disputes of creditors and debtors and other private differences.[27] Pescia was then confronting a grain shortage – the result of a poor harvest and an invasion by Niccolò Piccinino, who was then at war with Florence. To cope with the crisis, Manetti imposed strict controls on the grain supply; and, according to his biographers, he arranged to bring additional grain from Lombardy by making a loan to the community of 300 florins at no interest from his own funds.[28] 'Vicars and governors used to be sent out to console and assist their subjects', he liked to say.[29]

Manetti's offices in Pistoia and Scarperia were described in similarly glowing terms. At Pistoia he initiated a campaign against gambling, a vice he especially detested,[30] and he was so successful that 'no one gambled at all, and gambling was entirely extinguished' during his time in office.[31] His dealings with the two Pistoiese factions were so even-handed that both parties joined in sending an embassy to Florence with the controversial proposal – not approved by the Signoria – that Manetti's term be extended for another six months.[32] When his time in office came to an end, the Pistoiese voted to install Manetti's coat-of-arms in marble in an unusual place of honour on the cathedral bell-tower rather than in the customary place on the façade of the Governor's Palace, and as farewell gifts they presented him with a standard bearing his coat-of-arms and a helmet decorated with silver.[33] At Scarperia, the biographers tell us, Manetti found the region 'full of quarrels and differences – all, or the greater part of them, mortal feuds'.[34] And so he travelled in person from village to village and house to house, even in mountainous parts where the peasants 'were worse than beasts', hearing grievances and settling disputes.[35]

The descriptions of the biographers may be somewhat exaggerated, but other evidence generally confirms their accounts. Records of the meetings of the councils of Pescia and Pistoia survive from the periods

---

[26] Vespasiano, *Comentario*, II, p. 531. Compare also Antonio da Barga, *Liber de magistratibus et prelatis*, published in Kristeller, *Studies*, II, p. 555: 'non dona et xenia reportavit Florentiam sed amorem totius provincie, qui super hominem estimant virum'.

[27] Vespasiano, *Comentario*, II, p. 532.

[28] *Ibid.*, II, p. 530.   [29] *Ibid.*, II, p. 532.

[30] Vespasiano remarks on his dislike of gambling in *Vita*, I, p. 491; and *Comentario*, II, p. 586.

[31] Vespasiano, *Vita*, I, p. 499; *Comentario*, II, p. 548.

[32] Vespasiano, *Comentario*, II, pp. 548–9.

[33] *Ibid.*, II, p. 549; Naldi, *Vita*, col. 555.

[34] Vespasiano, *Comentario*, II, p. 584.   [35] *Ibid.*, II, p. 585.

in which Manetti was governor, and they document substantial local enthusiasm for his work. Although Manetti's personal loan to the commune of Pescia to supply the town with grain remains undocumented, the Pesciatine record states that soon after his *presentatio* Manetti was elected together with six Pesciatines to a commission with full powers to provide grain.[36] There is nothing in the register specifically to rule out the loan's taking place, and Antonio da Barga also mentions the loan in his work *On Magistrates and Priests*.[37] At Pistoia the campaign against gambling is confirmed by the sending of a letter from the Pistoiese Priors and Standard-Bearer to the Florentine Signoria supporting Manetti's punishment of a group of gamblers.[38] Manetti's popularity with the Pistoiese was no doubt enhanced by his creation of a new tax on future Florentine governors, who were required to donate a *palium* worth 16 lire to the town's chief charitable institution and treasury, the Opera of San Jacopo.[39] The marble coat-of-arms Vespasiano described no longer hangs on the bell-tower in Pistoia, but a very impressive terracotta version of Manetti's escutcheon, supported by two Donatellesque cherubim, can still be seen in Scarperia, in a position of honour at the left of the entrance to the Palace of the Vicars.[40] (See Frontispiece.)

Records at Pescia show the commune displaying its affection towards Manetti by means of a notable but quite traditional ceremony. Towards the close of his term a daughter was born to Manetti, whereupon the Pesciatine council voted unanimously, 'as a sign of the true and perfect friendship' between the commune and its Vicar, to elect a syndic to represent the entire community in raising the girl from the baptismal font, so that all Pescia should be considered her godparent.[41] Pescia had

---

[36] ASPe, Com., Delib. e rif., 24, 144v, 17 April 1440, records the appointment of Manetti 'una cum sex prudentibus viris [habentibus] baliam . . . providendi ut in dicta terra Piscie sit habundantia frumenti'. In fact the involvement with grain policy began with the day of his arrival, when the Florentine Signoria wrote instructing him to abolish gabelles on grain transported between Pescia and the nearby commune of Vellano; see the letter to Manetti in ASPe, Com., Lett. Sig. Fir., 89v, 2 April 1440.

[37] Antonio da Barga, *Liber de magistratibus*, p. 555: 'Item fuit prefectus in Valle Nebulae ubi in tempore famis providit populo de frumento de pecuniis suis'.

[38] ASPt, Com., Provv. e rif., 40, 3v, 29 September 1446.

[39] *Ibid.*, 29 September 1446.

[40] L. Brunoro Cianti, 'Stemmi dei vicari di epoca laurenziana', in Romby (ed.), *Nel vicariato di Scarperia*, p. 98, no. 127.

[41] ASPe, Com., Delib. e rif., 24, 164r, 24 September 1440: 'Quod Sanctes Antonii Turini intelligatur esse et sit sindachus communis Piscie ad elevandum de sacro fonte batismatis filiam noviter natam Gianozi Bernardi de Manettis, et quod insignia vere et perfecte amicitie inter dictum Gianozum et commune Piscie intelligantur esse et sint dicta'. The measure was approved by a vote of 29 to 0.

done this on at least one previous occasion, in 1404, when a daughter was born to Bonaccorso Pitti who was then serving as Vicar.[42] And other communities in the Florentine dominion, including San Gimignano and San Miniato, did the same for the newborn children of their governors.[43] This kind of godparenthood was an expression of the 'personality' of the commune, and as such it was practised by Florence, too, which in 1327 became godparent to a child of the Duke of Calabria and in 1390 sponsored the child of Bernabò Visconti of Milan.[44] But within the Florentine dominion of the fifteenth century the traditional rite became controversial: in 1456 a law forbidding the practice in the subject communes. The law's preamble stated that through godparenthood 'governors are made partisans of such places and also of single persons so as to represent or favour them contrary to the common good'.[45] The measure, which was passed three years after Manetti's departure from Florence in 1453, was no doubt sincere in its desire to combat corruption. But it also marked a curtailment in the ability of the subject communities to represent themselves symbolically as autonomous communes.

The biographers, and Manetti himself, tell us that the warm local response to his governorships resulted in jealousy and political trouble back in Florence, and it is easy to see how this might have come about.[46] Probably there were Florentines eligible to serve as Vicar at Pescia who would have been content to receive firewood and straw free of charge; it is doubtful that many were ready to make personal loans to supply grain for their subjects; and few can have liked the new tax on governors in Pistoia. However well their subjects may have liked him, it seems reasonable to assume many of Manetti's fellow Florentines thought he was setting uncomfortable precedents.

This was nowhere more evident than during the Pistoiese captaincy,

---

[42] Bonaccorso Pitti, *Ricordi*, in Branca (ed.), *Mercanti scrittori*, p. 346.

[43] San Gimignano became godparent to Luigi Pitti in 1414: Pitti, *Ricordi*, p. 347. San Miniato acted as godparent to Iacopo Niccolini in 1398: C. Klapisch-Zuber, *La maison et le nom: stratégies et rituels dans l'Italie de la Renaissance* (Paris, 1990), p. 79 n. 128.

[44] For the child of the Duke of Calabria, see Giovanni Villani, *Nuova cronica*, ed. G. Porta (Parma, 1990–1), II, pp. 547–8. For the child of Bernabò Visconti see Giovanni di Pagolo Morelli, *Ricordi*, in Branca (ed.), *Mercanti scrittori*, p. 229. The two cases were also noted by R. C. Trexler, *Public Life in Renaissance Florence* (New York, 1980), p. 285.

[45] The Florentine law of 25 October 1456 was discussed in Klapisch-Zuber, *La maison*, p. 128.

[46] Vespasiano, *Comentario*, II, p. 549; Naldi, *Vita*, col. 555; Manetti, *Historia pistoriensis*, col. 991.

when the Florentine Signoria turned down the Pistoiese request to renew Manetti's governorship. Records of the Pistoiese Council confirm the request, which was made by an embassy elected on 23 November 1446 that consisted of members of both of the rival Cancellieri and Panciatichi families.[47] The idea of a renewal in office was not unheard of, since in 1415 the Pisans had requested that their Captain, Palla di Nofri Strozzi, be retained for another six months,[48] although that earlier request, too, appears to have been denied.[49] Governorships were traditionally filled through a complex series of elections by lot, which meant that the citizen class jealously protected their few chances to serve in the coveted positions. What John Najemy called, 'the expectation of a share in political life, even if only a small one', was an underlying principle of the republican regime of the fifteenth century.[50] Granting the Pistoiese request in effect would have deprived each potential officeholder of an opportunity to be elected to one of the dominion's most desirable offices. Small wonder that Manetti became terrifically unpopular in some Florentine circles.

The Pistoiese embassy to Florence seems to have been formed without Manetti's knowledge – Vespasiano even cites a letter of Manetti's to that effect[51] – but evidently some Florentines thought otherwise. One sonneteer in particular, Paolo Soldino, took evident relish in lampooning the imagined ambitions of a man so famous for his learning, and he turned Manetti into a laughingstock with a poem that became the talk of the town:[52]

[47] ASPt, Com., Provv. e rif., 40, 14r, 23 November 1446. Q. Santoli, 'Giannozzo Manetti, Capitano di Custodia a Pistoia', *Bullettino storico pistoiese*, 28 (1926), pp. 47–56, is especially useful on the episode.

[48] The request was mentioned by Antonio da Barga, *Liber de magistratibus*, p. 557: 'Prefectus olim fuit in civitate Pisana. Ita splendide se habuit ut Pisani legatos mitterent Florenciam rogantes obnixe ut per alios sex menses eis concederetur'.

[49] According to ASF, Tratte, 983, 20r, Strozzi served only one term in Pisa, from 6 January to 6 July 1415.

[50] J. M. Najemy, *Corporatism and Consensus in Florentine Electoral Politics, 1280–1400* (Chapel Hill, 1982), p. 303.

[51] Vespasiano, *Comentario*, II, p. 549.

[52] For the Italian text, see Santoli, 'Giannozzo Manetti', pp. 53–4:

> Scienza è vero ch'è suprema richeza,
>   Se grave natural ne tien ghoverno;
>   Scienza in sé, se bene il ver discerno,
>   Senno non diè, né mai tolsse matteza.
> Per vanità, superbia et leggerezza,
>   Ti venne un falso albore di gloria eterno;
>   Onde ti seghue diligione et scherno:
>   Dimmi dove leggesti tal savieza.
> Fu testo ebraicho o greco o pur latino?

> Knowledge, it is true, is supreme riches –
>> so long as a serious nature keeps it under control.
>> But Knowledge by itself, if I understand correctly,
>> does not impart Wisdom, nor did it ever banish Madness.
> Out of Vanity, Pride and Thoughtlessness
>> there came to you a false glimmer of eternal Glory,
>> whence now you are pursued by Derision and Scorn.
>> Tell me, where did you acquire such Knowledge?
> From a Hebrew text? Or Greek? Or Latin?
>> Or was it the honourable vernacular
>> of the famous Florentine poet?[53]
> Or was it rather from lowly Scambrilla?[54]
>> For your renewal in office you dispatched
>> an embassy from the Cancellieri and Panciatichi.
> If I had known their message,
>> I would have promised you this terrible grief:
>> that with your own hands you would become homicide of
>> yourself.

It is easy to imagine Manetti felt relieved when he was called away from Pistoia before his term ended, to serve as ambassador to the newly elected Pope Nicholas V.[55]

III

It remains something of an anomaly that a prominent Florentine should have undertaken to write the history of a town ruled by Florence, and Manetti was certainly aware that his *Pistoiese History* was unusual. Most Renaissance histories concerned cities or principalities that were independent, and most were written by citizens of those places.[56] Manetti's unlikely work was motivated, so he tells us, by the controversy over the proposed renewal of his office. He explained in his Preface that the history was written in response to the 'envy' (*invidia*) of his fellow

> Fu l'opera vulghare degna d'onore
> Del famoso poeta florentino?
> Oppur fu lo Scanbrilla l'autore?
> Per la riferma inviasti a chammino
> Chancielliere et Pancaticho oratore.
> Se sapessi el tenore,
> Già terribil dolore are' promesso,
> Cholle man tue micida di te stesso.

[53] Dante Alighieri.

[54] Francesco di Giovanni Scambrilla was a Florentine vernacular poet of low repute.

[55] Santoli, 'Giannozzo Manetti', p. 55.

[56] E. Cochrane, *Historians and Historiography in the Italian Renaissance* (Chicago, 1981), pp. 26–7, 89–133.

Florentines and 'the womanly and insipid verses' of Soldino and 'in defence of the truth' (*pro defensione tamen veritatis*).[57] The major theme of the history was the exceptional problem of Pistoiese factionalism, and in his concluding remarks – when the narrative reached his own governorship – Manetti explained the attempt to keep him on at Pistoia as the consequence of his success in ending the rivalry of the two Pistoiese parties.[58]

But there may also have been a more subtle way in which Manetti's history defended the Pistoiese request, for the work also did much to buttress Pistoiese rights and sovereignty with respect to Florence. In an important essay on the historical writing of Leonardo Bruni, Riccardo Fubini argued that Manetti's *Pistoiese History* should be interpreted as something like a foil to Bruni's *Histories of the Florentine People*.[59] According to Fubini, fifteenth-century historical controversies about the founding of cities were not simply about competing republican and princely ideals, depending on whether a city was founded under the Roman republic or the Principate.[60] These scholarly debates of the Renaissance, he suggested, were also contests over the relation of customary law to Roman law. As Bruni saw it, the traditions and laws that were preserved in the statutes of the Tuscan communes and constituted their customary law were of Etruscan origin, since those cities were founded by the Etruscans. Florence, instead, was founded by the Romans, which meant the Florentine law was of Roman origin. Florentine law thus took the same precedence over the law of other Tuscan cities that Roman law did, and Florence's Roman founding consituted grounds for a claim to sovereignty under Roman law. Bruni's discussion of the Etruscans in the *Histories* thus affirmed what he

---

[57] Manetti, *Historia pistoriensis*, col. 991.

[58] *Ibid.*, cols. 1073–5.

[59] R. Fubini, 'La rivendicazione di Firenze della sovranità statale e il contributo delle *Historiae* di Leonardo Bruni', in P. Viti (ed.), *Leonardo Bruni cancelliere della repubblica di Firenze* (Florence, 1990), pp. 29–62, esp. 42–4.

[60] Compare N. Rubinstein, 'The Beginnings of Political Thought in Florence', *Journal of the Warburg and Courtauld Institutes*, 5 (1942), pp. 198–227; Rubinstein, 'Il Poliziano e la questione delle origini di Firenze', in *Il Poliziano e il suo tempo* (Florence, 1954), pp. 101–10; H. Baron, *The Crisis of the Early Italian Renaissance*, rev. edn (Princeton, 1966), pp. 61ff.; Baron, *In Search of Florentine Civic Humanism: Essays on the Transition from Medieval to Modern Thought*, 2 vols. (Princeton, 1988), I, pp. 43–67; R. G. Witt, 'Coluccio Salutati and the Origins of Florence', *Il pensiero politico*, 2 (1969), pp. 161–72; A. P. McCormick, 'Goro Dati and the Roman Origins of Florence', *Bibliothèque d'humanisme et renaissance*, 46 (1984), pp. 21–35. See also G. Cipriani, 'Il mito etrusco nella Firenze repubblicana e medicea dei secoli XV e XVI', *Ricerche storiche*, 2 (1975), pp. 259ff.

had elsewhere called the 'hereditary right' (*iure quoddam hereditario*) by which Florence administered Roman law in subject areas of Tuscany.[61]

Although Bruni's *Histories* made the Etruscans founders of the Tuscan towns, Fubini pointed out that Manetti's *Pistoiese History* returned to an older version, found in Dante and Villani, according to which Pistoia was founded by Roman followers of Catiline, after their defeat in the battle described by Sallust.[62] Fubini argued that Manetti's chief concern was to demonstrate the continuing validity of the great Florentine writers of the communal age.[63] But it is also possible that Manetti was attempting a more specific revision of Bruni. For if Pistoia's founders were themselves Roman, as Manetti maintained, then Pistoia was not comprised within Florence's 'Roman inheritance'; and she, too, might claim the legal autonomy that followed on Roman ancestry. It might be objected that there was something unsavoury in a Catilinarian founding, but the Pistoiese, who rather liked the idea that their own civil strife was descended from that of the Romans, prided themselves on the association.[64] And in a distant but not inconsequential way, this was also related to the question of Manetti's renewal in office, for if the Pistoiese request was a matter between two sovereign states and Florentine law did not take precedence, then there was nothing illegitimate about the proposal. Perhaps it was no accident that, in its decree thanking Manetti for the receipt of his *History*, Pistoia's Council emphasised his research into the 'origins and beginnings of the ancient inhabitants of the city'.[65]

IV

Giannozzo Manetti has often been considered an heir to the Florentine intellectual tradition Hans Baron called 'civic humanism'. According to Baron's great work *The Crisis of the Early Italian Renaissance*, there developed in Florence during the early fifteenth century an approach to

[61] Leonardo Bruni, *Laudatio florentinae Urbis*, ed. H. Baron in Baron, *From Petrarch to Leonardo Bruni: Studies in Humanistic and Political Literature* (Chicago, 1968), p. 244.

[62] See Manetti, *Historia pistoriensis*, cols. 998–1002. Cf. Sallust, *Bellum Catilinae*, 57.1ff.

[63] Fubini, 'La rivendicazione', p. 43.

[64] Local tradition held that Catiline was buried at Pistoia. The so-called 'Tower of Catiline' still stands in the central piazza.

[65] ASPt, Com., Provv. e rif., 40, 58r, 31 July 1447: 'cum labore dedit operam in reperiendo origines et principia antiquorum civitatis Pistorii'. Benedetto Colucci's *Lazareus*, which was dedicated to Giuliano de' Medici in 1468, revised Manetti's founding story in a Medicean vein. According to Colucci, Pistoia was founded by Etruscans before Catiline, although it failed to grow strong for want of a leader and because it was beset by pestilence. Cf. Benedetto Colucci, *Lazareus*, published in F. A. Zacharia, *Bibliotheca pistoriensis* (Turin, 1752), pp. 287–97, esp. 289.

classical studies that emphasised the active life, participation in government, and civic duty.[66] At the forefront of this new approach to ancient
learning stood Coluccio Salutati and Leonardo Bruni, two humanist
chancellors of Florence, who put their skills as scholars to work in service
to Florence. Clearly Manetti believed he was following in the footsteps
of Salutati and Bruni in a personal way: while Manetti was serving as
Vicar the Pesciatine Council voted to grant exceptional tax relief to
Salutati's son[67]; and it was Manetti who delivered Bruni's funeral oration
in 1444.[68] Manetti's opposition to the alliance with Francesco Sforza of
Milan promoted by Cosimo de' Medici, and his famous 1453 departure
from Florence for voluntary exile in Rome and then Naples, have been
interpreted as evidence of Manetti's deep-seated republicanism and
opposition to Medici tyranny.[69] The result has been a tendency among
some modern writers to see Florence in the 1430s, 1440s and 1450s as
divided between a republican or 'civic humanist' faction, which included
Manetti, and a Medici faction that favoured princely government. As a
consequence, the thought of a number of important humanists, from
Bruni and Poggio Bracciolini through Manetti and Matteo Palmieri,
often was imagined to have been opposed to Medicean government,
when in fact those writers generally supported the Medici.

The distortion has been especially strong in the case of Manetti. As
Mario Martelli argued, Manetti's political affiliations have been obscured
twice over by republican historiography – first in the fifteenth century,
by his biographers Vespasiano and Naldi, who were both close to the
anti-Medicean circles of the 1490s, and then in the twentieth century by
Hans Baron.[70] Manetti's career is too often interpreted retrospectively,
in the light of his dramatic decision of 1453 to leave Medicean Florence
for voluntary exile rather than pay tax assessments that were punitively
high. But this view has obscured much about Manetti's early career,
including his own role in the consolidation of the Medicean regime after
the return of Cosimo de' Medici from exile in 1434. To present Manetti
as the leader of a republican opposition to the Medici would be to
misunderstand both Manetti's relationship with the Medici party and
the nature of Medicean government in its first decades.

[66] Baron, *Crisis*, *passim*.
[67] ASPe, Com., Delib. e rif., 24, 149r–150v, 14–16 May 1440.
[68] Giannozzo Manetti, *Oratio funebris in solemni Leonardi historici, oratoris, ac poetae laureatione*, published in Leonardo Bruni, *Epistolarum libri VIII*, ed. L. Mehus (Florence, 1741), pp. lxxxix–cxiv.
[69] See especially Baron, *Crisis*, pp. 395–6, 400.
[70] M. Martelli, 'Profilo ideologico di Giannozzo Manetti', *Studi italiani*, 1 (1989), pp. 5–41.

The officeholding pattern offers a truer indication of Manetti's ties to the Medici. Throughout the Albizzi regime, indeed from 1374 until 1439, no members of the Manetti family served in the Signoria.[71] His father and grandfather compiled what Lauro Martines called a 'meagre administrative record'.[72] Giannozzo, instead, held many important Florentine offices, although only one of them, a term in 1429 with the Twelve Good Men, preceded the Medici's rise to power. After 1434, however, Giannozzo held office at a pace that was fast and furious. He served as Studio Trustee (1435), Sea Consul (1437), Defender of the Laws (1439–40), Regulator (1438), Night Officer (1447), Grain official (1435, 1443) – and ambassador to Venice, Genoa, Milan, Naples and the papacy, in addition to the governorships mentioned above. Manetti, moreover, was a member of the Medici balìe of 1434, 1438, 1444 and 1452, which oversaw the election process and determined who governed the state.[73] Thus it was as a privileged member of the group that came to power in 1434, not as a resistant holdover from the pre-1434 regime, that he pursued for two decades an extremely successful career in Florentine public service.

It is true that Manetti advocated preserving Florence's alliance with republican Venice (where he had commercial interests)[74] and opposed the Medici alliance with Sforza of Milan, but in this he was certainly not motivated by specifically republican principles, since he also favoured an alliance with princely Naples (where he also had commercial interests).[75] Indeed, jealousy and apprehension towards these extensive foreign ties probably contributed to the ill will that certain

[71] R. Pesman Cooper, 'The Florentine Ruling Group under the "Governo Popolare", 1494–1512', Studies in Medieval and Renaissance History, n.s., 7 (1984–5), p. 139.

[72] See L. Martines, The Social World of the Florentine Humanists, 1390–1460 (Princeton, 1963), p. 177, which discusses Manetti's career on pp. 176–91.

[73] N. Rubinstein, The Government of Florence under the Medici, 1434–1494 (Oxford, 1966), pp. 246, 259, 269 and 277.

[74] On Manetti's Venetian embassies, see N. Lerz, 'Il diario di Griso di Giovanni', Archivio storico italiano, 117 (1959), pp. 247–78; and F. Trivellato, 'La missione diplomatica a Venezia del fiorentino Giannozzo Manetti a metà Quattrocento', Studi veneziani, n.s., 28 (1994), pp. 203–35. His major commercial interest in Venice was an investment of 2,000 florins in a Venetian trading partnership he established with three other Florentines in 1441. The costituzione of the partnership, dated 2 November 1441, is preserved in ASF, MAP, 89, n. 289. (The document was also noted in F. W. Kent, 'The Making of a Renaissance Patron of the Arts', in Giovanni Rucellai ed il suo Zibaldone, 2 vols. (London,1960–81), II, p. 35 n. 4.)

[75] For references to Manetti's trading privileges in the Kingdom of Naples, see R. Fubini, 'Classe dirigente ed esercizio della diplomazia nella Firenze quattrocentesca. Rappresentanza esterna e identità cittadina nella crisi della tradizione comunale,' in I ceti dirigenti nella Toscana del Quattrocento (Florence, 1987), p. 176 n. 187.

members of the Florentine regime bore towards Manetti. In 1453 there was even a curious discussion in the Florentine Signoria of Manetti's essay *On the Dignity and Excellence of Man*, which some deemed treasonous because it was dedicated to Alfonso of Naples and seemed a 'justification' in his war against Florence.[76]

But despite a number of policy differences, Manetti seems to have remained on good personal terms with the Medici family and a faithful member of the Medici party. It is not even sufficient to attribute to Manetti the role of loyal opponent or internal adversary as has often been done in describing the role of Neri Capponi. Capponi and Manetti were friends and also politically close; and Capponi was among those who advised Manetti to leave Florence in 1453.[77] But during the great moment of crisis between Capponi and the Medici in 1444, after the Florentine Signoria's execution of Capponi's client, the mercenary captain Baldaccio of Anghiari, it was Manetti who went to explain the Signoria's action to Baldaccio's outraged employer, Eugenius IV.[78]

Confirmation of Manetti's generally good relations with the Medici family appears in the records from his Vicariate in the Mugello. The Mugello was the area from which the Medici family emigrated for Florence, probably in the twelfth century.[79] They maintained estates as well as a large network of clients in the region.[80] Documents from Manetti's term in the Mugello show him busily tending Medici interests in the very weeks that his own fiscal ruin was being plotted back in Florence. A letter of 6 October 1452 from Manetti in Scarperia to Cosimo de' Medici's son Giovanni, who looked after Medici patronage interests in the dominion, betrayed no sign of disagreement or rancour.[81] Instead, Manetti assured Giovanni that he had acted in accordance with the latter's wishes in mediating conflicts involving several Medici tenants and in settling some criminal cases. With respect to one Lolo di Piero from Peretola, Manetti wrote to Giovanni:

---

[76] E. Conti, *L'imposta diretta a Firenze nel Quattrocento (1427–1494)* (Rome, 1984), p. 349, described the discussion of 16 March 1453. Martelli, 'Profilo ideologico', pp. 30–3, explained what was offensive in such a seemingly innocuous treatise. Cf. Vespasiano, *Comentario*, II, p. 593.

[77] Vespasiano, *Comentario*, II, p. 587.

[78] Vespasiano, *Comentario*, II, pp. 535–6.

[79] G. A. Brucker, 'The Medici in the Fourteenth Century', repr. in his *Renaissance Florence: Society, Culture and Religion* (Goldbach, 1994), p. 2.

[80] See V. Franchetti Pardo and G. Casali, *I Medici nel contado fiorentino: ville e possedimenti agricoli tra Quattrocento e Cinquecento* (Florence, 1978).

[81] Published in H. W. Wittschier, *Giannozzo Manetti: das Corpus der Orationes* (Cologne and Graz, 1968), pp. 45–6. As Wittschier noted, Manetti's *Life of Nicholas V* was dedicated to Giovanni de' Medici.

'because he appeared and confessed what was contained in the charge, and because he has an unsavoury reputation, I should have kept him under arrest if not out of respect for you I cannot do otherwise than condemn him; but out of consideration for you, I will help him as much as I can while still preserving the court's honour'. The court record from Scarperia, which survives, shows that Lolo was tried, together with three accomplices, on 21 November 1452, six weeks after the date of Giovanni's letter.[82] They faced the possibly reduced charge of stealing raisin grapes (*uvas ad siccandas*) from the property of a Florentine landowner, Angelo Spini. In his sentence, Manetti fined Lolo 25 lire while his friends were fined 10 lire apiece. The register shows that for several years the fines remained unpaid.

Even in his voluntary 'exile', Manetti continued to serve the Florentine government – and he remained close to the Medici family. From Naples he corresponded with Giovanni di Cosimo de' Medici, thanking him for his help in arranging the marriages of two of Giannozzo's children.[83] Another letter to Giovanni de' Medici, also from Naples, explains the assistance Manetti had given in securing a captaincy at L'Aquila for one of Cosimo's clients.[84]

Clearly, the ultimate source of Manetti's problems with the post-1434 regime had little to do with the principled stand against Medicean tyranny that some have imagined. But why did he have such difficulties? It is not altogether true, as Martelli argued, that Manetti's departure from Florence was a 'pretended exile' prepared entirely in advance, since prior to his leaving there does seem to have been a concerted attack on Manetti's position within the regime.[85] Conti's research in fiscal records has established that Manetti was indeed the victim of Florentine fiscal assessments that were 'objectively excessive'.[86] Manetti's claim that high taxes forced him to leave Florence should actually carry credence. But rather than the Medici themselves, it appears to have been other enemies of a personal kind who created problems for Manetti within the regime. Who were they? The principal

---

[82] The actual court record of Lolo's case is preserved in ASF, GA, 106, 172r–v, 21 November 1452.

[83] ASF, MAP, 138, no. 54, Giannozzo Manetti to Giovanni di Cosimo de' Medici, 16 June 1459, published in Wittschier, *Giannozzo Manetti*, pp. 46–7.

[84] ASF, MAP, 9, no. 497, Giannozzo Manetti to Giovanni di Cosimo de' Medici, 13 September 1459, published in Wittschier, *Giannozzo Manetti*, p. 47, and re-edited in Martelli, 'Profilo ideologico', pp. 35–6.

[85] Martelli, 'Profilo ideologico', p. 34.

[86] Conti, *L'imposta diretta*, p. 348: 'Il coefficiente imposto al Manetti nella "cinquina" del 1452, confrontato con i coefficienti dello stesso nelle precedenti "distribuzioni", era obiettivamente eccessivo.'

person responsible for the unreasonable assessment, as Vespasiano and Naldi tell us,[87] was Luca Pitti, whose name appeared at the top of the list of the five members of the tax commission in 1452.[88]

There are many possible explanations for the enmity between Pitti and Manetti, but one possible early moment of conflict should not be overlooked. It happened during Manetti's term as Captain at Pistoia in 1446. Most subject towns in the Florentine dominion were administered by a single governor, but it so happened that Pistoia, as one of the largest towns with 996 households in 1442,[89] had two governors – a Captain and a Podestà.[90] During their six-month terms both officers received large salaries – although the Captain's was larger and he took precedence of rank. Each governor was accompanied by a separate retinue of soldiers and notaries. Although the jurisdictions of the two officers were distinct, the Captain being responsible for criminal justice and the Podestà overseeing civil suits, it was nonetheless natural that from time to time antagonisms and rivalry should have developed between the two Florentine rectors. Now it so happened that when Giannozzo Manetti arrived at Pistoia on 1 October, Luca Pitti was already serving there as Podestà.[91] The terms of the two officers overlapped for several months, until Pitti's departure on 28 November. Pitti was therefore present in Pistoia when the Pistoiese Council decided on 23 November to request Manetti's renewal in office; and, unlike Manetti, Pitti appears to have had a difficult time of it.

Possibly Pitti offended the Panciatichi faction at Pistoia – at least this is the likely significance of the 'not present' recorded at the final review of Pitti's books next to the name of Gualtieri Panciatichi, who was the leader of his faction and then serving as Gabelles Officer.[92] As Podestà, Pitti was supposed to receive 1300 lire in salary from the Gabelles Officer. According to a later record, shortly before his departure Pitti discovered that he was still owed 65 lire in salary by Panciatichi, so he raised most of the missing money in his role as Podestà by fining nine Pistoiese a total of 54 lire to be paid directly to Pitti's account with the Partini bank. It was not until March 1447, five months after Pitti's departure, that the accounts were squared.[93] Ill feeling between Pitti and

---

[87] Vespasiano, *Comentario*, II, p. 601; Naldi, *Vita*, col. 593.

[88] Matteo Palmieri, *Ricordi fiscali, 1427–1474*, ed. E. Conti (Rome, 1984), p. 156, listed Pitti first of the five members of the commission for the *Cinquina* of 1452.

[89] The figure comes from a catasto record preserved in the BFPt, FF, E 373, fasc. 7, part 1.

[90] Santoli, 'Giannozzo Manetti', p. 47.

[91] ASF, Tratte, 985, 6r. His term was from 29 May to 28 November 1446.

[92] ASPt, Com., Provv. e rif., 40, 15r, 29 November 1446.

[93] See *ibid.*, 34r, where a letter from the Priors and Standard Bearer of Florence to

Panciatichi is likely to have lingered: we know that Gualtieri later supported the anti-Medicean movement in Florence in 1466, for which he was sent into exile until his death in 1478.[94] It is not unreasonable to suppose that Manetti's clear success with the Pistoiese aroused in Luca Pitti a certain jealousy. We do not know whether after his return to Florence Pitti encouraged the malicious criticism that so troubled Manetti − it remains only a hypothesis that the enmity began at that point. But however the falling-out between the two men occurred, it needs to be kept in mind that it took place within the context of the Medici regime and party, of which Manetti remained a leading member.

Historians are still only slowly coming to realise that the Medici regime established in 1434 was no more repressive or less republican than the Albizzi regime it replaced.[95] Aspects of the post-1434 regime that sometimes troubled scholars in the past, such as the continued and indeed elevated role of Leonardo Bruni, indicate only how little was changed in Florentine factional politics in the transition from Albizzi to Medici control. The case of Bruni is particularly interesting, because in many respects Manetti saw himself as Bruni's intellectual heir. James Hankins recently criticised Hans Baron for feeling a need to apologise for the 'transgressions' implicit in Bruni's work for the post-1434 Medicean regime.[96] But Hankins' solution, which is to interpret Bruni as a rhetorician without ideological commitments, fails to appreciate the continuing strength of republicanism in Florence after 1434.[97]

Like his friend Manetti − and like Poggio and Palmieri for that matter − Bruni simply did not perceive what later generations sometimes took as historical gospel: that the return of Cosimo de' Medici to Florence in

Uguccione Capponi, then Podestà of Pistoia, dated 21 December 1446 and read in the Pistoiese Council on 23 March 1447, discussed these events.

[94] Gualtieri Panciatichi's exile in 1466 was mentioned in M. Phillips, *The Memoir of Marco Parenti: A Life in Medici Florence* (Princeton, 1987), p. 209. For the Panciatichi as anti-Medicean down to 1478, see W. J. Connell, 'Clientelismo e Stato territoriale. Il potere fiorentino a Pistoia nel XV secolo', *Società e storia*, 14 (1991), pp. 538–9.

[95] For a study of the electoral politics of the Albizzi regime that emphasised similarities with the later Medici period, see R. Ninci, 'Lo scrutinio elettorale nel periodo albizzesco (1393−1434)', in C. Lamioni (ed.), *Istituzioni e società in Toscana nell'età moderna*, 2 vols. (Rome, 1994), I, pp. 39−60.

[96] J. Hankins, 'The "Baron Thesis" after Forty Years and some Recent Studies of Leonardo Bruni', *Journal of the History of Ideas*, 56 (1995), pp. 309–38, esp. p. 325; and compare P. Viti, *Leonardo Bruni e Firenze: studi sulle lettere pubbliche e private* (Rome, 1992).

[97] He emphasises instead the similarities between Florentine oligarchy and princely rule elsewhere in the late fourteenth and fifteenth centuries. Cf. A. Field, 'Leonardo Bruni, Florentine Traitor? Bruni, the Medici, and an Aretine Conspiracy of 1437', *Renaissance Quarterly*, 51 (1998), p. 1135.

1434 marked the beginning of a Medicean tyranny. It is true that over time the regime became more closed and repressive towards those who opposed its policies. This was certainly true after the Medicean parlamento of 1458 – and even more so after the failed plots of 1466 and 1478.[98] But it is neither fair nor historically sound to interpret pre-1458 Florence in post-1494 terms. Giannozzo Manetti's departure for Naples was not a response to Medicean tyranny. The humanist's departure was the outcome of a factional operation internal to the Medici party. As such, it was typical of that heartbreakingly competitive and often corrupt system of politics known as republicanism – a system that, in Florence, in the early 1450s, was still very much alive.

[98] Rubinstein, *The Government of Florence*. See also W. J. Connell, 'Changing Patterns of Medicean Patronage: The Florentine Dominion During the Fifteenth Century', in G. C. Garfagnini (ed.), *Lorenzo il Magnifico e il suo mondo* (Florence, 1994), pp. 87–107, which showed that it was only after 1458 that the Medici family monopolised patronage over local governments in the dominion at the expense of other members of the Medici party.

CHAPTER 8

TERRITORIAL OFFICES AND OFFICEHOLDERS

LAURA DE ANGELIS

This chapter aims to provide stimulus to a debate already under way concerning the identities, activities, social origins and careers of the officials who administered the Florentine territory in the decades from the late fourteenth to the mid-fifteenth century. This was precisely the period that witnessed the intensification and fulfillment of a process whereby, over the forty years from Florence's acquisition of Arezzo in 1384 to that of Livorno in 1421, the Florentine territorial state attained the basic configuration it would retain down to the mid-sixteenth century. The study will discuss the composition of the body of officials who were dispatched by the state to administer the territory, their social and professional backgrounds, and Florentine attitudes towards them and towards the subject communities they were sent out to govern.[1]

The territorial state that took shape at the end of the fourteenth and beginning of the fifteenth century retained many institutional characteristics of the fourteenth-century Florentine state,[2] particularly the markedly Florentine composition of its corps of territorial officers.[3] Such a state was a product both of a predilection for ambitious projects that characterised Florence's rulers during the Albizzi regime, as well as of long-standing debates and creative encounters with subject communities, which retained a lively desire to preserve intact the privileges and fiscal immunities contained in their original pacts of submission.[4]

The government of the territorial state in this period became a

---

[1] On this point, see the observations of G. Chittolini, 'L'onore dell'officiale', *Quaderni milanesi*, 17–18 (1989), pp. 3–53; A. Zorzi, 'Giusdicenti e operatori di giustizia nello stato territoriale fiorentino del XV secolo', *Ricerche storiche*, 19 (1989), pp. 517–52; Zorzi, 'The Florentines and Their Public Offices in the Early Fifteenth Century: Competition, Abuses of Power, and Unlawful Acts', in E. Muir and G. Ruggiero (eds.), *History from Crime* (Baltimore, 1994), pp. 110–34.
[2] Zorzi, 'Giusdicenti', pp. 517–20.   [3] *Ibid.*, p. 521.
[4] A. Zorzi, 'Lo stato territoriale fiorentino (secoli XIV–XV): aspetti giurisdizionali', *Società e storia*, 13 (1990), pp. 799–825.

principal tool of Florence's ruling elite, which, in contrast with the
elites of other Italian states, reserved to itself the prerogative of
maintaining public order and administering justice throughout its
subject territories.[5] This ruling class, heterogeneous in its social and
professional origins, but largely devoid of precise juridical definition,
took the place of an earlier order of professional rectors who in the
communal period had governed the cities and territory then subject to
Florence, thus underscoring the essentially political rather than merely
administrative nature of the activities of territorial officials, and
favouring their role as representatives from the capital city over their
functions as officers of the localities themselves.[6] Territorial offices
became an exclusive appanage of the Florentine ruling class – to wit,
they were available to all those citizens who were qualified to hold
offices within the city walls. Even magnates and members of the minor
guilds were allowed to hold certain offices of lesser importance in the
territory, although they were required to pass through a narrow and
closely regulated double hierarchy, and they held office in the same
proportions as for similar offices in the city. The most prestigious offices
were instead reserved for members of the major guilds, and very often
were assigned to members of the ruling class's inner circle.[7]

The same mechanisms for qualification to civic offices applied to
those in the territory as well. Lists of citizens who met specific
requirements – not just citizenship but proven Guelf loyalty, regular
payment of taxes over a specified period of time, matriculation in a
guild, and a minimum age requirement – were drawn up by the
Standard Bearers of the militia companies and of the guilds, and by the

---

[5] A. Zorzi, 'Ordine pubblico e amministrazione della giustizia nelle formazioni
politiche toscane tra Tre e Quattrocento', in *Italia 1350–1450: tra crisi, trasformazione,
sviluppo* (Pistoia, 1993), pp. 419–74. For contrasts with Tuscany, see G. Castelnuovo,
Ufficiali e gentiluomini: la società politica sabauda nel tardo medioevo (Milan, 1994);
G. Chittolini, 'Governo ducale e poteri locali', in *Gli Sforza a Milano e in Lombardia e i
loro rapporti con gli Stati italiani ed europei (1450–1535)* (Milan, 1982), pp. 27–42;
P. Corrao, *Governare un regno: potere, società e istituzioni nella Sicilia fra Tre e Quattrocento*
(Naples, 1991); G. Cozzi, 'Politica, società, istituzioni', in G. Cozzi and M. Knapton,
Storia della Repubblica di Venezia: dalla guerra di Chioggia alla conquista della Terraferma
(Turin, 1986).

[6] See Zorzi, 'Ordine pubblico', pp. 459–60; Zorzi, 'Giusdicenti', p. 521.

[7] For officeholding among minor guildsmen and changes in their representation, see
L. De Angelis, 'La classe dirigente albizzesca a Firenze: fine XIV–primi decenni del
XV secolo', in R. Ninci (ed.), *La società fiorentina nel basso medioevo: per Elio Conti*
(Rome, 1995), pp. 93–114; De Angelis, 'La revisione degli Statuti della Parte guelfa
del 1420', in P. Viti (ed.), *Leonardo Bruni cancelliere della Repubblica di Firenze*
(Florence, 1990), pp. 131–56.

Captains of the Guelf Party.[8] They were then subjected to a scrutiny, that is, to a vote on each individual by a restricted assembly representing the principal agencies of the state. The names of the winners of the scrutiny, subdivided by category (major guilds, minor guilds, magnates), were placed in electoral pouches, one for each category for every office or group of offices of equal importance. Each time an office opened, names of eligible Florentines were drawn from the appropriate pouches according to a system of exact percentages and rotations.[9] The durations of territorial offices were limited, like those in the city, to terms of generally no more than six months and this, together with prohibitions (divieti) against repeat holding within a specified period of time, created an ongoing rotation of assignments. The entire territory was thus administered by a single Florentine ruling group, without distinction between internal and territorial offices.[10] As a result, administration in the territory was linked to domestic political developments, to changes in the 'state', the narrowing of the oligarchy, the shifting of political winds and the recurring pressures for reform that characterised Florentine political life from the last decades of the fourteenth century to the first period of Medici rule.

Scrutinies for territorial (or, as they were called, 'extrinsic') offices were held, with only a few exceptions, separately from those for internal offices. The balìa of 1393 divided the extrinsic offices into three groups according to their importance.[11] Different scrutinies did not always yield the same group of winners. The hierarchy of offices generally served to promote consensus within a fluid political system that was partially open to new entrants. However, the scrutinies also meted out penalties, exclusions or readmissions to members of the inner circle of the ruling class who in certain instances had fallen into political disgrace.[12] Holding extrinsic offices came to be regarded as an essential

---

[8] G. Guidi, Il governo della città-repubblica di Firenze del primo Quattrocento (Florence, 1981), I, pp. 313–19, III, pp. 183–91; G. Brucker, The Civic World of Early Renaissance Florence (Princeton, 1977), p. 252.

[9] De Angelis, 'La classe dirigente'; R. Ninci, 'Tecniche e manipolazioni elettorali nel comune di Firenze tra XIV e XV secolo (1382–1434)', Archivio storico italiano, 150 (1992), pp. 735–73; Zorzi, 'Giusdicenti', pp. 529–30.

[10] See also Zorzi, 'Giusdicenti', p. 522.

[11] ASF, Bal., 19, 38r.

[12] Such was the case of Giovanni di Pagolo Morelli, whose political tribulations are well known through his memoirs (ricordanze). Having failed to win in the Albizzi scrutiny of 1393, apparently on account of the calumnies of 'wicked neighbours' (Ricordi, in V. Branca (ed.), Mercanti scrittori (Milan, 1986), p. 232), Giovanni finally managed, after a decade of fruitless efforts, to have his name reinserted, for the scrutiny of 1404, into the pouches for internal as well as external offices, but only for the least important categories (ibid., p. 280).

part of any distinguished political career, which entailed alternating civic officeholding (whether of the highest offices or one of numerous other administrative or fiscal positions) with participation in the leadership of the Guelf Party, the merchants' court (*Mercanzia*) and the guilds, and for many required the additional commitment of carrying out diplomatic assignments. Preliminary findings of a prosopographical survey of Florence's ruling class in the period of Albizzi rule reveal a cadre of political functionaries who, though not professional civil servants, received nearly all of the commune's assignments to its various offices.[13] Surviving documentation also reveals considerable individual variation in the manner – rarely inspired – in which they carried out their duties. These were often, in fact, simply turned over to subordinates, or abandoned entirely after years of minimal accomplishments.

Membership in the ruling class's inner circle by no means signalled uniform levels of wealth, for professional circumstances could vary dramatically. Notable economic disparities are evident among members whose families engaged, on the one hand, in commerce, business or the professions, and those on the other hand who could count only on rents, and whose resources were often tied up in lands that produced only meagre revenues and left them chronically short of liquid funds. For these reasons, alongside the most important members of the ruling group who enjoyed great patrimonial wealth – men like Giovanni di Bicci de' Medici and his sons,[14] the Capponi family (particularly Neri di Gino and Giovanni di Mico, both owners of flourishing wool shops),[15] Sandro di Giovanni Biliotti (also a wool merchant in Via Maggio),[16] the brothers Niccolò and Giovanni di Messer Donato Barbadori (both bankers),[17] or Schiatta di Roberto Ridolfi,[18] to cite but a few examples – can be set the cases of Astorre di Niccolò di Gherardino Gianni, who in 1427 owned only half of the house where he lived and a small farm in the rural parish of Ripoli,[19] Niccolò di Cocco Donati who, despite having a large family to support, owned only the house he lived in, a

---

[13] For the time being this is limited to a survey only of those members of the major guilds whose names were inserted into the pouch (*borsellino*) of the gonfalonierate. It will be extended to include a survey also of members of the major guilds who won the scrutiny, to winners from the minor guilds, and to magnates present in the city councils in the decades under consideration. The political class here under consideration belonged for the most part to the guilds of bankers (*Cambio*), wool-merchants (*Lana*), and silk-manufacturers (*Por Santa Maria*).

[14] ASF, Catasto, 49, 339r–399r.

[15] Catasto, 18, 1177r–1180v; and Catasto, 65, 60r–63v, respectively.

[16] Catasto, 18, 1457r–1461r.

[17] Catasto, 18, 1170r–1171r; and Catasto, 17, 698r–705r.

[18] Catasto, 18, 1436r–1452v.   [19] Catasto, 15, 68r–v.

second that he rented out, and one third of a farm near Calenzano,[20] or, finally, Bernardo di Zanobi Serzelli who, having some years earlier already abandoned the goldsmith's profession that had earned him precious little, though owning some real estate in Florence and Alto-mena, complained of a regular lack of cash.[21]

Economic good fortune and professional prestige do not seem to have played essential roles in the selection of Florentine officeholders in these years. Astorre Gianni, though lacking a substantial economic base, enjoyed a solid standing within the ruling class in the first half of the fifteenth century. Not only did he win a place in all of the scrutinies from 1411 onwards, he also served on numerous occasions among the richiesti invited to advise the Florentine priors and was awarded every other major public office, alternating assignments in the city with offices in the territory.[22] Many other Florentine officials were intensely involved in public life, particularly, among those just mentioned, Schiatta di Roberto Ridolfi and Giovanni di Messer Donato Barbadoro (until his humiliating fall into political disgrace in 1430). A somewhat different political profile is offered by the silk merchant Goro di Stagio Dati, who, though his name had been imbursed for the office of Standard Bearer of Justice and he had been drawn several times to serve among the Priors and their Councillors, received few other less specifically political assignments.[23] In general, the most common tendency among members of Florence's ruling elite appears to have been towards almost continual engagement in the city's political life and

---

[20] Catasto, 17, 104r–108v.

[21] Catasto, 29, 76r–82r. Bernardo Serzelli submitted his Catasto declaration while he was away serving as Podestà of Castiglion Fiorentino, and to prove his lack of liquid assets complained that he had been able to furnish the Podestà's residence only by selling off his household belongings.

[22] He was drawn as a Prior in 1423 and 1431, served as one of the Dieci in 1418 and 1428, and was Standard Bearer of the Militia in 1420 and Standard Bearer of Justice in 1428. He served on the commissions of the Otto di custodia in 1413, 1424 and 1432, and of the Ten of Liberty in 1422. He was a communal accountant in 1414, a governor of the comune's Entrate e uscite in 1415, 1425 and 1429, a treasurer of the Camera del comune in 1416, provveditore of the Camera in 1419, an ufficiale delle carni in 1421, ufficiale della condotta in 1424, treasurer of the prestanzone in 1426, councillor of the Mercanzia in 1431, Defender of the Laws in 1431, Captain of Orsanmichele in 1417. As far as external (estrinseci) offices are concerned, he was Podestà of Colle Valdelsa in 1409, Captain of the citadel of Arezzo in 1411, Vicar of the Lower Valdarno in 1413, Vicar of the Val di Serchio and the Lower Valdarno in 1417, Podestà of Arezzo in 1422 and Captain of the citadel of Pisa in 1425 (ASF, Tratte, 170–1, passim).

[23] He served among the Ten of Liberty in 1405, and was one of the Officers of the New Gabelles in 1413, a provveditore of the Five of Pisa in 1417, and Podestà of Montale in 1424 (Tratte, 170–1, passim).

administrative affairs. The principal exceptions were the key figures of the regime who instead avoided accepting offices, particularly those in the territory that would have taken them away from Florence for long periods of time,[24] and people like doctors and lawyers whose professional activities required their continual presence in the city.[25]

Repeated inclusion among the political class at each new scrutiny, though by no means automatic for everyone holding the minimum necessary qualifications, was nevertheless not difficult for those who Morelli called 'persons of good standing and antiquity in Florence, especially the families',[26] particularly for those not too clearly marked by factional partisanship. Winning in the scrutinies was much more difficult, instead, for those upwardly mobile families and individuals seeking political acknowledgment of their new social standing, or for those who had fallen into political disgrace in earlier years and awaited long-sought readmission to political life, as was the case, among others, of Giovanni Morelli himself.[27] At such critical moments good relations with families in power would be exploited to the hilt, as they would be with friends, relatives and neighbours in the *gonfalone*, to assure at least that one's name was included on the list of those to be voted on in the new scrutiny, in a merry-go-round of personal ties, reciprocal obligations and enmities that were the foundation of the entire Florentine social world and the constant preoccupation of its members. The corps of officials for both internal and the so-called 'extrinsic' offices was formed by means of such personal and family dealings and obligations, which bound those in office to be ever mindful of the favours they owed.[28]

---

[24] Messer Maso di Luca degli Albizzi, for example, accepted only one territorial office, that of Podestà of Arezzo in 1407 (Tratte, 170). The same can be said of Cosimo di Giovanni di Bicci de' Medici, who never held an office in the territory.

[25] Two cases in point are the careers of the lawyer Messer Filippo Corsini (Tratte, 170–1, *passim*; L. Martines, *Lawyers and Statecraft in Renaissance Florence* (Princeton, 1968), p. 482) and the physician Maestro Cristofano di Giorgio Brandolini (Tratte, 170–1, *passim*).

[26] Ed. Branca: 'le persone da bene e antiche di Firenze e spezialmente le famiglie'.

[27] Morelli failed to win in the scrutiny of 1393, suffering, he thought, a great injustice for which he blamed his malevolent neighbours, despite the fact that he had never demonstrated partisan sympathies for the Alberti family. See Branca (ed.), *Mercanti scrittori*, p. 232. Morelli's name was reinserted in the electoral pouches in 1404, yet, so far as the scrutiny for the *Tre maggiori* was concerned, until his name was drawn in 1409, he was never sure whether all 'le preghiere che furono possibili a potere fare, e non si perdonò a niuna pratica, o ebbesi riguardo a niuna onestà d'improntitudine' (p. 280), had succeeded in their aim of having him and the other members of his family included in the new scrutinies.

[28] In a felicitous turn of phrase, Pagolo di Matteo Petriboni, in his 'Priorista', illustrated this feature by describing the sudden decision of the Signoria in 1417 to carry out an

As it developed in the Quattrocento, the Florentine territorial state followed institutional lines already laid out in the Trecento. The number of extrinsic offices grew in the first three decades of the fifteenth century as a result of Florence's subjection of such major centres as Pistoia, Arezzo, Cortona and Pisa, with their surrounding territories. But it soon began to contract, both as a result of Florence's efforts to rationalise its bureaucracy and, above all, owing to pressures from the subject communities themselves to reduce the costs of judges' salaries and those of their curial 'families'.[29] In the second half of the Quattrocento the number of extrinsic offices settled at around ninety, a figure not much greater than what it had been at the beginning of the century when Florence began the most dynamic phase of its territorial expansion.[30] Such modest numerical growth, and the corresponding increase in distribution of salaried positions in the hands of Florence's ruling class, are, in any case, scarcely sufficient to explain the profound change in attitudes towards public officeholding, both internal and external, that manifested itself among Florence's rulers in these years. The favourable light in which office was now viewed stimulated a new, more aggressive pursuit of territorial offices, which were no longer considered merely as necessary career steps in public life, burdened with inconveniences to be avoided whenever possible. Rather, they came to be seen as prizes to be won at all costs.[31]

Territorial offices assumed varying degrees of importance and value depending on the legal prerogatives that attached to them, producing not only differences in salary, but opening up various possibilities for turning additional profits by rendering special services and collecting commissions on fines that might be levied. Distinctions were created as well in the number and grade of assistants a judge might be obliged to take with him, whose salaries were paid from the salary of the office he assumed. Thus, for example, the Captain of Security at Pistoia in 1424

---

unannounced and unexplained scrutiny for internal offices and those in the territory. The decision was taken 'a utile di chi si trovò a farlo, che tutti s'aiutorno'; BNF, Conventi soppressi, C 4895, 97v.

[29] For figures on the number of extrinsic officials, see Zorzi, 'Giusdicenti', pp. 518–20.

[30] To this number must be added that of the castellanies, which at the beginning of the century came to 130. See *Statuta Populi et Communis Florentie publica auctoritate collecta, castigata et praeposita, anno sal. MCCCCXV* (Freiburg [Florence], bk V, tr. II, r. 172.

[31] Bonaccorso di Neri Pitti, writing his *Ricordi* in the early decades of the fifteenth century, briefly noted two characteristics of his father: first, the skill with which he managed his own affairs and business in the *Lana* guild and, second, his disinterest, bizarre in the eyes of Bonaccorso, in communal officeholding and his refusal of every position offered that it was possible to decline (Bonaccorso Pitti, in Branca (ed.), *Mercanti scrittori*, p. 356).

was assigned a half-year's budget of 3000 lire from which to pay himself
and his retinue or 'family' (Lat.: *familia*: It.: *famiglia*), which included a
professional judge (*iurisperitus*), a personal accountant, two other
notaries, four pages, two heralds, and twenty-five guards and attendants,
including a master groom to supervise the maintenance of six horses.[32]
In the same year, the Podestà of Mangona, a *podesteria* of the first order
embracing three notaries, four attendants and a horse, received a salary
of 700 lire, while the Podestà of Belforte, a second-tier assignment,
received 500 lire to pay a retinue of two notaries, four attendants and a
horse, and the Podestà of Caprese, a third-class posting, received 400
lire for six months for himself and a *famiglia* of one notary, three
attendants and a horse.[33] From the surviving documentation it is clear,
however, that these officials earned more from the percentages they
could collect on the fines they imposed, and from special services they
might perform, than from their salaries *per se.* Francesco di Iacopo del
Bene, in the meticulous entries he made in his account-books during
his term as Vicar of the Valdinievole in 1381, recorded extra income
derived from fines he imposed for fraud committed by the tax-farmers
who had purchased the gate gabelles, from the penalties imposed on
persons who violated a statute against exporting grain to 'Ghibelline'
regions, and from other revenues that for various reasons had been paid
over to him by his notary.[34] In 1375, among other extraordinary
revenues, Francesco was awarded substantial sums of money by the
citizens of Volterra for the capture of several criminals who were
wanted by Volterra and San Gimignano for illegally exporting grain
beyond the Florentine territory.[35]

---

[32] ASF, Tratte, 10.

[33] *Ibid.* Regarding the expenses that a judge was expected to bear before and during his
six-month term of office, it is necessary to remember that in the three months
between the time his name was drawn for office and his actual departure for the
locality to which he had been assigned, he was expected to pay a deposit, provide a
certain number of guarantors, recruit a *famiglia* (often from a variety of different
communes), prepare his own arms and mounts and, finally, provision a residence at
least with the furniture and household goods necessary for a sojourn of six months.
The official had also to enlist his own *famiglia* and to negotiate salaries with all of his
own assistants. To take one example, Francesco di Iacopo del Bene, Vicar of the
Valdinievole and Valleariana in 1381, paid 7 florins for two months' service for the
notary who was to serve also as his knight and companion, 20 florins for six months'
service for another notary, 3 lire a month on average for each of his servants, 4 florins
10 soldi a month for his cook, and 4 florins over six months for each of his pages;
ASF, CdB, no. 45. The expenses were much the same for the *famiglia* when
Francesco was Podestà of San Gimignano in 1375 and Captain of Montagna of
Pistoia in 1393–4; CdB, no. 46.

[34] CdB, no. 45, 32r–33v.   [35] CdB, no. 46, 1r–2r.

Thus, despite the inconveniences that sometimes accompanied officeholding, and the sensitivity of some positions, territorial offices from the 1380s onwards were increasingly sought after and appear to have carried growing political prestige. Case-studies of the preceding period indicate that so long as the selection of officers was carried out exclusively by means of electoral sortitions (formal elections being held only when an office had been declined three times and circumstances required a speedy appointment), the percentage of refusals was high, owing largely to Florentines' difficulty in accommodating their commercial and business interests during the prolonged absences required by extrinsic offices.[36] Territorial assignments must have seemed, in this early period, like honorific but inconvenient by-products of political life, particularly without those considerable economic incentives that later eased living outside of Florence and justified all the discomforts and nuisances caused by the practical organisation of a 'move', which involved the search for character witnesses, the enlistment of officers for the *famiglia* and the purchase of clothing, cuirasses and food to take to the site of the office. The account-books of the del Bene family for the early thirteenth century reveal that two captaincies in the city of Pistoia produced barely enough income to cover the cost of assuming the offices,[37] while a *podesteria* at Prato in 1359 generated only a slim margin of profit.[38] But a very different picture emerges from the later entries of Francesco di Iacopo del Bene, who twice held the vicariate of the Valdinievole in 1373 and 1381. During his first term of office he acknowledged having profited, all told, by 1020 lire, 18 soldi, 4 denari, and in his second by 1609 lire, 8 soldi.[39] Similar figures emerge from a del Bene notebook for the *podesteria* of San Gimignano in 1375, which carried a salary of 1800 lire meant to cover expenses that actually came to only 1652 lire, 18 soldi, 7 denari. By the end of the term, income from the office had actually reached 1544 lire, 16 soldi, 10 denari, yielding a profit of nearly 900 lire.[40]

This robust transformation of the economic prospect of holding territorial office meant that the offices were no longer shunned, but rather came to be actively pursued. As numerous petitions brought before the Signoria and the councils indicate, the offices became a valuable source of income, even if temporary, for disabled or

[36] ASF, Stipendiati del comune, 1–4.
[37] ASF, CdB, nos. 42, 43.
[38] CdB, no. 44.   [39] CdB, no. 45.
[40] CdB, no. 46. Iacopo Salviati recorded similar figures as Vicar of the Valdinievole and Podestà of Montepulciano; see Zorzi, 'Giusdicenti', p. 538.

incompetent relatives,[41] for youths lacking steady incomes or job
prospects, or for men who needed to raise a dowry for a daughter or
sister.[42] In the decade 1383–92 appointments to territorial offices were
sought and conferred as compensation for damages suffered under the
Ciompi revolt and in the tumultuous years that followed during the
government of the minor guilds (1378–82), the 'tempore alterius status',
as one member of the Bordoni family put it in appealing for a
castellany;[43] just as they might also be granted as rewards for exposing
plots against the government.[44] The opening of positions in the
territory, even less prestigious ones like castellanies and the lesser
podesterie, afforded the Florentines an opportunity to ease some of the
pressures of an unfavourable economic climate by transferring the
burden to subject communities. Territorial offices therefore had
become for many a source of income, sometimes the only one, and one
that was available as well to old and venerable families teetering on the
precipice of economic decline. No less a figure than Bonaccorso Pitti,
finding himself, in 1417, at the head of a family that included not only
his own numerous household but also those of his brother Luigi and of
his nephew Neri, both of whom had died in the plague that summer,
noted in his diary that 'I comfort myself with hope in the Lord, and of
offices to exploit.'[45]

The duties of Florentine officials varied according to the importance
of their offices, their strategic position within the Florentine territory,
and the political and military contacts that they might therefore maintain with neighbouring states. The principal duty common to all levels
of office was the administration of justice. However, judges also carried
out military tasks such as recruiting troops and monitoring the move-

---

[41] See the 'Ricordanze' of Leonardo Bartolini Salimbeni, who accepted the *podesteria* of
Empoli in 1375 in order to let his brother Salvestro have the post; cited in
R. Signorini, *Alle origini di una famiglia patrizia: Il libro di ricordanze di Leonardo di
Bartolini di Salimbene (1348–1382)*, tesi di laurea, Università degli Studi di Firenze,
Facoltà di Lettere e Filosofia of Florence (1995–6).

[42] See, among numerous possible examples, ASF, PR, 100, 133r, 5 February 1412;
141v–146v, 27 February 1413; PR, 124, 199v–207v, 29 August 1433; PR, 126,
418v–419r, 28 February 1436.

[43] PR, 76, 20 June 1387; PR, 75, 21 October 1388; PR 78, 12 April 1389.

[44] Such was the case of Cionetto Bastari, who in 1412 revealed a plot to the Signoria
that the Alberti were fomenting in Bologna. He was rewarded with a lifetime
stipend from the commune, five lances, and numerous other privileges, among
which was the election of two of his consorts to the office of Podestà in top level
podesterie for terms of a year each; ASF, Bal., 20).

[45] He made the entry, moreover, in the months in which he was preparing to assume
the *podesteria* of S. Gimignano, which he occupied in November of that year;
Bonaccorso Pitti, *Ricordi*, in Branca (ed.), *Mercanti scrittori*, p. 473.

ments of enemy forces. And they handled financial matters and political issues involving neighbouring lords (*signori*), allies, and the elites of the subject communities they were sent to administer. To judge from their correspondence with the central agencies of the Florentine state, the functions of territorial officers were, more than anything else, political, investigative and executive in nature, and hence their actions were carefully reviewed and severely judged by the central offices of the republic.[46] The officers were guided and checked by the central magistracies of Florence, not only by those specifically created to supervise the territorial administration but, above all, by the omnipresent Signoria itself. Innumerable cases can be cited of Florence's central magistracies intervening in the daily activities and decision-making of the officers in the territory, correcting them and bringing them into line with policies that placed the interests of a dominant Florence above every other consideration. No sooner had Florentines assumed their roles as extrinsic officers than they were confronted with a series of delicate tasks, the successful fulfilment of which required an enormous measure of political finesse in deciphering at every turn the courses of action most advantageous to Florence and, when disagreements arose with the central authorities, tremendous humility in adjusting immediately to their views.

If we look closely at a few examples of the relations between the Florentine Signoria and its officers in the territory, it is notable how often the former intervened to impose a precise line of conduct that left the latter with very little freedom of action. In November 1384, the Podestà of Bibbiena had begun a trial of two men of the *podesteria* accused of having participated in a plot against Florence to yield Bibbiena into the hands of a nearby lord, Guido da Pietramala. But the two men, betaking themselves to Florence, managed to convince the Signoria not only of their innocence, but that the accusations brought against them were treasonous slanders promulgated by their enemies. The Podestà was chastised not only for having listened to the calumnies, but also for having given them credence and for having failed to make every effort to warn the Signoria of a possible conspiracy. He was therefore ordered to continue investigating and to await precise orders, 'and we will inform you of our intentions before you do anything else'.[47] The Signoria made a similar intervention in April 1394, when it ordered the Podestà of Subbiano to annul a sentence he had imposed on two local soldiers who had run off to Florence during the period 'of

---

[46] ASF, Miss. I canc., 19–20, 22–6, 29, 35; ASF, Miss. II canc., 1.
[47] Miss. I canc., 20, 24r–v.

those disturbances', referring, in all likelihood, to an attempt made by several artisans the previous October to overthrow the state on behalf of the Alberti family (a plot that had resulted in the banishment of the Alberti and the formation of the Albizzi-led *balìa*). The Signoria ordered the Podestà to reverse his decision and to provide in whatever manner he found most appropriate 'that those, having come to the honour of the Guelfs, and of our Signoria, should come to no harm whatsoever'.[48]

Written in the same tone is a letter to the Captain of Pistoia, Silvestro di Messer Filippo Adimari, of March 1390, concerning some fines and penalties that he had imposed on some Pistoiese citizens that the Florentine Signoria wished to have revoked, and regarding which they had already written to the rector to scant effect. The second letter to Adimari therefore demanded immediate obedience to the Signoria's orders, on penalty of Adimari's being forced to pay out of his own pocket, once he returned to Florence, a sum equal to all of the fines he had levied in Pistoia.[49] Similarly, when a Captain of Pistoia, who already in July 1494 had balked at releasing several prisoners in accordance with the Signoria's orders, put another one in prison in contravention of their orders, he was commanded to release him immediately or face consequences that would be to his 'detriment and shame'.[50]

In his *Ricordi*, Bonaccorso Pitti himself noted two particularly difficult moments in the course of his many terms as a territorial rector. First, as Podestà of Pistoia in 1399, his ultimately futile efforts to defend the city's prerogatives and immunities very nearly got him arrested himself.[51] A second incident came about in 1420 when, as Podestà of Montepulciano, Pitti penalised a Sienese citizen, a native (*terrazzano*) of Montepulciano, for having exported grain from the city in violation of Florentine statutes. The *terrazzano*, by means of Sienese intervention, managed to get Florence to quash the condemnation, thanks to the fact that Florence owed the Sienese for a similar favour recently granted to a Florentine citizen, and thanks as well to the suasion that Bonaccorso's enemies had applied to the Signoria in an effort to undermine his authority. Pitti, convinced of being in the right, was prepared to disobey, and yielded only to the pleading of friends determined that he avoid political ruin and a massive fine.[52]

Guido Machiavelli, Captain of Pisa in 1426, went through an experience similar to Pitti's. For having failed to obey promptly an

---

[48] *Ibid.*, 24, 17r.   [49] *Ibid.*, 22, 45v.   [50] *Ibid.*, 29, 24r.
[51] Bonaccorso Pitti, *Ricordi*, in Branca (ed.), *Mercanti scrittori*, pp. 414–5.
[52] *Ibid.*, pp. 490–4.

order from the Ten of War (*Dieci di balìa*) for the immediate release of Mariano da Piombino's sequestered goods, he was accused of contempt for the magistracy and of having treated its letters like mere private correspondence. While venting their indignation on Machiavelli, the Ten acknowledged having been restrained from taking severe measures by the intercession of his powerful friends: 'and were we to treat your error at its face value you would get your just deserts, but, out of regard for others, we will let it rest for the moment, confident that you will correct the error and mend your ways'. Still, should there be further disobedience, 'we will set aside every other consideration and courtesy and take whatever measures we deem our honour to require'.[53]

Every such conflict that arose set off a process of taking sides in Florence, for and against the individual rectors in the territory, making the city an arena of continual personal and political clashes within the ruling class. Not surprisingly, extrinsic rectors tended to pay careful attention to domestic politics, focusing on the events unfolding at the centre and on the need to satisfy the wishes of friends and key citizens, to act on innumerable appeals for favour, and to respond positively to solicitations and recommendations of every sort – in a society in which personal relationships assumed vital importance, and everyone was at once a patron and a client.

The situation appears to have changed during the Medicean period, when Cosimo and the other members of the Medici family reinforced their position as dispensers of favour, above all among new entrants to the political class, and as points of reference in the activities of the rectors – so much so even as to force them to take actions against the law and their own consciences. Such was the case of the Podestà of Prato, Piero di Salvestro Ainardi who, having received an insistent letter from Cosimo on behalf of some inhabitants of Calcinaia whom he was about to sentence to death, immediately replied assuring Cosimo of his readiness to comply with his requests. Noting that he had always wanted to do something to please Cosimo, he promised his powerful patron that he would handle the case in such a manner 'that they will understand with perfect clarity how much your writing has benefited them; for, believing that I might do something to please you, you would find me absolutely tireless, even to the point of putting my own honour at stake'. The poor Podestà concluded his letter to Cosimo by promising to have a copy of the revised sentence sent to him shortly and, unable to conceal the embarrassment of the situation, he added,

---

[53] ASF, Dieci di balía, Missive interne, 2, 76v.

'I'll have the sentence drawn up quickly so as to be done with it, for it feels already like a thousand years to me.'[54]

Equally revealing is an anxious letter from Angelo Spini, Captain of Cortona in 1462, in which the writer wrestled with the delicate question of whether to enforce a prohibition against the circulation of foreign currencies within Florentine territory. This would have disrupted the lucrative trade that existed between Cortona and Perugia, and for this reason Spini's predecessors had simply ignored the law. Without openly indicating a position of his own, the Captain, in effect, sought Medici permission to let the situation in Cortona stand, rather than 'drain this land of money'. Indeed, Spini knew full well that with permission from the Medici family he might ignore a law of the communal councils, 'since I consider myself to have obtained this office, as well as every other honour and advantage that have come my way, by God's grace, as well as by that of you and your family; and, insofar as I follow your counsels, and those of the others members of your house, I can neither err nor fail to come out well'.[55]

The pressures and demands emanating from Florence were a fact of life that rectors could not avoid without political disgrace or even, in the most sensitive of cases, the loss of their political rights and exile. Such was the dilemma that confronted Palla di Palla Strozzi when, in 1436, he was serving as the Vicar of Firenzuola. Palla was well aware of the precarious political position of his family, part of which had been exiled in 1434. The fragile political fortunes of those who had managed to stay behind in the city lay at the mercy of their enemies, and thus they were desperately in need of the support not only of Cosimo and Lorenzo de' Medici, 'but of everybody we can latch onto'. Palla had promised at the outset of his office to behave 'in such a manner that nobody will talk about me; I'm not going to get tangled up in anything, but will simply let matters take their course'.[56] Still, his enemies in Florence 'and everybody else who does not feel they have been served by you or your office',[57] managed to find shortcomings in his behaviour and administration and to call them to the attention of the magistrates. The shrewd advice proffered by one relative, frightened of the consequences that these continual accusations might have, not only for Palla but for all of the house that remained in Florence, was to obey the orders coming from Florence, 'and accommodate them in these things, and don't wear yourself out, and try to make light of things in such a way, however, that you keep an eye on what's best for those of us who

54 ASF, MAP, XI, 568r (undated).   55 *Ibid.*, 534r, 7 June, 1462.
56 ASF, CS, ser. III, no. 25, 87r.   57 *Ibid.*

are in the spotlight, for you still have several months in office, so make yourself pleasing'.[58] To judge from the many other letters he received in the course of this vicariate, Palla Strozzi seems truly to have been the object of repeated attacks by various Florentine magistracies. The situation became so tense as to induce the lawyer Filippo di Andrea Balducci,[59] to whom Palla had turned for legal counsel concerning a dispute with the consuls of the wool merchants' guild, to advise him, given the ambiguity of the law, to adopt a politic course and yield to their demands. 'Yet even this, it seems to me, will not be easy for you', acknowledged Balducci, 'given that they will still speak ill of you, and will assume that you have yielded only out of greed, especially given the type of people who get into office these days.'[60]

For their part, the communities maintained frequent and personal contacts with Florence through their orators to the Signoria and to other magistracies and influential people in the city. The most frequent requests from the communities concerned the reduction of their fiscal burdens, the settlement of debts and acknowledgment of their immunities and privileges.[61] The communities were not shy to accuse Florentine rectors of harassment and extortion, but rarely did they get the satisfaction of a real investigation of the officers involved. Aside from a few famous cases easily attributable to the climate of open conflict prevailing among the Florentine ruling class in the third decade of the fifteenth century,[62] disciplinary measures were not taken against individual officials. Rather, every effort was made to defend their administration and honour wherever necessary. In 1412, the men of Modigliana rose up against their Podestà, Bernardo di Salvestro Nardi. At first, the Signoria asked the Captain of Castrocaro and the new Podestà of Modigliana to investigate the case and to interrogate the

---

[58] Ibid., 83r.

[59] L. Martines provides a brief biographical note in Lawyers, p. 502.

[60] ASF, CS, ser. III, no. 125, 99r, 1 September 1436.

[61] ASF, SC Delib. spec., 10, 15–16, 18, 26, 29, 32; Miss. I canc., 19, 23, 29, 30; ASF, Cinque del contado, 1–2.

[62] I refer in particular to a notorious case that developed during the war with Lucca involving one of the leading political figures of the Albizzi regime, the banker Giovanni di Messer Donato Barbadoro who, on his return from the podesteria of Montepulciano, was discovered at the city gates to be carrying 'armour, jewels and other valuables' (arnesi, gioie e altre cose di valuta) belonging to the natives of the place. A petition was brandished against him, 'and he was reputed among the greatest and most powerful criminals, and changed residence and quarter' (et rimase de' grandi et possenti per malificio, et mutò abitatione et quartiere). At the same time, the Defenders of the Laws received additional anonymous denunciations of Giovanni and his officers, who were sentenced to pay a collective fine of 1500 florins and return the goods they had carried back to Florence; BNF, Conventi Soppressi, C 4895, 127r.

leading men of Modigliana to get to the heart of the matter and find out why the population had risen up so violently. But, two weeks later, the Captain of Castrocaro was ordered to proceed against the guilty in such a way as to preserve the honour of the republic and to discourage further such actions, 'for offences committed against our officers may be said to have been committed against the Signoria itself'.[63]

The same reasoning led Florence to discourage the communities, usually already rather hesitant to take direct measures against their rectors, from making unfavourable representations against its officials. In 1395, the Captain of the Pistoiese Montagna was ordered to summon into his presence the syndics who had issued accusations against the last Captain and his knight and to order them to reimburse the previous rectors for every expense they had born on the Captain's behalf,[64] thereby discouraging any further efforts by the community to pursue the matter. A negative response was likewise waiting for the ambassadors of Colle Valdelsa when, in September 1415, they came to Florence to complain of their Podestà, Bartolomeo di Iacopone Gherardini. Recalled to Florence for further investigation and found innocent, Bartolomeo was sent back to Colle to complete his term of office.[65]

Without openly acknowledging accusations coming from subject communities, which Florentines understood as a challenge to their sovereignty, the central Florentine magistracies nevertheless responded to criticism of their officers' administration by taking steps that, on the one hand, aimed to develop and strengthen a centralised system that allowed strict control of officials' activities,[66] while, on the other, they promoted the passage of legislation to address the sources of local discontent. Thus, taking note of the accusations of extortion and abuse coming in from various communities in the Valdinievole, Florence promulgated a law prohibiting the Vicars and the members of their retinues from accepting money for any reason, and forbade every rector in the province as well from accepting grain or fodder for shipment to the city. The Signoria was assigned the task of drawing up a regulation preventing the Vicars from interfering in civil cases in the jurisdictions of the Podestà of the province, and set fixed tolls and taxes for the transport of goods.[67] Another general measure was passed in 1419 that prevented Vicars from interfering in cases concerning prohibited games,

---

[63] ASF, Miss. I canc., 29, 26v, 27r, 30r.
[64] *Ibid.*, 24, 165v, 166r.   [65] *Ibid.*, 29, 85v; Brucker, *Civic World*, p. 220.
[66] The process came to a head in 1429 with the creation of the magistracy of the Defenders of the Laws (*Conservatori delle leggi*), who were empowered, among other things, to supervise the operations of Florentine officers.
[67] ASF, PR, 74, 23 February 1386/7.

in order to put an end to what had become a common abuse of office. The Vicars and their deputies 'often harass subjects unduly by accusing them of playing prohibited games simply to collect the fines', with the result that subjects were frequently forced to flee simply to avoid prosecution by Florentine officials.[68]

Florentine policy thus appears to have been to defend the activities of its own representatives, especially of its leading and most influential citizens, rarely taking action against individuals and seeking instead to regulate the assignments and duties of every official in such a way as to prevent, or at least render more difficult, the repetition of certain abuses that impacted Florentine relations with the subject communities. The results were not always significant, given the general tenor of the system in which territorial officials operated. Only gradually, as the territorial state took shape, was the conduct of territorial rectors brought within sharper limits which, while facilitating good relations with the communities and leading families of the territory, also provided Florentine officials with a respectable income. It took time for officeholding to become an economic pursuit that did not provoke accusations of extortion, corruption, and the abuse of power, and that did not seem an extraordinary burden on the subject communities. At the same time, the rectors were strongly discouraged from resisting orders from Florence, whether from the Signoria or from other magistracies, above all in matters concerning the defence of the city's prerogatives as sovereign.

If territorial officials with more explicitly political duties were required by law to be Florentine citizens qualified to hold public office, the same limitations did not apply to the technical personnel that made up a rector's *famiglia*. The judges and notaries who accompanied rectors to their posts came for the greater part from various localities in the Florentine territory or even outside it, principally from the central and northern parts of the peninsula. This system allowed members of local elites, through the practice of law and related professions, to insert themselves into a broader regional ambit, as numerous current studies of small localities have demonstrated, and as we can see from a preliminary analysis of the composition of the retinues of the rectors. Full data on these 'families' is not easy to come by, but from a list (partially incomplete only with respect to the notaries) of the principal assistants for the *podesteria* of Pescia (which was absorbed in 1425 into the vicariate of the Valdinievole) from 1339 to the end of the fifteenth century,[69] some interesting facts emerge. The first point to note is the wide variety

---

[68] PR, 109, 13 October 1419.
[69] ASF, CS, ser. II, no. 75.

of the places of origin of the judges, a good percentage of whom did not come from the Florentine state. Of the judges, who totalled 157, fully sixty-eight came from localities outside the Florentine republic, generally from modern-day Emilia-Romagna, Umbria and Latium.[70] Among the judges of Tuscan origin, Florence, San Miniato, Pistoia and San Gimignano were the communities most often represented. Less variable, instead, was the place of origin of the notaries, nearly all of whom came from within the Florentine state and (unlike the judges) from minor rural locales.[71] The Florentine presence among the notaries and, especially, among the judges, declined over the course of the fourteenth century, but held steady for the other centres of greater prestige. Florentine notaries as well as judges seem to have preferred the less uncomfortable and perhaps more lucrative offices available on the Florentine market to those in the territory, which were by nature subordinate positions. For the Florentine rectors, instead, whose tours of duty were but part of a broader process of participation in public life both in Florence and the territory, the economic opportunities presented by territorial office were, in many cases, a form of *de facto* compensation for the discomforts of moving and residing outside of the city, and for the rigid control of their activity by the Signoria and the other offices of the central administration.

[70] Also worth noting are the three Piedmontese judges, a Milanese, two Romans and a German from Cologne, although the majority of the foreign judges came from cities in the central band of the peninsula, such as Bologna, Modena, Parma, Reggio, Cremona, Rimini, Perugia, Padua, Cesena, Forlí, Trevi, Tagliacozzo, Faenza, Fano, Foligno, Ferrara, Macerata, Orte, Terni, Bagnoregio, Ancona, Viterbo, Ascoli, Aquila, Sulmona, Gubbio, Todi, Spoleto, Fossombrone, Narni and Città di Castello; Zorzi, 'Giusdicenti', p. 546.

[71] Aside from Florence, San Miniato, Pistoia, San Gimignano and Prato, which have already been mentioned, a large percentage of the notaries came from such centres as Pratovecchio, Bibbiena, Barbialla, Castiglion Fiorentino, Poppi, Vicchio and Staggia; Zorzi, 'Giusdicenti', pp. 547–9.

CHAPTER 9

DEMOGRAPHY AND THE POLITICS
OF FISCALITY

SAMUEL K. COHN, JR.

Whether material conditions improved for the peasantry after the Black Death and into the fifteenth century remains an open question, not only for late medieval and Renaissance Florence, but for all of Europe.[1] Historians of a Malthusian bent have seen an economic golden age for the peasantry following in the wake of fourteenth-century pestilence.[2] From radically opposed perspectives, other historians such as the Marxist Guy Bois and the non-Marxist David Herlihy have also found prosperity for the peasantry at least in parts of Europe and for a portion of the fifteenth century.[3] However, more recently still other historians with various methods and political agendas have argued the opposite: the fifteenth century saw at best continued misery, not recovery, for the Florentine peasantry.[4]

[1] See, most recently, J. Hatcher, 'England in the Aftermath of the Black Death', *Past and Present*, 144 (1994), pp. 3–35, which considers the well-being of the peasantry only through the fourteenth century and only in England; and J. Bolton, ' "The World Upside Down": Plague as an agent of Economic and Social Change' in M. Ormrod and P. Lindley (eds.), *The Black Death in England* (Stamford, 1996), pp. 17–77. My argument is developed in my *Creating the Florentine State* (Cambridge, 1999).

[2] Most importantly, see E. Le Roy Ladurie, *Les paysans de Languedoc*, 2 vols. (Paris, 1966); and M. M. Postan, *Essays on Medieval Agriculture and General Problems of the Medieval Economy* (Cambridge, 1973), especially, 'The Fifteenth Century', pp. 41–8.

[3] See G. Bois, *Crise du féodalisme: économie rurale et démographie en Normandie orientale du début du 14e siècle au milieu du 16e siècle* (Paris, 1976); Hatcher, *Plague, Population and the English Economy 1348–1530* (London, 1977); and D. Herlihy, *Medieval and Renaissance Pistoia: The Social History of an Italian Town, 1200–1430* (New Haven, 1967), especially pp. 102–20; and his lectures, Herlihy, *The Black Death and the Transformation of the West*, ed. S. K. Cohn, Jr. (Cambridge, Mass., 1997). Bois' work is Marxist, whereas Herlihy's and Hatcher's demographic interpretations have been highly critical of both Marxist and Malthusian models.

[4] M. Ginatempo, *Crisi di un territorio: il popolamento della Toscana senese alla fine del medioevo* (Florence, 1988); S. Raveggi and M. S. Mazzi, *Gli uomini e le cose nelle campagne fiorentine del Quattrocento* (Florence, 1983); S. R. Epstein, 'Cities, Regions and the Late Medieval Crisis: Sicily and Tuscany Compared', *Past and Present*, 130

Yet, despite differences in political and methodological orientations, historians have posed these questions almost exclusively within the contexts of long-term social and economic causes; the affairs of state or politics more generally, especially at the level of specific events, largely have been left out. Was the condition of the Florentine peasantry during the Renaissance oblivious to changes in political regime – to the rise of the Albizzi's *governo stretto* in 1393 or the rise of the Medici in 1434? Or, did other political events have long-term consequences in shaping the fortunes of Florentine peasants?

This chapter will present data from a series of tax records from twenty-nine sample villages in the rural territory or (more precisely) the contado of Florence, from the Black Death through the fifteenth century. The trends sketched by these records show a picture of growing prosperity for large swathes of the countryside during the fifteenth century at least until the catasto tax of 1458–60.[5] This prosperity, however, did not derive solely from the population check of the Black Death of 1348 or even from the plagues that followed. Instead, political factors, I will argue, were as crucial in determining the fortunes of rural communities in the Florentine hinterland as were the mortalities due to plague.

To be sure, a long-term examination of Florentine tax registers from the late fourteenth through the fifteenth centuries is fraught with dangers. Not only do tax assessments for single years show the pitfalls of all tax records, past and present – evasion, deceit and missing records – but changes in the rules and even the culture of taxation compound the difficulties over time.[6]

(1991), pp. 3–50; and G. A. Brucker, 'The Economic Foundations of Laurentian Florence', in G. C. Garfagnini (ed.), *Lorenzo il Magnifico e il suo mondo* (Florence, 1994), pp. 3–15. For England, see L. R. Poos, *A Rural Society after the Black Death: Essex 1350–1525* (Cambridge, 1991), especially pp. 30–1. For an older essay on Tuscany, see P. J. Jones, 'From Manor to Mezzadria: A Tuscan Case-Study in the Medieval Origins of Modern Agrarian Society', in N. Rubinstein (ed.), *Florentine Studies: Politics and Society in Renaissance Florence* (Evanston, 1968), pp. 193–241.

5 The estimi for the Florentine contado known as the 'Capi di Famiglia' were redacted in 1355–6, 1365–6, 1371–2, 1383–4, 1393–4, 1401–2, 1412–14. Unlike the estimo, the catasto was instituted for the entire territorial state (city, contado and *districtus*) and not just the contado. My first analysis of the estimo records, 'Inventing Braudel's Mountains: The Florentine Alps after the Black Death', in S. K. Cohn, Jr. and S. A. Epstein (eds.), *Portraits of Medieval and Renaissance Living: Essays in Honor of David Herlihy* (Ann Arbor, 1995), defines my samples and techniques. My selection of sample villages depended on the survival of records for these villages in the various estimo, catasto and lira registers from 1365 through 1487.

6 For these changes, see C. M. de La Roncière, *Prix et salaires à Florence au XIVe siècle (1280–1380)* (Rome, 1982), pp. 643–60; D. Herlihy and C. Klapisch-Zuber, *Les Toscans et leurs familles: une étude du catasto florentin de 1427* (Paris, 1978), pp. 49–56.

The first records labelled as the *Capi di famiglia* (1364) differed little from earlier hearth-tax surveys common to Florence and other city-states of Italy dating back to the thirteenth century. But, by 1371, these records were the first in Florence and the earliest in Western civilisation (that I know of) to list all household members, not just family heads, and to give their ages. By the next survey, 1383, the listing of all family members and ages had spread thoroughly through the countryside, and by the time of the *Capi di famiglia*'s last redaction (1412–14) most aspects of the Renaissance catasti were firmly in place.[7]

To make inroads into the more than a thousand surviving volumes of tax records, called 'estimi' before 1427 and 'catasti' afterwards, I have selected villages according to altitude, comprising three samples, plains, hills and mountains. To simplify matters for this presentation, I will compare communities in the plains with those in the mountains. These samples cut two geographical trajectories: one, from the city walls of Florence through the rich plains of the lower Valdarno and the Bisenzio into the city of Prato; the other, from the Mugello highlands bordering the state of Bologna through the Alpi Fiorentine above Firenzuola and then across the Calvana mountain range into the former contado of Prato[8] (see Fig. 9.1).

My first results suggest that one of the oldest and most fundamental of debates in Renaissance Florentine history must be recast – that over tax policy and the relations between city and countryside.[9] My study of one survey, that of 1393, shows several unexpected findings for the history of taxation. The simple opposition – city versus countryside – fails to disclose the complex fiscal politics that defined the late medieval Italian city-state. In addition to the differences in Florentine tax policy and governmental control over its traditional contado and those subject cities newly incorporated into its *districtus*, the contado itself cannot be reduced to a single fiscal entity before the catasto of 1427. Not only can it be said that no standard tax rate existed for the contado; the inequalities from village to village were extraordinary. At the extreme, a mountain village in the upper Mugello, Mangona, was taxed at a rate thirty-two times that of villages touching the city walls of Florence.[10]

---

[7] See E. Conti, *I catasti agrari della repubblica fiorentina e il catasto particellare toscano (secoli XIV–XIX)* (Rome, 1966), p. 19.

[8] On these samples, see Cohn, 'Inventing Braudel's Mountains'.

[9] The literature on the relation between city and countryside is vast. For Florence, see the summaries of these debates in A. Molho, *Florentine Public Finances in the Early Renaissance 1400–1433* (Cambridge, Mass., 1971), pp. 23–5; and G. Dameron, *Episcopal Power and Florentine Society 1000–1320* (Cambridge, Mass., 1991), pp. 7–11.

[10] See Cohn, 'Inventing Braudel's Mountains', p. 404. The rate was calculated by linking the estimo documents with the lira registers. In 1393/4, the estimo base for

Fig. 9.1 The Florentine contado: sample villages

With a statistical method called regression analysis, used frequently by economists, I have sought to untangle the various determinants of the contado's tax rates. First, the tax on the countryside was highly regressive: the wealthier the peasant, the lower the tax rate. Second, larger families generally paid higher rates after adjustment for factors such as wealth. And third, matters such as the status, age, sex or physical condition of household heads made little difference to the tax rates. However, by far the most significant variables were geographic: distance from the city of Florence and, even more importantly, altitude. Mountaineers and those farthest from the city (often, but not always the same) paid much higher tax rates on their property than those closer to the city and in the lowlands.[11]

Nor was this mosaic of different tax rates a discrepancy of the 1393 tax survey (see Fig. 9.2[12]). Matters had been worse in the 1370s, when Florence appropriated 30,000 florins (roughly double the annual estimo assessment for the entire contado of Florence in the 1370s and 1380s[13]) to 'exterminate' the Ubaldini feudal lords, who ruled the upper Mugello.[14] The problem of tax income was further compounded by the fact that Florentine strategies of conquest were never restricted to military might. As Charles de La Roncière has argued, Florence tried as often to buy off its enemies as to defeat them in battle.[15]

In the early 1370s, Florentine policy took two directions: on the one hand, the commune bribed one branch of the Ubaldini lords with

Mangona was 11.96 per cent of its taxable wealth; for Santa Lucia Ognissanti fuori le mura it was 0.366 per cent.

[11] See *ibid*. To define the highlands and lowlands I have used the criteria assumed by Braudel and others: highlands villages as over 500 m and the lowlands as under 200 m. For the present sample, all of the lowland villages are under 100 m in altitude.

[12] The numbers on the *y*-axis are the assessments of taxable wealth found in the estimo records divided by the lira estimo base, which were later assessed by city officials using the village estimo returns.

[13] The rates varied from year–to–year, depending on the coefficients and whether an 'extraordinary' estimo was levied. I have not yet been able to find what the major councils set as the estimo 'distribution' in 1371, but for the next survey in 1383, it was set at 40,000 lire for the next ten years, ASF, PR, 72, 186r–187r, 24 November 1383. In 1373 – the year of the Florentine war against the Ubaldini – the 'ordinary' estimo was 12 soldi per lira and the 'extraordinary' 10 soldi per lira; PR, 61, 121r. Thus, the total expected return from the estimo would have been 44,000 lire or about 15,000 florins.

[14] ASF, PR, 61, 64r–66r, 30 May 1373.

[15] C. M. de La Roncière, 'Indirect Taxes or "Gabelles" at Florence in the Fourteenth Century: The Evolution of Tariffs and Problems of Collection', in Rubinstein (ed.), *Florentine Studies*, pp. 140–92.

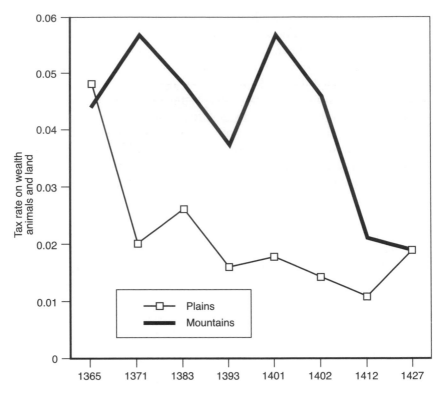

Fig. 9.2 Tax rates on wealth: propertied peasants

considerable sums;[16] on the other hand, it created the peasant commune of the Alpi Fiorentine by appropriating Ubaldini feudal holdings north of Firenzuola.[17] Florence sought to break these peasants' loyalties to their lords by granting them three-year exemptions on taxes and promising to defend them against any feudal obligations or other loans owed to the Ubaldini. In addition, except for members of the Ubaldini family, it pardoned any inhabitant from all previous crimes, including

[16] PR, 61, 101r–102r, 26 August 1373, 'Pro parte Andree, Guidonis, et Ugolini filiorum olim Actaviani de Ubaldinis qui vocantur "dale Pignuole".'

[17] On the Florentine 'new towns', see D. Friedman, *Florentine New Towns: Urban Design in the Late Middle Ages* (Cambridge, 1988); and C. Higounet, 'Les "terre nuove" florentines du XIV siècle', in *Studi in onore di Amintore Fanfani* (Milan, 1962), III, pp. 3–17. On the Ubaldini, see L. Magna, 'Gli Ubaldini del Mugello: una signoria feudale nel contado fiorentino', in *I ceti dirigenti dell'età comunale nei secoli XII e XIII* (Pisa, 1982), pp. 13–66. On the expansion of the commune of the Alpi Fiorentine, see ASF, PR, 61, 39r–42r, 28 April 1373.

homicide. Finally, it gave them the right to write their own statutes (subject of course to Florentine approval).[18]

However, as is made clear in later Florentine legislation (the *provvisioni*) and from calculations within the *estimi* themselves, when one community was granted exemptions, others in the district would have to make up the difference. Such was the case for the rocketing tax rates of 1371 imposed on the neighbouring villages of the communes of Barberino, Mangona, Montecuccolo and others[19] described as *prope Alpi*. Florentine taxation of the later middle ages and the early Renaissance was a zero-sum game. The target figure set by the tax board and approved by the Signoria had to come from somewhere in the contado – Florence's only direct taxpayers.[20] Yet, after the war against the Ubaldini lords of the early 1370s, the punitive tax rates against peasants in general and the mountaineers in particular eased. After the fall of the government of the minor guilds and their Ciompi sympathisers in 1382, the returning oligarchs did not immediately react with punitive fiscal policies; indeed, fiscal burdens on the peasantry lightened. Nor did the government of the Albizzi and the return of old aristocratic families to government in 1393 reverse this trend. Instead, the tax burden on the contado continued to decline and the differential in tax rates between the more privileged plains and the mountaineers slackened.

Yet, despite the continuity in regime and oligarchic dominance in the balance of city power, this trend was not to continue with the turn of the century. Here it was foreign, not internal politics, which proved decisive. The third war with Milan, which began to heat up in the mid-1390s, drained the Florentine state of reserves resulting in a fiscal crisis of unprecedented dimensions.[21] Although certain patricians argued in

---

[18] PR, 61, 39r–42r, 28 April 1373, 'Plebatium Cornaclarii et Camaioris et Bordignani alpium florentinorum'.

[19] See tables in Cohn, 'Inventing Braudel's Mountains'.

[20] See B. Barbadoro, *Le finanze della repubblica fiorentina: imposta diretta e debito pubblico fino all'istituzione del Monte* (Florence, 1929), pp. 78–80.

[21] On the military crisis, see H. Baron, *The Crisis of the Early Italian Renaissance: Civic Humanism and Republican Liberty in an Age of Classicism and Tyranny*, 2 vols. (Princeton, 1955), I, pp. 11–37; on the fiscal consequences, see M. B. Becker, 'Economic Change and the Emerging Florentine Territorial State', *Studies in the Renaissance*, 13 (1986), pp. 7–39; Becker, *Florence in Transition*, II, *Studies in the Rise of the Territorial State* (Baltimore, 1968), pp. 234–6; and Becker, 'Problemi della finanza pubblica fiorentina della seconda metà del Trecento e dei primi del Quattrocento', *Archivio storico italiano*, 123 (1965), p. 435. The trajectory of higher taxation can be plotted from the *Camera del comune* records and the *provvisioni* in the Florentine state archives. They show an increase in the tax rates based on the 'lira' distributions of more than ten times, from 10 soldi per lira in the 1380s to 4.5 florins at its peak in 1398 and 1401. See ASF, CCP, 1–32 (1383–1428).

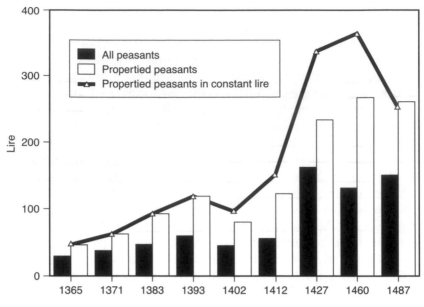

Fig. 9.3 Household wealth: animals and land

Florence's highest councils (the *Consulte e pratiche*) that citizens should once again share in the burden of direct taxes, social and fiscal conservatism prevailed: not only did the city shift its tax burden disproportionately onto the peasantry, the discrepancies in tax rates between the mountains and the plains deepened with the estimi of 1401–2 (see Fig. 9.2).

In terms of tax rates, wealth and, perhaps most importantly, tax inequalities, 1402 was a turning point. In the mosaic of unequal tax constituencies, those on or near the sensitive military frontiers along the northern mountain ridges of the Apennines – that is, many of the villages bought off earlier with tax exemptions in 1373 – were now charged the most. In addition, Florence continued to hammer those villages *prope Alpi* charged at extraordinarily unfavourable rates since the 1370s. From 1398 through 1401, Florence demanded that the Mugello highland village of Mangona hand over 66 per cent of its landed wealth in direct taxes in 1402 alone[22] and that on top of the salt tax, indirect

---

[22] By the 1393 estimo survey, the peasants of Mangona were forced to distribute an estimo that represented 11 per cent of its wealth. In the years 1398 through 1401, the coefficient of the 'extraordinary' estimo was 1.5 florins or 6 lira or six times the 'lira' calculated in 1393. (There were no 'ordinary' estimi for these years as reflected in the

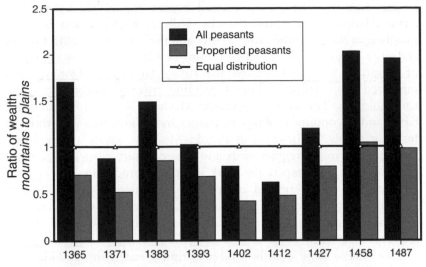

Fig. 9.4 Wealth, 1365–1487. Ratio: mountains to plains

taxes (gabelles) and other charges such as the Podestà's salary, castle duty and munitions, and wax for the Feast of San Giovanni[23] (see Figs. 9.2, 9.3 and 9.4[24]).

Why did Florence suddenly turn its tax policy aggressively against the mountaineers on its extreme northern borders? Thus far, I have found no direct testimony in the deliberations of the estimi, the statutes or the *provvisioni*. However, the logic or illogic of these patterns must have been linked closely with the micro-politics of patronage.[25]

Since Niccolò Machiavelli, historians have stressed the importance of patronage and *clientelismo* for understanding Florentine politics.[26] These

---

Camera del comune payments.) Thus, had these peasants paid their taxes in full, they would have been completely stripped of all their landed possessions by 1400.

[23] The schedules and amounts of these payments can be seen in the exemptions the commune of Florence granted villages in times of difficulty; for Mangona, see ASF, PR, 92, 215r–216r, 18 December 1403.

[24] For the estimi and the catasti, wealth has been calculated on the taxable 'sustanze'.

[25] In the last decades of the fifteenth century in Siena, the regime of Pandolfo Petrucci similarly used fiscal weapons to push small proprietors from the lands of the Sienese contado; see G. Pinto, *Città e spazi economici nell'Italia comunale* (Bologna, 1996), p. 180.

[26] See Niccolò Machiavelli, *Opere*, II, *Istorie fiorentine e altre opere storiche e politiche*, ed. A. Montevecchi (Turin, 1986); and N. Ottokar, *Il comune di Firenze alla fine del Dugento* (Florence, 1926). More recently, see the work of D.V. Kent, 'Dinamica del potere e patronato nella Firenze del Medici', in *I ceti dirigenti nella Toscana del Quattrocento* (Florence, 1987), pp. 49–62; Kent, *The Rise of the Medici: Faction in Florence, 1426–1434* (Oxford, 1978); D. V. Kent and F. W. Kent, *Neighbours and*

studies, however, have concentrated almost exclusively on patron–client relations both within the city walls of Florence and between members of the Florentine ruling elites and their agents in subject towns and cities. Yet as any reader of Florentine *ricordanze* knows, the tentacles of patronage extended beyond the ruling families of Florence and infiltrated those villages where Florentine citizens concentrated their rural holdings. The diary of Bernardo Machiavelli mixed entries of his farm hands' economic dealings, marriages and misfortunes with those of his own family.[27] Giovanni di Pagolo Morelli's advice to his future progeny demanded regular visits and rigorous surveillance over one's rural holdings, to compare the work habits and production of one farm with another and to reward and punish accordingly.[28] And Giovanni Rucellai's 'Il governo della famiglia' dealt exclusively with the ways his sons should administer their rural estates and how they should choose and treat their *fattori*.[29]

This *noblesse oblige* went beyond prescriptive statements and ideology and can be seen in the testamentary concerns of the Florentine elite. For instance, Paliano di Falco Falcucci in his testament of 20 June 1400, recorded in his own hand in his *ricordanze*, left equal amounts for dowries to fund poor girls in the city of Florence and in the Mugello, where he held several *poderi*. He further left sums to clothe the *mezzadri* on his estate in Borgo San Lorenzo after his death.[30] The devotion of Giovanni Rucellai was even more weighted towards the benefit of his peasants in relation to the pious sums he left to causes in the city. He bequeathed a dowry fund to benefit only young girls from the parish of San Piero a Quaracchi, the closer of his two rural estates to the citywalls.[31] In addition, he chose his place of burial not within his own

Neighbourhood in Renaissance Florence: The District of the Red Lion in the Fifteenth Century (New York, 1982); F. W. Kent, *Household and Lineage in Renaissance Florence: The Family Life of the Capponi, Ginori, and Rucellai* (Princeton, 1977); F. W. Kent and Gino Corti (eds.), *Bartolomeo Cederni and his Friends: Letters to an Obscure Florentine* (Florence, 1991); and A. Molho, 'Cosimo de' Medici: "Pater Patriae" or "Padrino"?', *Stanford Italian Review*, 1 (1979), pp. 5–33; R. Bizzocchi, *Chiesa e potere nella Toscana del Quattrocento* (Bologna, 1987); W. J. Connell, 'Changing Patterns of Medicean Patronage: The Florentine Dominion during the Fifteenth Century', in Garfagnini (ed.), *Lorenzo il Magnifico e il suo mondo*, pp. 87–107

[27] Bernardo Machiavelli, *Libro di Ricordi*, ed. C. Olschki (Florence, 1954).

[28] Giovanni di Pagolo Morelli, *Ricordi*, ed. V. Branca (Florence, 1956), p. 234.

[29] A. Perosa (ed.), *Giovanni Rucellai ed il suo Zibaldone*, I, '*Il Zibaldone Quaresimale*' (London, 1960), pp. 3–8.

[30] Paliano di Falco Falcucci, 'Ricordanze' (1382–1406), in ASF, CS, ser. II, 7, 59v.

[31] *Il Zibaldone*, p. 26: 'E' quali f.60 si debbono distribuire in perpetuo per la detta Arte [del Cambio] . . . E il resto per insino alla somma di f.60 si debbino chonvertire in maritare fanculle, dando l.40 per ciaschuna; le quali fanculle sieno nate e allevate nel

urban parish of San Pancrazio but in this rural parish.[32] By Rucellai's account, these ties of affection ran freely in both directions. His daily jottings announce proudly that, since the 'beauty and gentility of the Rucellai gardens gave [his peasants as much] fame', as they did to the Rucellai, 'of their own free will' the forty-three men of this village gathered in their parish church and voted to maintain these gardens at their own expense.[33]

Thus, when fiscal pressures demanded extraordinary levels of taxation, as in 1371 or 1402, those villages where patricians held their estates would be the ones offered tax advantages at the expense of others further removed, where Florentines possessed few landed properties if any at all and whose surplus hardly affected Florentine private interests.

Such concerns over the economic fortune and security of rural holdings may have proven even more problematic in the late Trecento than at any other time. After all, this was a period of acute labour shortages, especially of agricultural labour following in the wake of the plagues. Faced with low cereal prices and high wages, how were urban proprietors to maintain their rural investments in the plains and nearby hills? The *Capi di famiglia* reveals one solution practised at least since the 1370s: it was fiscal policy.

Radically inequitable tax rates forced highlanders more than others to forgo their independence and to abandon their homesteads. At the same time, the lowlands near the city were the very zones where taxes were low and where urban investment and the *mezzadria* system were expanding in the second half of the fourteenth century.[34] As repeated inducements passed by the Florentine ruling councils reveal, oligarchs from the city of Florence found themselves in dire need of agricultural

popolo di Sancto Piero a Quarachi, delle più miserabili, chome parrà a' chonsoli . . . e allo abate della Badia di Settimo . . . e a uno de' discendenti del detto Govanni . . . gravando le loro choscienzie in piglare buone informazioni delle più miserabili'.

32 *Ibid.*, p. 122. Similarly, various members of the Sirigatti family who died during the plague of 1417 chose to be buried in the parish of their rural estates in the Badia di Passignano; C. Bec (ed.), *Il libro degli affari proprii di casa de Lapo di Giovanni Niccolini de' Sirigatti* (Paris, 1969), p. 135.

33 *Il Zibaldone*, p. 23.

34 See C. Klapisch-Zuber, 'Mezzadria e insediamenti rurali alla fine del medio evo', in *Civiltà ed economia agricola in Toscana nei secc. XIII–XV: problemi della vita delle campagne nel tardo medioevo* (Pistoia, 1981), p. 154. Note also the land strategies of the Sirigatti family, whose purchases of rural real estate increased during the last decade of the Trecento and first two decades of the Quattrocento; C. Bec, 'Introduction', *Il libro degli affari*, p. 19. For the period between 1427 and 1469, the greatest increase in the *mezzadria* system was in the quarter of Santa Maria Novella, where the percentage of *poderi* with *mezzadria* contracts increased from 22.4 to 32.4 per cent; Herlihy and Klapisch-Zuber, *Les Toscans*, pp. 268–72.

labourers by the 1370s. With increasing regularity, the Signoria passed tax exemptions and moratoria on debts, first to induce foreign agricultural labourers to settle in the Florentine contado,[35] and, by 1399, to entice back Florentine agricultural labourers who had earlier skipped the border fleeing their debts and the Florentine tax official.[36] The earliest of these laws restricted exemptions to those who would work the land *ad medium vel affictu* and not as independent proprietors.[37]

Still, regardless of the commune's logic, another logic prevailed on the land. As might be expected, peasants were hard pressed to pay, and many did not. Their first means of resistance was with their feet. They did not move downward to greener valleys or to Florence – as historians of rural migration would have us believe and as the Florentine ruling class may have wished.[38] The mountain peasants instead migrated upward. Fleeing Florentine taxation altogether, they crossed the border into the higher villages of the Pistoiese (not burdened by the estimo[39]) and more significantly into villages in the Bolognese Apennines.[40]

Indeed, 1402 was the pinnacle of migration out of the Florentine contado and the nadir of in-migration to the city of Florence (see Fig. 9.5[41]). For a mountain village such as Mangona, taxation appears to

---

[35] ASF, PR, 52, 34v, 8 August 1364; PR, 72, 171r, 20 October 1383; PR, 74, 204r–205r, 8 December 1385; PR, 80, 197r–198r, 2 December 1391.

[36] ASF, PR, 88, 226r–227r, 7 November 1399, 'Laboratores absentes possint redire': 'Laboratoribus terre jam absentibus propter debita succurrere cupientes cum etiam ex reditu ipsorum videatur utilitas varijs respectibus perveniret.'

[37] ASF, PR, 52, 34v.

[38] More generally, see F. Braudel, *The Mediterranean and the Mediterranean World in the Age of Philip II*, trans. S. Reynolds (New York, 1966 [Paris, 1949]), I, pp. 44 and 47; and the remarks of P. P. Viazzo, *Upland Communities: Environment, Population and Social Structure in the Alps since the Sixteenth Century* (Cambridge, 1989), pp. 1–15. For Florence, see La Roncière, *Prix et salaires*, pp. 661–80.

[39] Indeed, the *provvisioni* to attract foreign agricultural labour into the contado and district of Florence specified that immigration to the former contadi of Pistoia and Volterra would not result in forgiving past debts and taxes. For these *provvisioni*, see note 35.

[40] For the estimo of 1393, it is possible to trace the final destinations of many of these Florentine mountain dwellers who fled the tax officials. Some of the villages recorded in the registers of these 'usciti' are: Quinzano (622m), Castel dell'Alpi (694 m), Sant'Andrea in the Val di Sambro (589 m), San Damiano (691 m), Baragazza (675 m), Qualto (762 m), Bruscoli (765 m) and Pietramala (851 m – then, within the confines of the Bolognese state).

[41] Between 1383 and 1412, the estimi allow the historian to chart the migratory movements of the villagers. The estimi divided their ledgers into four categories: 'stanti', 'venuti', 'usciti' and 'morti', that is, those in the village who had stayed, come, left and died. With the 'venuti' the officials consistently specified the village where they had last resided. With the 'usciti', the places of emigration given were

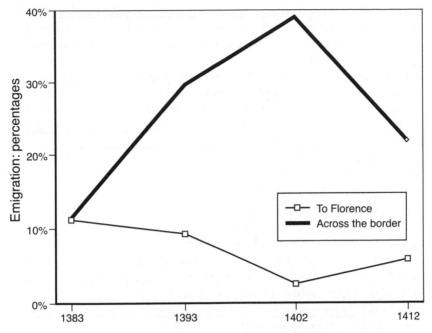

Fig. 9.5 Peasant migration: percentage of emigration

have been a more crucial variable in its late medieval demographic history than even the plague. This super-taxed commune experienced the sharpest decline in population of any of the villages I have sampled. In 1365 it was one of the largest villages in the contado, twice the size of Sesto, with well over 200 families (or nearly 1000 individuals);[42] by 1401 it had shrunk to a quarter of its post-plague population, with eighty-six families and 278 persons. After the further onslaughts of war and migration in 1402, its population was cut in half again, falling to its

not as precise, but often the villages were listed, even when the peasants moved across state borders.

[42] No returns survive for the church (*plebis*) of San Martino a Sesto in 1356, but in the next survey, of 1365, it posted 125 households. The disparity in the population of Mangona relative to Sesto and other large villages in the Florentine lowlands may have been even greater before the Black Death of 1348. In the *provvisioni* registers of that year, Mangona was the only village singled out as particularly badly struck by the pestilence ('mortiferam pestem') and in need of special consideration. The *provvisione* claimed that three-quarters or more of its population had been wiped out. See ASF, PR, 36, 8v–10v, 12 September 1348.

lowest ebb in 1412 counting only forty-seven families and 138 individuals or about a quarter the size of Sesto, which had been able largely to preserve its post-1348 population over the course of the later half of the fourteenth century.

From indications of propertied wealth, population, family size and skewed sex-ratios, the Alpi Fiorentine appear to have been headed towards ecological disaster during the late decades of the fourteenth and the first years of the fifteenth centuries. The exodus from the mountain hamlets meant even higher tax burdens on those who stayed behind. As a consequence, the years 1401–6 saw a new wave of resistance. This time, the effects went beyond demography. Assisted by the invading troops from Milan and rebel outposts in the Montagna Pistoiese, peasant uprisings spread across the Apennines from the Alpi Fiorentine to the Romagna zones recently incorporated into the Florentine territory and then down the Casentino highlands of Arezzo.

Unlike the much better-known urban artisan revolt a generation earlier – the Revolt of the Ciompi, 1378 – these peasant revolts were successful. Again, unlike the Revolt of the Ciompi, for reasons not yet clear to me, these events have left few traces in contemporary histories, and with the exception of the Pistoiese revolt, which began as an urban factional feud among patricians in 1401, these waves of insurrection remain completely unknown to present-day historians.[43]

But the criminal courts and the day-to-day record-books of Florence's highest councils, the *provvisioni,* reported them in great detail. Between 1403 and 1406, these legislative acts became transformed. Previously, petitions from peasant communes rarely exceeded eight a year (less than 3 per cent of the Priors' case loads[44]), whereas between 1403 and 1406 certain sessions of the *Tre Maggiori* were dominated by negotiations and grants of tax relief to peasant communes largely located in the traditional Florentine contado. The usual day-to-day matters of Florentine citizens – petitions over forced loans, bankruptcies, and pressing governmental matters such as how much to feed the town's lions – suddenly had to be shoved aside to evaluate peasant demands.[45]

---

[43] On Ricciardo Cancellieri's urban revolt in Pistoia and the capture of Sambuca in the Montagna Pistoiese, see G. Chittolini, 'Ricerche sull'ordinamento territoriale del dominio fiorentino agli inizi del secolo XV', in Chittolini, *La formazione dello stato regionale e le istituzioni del contado: secoli XIV e XV* (Turin, 1978), p. 313; and Stephen Milner in chapter 15, this volume.

[44] For instance, in 1393, when war was beginning to break out with Milan, the councils approved only seven petitions from the rural villages of Florence's hinterland.

[45] See for instance the session of the Council of the Popolo on 20 December 1403 (ASF, LF, 47, 174r–v) when fifteen of the nineteen petitions brought before the councils of the people and the commune were from rural villages asking for tax

In these years tax exemptions were granted to over 200 rural villages, and some of these villages such as Casaglia and the communes of the Alpi Fiorentine appeared as recipients of Florence's benevolence as many as nine times. Such immunities and reductions of past taxes then spread from the north-eastern frontier of the Florentine contado, east-ward and southward to other war-weary, depopulated and impover-ished villages along the Florentine periphery.

These exemptions, moreover, cut a distinctive topography. They came from those places most overburdened by Florence's tax policies of the last years of the fourteenth century: first, mountain communities and second, places distant from the capital, Florence. In terms of distance, the petitions plot a ring around the Florentine contado. The only exception was the rich alluvial plains of the lower Valdarno, from Prato to Gambassi[46] (see Fig. 9.6). On the other hand, the densest concentration of peasant demands centred on the highest and furthest-removed outposts of the Florentine contado: first the Alpi Fiorentine, next the Montanea Florentina on the back slopes of the Pratomagno, and then the Chianti mountains mostly beyond the borders of the present-day *provincia* of Firenze. Few places close to the city or in the plains and lower hills appear.[47]

The character of and reasons for these exemptions differed widely over the mountainous zones of the Florentine periphery. The first to appear came from the Alpi Fiorentine and other villages in the Mugello highlands such as Casaglia and Castro, which since the 1370s had shouldered the heaviest tax burdens found in my samples. The language and substance of these exemptions are completely new. For instance, when war with Milan had earlier flared over the northern mountain passes in 1393, Florence had granted immunities to seven communities. Though formulaic, the reasons for these exemptions were spelled out clearly − 'impotence, poverty and for the damages suffered during the war' − and because of Florentine *clementia* and *misericordia*, these rural communities were granted exemptions from some of their back taxes and given extended deadlines for paying others.[48]

---

exemptions. Most of these villages were within the traditional boundaries of the contado, and all fifteen were approved.

[46] Empoli appears four times between 1400 and 1405; Pontormo and its parishes, three times.

[47] The closest village to the city that petitioned successfully for tax exemptions in the period 1400−6 was the ancient hillside parish of Rignano (about 20 km from the city); ASF, PR, 95, 169r, 8 August 1406.

[48] See for instance the long list of parishes − one group from the Casentino, the other from the Chianti − which petitioned for and won tax relief in a provision of 20 May 1405, ASF, PR, 94, 31v−35v.

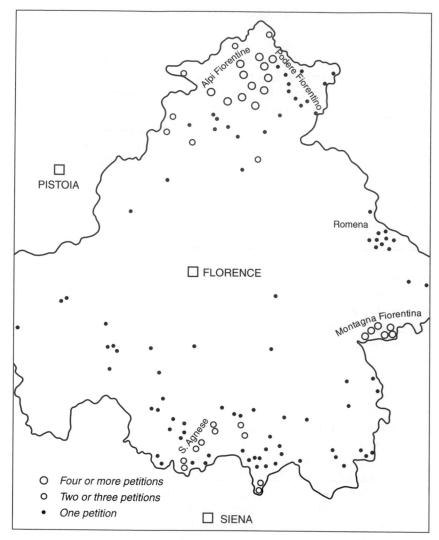

Fig. 9.6 Tax exemptions, 1400–6

By contrast, the exemptions of 1403 did not arise from the state's clemency or *gratia* but derived from the villagers' positions of strength and from negotiations with peasant *ambaxiatores*.[49] Moreover, this wave

---

[49] I know of no recent discussions of these peasant ambassadors and their negotiations. For contemporary references see Franco Sacchetti, *Trecentonovelle*, ed. A. Lanza (Florence, 1975), no. XXXI, 'Due ambasciadori di Casentino sono mandati al vescovo Guido d'Arezzo'.

of grants went far beyond the one- to three-year exemptions on certain taxes or rescheduled payments. Places like Castro, Casaglia, Cavrenno, Cornacchiaia and Pietramala (in the Alpi Fiorentine) negotiated successfully for exemptions of up to fifteen years on all gabelles and estimi and won promises to be protected from past debts of any kind. Second, these villagers were absolved of any crimes or acts of rebellion 'from all and sundry acts of war and rebellion, from plunder, incendiary deeds and any other excessive crimes of violence and malice'. Further, in grants made to the villages of Castro and Casaglia, the peasant ringleaders were singled out for special treatment, but not of the usual sort seen in the criminal records – death by torture, live burials and the confiscation or destruction of all their properties.[50] Instead, after being absolved of any crimes of rebellion including murder, they were granted lifetime rights to carry arms anywhere in the Florentine state (a privilege usually reserved only for the most powerful families of the city) and the right to pass these rights down through their male lineages. These peasant insurgents were absolved of personal debts going back as far as 1394, and for themselves and their families they gained exemptions from all taxes of any sort. Moreover, better than the humanist-statesman Leonardo Bruni (who was later granted tax exemption for life for his services to the Florentine state), these peasants were able to pass these special privileges down to their children and afterwards through their male lineages in perpetuity. Finally, the Florentine state granted the peasant leaders (some of whom had earlier fled Florentine taxation and had migrated to villages in the Bolognese Apennines) lifetime sinecures and salaries as 'stipendiaries' of the Florentine state.[51]

Along with the criminal acts of the Podestà, the Captain of the Popolo and the new Vicariate courts of the Florentine territory, the *provvisioni* report other peasant rebellions in 1402 and 1403. These range in military importance from the siege and destruction of the city of Firenzuola,[52] the building of new military bastions in the Alpi,[53] the torching of houses, lands and villages throughout the Alpi and the

---

[50] These penalties were discussed in chapter 6 of my *Women in the Streets: Essays on Sex and Power in Renaissance Italy* (Florence, 1996).

[51] ASF, PR, 92, 87v–90v, 22 April 1403. See also, PR, 92, 248v–251r, 22 December 1403; PR, 93, 4r–5v, 18 April 1404; *ibid.*, 46v–47v, 9 June 1404.

[52] ASF, Cap. Pop., 2199, 45r–47r, 1403; Cap. Pop., 2207, 3v–6v; 26r–v; 37v–39v; 58r–60r; ASF, Pod., 3886, 9r–10v, 12 February 1402.

[53] In addition to the criminal sentences above, see ASF, Cap. Pop., 2199, 34r–38v, 23 May 1403; ASF, Pod., 3886, 28v–29r, 1 April 1403; *ibid.*, 84r–85r, 22 December 1402.

Podere Fiorentino,[54] the capturing of old feudal castles such as that of
Castel Pagano north of Susinana,[55] to numerous cattle raids and
kidnapping used to acquire money and materiel for the peasants' war
efforts.[56]

While the *provvisioni* and criminal records show the peasants on the
northern borders of the area *prope Alpi*, the Alpi Fiorentine and the
Podere Fiorentino to have been the most militant and successful of the
insurgents, tax breaks given in the Casentino were less extensive and
came about for different reasons. Here, rebellion was more a feudal
reaction. Unlike the Ubaldini, who had been crushed by Florentine
forces in the 1370s,[57] the Casentino feudal lords, the Ubertini and
Guidi counts, remained entrenched in their territories and could still
call on the support of their peasant *fideles*, despite the recent sale of
their castles to Florence.[58] With the support of Bolognese and
Milanese troops, these counts reconquered their old feudal territories.
And, in 1404, the Florentine state had to buy them back again.[59] In
addition to handing over large sums of money to the Ubertini,
Florence also had to grant tax exemptions to the mountain villagers of
the Montagna Fiorentina who had battled against Florentine rule and
its high direct taxes.[60]

The exemptions given to the Chianti peasants along the southernmost mountains of the Florentine territory form yet a third group.
These begin later, appearing in 1404 with the intensification of war
between Florence and Siena.[61] Here, the formulaic phrases of pity and

[54] See ASF, PR, 92, 87v–90v, 22 April 1403.
[55] For the castle at Mangona and other 'bastie' in the Alpi Fiorentine, see ASF, Cap.
Pop., 2183, 31r–v, 1402; Cap. Pop., 2199, 34r–38v, 23 May 1403; for Susinana and
Pagano, Cap. Pop., 2206, 10r–11r, 16 August 1403; *ibid.*, 17v–19v, 16 August 1403;
Cap. Pop., 2203, 140r–141r, 1 August 1403.
[56] ASF, Cap. Pop., 2188, 20r–21v, 2 November 1402; *ibid.*, 70r–73r; Cap. Pop.,
2192,15r–v, 10 January 1402; Cap. Pop., 2203, 12r–14r, 18 April 1403; Pod., 3886,
67r–68r, 2 May 1403; ASF, Pod., 3856, 10r–11r, 4 August 1402.
[57] In the sentences and inquisitions of the *Capitano del popolo* and the Podestà for the
first years of the fifteenth century, members of the Ubaldini clan still appear as
among those charged with conspiracy and insurrection. But, unlike the lords of the
Casentino, Florence did not grant them special rights, money, tax exemptions or
renunciations of capital punishments.
[58] See ASF, PR, 90, 56r–57v, 7 April 1401; PR, 91, 160r–162r, 19 October 1402; PR,
92, 38r–39r, 26 April 1402; *ibid.*, 113r–115r, 27 August 1403.
[59] ASF, PR, 93, 27v–28v, 19 April 1404.
[60] ASF, Pod., 2192, 28v–30r, 26 February 1402. From 1374, Florence had imposed the
estimo on the 'homines, fideles seu vassalli dicti comitis Roberti', ASF, PR, 62,
61v–62r, 16 June 1374.
[61] The first of these petitions dates from 22 December 1404, ASF, PR, 93, 178r–180v.
It rescheduled and reduced the payments for a number of parishes within and around

supplication appear once again in the place of negotiation. But these petitions do not reflect a return to the formulaic exemptions that had sprinkled the *provvisioni* before the northern peasant insurrections of 1400. First, Florence doled out far more exemptions and rescheduled more peasant debts than at any time found in these records before 1427; second, the rhetoric of the Chianti peasants' petitions differed from those prior to 1400. The Chianti petitions of 1404–6 not only pointed to the destruction wrought by war and booty as the reasons for needing tax cuts; they also charged the Florentine state directly as the source of their misery, claiming that they had suffered as much 'from the vexations of overzealous and dishonest tax collectors as they had at the hands of enemy troops'.[62] Because of these disasters, these peasants explained that they were forced either 'to wander through the world begging with their families or to die in prison', neither of which, they explained, 'would be of utility to the Florentine Commune'. They then threatened to leave their homesteads, fleeing into the lands of Florence's enemy Siena, and presented the Florentine oligarchs with an ultimatum: either they should cancel these peasants' earlier tax debts and penalties or Florence would lose these peasants altogether as taxpayers.[63]

The frequent passage of Florentine laws over the past two decades makes it clear that such threats would have touched sensitive nerves in the highest chambers of the Florentine state. As repeated legislation passed to lure back agricultural labourers and to attract new foreign ones make clear, the city fathers had become painfully aware of the encroaching demographic and ecological crises in the outlying zones of

the *plebis* San Leolino, 'along the confines of the city of Siena, where war was raging'.

[62] Indeed, new provisions were passed in these years to regulate more closely the behaviour of these Florentine 'nuntii'. See, for instance, ASF, PR, 90, 429v–431r, 21 March 1401, 'Pro taxatione comitatus'; PR, 92, 274v–275v, 28 December 1403.

[63] See the 1404 petition of the parishes of San Marcellino and San Polo in Chianti, ASF, PR, 93, 218v–222r, 'Plurium populorum plebatus Sancti Marcellini et plebatus Sancti poli de partibus chiantis': 'de ipsis infrascripis populis alterum eligere aut se absentare et cum eorum familiis per mundum pergere mendicando aut in carceribus mori quod ut putatur esse contra voluntatem dominationis vostre. Et quod propter exactorum vexationes multa danna sine ultilitate comunis florentie eis inferuntur.' And also the petitions of 21 February 1404, again to the parishes of San Marcellino, PR, 93, 251r–v: 'sine utilitate comunis florentie cum eorum maximis expensis et dannis ab exactoribus comunis florentie vexantur et molestantur . . . Et illi qui ibidem remanserunt cogentur et se absentare timentes in carceribus mori.' According to Pinto, *Città e spazi economici*, p. 62, similar threats can be found in the post-plague peasant petitions in Siena, Genoa and elsewhere; however, the timing in the appearance of such threats has yet to be charted.

the Florentine contado.[64] The demographic context mixed with war and peasant insurrection had caused Florence to come to an about-face in the control of its contado.

The war with Milan and the waves of peasant rebellion and tax protest that followed, moreover, had deeper and longer-lasting consequences than tax concessions and exemptions won by individual peasants or particular villages. First, the assessments of 1401/2 marked the watershed in community tax inequalities; afterwards, not only did tax rates decline, the difference in rates from village to village narrowed progressively until the catasto of 1427, when universal guidelines were instituted throughout Florence's contado (see Fig. 9.2). Nor would the Medici's system of clientage reverse this cardinal principle of taxation as it did for those who resided in the city.[65] The rise of the Medici in 1434 appears not to have affected long-term demographic and economic trends for the Florentine peasants in the least. Furthermore, as these graphs suggest, the catasto of 1427 did not spring solely from the political, military and fiscal crises that ensued from a new wave of Milanese wars in 1424. The attack on unequal taxation (at least in the countryside or more precisely in Florence's traditional contado) originated with the mountain revolts of 1401–6.

These events marked other long-term consequences for Florentine

---

[64] See ASF, LF, 47, 5 April 1400–1 April 1404. In these years, slightly more than three-quarters of all the petitions (939 of 1232) were approved by the Councils of the *Popolo* and the *Comune*, but 97 per cent of the petitions from rural communes were approved (91 of 94). Of the three rural petitions rejected ('displacuit'), two were from the *districtus*, the communes of the Valdinievole and Volterra, and the other came from the ancient *pieve* of Ricasoli, relatively near the city of Florence: LF, 47, 160r, 30 August 1403; *ibid.*, 41r, 30 December 1400; and *ibid.*, 22r, 23 August 1400, respectively. Of those petitions approved, some, such as one from 'Plurium populorum plebatus Sancti Marcellini et plebatus Sancti poli de partibus chiantis', comprised and listed individually the grievances and pleas of as many as twenty separate communities and parishes, PR, 93, 218v–222r, 21 February 1404.

[65] For the effects of Medici clientelage on taxation see Kent and Kent, *Neighbours and Neighbourhood*; E. Conti, *L'imposta diretta a Firenze nel Quattrocento (1427–1494)* (Rome, 1984); A. Molho, 'Fisco e società a Firenze nel quattrocento (a proposito di una ricerca di Elio Conti)', *Società e storia*, 8(30) (1985), pp. 929–36; Molho, 'Fisco ed economia a Firenze alla viglia del Concilio', *Archivio storico italiano*, 148 (1990), pp. 807–44; Molho, 'The State and Public Finance: A Hypothesis Based on the History of Late Medieval Florence', in J. Kirshner (ed.), *The Origins of the State in Italy, 1300–1600* (Chicago, 1996), pp. 87–135; G. Ciappelli, 'Il cittadino fiorentino e il fisco alla fine del Trecento e nel corso del Quattrocento: uno studio di due casi', *Società e storia*, 46 (1989), pp. 823–72. On Medici patronage more generally, see F. W. Kent and P. Simons (eds.), *Patronage, Art and Society in Renaissance Italy* (Oxford, 1987); and D. V. Kent, *The Rise of the Medici*.

peasants. From its nadir in 1402, household size, population and, most notably, wealth, as measured by the assessments of landed property and animals, began to climb throughout the contado (see Figs. 9.3 and 9.4). This was especially true for propertied peasants. In the space of less than sixty years, the average values of their holdings more than trebled in nominal terms from 80 to 267 lire. Relative to the price of grain, they increased still more, by three and a half times. Nor was this increase simply an artifact of inflated land values in this deflationary epoch of more careful tax accounting. The survey of 1401/2 was the first to institute the itemisation of all peasant holdings, specifying the land's measurements and contiguous boundaries as opposed to a single figure for the property's value. Yet, for the reasons outlined above, this date witnessed the low point of peasant well-being from the Black Death through the early Renaissance. Nor did one of the most painstaking of tax surveys from the entire history of preindustrial Florence, the catasto of 1427,[66] mark a sudden surge in peasant property values that might have resulted from more scrupulous care in assessment along with the curbing of corruption on the part of tax officials in the countryside and the city.[67] Instead, from 1402 to 1460 the average property values, at least of landed peasants, show a steady linear progression.[68]

These increases in peasant property values from the turn of the century to 1460 were not, however, evenly distributed throughout the contado; rather the mountaineers benefited the most – especially those who, in the early crisis years of the fifteenth century, were without any holdings (see Fig. 9.3[69]). These trends run contrary to the near timeless

[66] See Herlihy and Klapisch-Zuber, *Les Toscans et leurs familles*, pp. 77–106.

[67] See the cases from the vicarial courts of the Florentine territory, ASF, GA, no. 76, 479v–487r, 30 August 1427; and *ibid.*, 562r–v, 20 December 1427, where the vicariates of the Valdinievole and Marti (in the former contado of Pisa) cracked down on five rural communes, and over fifteen men were charged with taking bribes from men in these communities in exchange for lower estimo assessments. From these records, such corruption appears to have been a long-established practice in the outlying areas of the Florentine periphery. See also Herlihy and Klapisch-Zuber, *Les Toscans et leurs familles*, pp. 71–2.

[68] These advances in the wealth of peasants do not appear to be a simple trick of the documentation whereby government officials may have inflated peasants' property values as a means of collecting more taxes. Parallel to the rise in tax values, I have found a similar rise in the values of peasant dowries in the plains and mountains of the quarter of Santa Maria Novella. These dowries were found in notarial documents. See my 'Marriage in the Mountains: The Florentine Territorial State, 1348–1500', in T. Dean and K. J. P. Lowe (eds.), *Marriage in Italy, 1300–1650* (Cambridge, 1998), pp. 174–96.

[69] The horizontal line indicates an equal distribution of wealth between the mountain and plains villages found in my samples. If the mountain bar at a certain date is under

picture of mountain poverty painted by Fernand Braudel and affirmed more recently in the writings of Giovanni Cherubini for the mountains of Tuscany from the later middle ages through the early modern period.[70] In the earliest post-plague records, peasants in the mountains were more than one-and-a-half times as wealthy as those in the plains. But with war, migration and unequal taxation, the mountaineers' property values declined absolutely and relative to the plains through much of the late Trecento so that by 1402 their worth amounted to less than half that of plainsmen (see Fig. 9.4).

Did these ups and downs result from climate changes or plagues that may have destroyed men and crops more in the mountains than in the valleys? Perhaps. But it is man-made forces that emerge from the documentation: war, which ravaged the mountains; and, more significantly, Florence's differential taxation, resulting from its deep-seated micro-politics of *clientelismo,* which hit the mountain communes hardest. As taxes increased, the poverty of the mountains deepened both in absolute terms and relative to the more favoured peasants further down the slopes and nearer to the city of Florence (see Figs. 9.3 and 9.4).

These differentials in the timing and geographical patterns of recovery suggest that early fifteenth-century prosperity in the Florentine country-side was not simply the result of that epoch's most dramatic exogenous variable – plague.[71] In other areas of Europe, population began to recover economically from the initial shock waves and dislocation of the plague by the 1370s.[72] The heavy burden of Florentine tax policy not only retarded the economic recovery of its contado; it led to a further emptying of the countryside, especially in the mountain districts.

After the peasant uprisings of 1401–6, these patterns changed. But less harsh taxation did not improve economic conditions evenly

---

this line, it means the taxable wealth of mountain communities at that point in time is less than the wealth of the villages in the plains by the ratio indicated on the y-axis.

[70] In addition, Tuscan historians have argued that throughout the Quattrocento peasants lived in misery. See note 4, above, and in particular Mazzi and Raveggi, *Gli uomini e le cose.* Their research has used records such as inventories more to tell stories of individual misery than to compare changes in peasant poverty or well-being over time.

[71] On plague as an 'exogenous variable', see B. Campbell, 'Population-Pressure, Inheritance and the Land Market in a Fourteenth-Century Peasant Community', in R. M. Smith (ed.), *Land, Kinship and Life-Cycle* (Cambridge, 1984), pp. 87–135, esp. pp. 120, 127; and Herlihy, *The Black Death.*

[72] Campbell, 'Population-pressure', pp. 122–3; J. Hatcher, *Plague, Population and the English Economy 1348–1530* (London, 1977), pp. 100–1; Hatcher, 'England in the Aftermath of the Black Death'; A.R. Bridbury, 'The Black Death', *Economic History Review,* 2nd ser., 26(4) (1973), pp. 584–92.

throughout the Florentine countryside; household wealth increased faster in the mountains than in the plains, especially when all peasant holdings are taken into account. In 1412, the worth of plains peasants was almost double that of the mountaineers. By 1460, the relations had reversed: mountaineers were twice as wealthy as the plainsmen. At the same time, these graphs show a steady progression in the worth of propertied peasants. By 1460, average household wealth in the mountains surpassed that of the lower valleys for the first time. Nor did these increases in property holdings merely reflect an increase in the prices of property with no corresponding relationship to the income or produce from the property. First, land prices remained stable throughout the first half of the fifteenth century or may have even dropped in Tuscany as well as across Europe.[73] Second, with the catasto of 1427 (and probably earlier), the tax officials calculated property values, not by the notarised prices that properties fetched, but from assessments of the properties' annual production in grain, wine and other commodities.[74]

Certainly, mountaineers must have prospered from other factors during the first sixty years of the fifteenth century. From the French Cévennes[75] to the Val Demone in north-east Sicily,[76] highlanders benefited from rising meat prices and crops other than cereals common to the lowlands. But economic trends cannot by themselves explain the mountain prosperity of the Renaissance. For Florence the decline in warfare favoured the mountain zones first and foremost, since earlier the mountains had been the battlefields of the late Trecento, causing mountaineers to bear a disproportionate brunt of the damages to crops, buildings and manpower.[77]

---

[73] I do not know of any price series for land in Tuscany for the later Middle Ages and Renaissance. On the low profits from land from the late fourteenth through the early sixteenth centuries, see R. Goldthwaite, *Private Wealth in Renaissance Florence: A Study of Four Families* (Princeton, 1968), pp. 246–51; and, for Europe more generally, see B. H. Slicher Van Bath, *The Agricultural History of Western Europe, 500–1850*, trans. O. Ordish (London, 1963), pp. 140–5, who recorded the fall of land rents through 1450.

[74] Herlihy and Klapisch-Zuber, *Les Toscans et leurs familles*, pp. 9–67.

[75] Le Roy Ladurie, *Les paysans de Languedoc*, I, pp. 167–8.

[76] S. R. Epstein, *An Island for Itself: Economic Development and Social Change in Late Medieval Sicily* (Cambridge, 1993), p. 220.

[77] On the chronology of warfare in late medieval Tuscany, see Molho, 'Fisco ed economia a Firenze alla vigilia del Concilio', pp. 824–7, for warfare in the 1430s and 1440s in the Florentine territory; and Molho, 'The State and Public Finance', p. 123, for the years 1470–90. Also, see the remarks of Giovanni Rucellai, *Zibaldone*, p. 122: 'E per chagone che lla nostra città era stata in ghuerra e in grave spesa anni trenta, cioè dal 1423 al 1453 . . . che ssiamo stati in tranquilla pace anni 20 di tenpo, cioè dal 1453 al 1473, eccetto un anno solo del 1467, ch'avemmo ghuerra in Romangna.'

Furthermore, taxes, once the bane of the mountaineers' existence
and the reason for their mass emigration of the late Trecento, may have
come to favour them over valley peasants after the catasto of 1427. As
mentioned earlier, one of the long-term effects of this tax reform, not to
be dismantled by the Medici, was a system of taxation that burdened all
households in the Florentine contado according to the same principles
and rates. But a decline in the rigour and efficiency of tax collecting,
especially of liquid and mobile wealth, may well have favoured the
remote mountain communities:[78] first because of their inaccessibility;
and second because a greater proportion of the mountaineers' wealth
relative to that of the valley peasants was invested in livestock more
difficult to find and to assess.[79] Thus, the mountaineers may well have
been prospering through the first half of the fifteenth century even
more than their tax returns tell!

In conclusion, social, economic and demographic trends in the Florentine countryside appear to have been oblivious to fundamental shifts
in political regimes of the early Renaissance – the oligarchic consolidation of power in 1393 and the rise of the Medici in 1434. Yet, neither a
hidden history of micro-parasitic struggle, nor a Braudelian division of
historical time, in which affairs of state dance on the surface of history,
can explain the timing or geography of these long-term trends. Instead,
politics – war, taxation, patronage and even (dare I say) class struggle
between the mountains and the Florentine oligarchy[80] – constituted the
immediate causes that explain why 1402 and not 1348 or 1375 (as in
England) was the nadir in peasant well-being, and why mountaineers
and not lowland peasants made the most remarkable strides in the
accumulation of wealth over the fifteenth century.

[78] See chapter 4 by Giuseppe Petralia in this collection, and for the sixteenth century
and the problems of taxing and ruling mountain dwellers, see C. J. Wickham, *The
Mountains and the City: The Tuscan Apennines in the Early Middle Ages* (Oxford, 1988),
pp. 370–80.
[79] See Braudel, The Mediterranean, I, pp. 39–41; and Wickham, *The Mountains and the
City* (Oxford, 1988), pp. 349–80, on Florence's difficulties disciplining the local
elites in the Garfagnana highlands during the sixteenth century.
[80] See my *Women in the Streets*, ch. 6.

CHAPTER 10

FLORENTINES AND THE COMMUNITIES OF THE TERRITORIAL STATE

PATRIZIA SALVADORI

The study of urban history has increasingly focused on the reconstruction of ties of kinship, neighbourhood and the issue of social patronage generally. Although the conclusions reached have often differed, the result of such study has been the emergence of an image of Renaissance man bound into a multitude of social network systems that fundamentally conditioned both the practice and conceptualisation of daily life. More recently, patronage studies have moved beyond the walls of Florence itself to consider the city's territorial state, paying particular attention to the complex interrelations between the Florentines and the inhabitants of the subject communities.[1] With the territorial expansion of the Florentine *dominio*, the numbers of Florentines in the cities and rural communities of Tuscany increased with respect to the recent past. Significantly, many Florentines occupied positions as resident judicial officials in the subject towns for a period of several months, whilst merchants and rich bankers invested capital in the fertile Arno valley and along the coast, or built their country retreats in the areas from which their families originated. Many of these Florentines demonstrated their growing interest in the territories by establishing private networks with the indigenous populations and they were often in a position to

---

[1] See R. Black, 'Lorenzo and Arezzo', and S. J. Milner, 'Lorenzo and Pistoia: Peacemaker or Partisan?', both in M. Mallet and N. Mann (eds.), *Lorenzo the Magnificent, Culture and Politics* (London, 1996), pp. 217–34, 235–52, respectively; W. J. Connell, 'Clientelismo e stato territoriale. Il potere fiorentino a Pistoia nel XV secolo, *Società e storia*, 14 (1991), pp. 524–43; Connell, 'Changing Patterns of Medicean Patronage. The Florentine Dominion during the Fifteenth Century', in G. C. Garfagnini (ed.), *Lorenzo il Magnifico e il suo mondo* (Florence, 1994), pp. 87–107; P. Salvadori, 'Rapporti personali, rapporti di potere nella corrispondenza di Lorenzo il Magnifico', in G. C. Garfagnini (ed.), *Lorenzo il Magnifico e il suo tempo* (Florence,1992), pp. 127–46 and Salvadori, 'Lorenzo dei Medici e le comunità soggette, tra pressioni e resistenze', in R. Fubini (ed.), *La Toscana al tempo di Lorenzo il Magnifico: politica Economia Cultura Arte*, 3 vols. (Pisa, 1996), III, pp. 891–906.

exercise influence over the political and administrative life of the subject towns themselves.

The Florentine state of the Quattrocento was a recent phenomenon. Although the institutional framework had been largely defined during the early years of the century, there remained space for the process of negotiation, the possibility of informal contact, and the formation of networks of mutual interest. It is this privileged realm of social and political operation that constitutes the focus of the present study.

SOURCES AND METHOD

The following analysis began with an examination of the spheres of interest and clientage networks established by the Medici in the subject territories, focusing especially on the Laurentian period. Archivally, the point of departure was the *Medici avanti il Principato* collection which contains thousands of letters sent from the territories to the Medici by local governing councils, the inhabitants of the territories and also the Florentine judicial and administrative officials serving within the subject cities.[2] The richness of these letters as a source lies in the numerous leads and the quantity of information they furnish; yet, there are also whole areas where they remain silent. This is because of either lost correspondence, deliberate ambiguity or studied reticence on the part of the correspondents. An additional complicating factor lies in the linguistic conventions governing the composition of such missives, for they are often composed with the specific aim of securing a favour. Consequently, they normally depict the patron as being far more powerful than he really is, and thus he needs to be put back into perspective.[3] It should also be borne in mind that the *Medici avanti il Principato* archive as a source only makes passing references to the patronage networks of other leading Florentine families.

Such difficulties can be overcome, however, with the rich documentary material conserved in the Tuscan archives, especially in the subject communes' council deliberations. These permit the reconstruction of the principle characteristics of political and administrative life in the subject communities, in some cases stretching back over many centuries.

---

[2] For the inventory of the archive preserved in the Archivio di Stato in Florence, see F. Morandini and A. d'Addario (eds.), *Mediceo avanti il Principato. Inventario*, 4 vols. (Rome, 1951–7). For the results of this research, see P. Salvadori, *Dominio e patronato: i Medici e la Toscana nel Quattrocento*, forthcoming.

[3] See V. Ilardi, 'Crosses and Carets: Renaissance Patronage and Coded Letters of Recommendation', *The American Historical Review*, 92 (1987), pp. 1127–49.

A critical analysis of the deliberations of several villages and cities of the territories has revealed how the letters tend either to oversimplify or to confuse further the reality of any particular scenario.[4] They also help define more clearly the nature of the Medici's relations with the subject communes. Often their requests are put under scrutiny, discussed and even refused within the communal councils. Such archival documentation throws light on the process of negotiation, the means of resistance, the compromises reached and the role played by other Florentines. Few of the other leading families within the Florentine patriciate of the Quattrocento have their records and papers as systematically conserved and catalogued as the Medici, but within the volumes of communal deliberations, traces of other families' influence still remain.

An attempt has therefore been made to reconstruct the parameters of institutional power, at both the central and local level, with the aim of defining the scope for the evolution of clientage and informal government within those constraints, through a study of a sample of subject communities. Having established such a framework, it becomes possible to quantify the effective potency of the influence wielded by the Florentines on the political and administrative life of the subject towns, especially in areas that came under local jurisdictional control. At the same time, attention has been paid to the letters sent from the subject communes and the specific objectives sought after by the councils or eminent families who wrote directly to members of the Florentine patriciate. As one might expect, the cost of widening the scope of the study to encompass the whole *dominio* would have been the loss of particularity and local variations within the territorial state. Yet even given this limitation, it is still possible to put forward a model that is capable of identifying the use of patronal practices in the exercise of power and their role in the formation of the Florentine territorial state.

THE EXTENT OF LOCAL AUTHORITY AND FLORENTINE INTERFERENCE

As a consequence of the expansion of the territorial state at the start of the fifteenth century, Florence assumed new governmental responsibilities, placing some sectors of territorial administration under centralised

---

[4] Research was based on the deliberations of several cities and smaller communes within the territorial state (Arezzo, Pistoia, Pisa, San Gimignano, Fucecchio, Prato, Borgo San Sepolcro, Colle Valdelsa, San Miniato, Poggibonsi), in addition to documentation conserved in the Florentine State Archive relating to other smaller centres within the territories that can be found in the collections of *Statuti, Provvisioni,* the *Carteggi della Signoria,* and elsewhere.

control. As a result, many local statutes were redrafted and jurisdictional boundaries redefined. In this guise, Florence arrogated to itself total authority in all military matters whilst also assuming the right to tax all subject territories.[5] In addition, all territorial judicial posts were occupied by native Florentines.[6] Once these strategic positions and functions had been assumed, however, the Florentine republic did not suspend all local jurisdictional and political powers. Given its recent formation, the territorial state was by no means secure, and several subject cities, conscious of their past, never fully accepted Florentine domination, seeking to free themselves whenever the opportunity presented itself. These cities and communes had their own administrative and political structures, with magistracies and laws designed to regulate communal life.

For the Florentines, it was neither conceivable nor convenient to disrupt this delicate and valuable political and administrative framework. Florence left the subject cities and communes to live under their own laws, the extent of local autonomy as defined within local statutes remaining considerable, and encompassing the determination of political and administrative affairs, the running of charitable institutions, the management of communal goods and the regulation of communal ritual. However, the picture of a clear-cut differentiation between central and local powers that emerges from a reading of the relative statutes requires some form of qualification. In order to secure a more detailed impression, therefore, the more informal networks of private relations need to be added, and considered in tandem with the complex of institutional structures.

Florentine interference in the administrative framework of the territorial communities is most clearly discernible in the pressure exerted through local magistracies to ensure the election of candidates preferred by the Florentines to key administrative posts. Such offices were extremely important at the local level, especially those of communal chancellor and notary of the *danni dati*, both of which impinged directly

---

[5] On the Florentine territorial state in the fifteenth century see G. Chittolini, 'Ricerche sull' ordinamento territoriale del dominio fiorentino agli inizi del secolo XV', in Chittolini, *La formazione dello stato regionale e le istituzioni del contado. Secoli XIV–XV* (Turin, 1979), pp. 293–352; E. Fasano Guarini, 'Città soggette e contadi nel dominio fiorentino tra Quattro e Cinquecento: il caso pisano', in M. Mirri (ed.), *Ricerche di storia moderna*, I (Pisa, 1976), pp. 1–94; A. Zorzi, 'Lo stato territoriale fiorentino (secoli XIV–XV): aspetti giurisdizionali', *Società e storia*, 50 (1990), pp. 799–825. On the Italian states see J. Kirshner (ed.), *The Origins of the State in Italy, 1300–1600* (Chicago, 1996).

[6] See A. Zorzi, 'Giusdicenti e operatori di giustizia nello Stato territoriale fiorentino del XV secolo', *Ricerche storiche*, 19 (1989), pp. 517–52.

on fundamental areas of communal life. In contrast with other political and technical offices, the offices of chancellor, notary of the *danni dati*, schoolmaster and physician were generally secured by non-residents, and required a degree of professional competence. These positions were filled by a small group of professionally trained men, the majority of whom came from within the territorial state, were usually from influential families and had undergone some form of specialised training. They were elected by the communes who also paid their salaries. Nomination to such posts normally occurred through the traditional electoral sortition and extraction, even though the procedures governing such elections were subject to numerous reforms and varied considerably from place to place and over time. Their jobs were nominally temporary in nature, ranging from six months to just over a year, in keeping with the communal tradition of regular rotation of office.

During the course of the century, these professionally trained and qualified itinerant officeholders sensed that their profession constituted a useful means of securing promotion and social advancement. Through adherence to the powerful families at the centre they envisaged the possibility of establishing successful careers, and the potential for relaxing their adherence to rigid bureaucratic precepts, whilst also enjoying the benefits of the additional prestige and power which came from association with an authority beyond the commune itself.[7] Offices within the territorial state were therefore keenly contested by ambitious candidates who often sought prior sponsorship and protection from amongst the leading members of the Florentine oligarchy. Hence, it was not uncommon to find a Florentine rector recommending a notary who had served as one of his staff. From the mid-1450s onwards, members of the two most influential Florentine families, the Pitti and the Medici, were deeply implicated in this complex web of informal relations, a scenario that lasted until the uprising of 1466. From that point onwards, however, Lorenzo de' Medici gradually imposed his own personal pre-eminence.[8]

In the struggle to secure positions as chancellors, notaries, doctors and communal schoolmasters Laurentian intervention was not infrequent, and took a variety of forms. On occasion Lorenzo simply

---

[7] On this issue see R. Fubini, 'Antonio Ivani da Sarzana: un teorizzatore del declino delle autonomie comunali', in *Egemonia fiorentina ed autonomie comunali nella Toscana nord-occidentale del primo Rinascimento: vita, arte, cultura* (Pistoia, 1978), pp. 113–64.

[8] See the studies listed in the first note and the many examples cited in Lorenzo de' Medici, *Lettere*, ed. R. Fubini (vols. I–II, 1460–78), N. Rubinstein (vols. III–IV, 1478–80) and M. Mallett (vols. V–VII, 1480–4) (Florence, 1977–98).

indicated his preferred candidate for a particular office, following an
established practice that was periodically permitted by statutory regulation. However, his interventions were not always so deft and readily
acceptable, or at least bearable, by the communes in question.[9] On
several occasions, his actions were characterised by direct and forceful
interference that not only compromised existing laws, but also destabi-
lised the local balance of power and broke with established custom. The
most unpopular interventions were above all those that ensured favourable treatment for a candidate through either the prolongation of an
office or the granting of a reward of some kind. These privileges, which
were clearly in opposition to local communal interests, combined to
increase the resentment felt against individuals who had only been
granted a grudging acceptance from the outset. It is no coincidence that
the biographies of many of these Laurentian clients are full of complaints
from local communities, especially as many of them failed to administer
their duties adequately once they had secured such prestigious
backing.[10]

Although territorial offices clearly remained in the hands of the
communes in both the fifteenth and the sixteenth centuries, the
pressures exerted by the Florentines constituted the first indication of
the diminishing control of local communes relative to the increasing
influence of the officials sent to oversee their administration. The
chances of being elected or reconfirmed in office still largely depended
on the officials' ability to carry out their offices, the final word often
lying with the local communal magistracies. The key to a career in
public administration within the territories or within Florence itself,
however, clearly lay in adherence to a powerful Florentine family, and
most notably to the Medici.

Many of the communities within the territories housed institutions
concerned with the distribution of alms and charity within the communes. Although independent, many of these were either directly or
indirectly subject to communal control. Such institutions generally
depended upon the communes to oversee their activities, and supervise
the nomination and election of their officials, and the auditing of their
accounts. In light of the substantial riches amassed through endowments
and bequests, such hospitals and charitable institutions were keenly
contested spheres of political power.

Administrative positions within these charitable institutions were
much coveted as they were more profitable and of longer duration than

---

[9] See Salvadori, 'Lorenzo dei Medici e le comunità soggette', p. 897.
[10] *Ibid.*, pp. 897–8, and Salvadori *Dominio e patronato*, ch. II.

political offices. They also allowed the holders to exercise a profound influence upon local communal life. Consequently, the appointment of rectors to charitable foundations provided an arena within which conflict between eminent families of the area could be played out, especially where local factional animosities prevailed, as was the case in Pistoia. In fact, although the Panciatichi and Cancellieri were excluded from holding political offices because of their magnate status, they exercised their power indirectly through families associated with them by familial or patronal ties.[11]

As a result of the recurring disputes concerning such posts, eminent Florentines were often entrusted with the task of electing the rectors of such institutions on behalf of the communes, and of overseeing the reforms intended to placate internal dissent. Consequently, members of the ruling elites within the communes themselves sought to ensure the backing of such families through their networks of informal relations in order to secure such positions. This pattern of behaviour therefore presented the opportunity for the centre to intervene in the running of charitable institutions on a larger scale. Within the space of a hundred years, and in a wholly different institutional context, charitable foundations were held accountable to central bodies within Florence and often administered by governors selected directly by the Grand Dukes.

The management of communal lands and overseeing of civic prerogatives also fell under local jurisdiction and, in many places, constituted one of the primary sources of income for the communal treasury. Access to communal lands often provided a means of subsistence for the propertyless, who benefited from rights to grazing, wood, hunting and fishing. The sequestration of communal lands and the limitation of hunting and fishing privileges could take place only with the agreement of local governmental organs.[12] Even within this important and jealously guarded sphere of local jurisdiction, Medicean interference was evident. Through sequestration and gifts, Lorenzo obtained property owned by the communes as part of a larger programme of property investment that anticipated the regeneration of lands which had deteriorated through neglect but which were potentially highly productive.[13]

---

[11] See Connell, 'Clientelismo e stato territoriale', Milner, 'Lorenzo and Pistoia', pp. 248–50, and Medici, *Lettere*, I, pp. 160–4.

[12] On communal lands, see D. Pesciatini, 'Continuità e transformazione: le comunità nel contado di Pisa nel sec. XVII', in M. Mirri (ed.), *La città e il contado di Pisa nello Stato dei Medici (XV–XVII)* (=*Ricerche di storia moderna*, III) (Pisa, 1984), pp. 293–390, especially pp. 355ff.

[13] See Salvadori, 'Lorenzo dei Medici e le comunità soggette', p. 900 and *Dominio e*

The problem of communal holdings should be analysed in the context of a broader survey of the expansion of Florentine landholding within the territories.[14] With the expansion of the territory under centralised control, Florentine bankers and merchants finally had the chance to invest their own capital in the surrounding countryside, and into areas where land purchase had previously been precluded, or at least resisted, by the neighbouring city-states until as recently as the mid-Trecento. The consequence of such marked spatial expansion in the territories was the growth of a considerable regional market during the course of the fifteenth century, which in turn was augmented by the annexation of Pisa and of other ports along the coast that guaranteed access to the sea.

The newly annexed territories along the coastline and in the Pisan interior, and the fertile farmland of the small Tuscan valleys consequently fell into the possession of the rich Florentine patriciate. Moreover, the tendency to form large territorial holdings in the area around Pisa was characteristic of many families in the Florentine oligarchy. The Medici, especially from Lorenzo the Magnificent onwards, spent a considerable amount of time in Pisa and its contado where many of their landholdings were gathered, whilst the Martelli held similar holdings in Cascina, the Salviati in Ponsacco and Peccioli and the Rucellai in Collesalvetti. In these regions, where Florentine interests were most concentrated, one can perceive the first attempts by the Florentine republic at environmental regeneration as attempts were made to release the potential latent in lands that previously had been poorly cultivated.[15]

The interests of Florentine proprietors undoubtedly conditioned the programme of drainage and land reclamation undertaken by the republic. In addition, their presence probably also impacted upon the lives of the subject populace. Even if there were some who managed to secure preferential treatment through their connections with the Florentine elite, there were many others who, in the realignment of long

---

patronato, ch. VI. On the subject of Medicean possessions, see V. Franchetti Pardo and G. Casali, *I Medici nel contado fiorentino: ville e possedimenti agricoli tra quattro e cinquecento* (Florence, 1978); and A. Lillie, 'Lorenzo de' Medici's Rural Investments and Territorial Expansion', *Rinascimento*, 33 (1993), pp. 53–67.

[14] I began research on this theme, upon which work is still in progress, during the year spent as Fellow at The Harvard University Center for Italian Renaissance Studies at Villa I Tatti, 1994–5.

[15] M. Mallett, 'Pisa and Florence in the Fifteenth Century. Aspects of the period of the First Florentine Domination', in N. Rubinstein (ed.), *Florentine Studies: Politics and Society in Renaissance Florence* (London, 1968), pp. 403–31; and Fasano-Guarini, 'Città soggette', pp. 39ff.

held positions, lost out in the early encounters of a struggle that was destined to continue into the following centuries.

THE EXTENT OF CENTRAL AUTHORITY: NEGOTIATIONS

The pressures exerted by the Florentines on affairs which lay within the jurisdictional remit of the territorial communes constituted a form of interference in territorial political and administrative life, and resulted in the tangible erosion of local autonomy.

There was considerable resistance to such piecemeal attempts to assume control. Such resistance is clear from the number of obstacles that were periodically placed in the way of the Florentine elite when making specific requests. Occasionally, securing a post for a specific client was rendered unusually problematic, and these attempts often failed after extensive and prolonged negotiation, during which local magistrates appealed to every minor rubric contained in the local statutes. Statutory provisions that had previously gone unobserved could in fact prove to be insurmountable obstacles when faced with unpopular requests like a call for the increase in a chancellor's salary or the prolongation of his office. However, the nature of resistance and the forms of defence assumed against centralised authority did not solely involve maintaining the formal framework of self-government. Complex strategies were also developed by the subject communities with the scope of reconfiguring the nature of their relations with Florence as the centre.

Mention has already been made of the attempts by individuals or families who were motivated by ambition and personal interest to establish links with powerful families of the Florentine oligarchy. However, this behavioural pattern was also replicated at the communal level, with local governments seeking to form direct contact with a number of Florentine patricians from whom they sought benefit. The intention was to establish a bargaining position that would enable the territorial communes to enter negotiations regarding matters that no longer lay within their jurisdiction.

The instructions given to ambassadors charged with the task of seeking out the residencies of members of the Florentine patriciate in order to present their commune's petition are often registered within the volumes of communal deliberations. As a source, they are not particularly informative, as there is often little detail in the actual mandates issued, but they permit the identification of the principal problems that afflicted the subject communes, problems which the communes hoped to solve through the intervention of powerful

Florentine 'benefactors'. These were often sensitive and important issues: the easing of fiscal levies, the financing of public works, licences for markets, and the provision of supplies to alleviate food shortages.[16]

Central government seems to have operated in a discriminating manner regarding such sensitive areas (tax, the victualling board and local markets), reacting to practical considerations dictated by local variations within the areas under their jurisdiction. Every village or city was a constitutive part of the *dominio* in its own right, and there was no sense, especially in the second half of the fifteenth century, of a concerted plan to ensure uniformity between the various communes. An extremely heterogeneous body of legislation that was subject to constant changes took account of practices characterised by their flexibility and adaptability. Whilst the principal objectives of securing the necessary fiscal income and safeguarding the marketplace and essential supplies were kept firmly in mind, central government never seemed to forget the need to maintain political control over a recently acquired territory where profound and irremediable differences could easily arise. In this context, the granting of one-off concessions capable of being periodically extended could become a subtle governmental tool.

Within this complex matrix of personal relationships, the subject communes sought out Florentine patriciates as a point of reference within the central power base in order to open up a wider margin for manoeuvre and negotiation and establish more scope for mediation and arbitration. As a result, relations with members of the Florentine oligarchy, and especially with the Medici, presented the subject communes with the opportunity to redefine their relations with Florence regarding questions that were particularly pertinent to the communes themselves, thereby recuperating precious fragments of their long-lost legislative powers.

The administration of justice within the territorial communities certainly fell within the ambit of Florentine power. The *rettore forestiero* who oversaw the execution of judicial affairs was a well-established figure of political life within the Tuscan cities and communes even prior to Florentine subjection. Prior to subjection, such *rettori* were directly selected by the local magistracies that drew on a nucleus of

---

[16] See the recent considerations of these themes in S. R. Epstein, 'Stato territoriale ed economia regionale nella Toscana del Quattrocento', in Fubini (ed.), *La Toscana al tempo di Lorenzo il Magnifico*, III, pp. 869–90 and G. Petralia, 'Imposizione diretta e dominio territoriale nella repubblica fiorentina del Quattrocento', in *Società, istituzioni, spiritualità: studi in onore di Cinzio Violante* (Spoleto, 1994), pp. 639–52, including a detailed bibliography.

itinerant professionals who came from other Italian states. Once under Florentine control, however, these officials were definitively replaced by Florentine citizens.

The *rettori* were chosen by central government following the traditional procedure of selection through extraction, whilst the subject communes were responsible for meeting their salaries. The majority of these Florentine officials were from a narrow band of families who made up the urban ruling elite, and were usually furnished with sufficient legal training. Recent studies have stressed the representative and arbitrational role fulfilled by these officials, for the function of the rector was to represent *in situ* the ethos of the ruling elite within Florence and guarantee the surveillance of local political and administrative life, in addition to securing public order and the security of the republic as a whole.[17]

It was through these channels that requests for intervention in judicial proceedings, mostly penal in nature, or in the settling of disputes, arrived at the door of the Medici and other leading members of the Florentine oligarchy. Generally these petitions were sent by friends or relations of the suspects, or took the form of requests by representatives of local government for intervention *pro parte* in pending court cases. In the latter instance, they usually wrote in defence of their fellow citizens who had been charged, acting as character witnesses to their integrity and good nature. Requests for the release of prisoners rarely met with success in serious cases such as murder, but this was often probably not the intention of the writer in the first place. It was more likely that they constituted a means of raising the stakes in a game with unwritten rules. Less serious cases, however, could end with the release of the suspect without the trial even being called, so long as this was possible without compromising the 'honour' of the official involved.[18] Once the administration of justice, a key function at the local level, had been lost, the only way to secure a voice in judicial matters was through requests and petitions addressed to the Florentine oligarchy who were in a position to influence the *ufficiali estrinseci* in their capacity as fellow Florentine citizens.

THE ALBIZZI AND MEDICI PERIODS

The practice of forming patron–client relationships which extended into the territorial state, although a factor in the formation of Medici

---

[17] See Zorzi, 'Giusdicenti ed operatori'.
[18] Salvadori, *Dominio e patronato*, ch. IV.

power, was certainly not their exclusive preserve. The importance of informal means of exercising power needs to be considered within the context of a process of transformation that affected the entire structure of governmental forms during the course of the fifteenth century. By the time Lorenzo the Magnificent assumed pre-eminence, the formative stage in the evolution of the Florentine state had ended and the basic structure was in place. The process of territorial expansion had been initiated by the Florentine republic during the previous century, and resulted in a profound alteration in the geographical configuration of the territories between the Tre- and Quattrocento. This was aided by the creation of central magistracies formed to govern the *dominio* and reform local administrative and political structures.

After this period of substantial change, there followed a phase of consolidation during which new equilibriums were established, for jurisdictional parameters had to be clearly defined and absorbed prior to the establishment of procedures regulating negotiations, compromises, and the trading of favours between the centre and the subject communes. In addition, the increasing presence of Florentines in the territories during the course of the century (*rettori*, holders of ecclesiastical benefices and landholders) facilitated the creation of concrete ties between citizens from Florence and those who lived in the territories.

It was only at a later stage that the Florentine patriciate's practice of gradually extending their authority through patronage networks assumed major significance, aimed, as it was, at the creation of a framework for reciprocal exchange between the local elites and as an alternative means of influencing the civic life of the subject communes. Such strategies were also customary during the Albizzi period (and presumably even earlier), but they were less frequent and had less of an impact on the life of the subject communities. As under the Medici, chancellors and notaries were also elected as a result of Florentine patronal pressures during the Albizzi period, normally through the intervention of a rector or a relation, but their influence was usually temporary. Whilst the protagonists in this game were traditionally numerous, the rules were enforced by the local magistracies. It was only in the Laurentian period that cases like the one that arose in Fucecchio, where Lorenzo controlled the election of the chancellor for over twenty years, actually took place.[19] The participants were still numerous, but the rules were no longer impartially applied and, more

---

[19] See Salvadori, *Dominio e patronato*, ch. II. For Arezzo, see Black, 'Lorenzo and Arezzo'.

importantly, arbitration increasingly fell out of the hands of those attributed the role according to the statutory rubrics.

Lorenzo de' Medici therefore built on a pre-existing practice established by the Florentine patriciate, including his own ancestors. Although their influence was less marked, Lorenzo's actions merely accelerated existing tendencies. If the governmental practices established by Lorenzo in the territories seemed to fail in the short term, the changes he initiated proved to have deep roots. In the space of just a few decades, and in the context of a radically altered governmental structure, the bond between subjects and prince was engendered thanks to practices that originated during the republican period.

There were many differences between the Albizzi and Medici periods, partly because of the different conditions faced before and after the 1430s. However, it is possible to discern continuity between the two regimes as they sought to establish an acceptable means of maintaining the *dominio*. During the Laurentian period, this tendency was strengthened as a consequence of the centralisation that took place under Lorenzo.

1466: THE DECLINE OF THE PITTI AND THE BEGINNINGS OF LAURENTIAN HEGEMONY

Florentine political affairs at both a communal and private level had a direct impact on what happened in the territories. This is especially evident in relation to dealings with the Medici, where the alignment of forces within Florence was clearly felt.[20] On the occasions when Lorenzo's standing fell, reactions within both Florence and the territories ranged from a cooling of relations between Lorenzo and local territorial governments to direct citizen involvement in uprisings organised by Florentine exiles. The significance of these patterns of behaviour lie in their witness to the close attention paid by subject communes to the political manoeuvrings at the centre and their consciousness of the precarious nature of existing political alignments. What it also indicates is the extent of their resolve to secure the best possible outcome and derive the maximum possible benefit from any situation that might arise.

Such considerations are useful in identifying several key moments in the history of Florentine government. As regards relations with the subject communes, for example, 1466 stands out as an extremely significant date. It was the year that signalled the beginning of Medicean

[20] Salvadori, 'Lorenzo dei Medici e le comunità,' p. 901; and Medici, *Lettere*, I, p. 309.

pre-eminence and hegemony, based on their successful exploitation of patronage networks. As has already been noted, there were many Florentines involved in territorial affairs and each subject commune was capable of having a different patron within the Florentine elite. From the mid-fifteenth century onwards the members of two families in particular stood out from this nucleus, the Pitti and the Medici. Their names frequently appear within subject communes' deliberations and they were clearly treated with respect. Their letters of recommendation concerning the election of notaries and chancellors were often heeded and their requests met.[21]

Even after Cosimo's death, the two families continued to figure prominently in the territories, a fact which doubtless reflected the balance of forces within Florence itself at that time. Luca Pitti was probably the only citizen capable of matching Piero di Cosimo's leadership in Florence during that period, and definitely one of the most influential men within the contado and distretto. After the failure of the 1466 coup and Luca's political isolation, his name no longer continued to appear in the deliberations of the subject communes, not even in those cities which had shown him particular reverence.[22] In fact, in the letters sent to Lorenzo, 1466 became a watershed in the memory of the inhabitants of the territories. Frequent references were made to this date either to underline fidelity to the Medici cause or to stress the infidelity of others.[23] From 1466 onwards the Medici's pre-eminence is clearly defined not only centrally, but also at the regional level.

CLIENTAGE PRACTICES AND GOVERNMENTAL PRACTICES

In recent years, the history of political association has undergone profound change. It is no longer enough to describe institutional structures and governmental practices as articulated in formal statutes and political tracts. Many studies on the Italian states of the medieval period have focused on individuals, structures and practices that have little to do with the institutionalised framework of public government. Instead, questions of kinship, clans, factions and the environment of the

---

[21] See the works cited in note 1 above.

[22] On the 1466 uprising, see N. Rubinstein, *The Government of Florence under the Medici (1434–1494)*, 2nd edn (Oxford, 1997), pp. 155–98 and R. Fubini, *Italia quattrocentesca: politica e diplomazia al tempo di Lorenzo il Magnifico* (Milan,1994), pp. 220–52.

[23] For a typical example see the letter from an inhabitant of Montaione to Lorenzo referring to the commune of Palaia: 'questo comune e questi huomini non funno mai amici della vostra casa, che nel sesantasei costoro andonno a casa di Messer Lucha Pitti e sempre funo suo partigiani', Niccolaio da Montaione a Lorenzo dei Medici, Palaia 19 April 1474, in ASF, MAP, 23, no. 573.

court and the practices they gave rise to (clientage, corruption, favouritism and mediation) have assumed increasing importance.[24]

Although previously considered of marginal importance in the face of the onward march of the rationalising modern state, such forms of power have increasingly become the focus of scholarly investigation, where the stress has been on their profound impact on social life and political decision-making. The result has been the construction of models of political organisation based upon a nexus of private associations, where effective power was exercised through these networks that stood independent of any state-constituted magistracies.

A knowledge of public institutions and the apparatus of state is certainly insufficient to provide an understanding of the organisational principles which underpin a political system. By the same token, this shortcoming is not overcome by studies based solely on informal power structures, for it is within the framework of such institutional structures that such power blocks form and develop strategies of opposition and compromise. Instead of insisting on the opposition public/private, it is perhaps more useful to consider the whole complex of political forms and groupings and study how they function in their interrelation.[25]

In the Florentine state of the fifteenth century a well-defined institutional structure took shape with clearly differentiated areas of jurisdiction. Yet it was flexible at both a central and local level, leaving ample scope for interventions based on personal ties. Structurally it was capable of offering, and in part did offer, advantages to a host of individuals. In practice, however, it further enforced the controlling influence of the Florentine oligarchy.

The web of personal ties that the Florentine ruling elite spread over the *dominio* was a fairly subtle and flexible instrument of government based on understandings and mutual interests, and designed to secure greater control of the territories and reduce internal opposition. However, clientage did not constitute an alternative to the traditional institutional channels. Rather, it proved to be a useful tool in maintaining the *dominio* and an efficient way of eroding local autonomies that were protected by statute.

Florentine interference in areas that lay within the competence of the local communes grew increasingly pervasive, especially in relation to territorial offices. The authority which local governmental agencies

---

[24] On this theme see the contributions in Kirshner (ed.), *Origins*, especially G. Chittolini, 'The "Private", the "Public", the State', pp. 34–61. See also D. Andreozzi, 'Valli, fazioni, comunità e Stato', *Società e storia*, 67 (1995), pp. 129–40.

[25] Chittolini, 'The "Private", the "Public", the State', pp. 50–61.

possessed regarding the distribution of posts within their gift came under increasing pressure from powerful patrons at the centre. Such pressure was actually capable of affecting the formation of the territorial administrative apparatus on a piecemeal basis. The tendency towards the creation of a small nucleus of offices which were more stable and easily managed by the centre, the lengthening of their tenure, and above all the assumption of the right to elect certain officials constituted the first signs of a process that assumed greater significance during the following centuries. For example, the task of electing chancellors, so keenly contested during the Laurentian period, was taken out of the hands of the local communities in the sixteenth century, and granted to a Florentine magistracy and ultimately to the Grand Duke.[26] As a consequence of this shift, the competition between rival Florentine landowners for control over communal territory became increasingly fierce during the following centuries.[27]

CENTRE AND PERIPHERY

The study of the mutual dependence between state institutions and local communities has led to the overhauling of the dichotomy centre/periphery which has long held sway over investigations into the formation of the Renaissance states.[28] This development has been especially valuable in revising the characterisation of the periphery as an undifferentiated and passive unity that only reacted to the centralising influence of the dominant power eroding its liberties.

The nature of relations between different territorial communes and Florence varied and were subject to continual change. Significant issues such as fiscal arrangements, and conditions governing local markets and food supplies, could be renegotiated through the careful marshalling of informal contacts. In this context patronage networks with the Florentines assumed particular importance. Studies of the Florentine territorial state in the fifteenth century initially focused on the chronology and means of territorial conquest, furnishing valuable information concerning the local governmental institutions that the Florentines subsequently made their own. Having mapped the roads that radiated

---

[26] E. Fasano Guarini, 'Potere centrale e comunità soggette nel granducato di Cosimo I', *Rivista storica italiana*, 89 (1977), pp. 513–38.

[27] Pesciatini, 'Continuità e trasformazione'.

[28] See the comments of E. Fasano Guarini, 'Center and Periphery', in Kirshner (ed.), *Origins*, pp. 74–96; and A. Torre, 'Società locale e società regionale: complementarietà o interdipendenza?' *Società e storia*, 67 (1995), pp. 113–24.

from the centre to the periphery, the emphasis now lies on exploring the pathways that led from the margins back to the centre.[29] By focusing on particular cases it is possible to define more clearly the advantages each territorial commune managed to secure through negotiation, and the concessions they periodically wrested from the centre through mediation between both the relevant institutions and their Florentine patrons.

In shedding light on the complex nature of the reciprocal networks of influence and how they operated, as well as the strategies adopted by the ruling elite within Florence to alter them, it should be possible to estimate whether, and by what means, the subject communes themselves have contributed to the delineation of the Florentine territorial state.

RULED AND RULERS

The danger in focusing on the reciprocal nature of relations between local communities and central authority in the pre-modern age is that it fosters a vision of peace, in which conflict is reduced and the violent break with the past minimised. Such a vision would be a misrepresentation. Although Florence pursued a policy that was open to compromises, mediation and alliances with local ruling elites, it was also a policy, as has been noted, directed towards the erosion of local autonomies. In order to maintain a territory – especially one like Tuscany that was difficult to subdue – it was not enough to conquer or purchase land, or institute laws and demand they were observed. The establishment of a basis for negotiation and exchange was also necessary, for it was here that personal contacts and informal relations between governments and successive Florentine elites could bear most fruit.

In this context, it was extremely important to secure the backing of individual sponsors. Differences of class and social standing clearly existed between those being ruled. Increasingly during the fifteenth century, players from the subject communes saw the possibility of social advancement through adherence to powerful individuals at the centre. Such alliances enabled them both to maintain their pre-eminence within their own communities and to take up positions

---

[29] In addition to the studies cited in note 1, and those in the present volume, see J. C. Brown, *In the Shadow of Florence: Provincial Society in Renaissance Pescia* (New York, 1982); L. Fabbri, 'Autonomismo comunale ed egemonia fiorentina tra '300 e '400', *Rassegna volterrana*, 70 (1994), pp. 97–110.

within the public administration of the territories or even within
Florence itself.

The reorientation of local powers towards the centre presents a
complicating factor in the relation between rulers and ruled. The
network of social ties between local and Florentine elites could fragment
opposition to the centre, leading to a form of assimilation. More closely
bound to their Florentine rulers, such individuals could find their
associational allegiance compromised, for, in pursuing their own interests and ambitions, they could periodically find themselves acting as
spokesmen for policies which were detrimental to their communities of
origin.

The increasingly burdensome nature of political authority, combined
with patterns of intervention in local administrative affairs that were
almost officially sanctioned, offered an equal number of further channels
for advancement at a variety of levels. Cumulatively, these tendencies
resulted in the gradual formation of culturally homogeneous practices
amongst officeholders within the administrative structure of the state.
The officeholders, although themselves active, became the instruments
used to deprive local communities of their liberties.

On the positive side, the links established with the Florentines carried
the expectations of local communes and individuals alike, and probably
helped secure special prerogatives for certain communities and affected
the destinies of a limited number of subjects. The drawback, however,
was the progressive erosion of liberty in every subject community.
Territories accustomed 'to living freely and under their own laws'[30] saw
the scope for self-determination diminish ever faster under the Grand
Dukes; yet the foundations for this gradual erosion of local power were
clearly laid during the fifteenth century.

[30] Niccolò Machiavelli, *The Prince and Other Political Writings*, trans. and ed. S. J. Milner
(London, 1995), ch. 5, p. 51.

CHAPTER 11

PATRONAGE AND ITS ROLE IN GOVERNMENT: THE FLORENTINE PATRICIATE AND VOLTERRA

LORENZO FABBRI

Volterra represents a remarkable anomaly in the formation of the Florentine territorial state. It may be impossible to detect a general pattern in the incorporation of the communities into the large dominion emerging in fourteenth- and fifteenth-century Tuscany. However, the case of Volterra seems atypical for many reasons, the first of them being the late date of its formal submission to Florence (1472), which makes this town the only significant case of enlargement of the Florentine state in the Medicean period. On the other hand, this submission was only the final act of a long process begun in 1361.[1]

And yet, precisely this atypicality, and in particular the persistence for over a century of a fundamental ambiguity in the relationships between 'quasi-ruler' and 'quasi-subject', makes it possible to distinguish with greater clarity some important elements relating to the general theme of this volume. I refer here, for example, to the divergence between juridical forms and political realities, to the complex relationship between institutional framework and practice of government, to the combination of regional policy with day-to-day local relations, and to the ubiquity of formal as well as informal negotiations.

Before discussing Volterra's case in broader terms, it may be opportune to outline the principal stages of its subjugation.

I

Florentine hegemony over Volterra, only intermittently established in the thirteenth century and in the first half of the fourteenth,[2] was put on

---

[1] This chapter is based on my doctoral dissertation, 'La sottomissione di Volterra allo stato fiorentino. Controllo istituzionale e strategie di governo (1361–1435)', University of Florence (1994).

[2] On Volterra before 1361, the fundamental study remains G. Volpe, 'Vescovi e

a solid and durable basis beginning in 1361. At the end of that year, amidst the death-throes of the Belforti regime (they were a local family who had dominated Volterra since 1340), the ancient competition between Pisa and Siena for the control of Volterra was resolved in favour of Florence. Intervening opportunely in support of a rebellion against the Belforti, the Florentines were in an ideal position to conclude an exclusive alliance with the new communal rulers.[3] This agreement (signed without delay by the two parties to seal their compact) constituted the first and decisive political-juridical foundation of Florentine *superioritas*.[4] Formally, it inaugurated a kind of temporary military protection, conceding to Florence the administration for ten years of the civic fortress, but in fact Volterra was degraded to the level of a city under Florentine hegemony. The implications of this pact went far beyond its literal terms.

Over the following ten years the Florentine republic strengthened its supremacy especially through a policy of pacifying Volterran factions, involved after 1361 in bitter strife both inside and outside the city. This enhanced conflict was overcome by means of a long and arduous diplomatic campaign on the part of the Florentine republic: in this way its hegemony was not only safe-guarded against the intrigues of volatile local politics, but was even buttressed by the acquisition of a unique role as guarantor and patron of Volterra's civic peace.[5]

This fervent political and diplomatic activity was not accompanied by a correspondingly decisive effort to systematise the institutional relations between the two communes. The only significant attempt of this type focused on the office of the Captain of the People: after 1361 this official, who shared with the Podestà the highest judicial authority, came gradually to assume the role of local representative of the ruling power. This process was begun by restricting the office to Florentine citizens, and was carried further by granting to the Captain important

comune di Volterra', in his *Toscana medievale (Massa Marittima, Volterra, Sarzana)* (Florence, 1964), pp. 141–311, reprinted from the 1923 edition. See now as well E. Cristiani, 'Vescovo e comune a Volterra nella prima legislazione statutaria', *Rassegna volterrana*, 70 (1994), pp. 75–82, and D. Balestracci, 'La politica di Volterra fra Pisa e Siena', *ibid.*, pp. 83–96.

[3] Matteo Villani, *Cronica*, ed. G. Porta, II (Milan, 1995), pp. 537–41 (bk 2, ch. 67).

[4] ASF, Cap., 13, 134r–135v, 30 September 1361; A. Gherardi (ed.), *I Capitoli del Comune di Firenze: inventario e regesto*, II (Florence, 1893), pp. 328–9.

[5] Alamanno Salviati laid the cornerstone of Volterra's pacification during his embassy of June 1369, establishing the Florentine Signoria as arbiter between the factions: see ASCV, A nera, 21, 1, 25v–29r. See my 'Autonomismo comunale ed egemonia fiorentina a Volterra tra '300 e '400', *Rassegna volterrana*, 70 (1994), pp. 97–110.

prerogatives with regard to pacification.[6] In 1385 this development culminated in the transformation of the Captain of Volterra into one of the territorial officials of the Florentine republic, drawn by lot in Florence.[7]

Albeit restricted to the control of the civic fortress and the role of the Captain, the Florentine regime succeeded in exercising effective political dominance over Volterra, despite the fact that important communal prerogatives, such as the exploitation of economic resources – in particular, the deposits of rock salt – and the administration of the contado and of the communal fisc, remained in local hands. Apart from a brief interval between 1429 and 1431, when communal liberties were suppressed in the wake of the Volterran rebellion against the imposition of the catasto, the political parameters existing between Florence and Volterra remained unchanged until 1472. It was only as a result of the war over the alum deposits, newly discovered in Val di Cecina, that Volterra's subjection was completed, leading to full integration into the Florentine territorial state.[8]

II

The survival for a relatively long time of many of the commune's traditional rights, as well as of its formal autonomy, shifts the focus of this study to the sphere of political realities.

We have already pointed to the fundamental importance of Florence's policy of internal reconciliation after the fall of the Belforti lordship (signoria). Having favoured the new regime, the general inclination of the Florentine government was from the start towards a role, super partes, of mediator between victors and vanquished.

Negotiations with the exiled Belforti party, who were strongly opposed by the new regime in Volterra, developed in the context of Florentine diplomatic activity preceding the impending war with Pisa. In fact, contacts between the Pisans and the leaders of the Belforti family, besides placing the outcome of the war in doubt, jeopardised Florentine control over Volterra and its contado: the debates of the

---

6 By virtue of the laws of 1370, the Captain, now called 'Capitano di Custodia', gained jurisdiction over conspiracies against the state; moreover, he was entrusted with the keys to all city gates: ASF, Dipl., Comunità di Volterra, 19 October 1370; Gherardi (ed.), I Capitoli del Comune, II, pp. 330–3; L. A. Cecina, Notizie istoriche della città di Volterra, annotated by F. Dal Borgo (Pisa, 1758 [repr. Bologna, 1975]), pp. 182–4.

7 ASF, Cap., 13, 144v–148v (30–31 December 1385; 20 January 1385/6). Another copy: Cap., 21, 23r–25v; Gherardi (ed.), I Capitoli del Comune, II, pp. 335–8.

8 The fundamental study remains E. Fiumi, L'impresa di Lorenzo de' Medici contro Volterra (1472) (Florence, 1948).

consulte clearly reveal Florence's urgent concern to convince the Belforti to abandon the Pisan alliance in exchange for an advantageous settlement with the Volterran regime.[9]

Nevertheless, even after the Pisan war ended in 1364, the strategy of pacification remained at the heart of Florentine policy towards Volterra. Both the city and the territory continued to be the scene of conspiracies and revolts, which aimed at removing from communal control a series of castles which had fallen into opposing hands. Only Florentine intervention was able to close the rift between the *intrinseci*, i.e. the present communal regime, and the *estrinseci*, focused on the exiled signorial family, thus re-establishing political equilibrium. It was an equilibrium, however, that depended totally on an external power which, while providing peace, ended also by inescapably imposing its own hegemony.

On the other hand, the documentation that we have, and in particular the correspondence between the two governments,[10] makes it clear that the process of peace, which was completed by a series of arbitrations signed by the two factions between 1369 and 1371,[11] resulted not so much from local wishes as from the will of Florence. The policy of reconciliation, in fact, emerged as part of a strategy of domination: instead of promoting its own allies, the Florentine government preferred to enhance its supremacy by assuming the mantle of mediator between the local factions. For that purpose it manoeuvred not only to heal the existing conflict, but also, in a certain sense, to keep that conflict alive. This is demonstrated, precisely in those years, by the creation of an electoral system based on equal partition of offices between the two factions.[12] Florentine policy thus reached the aim of crystallising an inflamed and unpredictable partisan conflict, by splitting the local oligarchy into two established parties.

The success of this strategy, and the achievement of political control which went well beyond the contractual limits of the accord of 1361, enabled the Florentines to put their relations with Volterra on a firmer and more hierarchical footing. At the end of 1385 it was possible to introduce the one important modification to the communal constitution, i.e. the reform of the office of Captain of Custody mentioned above. And in the following year the most notable aspect of Florentine domination of Volterra begins to come to the forefront: taxation.

---

[9] ASF, CP, 3, *passim*.

[10] ASF, Miss. I canc., 13, *passim*.

[11] ASF, Dipl., Comunità di Volterra, 24 August 1369; *ibid.*, 4 February 1370.

[12] The two factions now assumed the names 'volere dell "A" ' and 'volere del "P" ': Fabbri, 'Autonomismo comunale', p. 103.

III

If we were to describe in a few words the real status of the commune of Volterra during the Albizzi period, we should have to speak of a tributary subject of the Florentine republic. From 1386 Volterra appears regularly among those subject cities required to pay frequent taxes. Among these the most important was the so-called *tassa delle lance*, a subsidy collected by the Florentine Camera in order to maintain Florence's mercenary army.[13] In fact, even at the beginning of the fifteenth century this was transformed into an ordinary tax intended to reduce the Florentine public debt: thus the duties of collection, previously carried out by the Camera, were now taken over more and more by the officials of the Monte Comune.[14] Theoretically, the *lance* tax did not imply political subjugation, tied as it was to the military protection exercised by Florence over all Tuscany, and even extending beyond its direct dominion.

Up to 1385 Volterra had been forced to make only sporadic contributions, occasioned by military commitments.[15] But in 1386, with the introduction of a *lance* tax for five years, which was then extended to 1393, a series of almost permanent payment demands was initiated. Through these Volterra found itself one amongst a group of subject communities, differentiated by the amount of the requests, but still liable to a common series of obligations, deadlines and sanctions, all of which constituted a first step towards fiscal uniformity in the diversified territory outside the Florentine contado.

The area subject to the tax of 1386 appears relatively large with respect to the actual extent of the Florentine distretto at the time. Included was the commune of Pistoia, which, with an annual levy of 12,000 lire, contributed almost half of the total tax. The other areas affected were the 'province' of Valdinievole, subdivided into eleven communes, the vicariate of Galeata and Modigliana in the Florentine

---

[13] The tax was actually intended for the office of the 'Condotta degli stipendiari'. On territorial finances, see G. Petralia, 'Imposizione diretta e dominio territoriale nella repubblica fiorentina del Quattrocento', in *Società, istituzioni, spiritualità nell'Europa medievale: scritti in onore di Cinzio Violante* (Spoleto, 1994), pp. 639–52.

[14] J. C. Brown, *In the Shadow of Florence: Provincial Society in Renaissance Pescia* (New York, 1982), pp. 216–18.

[15] After the agreements of 1361, Volterra contributed to various Florentine military enterprises, but beginning in the 1370s Florence's tax demands became primarily financial, under the guise of contributions to sporadic military campaigns. See for example, ASF, Miss. I canc., 16, 7v (letter from the Florentine Signoria to the Priors of Volterra, 16 August 1375). Nevertheless, requests for armed contingents never stopped completely.

Romagna, the communities of the lower Valdarno, and the communes of Colle Valdelsa, San Gimignano, Foiano and Castiglion Fiorentino. With an annual tax of 3500 lire, Volterra took second place amongst the communes most heavily taxed, albeit far behind Pistoia.[16]

In following years, Volterra's tax burden increased almost continually, a process which ceased only with the fall of the Albizzi regime and the rise to power of Cosimo de' Medici. During this long period the commune, like many others, had to sustain a series of extraordinary impositions, thus aggravating the pressure on Volterran finances and leading to increased bitterness. To this was added, in 1429, a triennial tax based on the catasto, the so-called *danaio per lira*, which, however, like other taxes of this period, was never paid by the Volterran commune.[17]

From the end of the fourteenth century up to the rise of the Medici, fiscal concerns came to dominate relations between the two cities, besides being – as is shown clearly by local documentation – Volterra's own particular preoccupation. The four-monthly deadlines with the Florentine *Camera* or Monte constantly gave rise to animated debates in civic councils, summoned to come up with the required funds. Throughout the registers of the communal deliberations the enormous difficulties encountered by local finances in the face of these demands are clearly evident. Some gabelles were regularly devoted to this purpose, while, from time to time, various *ad hoc* expedients were contrived to raise the necessary money. These however were not enough to solve the problem and to avoid the necessity of continually seeking new sources of revenue.

Similar financial pressures induced the local government to consider various ways of reducing expenditure and restructuring the financial organisation of the commune.[18] In fact, however, the chronic impecuniosity of the Volterran treasury gave rise to increasing arrears to the Florentine fisc, a situation that became insoluble in 1429 at the time of the revolt against the catasto. On the other hand, it was precisely this financial weakness that permitted the Florentine government to

---

[16] ASF, CCP, 3, 411v–415r.

[17] Omitting the question of the actual sums collected, I list here the total direct taxation demanded from Volterra between 1386 and 1435: 1386–95: 15,251 florins; 1396–1405: 13,518 florins; 1406–15: 22,702 florins; 1416–25: 22,948 florins; 1426–35: 30,459 florins. This information was taken from: ASF, CCP, 3–25, 53; ASF, MC, 1090–7, 1103; ASCV, A nera, 23–37. For the 'danaio per lira', see ASF, PR, 123, 386v.

[18] Such proposals are found particularly between 1414 and 1416, occasioned by the need to settle debts with Florence: 'ut parata pecunia, cum terminus huiusmodi taxarum advenerit, semper habeatur et solvi possit' (ASCV, A nera, 32, III, 134r).

strengthen its political control. But above all this situation enabled the Florentine patriciate to establish relations – both formal and informal – with communal magistracies and with the local ruling group.

IV

In recent years many historians, seeking to define the nature of Florentine domination over its territory, have underlined the importance of the relations which oligarchs and their families gradually established with the subject localities of the Florentine state. Extending their clientage and alliances beyond the walls of their native city, the leading protagonists of Florentine public life and their relatives established ties with large segments of the ruling classes of cities such as Arezzo or Pistoia, and in this way contributed to strengthening the links of these subject centres to the Florentine state.[19]

This phenomenon is also apparent in Volterra, where the slender institutional apparatus of Florentine power gave ample room for development of informal relations and thus allowed for greater intervention by influential figures. The problems pertaining to fiscal pressure and to the particular kind of subjugation that they established in Volterra provided an ideal climate for the growth of such connections. In the first place, there were links with Florentine bankers, to whom the Volterrans turned as a last resort in order to meet the fiscal deadlines imposed by Florence. Before 1386 the commune had occasionally had recourse to foreign moneylenders, but with the introduction of taxes levied more than once a year and with the continual flow of money into Florence, these relations with private financiers became more and more regular, leading to particular ties with favoured bankers.[20]

In the first half of the fifteenth century, bankers such as Niccolò Serragli, Neri di Gino Capponi, Esaù Martellini and the brothers Berto and Ridolfo di Bonifacio Peruzzi acquired an inordinate influence over Volterran finances, one which often spilled over into the political arena. Serragli in particular had a fundamental role in relations between Florence and Volterra. From 1400 to 1425, when his bank collapsed amidst a wave of bankruptcies,[21] he was at the centre of all major

---

[19] See for example W. J. Connell, 'Clientelismo e stato territoriale. Il potere fiorentino a Pistoia nel XV secolo', *Società e storia*, 14 (1991), pp. 523–43 and R. Black, 'Cosimo de' Medici and Arezzo', in F. Ames-Lewis (ed.), *Cosimo 'il Vecchio' de Medici, 1389–1464* (Oxford, 1992), pp. 33–47.

[20] For an analogous case, related to Pescia, see Brown, *In the Shadow of Florence*, pp. 166–7.

[21] The bankruptcy of the company, headed by Niccolò di Agnolo and Goro di

financial operations of the commune, especially those connected with
Florence; in particular, he was involved with the payment of taxes and
the receipt of revenue connected with Volterran salt, imported by
Florence. In these twenty-five years there were few transactions with
Florence that failed to pass through his hands. In many cases, it was his
bank which, on the simple order of the Volterran authorities, made
payments to the Florentine *Camera* or Monte.[22]

After his departure, banking operations by the Volterran commune
were undertaken by other Florentine companies. Among these, the
bank of Berto and Ridolfo Peruzzi figured prominently, achieving a
monopoly similar to that previously attained by Serragli.[23]

Besides this mediating activity by Florentine bankers – very important, but limited to a specific field of interests – documents reveal the
presence of other figures who contributed to consolidate the ties
between periphery and centre. Part of the Florentine patriciate thus
found itself directly involved in ruling Volterra, by means, above all, of
ties with the local ruling class. Here it was a question of relations
involving personal or family interests, or political and diplomatic affairs,
and which ended by confounding personal and private elements in the
developing relations between Volterra and Florence.

From the 1360s onwards there was a tendency for the commune of
Volterra to seek help, advice and sometimes even direct instructions
from influential Florentines. This developed from the need to establish
more stable links with the government of the Florentine republic, in
view of the rapid rotation of principal offices there. Evidently the
pursuit of political continuity through personal ties emerged, at least in
part, as a quest for protection, to safeguard rights and further petitions at
the political centre.[24]

The work of these Florentine contacts therefore had a significant role
in forging relations between centre and periphery, constituting an
important means for integrating the local community into the Florentine state. Their scope was not always purely political, because
frequently private interests, directly or indirectly, played a notable part.

Antonio Serragli, occurred on 23 December 1425: see ASF, Merc., 10872 (not
foliated; see date for reference).

[22] For many instances of this type, see ASCV, A nera, 28–35, *passim*. On banking
activity in Volterra, see M. Luzzati and A. Veronese, *Banche e banchieri a Volterra nel
Medioevo e nel Rinascimento* (Pisa 1993).

[23] In 1430 the Peruzzi bank was the commune's creditor for 2,800 florins: ASF,
Catasto, 240, 386r–387r.

[24] For the importance of clientage relations in Volterra's submission, see A. K. Isaacs,
'Volterra nel Cinquecento: alcune prospettive di ricerca', *Bollettino storico pisano*, 58
(1989), pp. 197–8.

The natural recourse for Volterrans was the Captain of Custody, who not only was meant to be an able and honest official, the defender of communal interests, but who also had to act as a link with the Florentine government and therefore to represent the interests of Volterra. The Captain, who was in the first instance a Florentine officer and as such the representative of the Florentine Signoria, was therefore to a certain extent an ambivalent figure, placed as he was at the heart of relations between the two cities. The delicacy of his position favoured the forging of firm personal ties with the exponents of the local patriciate, likely to endure well beyond his term of office. It is not surprising, therefore, that the greater part of those Florentines in whom Volterra placed its trust were ex-Captains and their families.[25]

Protection and trust, constantly sought by the local community for its informal ties, had, nevertheless, a price – a price that was paid in the currency of political autonomy. A striking example can be seen in the choice of foreign officials of the commune. On 4 November 1394 the communal councils approved a petition from Maso degli Albizzi, then Captain of Custody, seeking the election of Matteuccio di Cecchetto dalla Pergola as Podestà, notwithstanding the existing statutory procedures.[26] Thenceforth even jobs reserved for foreigners, from which Florentines had been debarred, came under their indirect control: promoting their own candidates and systematically suspending normal electoral procedures, they *de facto* stripped the commune of its electoral prerogatives. In practice, through a continuous series of petitions similar to Maso degli Albizzi's, about eighty Florentine citizens, including Captains and ex-Captains, their families and other eminent figures, managed to take advantage of the Volterrans' need for protection by including these offices in the circle of their patronage exchanges.

The significance of this practice is demonstrated by its widespread use. From 1394 to 1429 there were sixty-eight appointments of this type to the office of Podestà.[27] It is true that the frequency of these extraordinary elections led to long queues and that therefore some of the Podestà thus chosen never served in office; nevertheless, it is striking that so many nominations of this type were made in merely seventy six-monthly terms of office. A similar proportion is to be found in other offices reserved for foreigners, in particular that of the Captain of the

---

[25] Beginning in the first decades of Florentine hegemony, the families of various captains – the Adimari, Ricci, Salviati, for example – established notable relations with Volterrans.

[26] ASCV, A nera, 24, 328r–v.

[27] This information is taken from Volterra's communal deliberations, ASCV, A nera, 24–37.

Priors' Household and of the Notary of the *danni dati*.[28] All this is a sign of the attitude of Florentines to Volterra: they left intact the constitutional structures of the commune, while attempting in so far as possible to deprive them of substance through a process of infiltration.

The systematic use of extraordinary procedures is a clear indication of how Volterra's autonomy, albeit fully protected in an institutional and formal sense, was opened to Florentine control through political relationships whereby the ruling city's superior position could find greater scope for action. The penetration into local political life by influential Florentine citizens was not merely a consequence of the domination exercised by their city, but actually represented the process of domination itself. It was precisely the interference by the Florentine patriciate that most effectively served to secure Volterra's political integration.

The principal practitioners of these alternative electoral methods, as has been stated, were incumbent Captains of Custody. The regularity with which they exploited such means suggests how key officials, mediating between centre and periphery, could add a series of informal powers to their statutory prerogatives.

This emerges most clearly from the identity of the candidates proposed by the Captains for the above-mentioned three magistracies (Podestà, Captain of the Household of the Priors, and Notary of the *danni dati*). It is possible to observe not only an almost systematic recruitment from members of their own staff, but even a direct correspondence between the job held in the service of the Captain and the new office for which nominees were destined. Thus, there was a marked tendency for the collateral judge of the Captain to become the Podestà, for one of the companion knights to become Captain of the Household, and for one of the notaries of the Captain's staff to become Notary of the *danni dati*.

This was a phenomenon that symbolised the function of clientage relations in the formation of the territorial state: the political ascendancy and personal ties of the rectors sent by Florence could be transformed into an extraordinary instrument to direct and channel that vast and

---

[28] As far as the Captaincy of the Household of the Priors is concerned, there are at least ten such cases between 1397 and 1411, a striking number in view of the fact that it was an annual office. In 1411, perhaps in order to limit this Florentine interference, the commune decided to reform the office, restricting it to locals and limiting its term to two months, which thus corresponded to individual priorates (ASCV, G nera, 18, 23v). Florentine interest in the Notary of the *danni dati* developed later, beginning only in 1405, but thereafter intervention was constant, leading to twenty-six appointments of this type up to 1423.

dispersed mass of functionaries, coming from various parts of Italy, who came to constitute the personnel of the judicial, administrative, police, sanitary and educational apparatus of so many Italian communes. Florentine interference therefore favoured the development of local roots on the part of these errant officials, who tended to exploit proven channels in the furtherance of their own careers. These tendencies were still largely haphazard and irregular, but in them I believe it is possible to detect the seeds of a diffused territorial bureaucracy, operated directly by the central government of the state.

With regard to Volterra, these phenomena are symptomatic of a tendency to assimilate the commune into a system of domination that was taking shape in the region, although it stood in theory at the margins of this process, by virtue of the limits placed on its own obligations through the above-mentioned bilateral pacts. The Florentine republic had to accept many analogous compromises in subjugating its territory, which therefore still remained fragmented amongst a mass of local rights and prerogatives. And it is precisely with regard to this political reality that the mediating work undertaken by the Florentine patriciate appears to have been particularly decisive. The exercise of patronage tended, in fact, to reinforce the internal homogeneity of the dominion, even where formal relations with single communities did not allow for direct governmental intervention. In conclusion, we can say that recourse to this indirect form of domination favoured the political–institutional progression, but, at the same time, it was symptomatic of the objective limits of Florentine state-building in the Albizzi period.

V

Even Volterra, albeit to a limited extent, felt the impact of those centralising and unifying currents which affected all the Florentine dominions between the end of the fourteenth and the first decades of the fifteenth century. The reform of the office of Captain of Custody and the incorporation of the commune into the republic's fiscal system signalled the transition from a political and military type of hegemony to a more organic and hierarchical relationship, one in which the controlling influence of the ruling power was made more effective while the obligations of the subject commune became clearer and more definite. The commune of Volterra entered therefore into a wider political system. It is true that its dependence continued to be based on contractual, bilateral pacts which allowed for wide areas of autonomy. But it was on the level of practical politics, including informal contacts, that ties with Florence were reinforced, thus favouring the process of integration into the territorial state.

Such a system of relationships, always retaining a balance between effective dominion and formal recognition of autonomy and subject to continual renegotiation through a series of public and private links, was able to function as long as certain equilibriums and limits were safeguarded and respected. Nevertheless, the prevalence of negotiation and of clientage did not mean that the relationship between Florence and Volterra was without tensions, ones which could at times even become embittered. Questions such as the pacification of Volterra's factions and the reform of the office of the Captain, or the repeated attempts by the Florentine government to impose a salt gabelle, as well as its frequent requests for military subsidies and contingents, led to sharp differences, even if they were ultimately resolved through negotiation. The choice of peaceful means thus did not imply the absence of conflict. On the contrary, negotiation itself and even patronage in many cases acted as integrating elements in the context of daily conflicts fought by each party in order to reach an acceptable equilibrium.

The imposition of the catasto of 1427 constituted a clear attempt to upset this balance, to achieve a new kind of relationship between the two cities, creating the preconditions for an effective and definitive assimilation of Volterra and its territory into the Florentine state.

This new method of taxation represented the high-water mark for Albizzi policy in the dominion, soon to be frustrated by reverses in the war against Lucca and by the triumph of the Medici faction.[29] It shook some of the fundamental cornerstones of local autonomy, undermining both the link between the city and its contado and the power of the commune's ruling group. In particular, it inaugurated a direct relationship between the Florentine government and the individual contributors of the district, relieving the local authorities, up to then in full control over the distribution of the local tax burden, of their status as

[29] On the introduction of the catasto in 1427 and the political debate associate with it, see P. Berti, 'Nuovi documenti intorno al catasto fiorentino per quali vien dimostrato che la proposta del medesimo non fu di Giovanni dei Medici', *Giornale storico degli archivi toscani*, 4 (1860), pp. 32–62; E. Conti, *L'imposta diretta a Firenze nel Quattrocento (1427–1494)* (Rome, 1984), pp. 119–37; A. Molho, *Florentine Public Finances in the Early Renaissance, 1400–1433* (Cambridge, Mass., 1971), pp. 79–81; D. Herlihy and C. Klapisch-Zuber, *Les Toscans et leurs familles: une étude du catasto florentin du 1427* (Paris, 1978), pp. 34–42; D. V. Kent, *The Rise of the Medici: Faction in Florence, 1426–1434* (Oxford, 1978), p. 6; G. A. Brucker, *The Civic World of Early Renaissance Florence* (Princeton, 1977), pp. 483–486. The law instituting the catasto was published by O. Karmin, *La legge del catasto fiorentino del 1427 (Testo, introduzione e note)* (Florence, 1906).

intermediaries. It was clearly a fundamental issue regarding the status of the subject commune within the dominion created by Florence, not to mention the local power structure within the commune itself.

The conflict with Volterra over the catasto lasted for more than two years, culminating in the anti-Florentine revolt of October 1429, headed by Giusto Landini; its result was definitively to upset those assumptions and balances which had for many decades propped up relations between the two cities.[30]

In the last analysis, the struggle between Florence and Volterra involved the conception that each city had of its reciprocal relations, assuming eventually a strongly ideological dimension. The Volterrans forcefully upheld the contractual nature of the relationship, confirmed by the bilateral pacts of 1361, which they understood as the sole basis of – and therefore also as a limit on – Florentine superiority; they continually referred to those agreements to justify their conduct.[31] A similar conception could have commanded support among a part of the Florentine oligarchy, inspired either by legalistic idealism or political calculation; nevertheless, in Florence a different view prevailed, upholding the superior rights of the dominating power *vis-à-vis* the subject communities, even in the teeth of the juridical implications of various acts and agreements.

It is from this perspective that one must see the intransigence of the Florentine authorities in the face of the tenacious resistance by the Volterrans, not to mention the punitive provisions adopted towards the city in the aftermath of the revolt.

In the *consulta* called by the Signoria on 24 October 1429, immediately after the news of the events of Volterra reached Florence, and in a later meeting of 14 November, a clear contrast emerged between those in favour of exemplary repression, on the model of that earlier imposed on the Pisans, and those who, thinking perhaps of the social and economic consequences already evident in Pisa, favoured negotiation

---

[30] There survive a number of contemporary accounts of the revolt against the catasto, but these are almost exclusively Florentine. The only Volterran version, albeit composed about fifty years after the events, is the 'Cronichetta volterrana di autore anonimo dal 1362 al 1478', ed. M. Tabarrini, *Archivio storico italiano*, App., III (1846), pp. 320–2. The most detailed account is by Giovanni Cavalcanti in his *Istorie fiorentine*, ed. F. L. Polidori (Florence, 1838), I, pp. 276–91. For relevant documents, see Cecina, *Notizie istoriche*, pp. 220–9, and C. Guasti (ed.), *Commissioni di Rinaldo degli Albizzi per il comune di Firenze dal MCCCXCIC al MCCCCXXXIII*, III (Florence, 1873), pp. 173–86. This subject has been little studied. See Herlihy and Klapisch-Zuber, *Les Toscans et leurs familles*, pp. 89–90, 92–4.

[31] ASCV, A nera, 37, I, 43r–298r, *passim*; Cavalcanti, *Istorie fiorentine*, I, pp. 257–8.

and renewal of the ancient agreements.[32] The provision of 23 and 24 December demonstrates how the hardliners, identifiable with the Albizzi faction, prevailed: the abolition of the Podestà, with consequent transferral of civil jurisdiction to the Florentine Captain, and above all the separation of Volterra from its contado, which was incorporated into that of Florence, represented the logical conclusion of this wish to 'normalise' the anomalous position of an area which, within the Florentine state, had maintained until that time an undoubtedly privileged position.[33]

Volterra was therefore on the point of undergoing the same fate which, twenty or thirty years before, Florence had meted out to other subject cities. But this now was taking place in an altered context: the last phase of territorial and institutional development of the Florentine republic was frustrated by the ill-fated campaign against Lucca at the very moment that the internal conflict between Albizzi and Medici factions was intensifying. In the course of two years, Volterra regained all its liberties and privileges, including exemption from the catasto, thus completely nullifying the penal provisions enforced after the revolt.[34] All this was a clear symptom of how weak the impulse towards the formation of a regional state had grown.

VI

The advent to power of the Medici in 1434 marked a significant turning point for Volterra.[35] As early as the catasto crisis, special links had been forged with Cosimo, who had assumed the role of great patron of the

---

[32] Guasti (ed.), *Commissioni di Rinaldo degli Albizzi*, III, pp. 174–6, 184. An eloquent advocate of leniency was Neri di Gino Capponi: 'Serventur pacta pristino modo Vulterranis; utilius est isto modo tenere, quam recipere in dominium; quia cito destruentur. Et fiat fortilitium. Et grate recipiantur et tractentur Vulterrani. Aliter cito destruentur, propter paupertatem, sterilitatem et desperationem civium' (p. 184).

[33] ASF, PR, 120, 406r–409r. It is noteworthy that the provision was approved by the councils with the minimum two-thirds majority (409v, 426v).

[34] The catasto, the original cause of the conflict, was the first object of clemency: the Volterrans' exemption was approved on 9 April 1431 (the act was published by Cecina, *Notizie istoriche*, pp. 220–1). On 25 October 1431, the provision of December 1429 was repealed: ASF, PR, 122, 231r–232r.

[35] On Volterra in the Medici period, and particularly under Lorenzo, see E. Insabato and S. Pieri, 'Il controllo del territorio nello stato fiorentino del XV secolo. Un caso emblematico: Volterra', in M. A. Morelli Timpanaro, R. Manno Tolu and P. Viti (eds.), *Consorterie politiche e mutamenti istituzionali in età laurenziana* (Florence, 1992), pp. 177–211.

Volterran cause,[36] evidently in opposition to his political adversary, Rinaldo degli Albizzi, who had been the major advocate and architect of the policy of repression.[37] The benefits were not long in coming after the Medicean ascent to power: as early as June 1435 the Florentine government approved the remission of all fiscal debts accumulated by Volterra over the preceding six years. At the same time there was a drastic reduction in the annual lance tax from 2340 to 1000 florins,[38] not to mention the willingness, later shown several times, to suspend this exaction at moments of particular hardship for Volterra and its territory.[39]

Beginning in the 1450s, visits to Volterra by some members of the Medici family opened new channels between the two cities. Figures such as Piero di Cosimo and his wife Lucrezia Tornabuoni,[40] but especially Giovanni di Cosimo, who repeatedly stayed in Volterra,[41] led to friendly relations with various local notables as well as with wider segments of the population of the city and contado. This personal presence, forming deep roots within society, consolidated Medicean ascendancy, shifting notably the axis between Florence and Volterra with regard to formal and extra-institutional relations. Even the very figures who ought to have enshrined the official character of Florentine dominion, such as the Captain of Custody, in fact acquiesced to this new state of affairs, participating directly in the exchange of favours, recommendations and personal pressures. As early as 1435, for example, a number of letters directed to Cosimo de' Medici illustrate how his pioneering indirect involvement in mining activities in the Val di

---

[36] It seems that Cosimo became Volterra's principal advocate at the end of 1428, in the midst of the catasto controversy, when the Volterran government decided to write to him, 'ipsum rogitando quod pro tutela et defensione iurium comunis Vulterrarum suos favores propicios interponat'; ASCV, A nera, 37, I, 256r.

[37] Rinaldo's role emerges immediately after the rebellion, during the *consulta* of 24 October 1429. Subsequently he was one of the *balìa* of ten appointed to deal with the revolt, and, together with Messer Palla di Nofri Strozzi, he undertook the command of military operations as the republic's commissioner. It was he who, on 5 November, entered Volterra and formally took control of the city: Guasti (ed.), *Commissioni di Rinaldo degli Albizzi*, III, pp. 173–86.

[38] ASF, PR, 126, 100v–101v.

[39] This occurred, for example, in December 1449, when, in view of the devastation caused by the Aragonese army in the area, Volterra gained remission from two preceding annual taxes and a further exemption for five years: ASF, PR, 140, 202v–204r.

[40] The regular visits by Cosimo's daughter–in–law to Bagno a Morbo, in Volterran territory, are fully documented in Lucrezia Tornabuoni, *Lettere*, ed. P. Salvadori (Florence, 1993).

[41] See his abundant correspondence with Volterran friends in ASF, MAP, *passim*.

Cecina was supported not only by Volterran clients, but also by the prompt action of the Captain Giovanni di Astorre Gianni.[42]

A key role was taken in this sense moreover by the bishops of Volterra, carefully chosen by the Florentine government from its own citizenry.[43] They always maintained a certain autonomy of judgment and action, befitting their lofty political and spiritual prestige, a position which was preserved over centuries and which still guaranteed them a series of important jurisdictional prerogatives. Nevertheless, as is revealed by the correspondence between the Medici and Giovanni Dietisalvi Neroni, bishop of Volterra from 1449 to 1462, before becoming archbishop of Florence, it is clear how much the presence of a philo-Medicean bishop could affect the distribution of ecclesiastical benefices and, on a more general level, influence the functioning of clientage in the dominion.[44]

With the supremacy of the Medici, therefore, in place of the now outdated scheme of completing the subjugation of the city, there emerged an idea of control based above all on political consensus and on a network of interpersonal ties between the governing family of Florence and the citizen class that controlled Volterra. This phenomenon was certainly not limited to one particular locality, and indeed represented an important aspect in the evolution of the Florentine state in the fifteenth century. Nevertheless, Volterra's case helps to clarify how the dichotomy between the Albizzi and Medici models cannot be explained simply in terms of changed political and military contexts. Indeed, those features which would characterise the second model in contrast to the first were notable as early as the 1420s.

The intense relations between members of the Medici family and some sectors of the local ruling group introduced, however, an element of weakness, which previously had been missing in relations between the two cities. With the *reductio ad unum* of the Florentine patronage

---

[42] ASF, MAP, 12, n. 122, Giovanni di Astorre Gianni, Captain of Volterra, to Cosimo de' Medici in Florence, Volterra, 5 October 1435. The letter has been published in A. Molho, 'Three Documents Regarding Filippo Brunellischi', *The Burlington Magazine*, 119 (1977), pp. 851–2. Cosimo had an interest in the copper mines of Serrazzano. On this, see two other letters: ASF, MAP, 12, n. 113, Stefano de Valone to Cosimo de' Medici in Florence, Volterra, 3 October 1435; and *ibid.*, n. 124, Potente di Bartolomeo di Ser Potente Baldinotti to Cosimo de' Medici in Florence, Volterra, 5 October 1435.

[43] On the role of Florentine political authorities in the election of the bishops of Tuscan sees, see R. Bizzocchi, *Chiesa e potere nella Toscana del Quattrocento* (Bologna, 1987), pp. 225–39.

[44] See the correspondence of Giovanni Neroni with members of the Medici family during his Volterran episcopate: ASF, MAP, *passim*. On Neroni, see Bizzocchi, *Chiesa e potere*, p. 211.

system, which at one time had been fully pluralistic, there emerged a philo-Medicean party amongst some of the principal families of the city, including the Inghirami, Minucci, Riccobaldi, Caffarecci, Lisci and others.[45] This could not but impinge on the equilibrium and the stability of power relations within the governing class – both of which had been scrupulously nurtured by the previous regime. The conflicts between the old families, long appeased by the *pax florentina*, once again came to the fore. And the discovery of alum deposits in the contado of Volterra, which enabled the philo-Medici group, some of whom were directly involved in the enterprise, to reinforce its own economic and political pre-eminence, lit the spark of a new and violent confrontation between the factions. This time, however, the Florentine government, itself party to the conflict, was unable to play the role of conciliator above the factions. Indeed, its intervention, instead of restoring peace as in the past, led to a harsh and definitive submission of Volterra to the territorial state.[46]

---

[45] Insabato and Pieri, 'Il controllo del territorio', pp. 193–4; R. Fubini, 'Lorenzo de' Medici e Volterra', *Rassegna volterrana*, 70 (1994), pp. 177–8. On Volterran families, see E. Fiumi, 'Popolazione, società ed economia volterrana dal catasto del 1428/1429', in his *Volterra e San Gimignano nel Medioevo*, ed. G. Pinto (San Gimignano, 1983), pp. 194–260 (previously published in *Rassegna volterrana*, 36–9 (1972), pp. 85–161).

[46] Besides Fiumi, *L'impresa di Lorenzo de' Medici*, see now P. Airaghi, A. Osimo and G. Cagliari Poli, 'Documenti sul sacco di Volterra del 16 giugno 1472 che si trovano presso l'Archivio di Stato di Milano', *Rassegna volterrana*, 69 (1993), pp. 79–96, and Fubini, 'Lorenzo de' Medici e Volterra', pp. 171–85. On developments after 1472, see E. Insabato and S. Pieri, 'Tra repressione e privilegio: i rapporti tra Volterrra e Firenze dal 1472 al 1513', in L. Borgia, F. De Luca, P. Viti and R. M. Zaccaria (eds.), *Studi in onore di Arnaldo d'Addario* (Lecce, 1995), IV, 1, pp. 1215–44.

CHAPTER 12

SAN MINIATO AL TEDESCO: THE EVOLUTION OF THE POLITICAL CLASS

FRANCESCO SALVESTRINI

A sector of studies by now decades old, which has developed out of a renewed attention for the first constitutive circumstances of the State, has concentrated on the Florentine dominion and its definition as a subregional entity, as well as on the structures of its territorial government. Research has revealed, both on a general level and in the course of categorical and local studies, that the progressive growth of the old 'contado' (Lat. *comitatus*) that had belonged to the Florentine republic at the height of the communal period experienced, apart from any teleological considerations, a strong acceleration, and was more dense with changes beginning, more or less, in the late fourteenth century, with particular intensity during the Albizzi period. It has been remarked, in fact, that between 1300 and 1400 there took place both an institutional redefinition of the ruling city and a more *organic* structuring of the existing relations between centre and periphery.

In particular, it has been shown that the relations between Florence and the subject communes underwent, in the decades of most rapid expansion, a profound re-elaboration of the institutions of government and of the methods of administration applied to the territory, even in the sense of an opening at a broader scale of the preceding organs for the administration of power, with a planning impulse in the institutional area that expressed an orientation towards forms of control and conduct that were more centralised.[1]

---

[1] M. B. Becker, *Florence in Transition*, II, *Studies in the Rise of the Territorial State* (Baltimore, 1968); G. Chittolini, 'Ricerche sull'ordinamento territoriale del dominio fiorentino agli inizi del secolo XV', in his *La formazione dello stato regionale e le istituzioni del contado. Secoli XIV e XV* (Turin, 1979), pp. 292–352; D. Herlihy, 'Le relazioni economiche di Firenze con le città soggette nel secolo XV', in *Egemonia fiorentina ed autonomie locali nella Toscana nord-occidentale del primo Rinascimento: vita, arte, cultura* (Pistoia, 1978), pp. 79–109.

It has also been seen, however, that a more stable vigilance on the part of the Florentine rulers over the congeries of political organisms pre-existing and absorbed over time in the dominion of the republic was actuated not only through the construction of a more organic and unitary constitutional model, but rather, above all, thanks to a capable policy of pragmatic adaptation to local conditions. It has emerged, therefore, that the Florentine state, as it created itself over the cusp of the two centuries, was not so much a coherent jurisdictional reality, stamped with integration and administrative uniformity, but rather a coming together of local situations controlled politically by the Arno city through ductile and consensual practices of government.

It is an accepted historical datum that the effective exercise of power over the territory passed through channels that were not institutionalised and were of a more political rather than an administrative nature, such as the widely diffused phenomenon of patronage. Patronage provided both a structure and a dynamic of the social relations within the city during the early Renaissance.[2] The eminent families of the Florentine patriciate extended it, above all from the mid-1400s, also to relations with the society of the contado.[3]

Studies on this subject have been conducted from two points of

[2] There is a vast literature on this subject. See especially, C. Klapisch-Zuber, ' "Parenti, amici e vicini": il territorio urbano d'una famiglia mercantile nel XV secolo', Quaderni storici, 33 (1976), pp. 953–82; Klapisch-Zuber, 'Compérage et clientélisme à Florence (1360–1520)', Ricerche storiche, 15 (1985), pp. 61–76; A. Molho, 'Cosimo de' Medici: "Pater Patriae" or "Padrino"?', Stanford Italian Review, 1 (1979), pp. 5–33; R. Weissman, Ritual Brotherhood in Renaissance Florence (New York, 1982); D. V. and F. W. Kent, Neighbours and Neighbourhood in Renaissance Florence: The District of the Red Lion in the Fifteenth Century (Locust Valley, 1982). A critical examination of some of these studies may be found in Molho, 'Il padronato a Firenze nella storiografia anglofona', Ricerche storiche, 15 (1985), pp. 5–16.

[3] Cf. D. V. and F. W. Kent, 'Two Vignettes of Florentine Society in the Fifteenth Century', Rinascimento, 34 (1983), pp. 237–60, esp. pp. 247 and 249–52; W. J. Connell, 'Clientelismo e stato territoriale. Il potere fiorentino a Pistoia nel XV secolo', Società e storia, 14 (1991), pp. 526–33; R. Black, 'Cosimo de' Medici and Arezzo', in F. Ames-Lewis (ed.), Cosimo "il Vecchio" de' Medici, 1389–1464 (Oxford, 1992), pp. 33–47; L. Fabbri, 'Autonomismo comunale ed egemonia fiorentina a Volterra tra '300 e '400', Rassegna volterrana, 70 (1994), pp. 97–110, at pp. 106ff. In general, see G. Chittolini, 'Stati padani, "Stato del Rinascimento": problemi di ricerca', in G. Tocci (ed.), Persistenze feudali e autonomie comunitative in stati padani fra Cinque e Settecento (Bologna, 1988), pp. 9–29, esp. pp. 15–16. For the evolution of the phenomenon in the Medicean period, see Connell, 'Clientelismo', pp. 538ff.; Connell, 'Changing Patterns in Medicean Patronage. The Florentine Dominion During the Fifteenth Century', in G. C. Garfagnini (ed.), Lorenzo il Magnifico e il suo mondo (Florence, 1994), pp. 87–107; P. Salvadori, 'Rapporti personali, rapporti di potere nella corrispondenza di Lorenzo dei Medici' in G. C. Garfagnini (ed.), Lorenzo il Magnifico e il suo tempo (Florence, 1992), pp. 125–46.

view: a general plan, from the perspective of the centre, for the entire layout of the dominion;[4] and a particular plan, which looks at lesser cities and centres.[5]

The second key for reading these phenomena, that is of the forms of submission realised locally and at the margins of autonomy that remained in subject areas, appears interesting, because it offers the possibility of verifying and enriching general syntheses, contributing to the definition of a political layout which, as we have said, was especially varied.

The study of the political and social transformations that took place at San Miniato al Tedesco, a smaller city located halfway between Florence and Pisa, in the period when it became part of the Florentine dominion, can furnish several points of reflection. It has often been shown that Florentine hegemony, above all in the course of the fourteenth century, was affirmed through the insertion of representatives of the ruling city in the socio-political context of the controlled cities and in the struggles of factions that often lacerated them, assuming, in various ways, a position *super partes*, with the intention of carrying out a local pacification. Scholars have also shown that the strategies of

---

[4] In addition to the works cited in note 2 above, see P. Benigni, 'L'organizzazione territoriale dello stato fiorentino nel '300', in *La Toscana nel secolo XIV: caratteri di una civiltà regionale* (Pisa, 1988), pp. 151–63; R. Fubini, 'Dalla rappresentanza sociale alla rappresentanza politica: alcune osservazioni sull'evoluzione politico-costituzionale di Firenze nel Rinascimento', *Rivista storica italiana*, 102 (1990), pp. 279–301; A. Zorzi, 'Lo Stato territoriale fiorentino (secoli XIV–XV): aspetti giurisdizionali', *Società e storia*, 13(50) (1990), pp. 799–825; A. Zorzi, 'Ordine pubblico e amministrazione della giustizia nelle formazioni politiche toscane tra Tre e Quattrocento', in *Italia 1350–1450: tra crisi, trasformazioni, sviluppo* (Pistoia, 1993), pp. 419–74. On the initial phases of the process, see A. Zorzi, 'L'organizzazione del territorio in area fiorentina tra XIII e XIV secolo', in G. Chittolini and D. Willoweit (eds.), *L'organizzazione del territorio in Italia e Germania: secoli XIII–XIV* (Bologna, 1994), pp. 279–349. On the limits to territorial consolidation, see W. J. Connell, 'Il commissario e lo stato territoriale fiorentino', *Ricerche storiche*, 18 (1988), pp. 591–617, esp. pp. 592–3.

[5] Other examples to be compared with San Miniato include M. Mallett, 'Pisa and Florence in the Fifteenth Century: Aspects of the Period of the First Florentine Domination', in N. Rubinstein (ed.), *Florentine Studies: Politics and Society in Renaissance Florence* (London, 1968), pp. 403–41; D. Herlihy, *Pistoia nel Medioevo e nel Rinascimento, 1200–1430*, Ital. trans. (Florence, 1972), pp. 250ff.; J. C. Brown, *Pescia nel Rinascimento: all'ombra di Firenze*, Ital. trans. (Pescia, 1987); G. Pampaloni, 'L'autonomia pratese sotto Firenze (1351–1500)', in F. Braudel (gen. ed.), *Prato. Storia di una città*, I, *Ascesa e declino del centro medievale (dal Mille al 1494)*, ed. G. Cherubini (Florence, 1991), pp. 737–60; Connell, 'Clientelismo'; Black, 'Cosimo de' Medici'; Fabbri, 'Autonomismo'; L. De Angelis, 'La fine della libertà pistoiese', in L. Borgia, F. De Luca, P. Viti and R. M. Zaccaria (eds.), *Studi in onore di Arnaldo d'Addario* (Lecce, 1995), IV, 1, pp. 1157–65; O. Muzzi, 'Attività artigianali e cambiamenti politici a Colle Val d'Elsa prima e dopo la conquista fiorentina', in R. Ninci (ed.), *La società fiorentina nel basso medioevo. Per Elio Conti* (Rome, 1995), pp. 221–53.

subjugation adopted before the 1370s did not involve institutional reforms intended to deprive cities of jurisdiction over their contadi. This may have been due, in part, to the desire to avoid local turmoil, but it was also probably the result of an inability on the part of the central government to conceive of new forms of territorial hegemony. Thus, even factoring in the multiplicity of the different situations, often an accord was reached with the former ruling classes, the various factional struggles were frozen, there were attempts to shrink social conflict and the preceding territorial organisation was allowed to stand.[6]

With respect to San Miniato there are several differences from this general outline, however. The change from pacts that established a Florentine political protectorate to the definitive passage of San Miniato into the jurisdiction of the Florentine republic took place through a conquest and a military occupation in 1369–70. The particular socio-political situation of the place, together with a change in Florentine strategies, and the emerging war with the Visconti, determined immediate institutional reforms that radically overturned the local *reggimento*, with respect to both the city and the surrounding territory. Such an action, destined to repeat itself on subsequent occasions, above all with the occupations of Arezzo and Pisa, had not been usual in the preceding period;[7] and, from certain points of view, it seems to have been first tried out at San Miniato. What is most significant about the case we are studying, moreover, is that at San Miniato the initial accords that were reached with the local elite were only partial and transitory and the conquerors achieved a rapid and almost total substitution of the

[6] This seems to be the case at Pistoia, where, as underlined by Connell, 'Clientelismo', pp. 526–9, 533–4 and 537–8, from the 1370s members of important Florentine families adhered to one or the other of the two factions that divided the city. On the other hand, the Florentine government, which made use of the factions in governing on the local level, did not attempt to suppress the factions. (See also Chittolini, 'Ricerche', p. 313; De Angelis, 'La fine', p. 1158.) At Volterra, too, during the first phase of Florentine control (beginning in 1361), the republic acted as peacemaker between the local factions without drastically affecting the local magnates (Fabbri, 'Autonomismo', pp. 100–3). At Pescia, the exile of the local Ghibellines after the town's submission in 1339 does not seem to have resulted in a sudden change in the social or political make-up (Brown, *Pescia*, p. 85). Even at Pisa, notwithstanding her violent conquest and the emigration of many patricians (G. Petralia, ' "Crisi" ed emigrazione dei ceti eminenti a Pisa durante il primo dominio fiorentino: l'orizzonte cittadino e la ricerca di spazi esterni (1404–1460)', in *I ceti dirigenti nella Toscana del Quattrocento* (Florence, 1987), pp. 291–352), there were many leaders of the anti-Florentine resistance who still owned their lands at the time of the Florentine catasto of 1427 (Mallett, 'Pisa', pp. 404–8 and 415–18).

[7] Thus Pistoia, although controlled by Florence from 1329, preserved, at least until the 1370s, jurisdiction over her own territory (Chittolini, 'Ricerche', pp. 295–7). Similarly, too, at Volterra (Fabbri, 'Autonomismo', pp. 99ff. and 103).

former class of notables. There took place, consequently, the complete suppression of the dialectic of the city's factions, together with important social changes that involved the entire Samminiatese citizenry. The reasons for choices of this kind belonged in part to the distant past, and in part to developments that were more recent. The aim of this chapter is to attempt to sketch them, taking into account that San Miniato al Tedesco claimed a notable strategic importance on the principal road from Florence to the sea; and that in the past it was a 'quasi-city' – in accordance with the definition coined by Giorgio Chittolini.[8] It is estimated, in fact, that until the crises of the Trecento, San Miniato had about 5000 inhabitants. But at the time of the conquest, it had become a secondary centre, of small demographic weight and lacking any particular areas of economic strength.[9] Such a situation allowed the Florentines to intervene with decisiveness in the local context, without those cautions that doubtless would have accompanied the assimilation of larger cities.

From the first half of the fourteenth century San Miniato, which had been seat of the imperial vicariate furnished with jurisdiction over central Italy, was the principal city at the heart of the lower Arno valley. The regime was Guelf and popular, and it was connected with a dialectical alliance with the Florentine republic.[10] However the prevalently Ghibelline orientation had never been reduced in the local context, involving above all the old aristocratic class, which, created through the patronage of the Imperial Vicar and documented from the later twelfth century, had played a fundamental role in the first delineation of communal institutions.[11]

---

[8] G. Chittolini, ' "Quasi-città". Borghi e terre in area lombarda nel tardo Medioevo', *Società e storia*, 13 (1990), pp. 3–26.

[9] According to the Florentine estimo of 1383 there were 772 families, for a total of roughly 2,700 persons, which dropped to fewer than 1,500 (324 hearths) in the years of the Florentine catasto of 1427–30. See ASF, Estimo, 243, 1353r–1449v and 1482r–1535v; Catasto, 167, 356v–488r; and M. Ginatempo and L. Sandri, *L'Italia delle città: il popolamento urbano tra Medioevo e Rinascimento (secoli XIII–XVI)* (Florence, 1990), pp. 41, 53ff., 107–10 and 148.

[10] Since San Miniato is little known to historians, it will be useful to note certain elements of its sociopolitical structure in the communal period.

[11] On the period of the Imperial Vicars (eleventh–thirteenth centuries), on the birth of the commune, and in general for the town's history before 1350, see F. Salvestrini (ed.), *Statuti del Comune di San Miniato al Tedesco (1337)* (Pisa, 1994), pp. 11–42, 'Introduzione'. For the first Florentine *balìe* (1329 and 1347), see ASF, Dipl., Comune di San Miniato, 26 September 1329; G. Villani, *Cronica*, bk XII, ch. 72; M. di Coppo Stefani, *Cronaca fiorentina*, ed. N. Rodolico, in *Rerum Italicarum Scriptores*, 2nd edn, XXX, pt I, fasc. 18–19 (Città di Castello, 1903), rub. 282, p. 106; 294, pp. 109–10; 359, p. 132; 580, p. 206; ASF, Dipl., Comune di San Miniato, 17 October 1347, 8 August 1348. See, too, R. Davidsohn, *Storia di Firenze*, Ital. trans., 5

Notwithstanding the influence of the municipal order and the existence of anti-magnate legislation,[12] this strong class, boasting counts as ancestors, and in particular the two *consorterie* with the emblematic names Ciccioni and Mangiadori, still preserved a notable influence over the political life of San Miniato in the fourteenth century.[13]

Such nuclei of relatives were extrinsic, at least in large part, to commercial activity; and, since they were in constant combat among themselves, these resulted in enmities that generated two opposing factions.[14] Notwithstanding this, certain leaders of this order had held political office, whether on behalf of the commune or outside the city, at least from the early thirteenth century.[15]

The families possessed landed patrimonies that placed them at the top of the social scale. They in fact owned many factories rented out within the city walls and a large share of the lands of the contado and the district.[16] The territory, in particular, appeared dotted with their strong-

---

vols. in 8 (Florence, 1956–60), IV, pp. 1199, 1202; V, p. 361; Zorzi, 'L'organizzazione', p. 347. On methods for watching over smaller centres not yet subject to Florence, see Zorzi, 'Lo Stato territoriale', pp. 800–2.

[12] See *Statuti del Comune*, lib. II, rub. XXIIII, pp. 144–5; XLIIII, pp. 164–5; LXXXVIII, pp. 203–6; LXXXXI, pp. 207–8; lib. IV, rub. 28, p. 319; 29, p. 320; 34, pp. 324–5; lib. V, rub. 28, pp. 431–2; and ACSM, Statuti di San Miniato (1359), 2249, lib. I, rub. LXVI, LXVII; lib. II, rub. XXXVII, LIII, LXXXII, CVI; lib. IV, rub. XVII, XL, XLII, XLVIII, XLVIIII, LI, LXI, LXIII; lib. V, rub. IV, V, VI, XXXV.

[13] There were roughly ten magnate families. Their names (Ciccioni, Mangiadori, Orlandini, Scornigiani, counts of Collegalli, Lucardesi, Traini, Rustici, Bottecci, Gigliori) appear in certain rubrics of the commune's statutes (*Statuti del Comune* lib. II, rub. LXXXVIII, pp. 203–6; ACSM, Statuti (1359), lib. II, rub. CVI, 30r). On the families, see ASF, Carte Ceramelli Papiani, 2918 (Malpigli), 2938 (Mangiadori), 5436 (Ciccioni); BNF, Poligrafo Gargani, 352, fol. 45; 577, fol. 84; 599, fols. 21, 31, 41; and 1199, fols. 196–245. Aside from the magnates, there were also the so-called 'grandi di popolo', especially the Bonincontri and the Borromei, who, while engaged in commerce, are poorly documented. On the Borromei, see F. Melis, 'L'economia delle città minori della Toscana', in *Le zecche minori toscane fino al XV secolo* (Pistoia, 1967), pp. 20–1; and the articles by F. Edler and G. Chittolini in *Dizionario biografico degli italiani*, XIII (Rome, 1971), pp. 45–6, 48–9, 53–5, 63–4, 72–4.

[14] For the division of the magnates, and of part of the remaining citizenry into two factions, led by the Ciccioni and the Mangiadori, see G. di Lelmo da Comugnori, *Diario cittadino (1299–1320)*, ed. L. Passerini, in *Documenti di storia italiana*, VI (Florence, 1876), pp. 157–205.

[15] See G. Rondoni, 'Il franco ed esperto cavaliere Messer Barone dei Mangiadori', *Archivio storico italiano*, ser. 4, I (1882), pp. 350–61; Davidsohn, *Storia*, IV, p. 383; F. Salvestrini, *Società ed economia a San Miniato al Tedesco durante la prima metà del secolo XIV* (Pisa, 1995), p. 10.

[16] ASF, NA, 7170, 13 July, 30 November and 7 June 1309 (houses rented by the Ciccioni for 30–50 lire annually); 3818, 18 February 1326 (residences leased out by the Mangiadori). See also ACSM, 2248, copies of notarial contracts from 1350–2.

houses, topped by towers, which were centres of signorial power beyond the control of the popular magistracies.[17]

In the decades after the fall of the Swabians, there were various attempts by the Samminiatese nobles to obtain control of the city by force.[18] The particular situation of the Frederician commune, by virtue of its imperial ancestry, determined the survival, well into the fourteenth century, of a clear opposition between Guelfs and Ghibellines, coinciding, for the most part, with the division between magnates and *popolari*.[19]

The presence of an active aristocratic component, and the absence of a correspondingly powerful commercial class which might have adequately supported the popular regime, favoured a certain intolerance for the Florentine treaty (*accomandigia*), making problematic and substantially unstable the support the Samminiatese were able to offer the Tuscan Guelf Party. There were frequent declarations of fidelity to all of the emperors who descended into Italy, and also, in the mid-fourteenth century, the explicit request for the protection of the Visconti of Milan.

But these were not the only factors that nourished the interest of the Florentines in neighbouring San Miniato. What for some time worried the merchants of the city were the tolls (*dazi*) imposed by the Samminiatese commune, by virtue of a privilege of Frederick II, on goods in transit on the road to Pisa.[20] On the other hand, the

---

[17] We know, for instance, from an inventory of possessions drawn up *c.* 1375 (ACSM, 2252, 'Beni che furono incorporati per la Parte Ghuelfa di Firenze . . .') that still at that date Jacopo Mangiadori (one of the rebels in his consorteria) owned at least eleven houses in the city and countryside, one mill, and about 2,000 *staiora* of land concentrated in the southern part of the Samminiatese territory, with four fortified structures (211). Lodovico Ciccioni possessed twelve houses and almost 900 *staiora* of land. Ser Filippo Lazzerini, a leader of the anti-Florentine resistance and one of the *grandi di popolo* of the Borromei consorteria, owned numerous parcels of land in various areas of the Samminiatese contado and distretto, totalling more than 1,200 *staiora*, twenty-four houses, two towers and a mill on the river Elsa. And Francesco dei conti di Collegalli, a noble from the distretto, owned roughly 4,200 *staiora* of land and nine houses. (1 Florentine *staioro* corresponded approximately to 0.5 hectare.)

[18] Among the most notable was the *coup d'état* effected in 1308, which nullified the first statutes drawn up by the popular regime (*Statuti del Comune*, p. 31).

[19] It is not possible at San Miniato, not unlike other Tuscan communes, to equate the aristocratic class with the magnate class. There were, as we have said, the 'grandi di popolo', whom the antimagnate laws treated like counts, and, on the other hand, there were counts who, feuding with their *consortes*, declared themselves as Guelfs belonging to the popolo. See my remarks in 'Società ed economia', pp. 8–11.

[20] The privilege (Ulm, February 1217, ind. V) was edited in J. L. A. Huillard-Bréholles, *Historia diplomatica Friderici secundi* (Paris, 1852–61), I, pt. 2, pp. 497–99. For the

republic could not help but try to make her presence more active in
the lower Valdarno, an area that lacked important urban centres, but
which had a certain number of autonomous communes of a certain
demographic and economic consistency, forming an important political
block that was sufficiently compact, separating Florence from Pisa and
Lucca.[21] The control of the ancient imperial citadel signified, without
doubt, for the republic of St John the Baptist the guarantee of more
stable and secure connections along the roads that led to the Tyrrhenian Sea.

If, on the other hand, one looks at the definitive submission, it can be
seen that it took place during a crucial period, in which Florentine
primacy over this part of the region, crossing the limits of a 'defensive
conquest',[22] was directed towards forms of territorial domination, the
first truly lasting outcome of which happened with the taking of San
Miniato.[23]

As is well known, Florence began to face the menacing expansionism
of the lords of Milan from, more or less, the middle of the fourteenth
century. The contrast with the centre of power in Lombardy determined in notable measure the growing dynamism of the republic in
extending its control over the Tuscan territory.

In 1364 there was present at San Miniato a Florentine *chomesaro*.
Perhaps he was sent to defend the city on the occasion of the recent war
with Pisa (1362–4).[24] A castellan representing the republic *in loco* still
governed the imperial fortress in 1367.[25] But in successive years, while
the Visconti aimed at the consensus of those Tuscan centres that feared
or had experienced Florentine hegemony, San Miniato confirmed its
'Ghibelline' faith and hosted the garrisons of the allied lords.[26] The local

---

complaints of the Florentine merchants, see A. Gherardi, *Le consulte della Repubblica
fiorentina dal 1280 al 1298* (Florence, 1898), II, p. 394 (1293); ASF, LF, 14, 53v (1330);
and C. M. de la Roncière, *Florence, centre économique régional au XIVe siècle* (Aix-en-
Provence, 1976), p. 865. On the Samminiatese dazio, see F. Salvestrini, 'San Miniato
al Tedesco. Le risorse economiche di una città minore della Toscana fra XIV e XV
secolo', *Rivista di storia dell'agricoltura*, 32(1) (1992), pp. 95–141, esp. pp. 97–100.

21 Compare Chittolini, 'Ricerche', pp. 318–21.
22 Chittolini, 'Ricerche', p. 293.
23 Zorzi, 'Lo Stato territoriale', pp. 810–11.
24 Connell, 'Il commissario', pp. 597–8, esp. note 21.
25 Cf. ASF, PR, 55, 56r–v, 174r–175r.
26 Between 1368 and 1369, when Charles IV entered Italy, Bernabò Visconti had
   himself named Imperial Vicar of Pisa, Lucca and San Miniato; L. Bonincontri,
   Annales, in *Rerum Italicarum Scriptores*, ed. L. A. Muratori, XXI (Milan, 1732), p. 16;
   Rondoni, *Memorie storiche di S. Miniato al Tedesco* (San Miniato, 1876; repr. Bologna,
   1980), pp. 150–1.

magnates took power, threw out the popular magistracies, and openly challenged the republic of the Baptist.[27]

At the same time, the city of the lily, worried not only by the successes of the Visconti, but also by the contemporary growth of papal power in bordering areas of Umbria and Emilia, decided to accelerate the annexation of the Valdarno.[28] The small capital of Frederick II, situated for effective control of the road to Pisa, thus paid the price of the new strategy. The Florentines, by now, could not accept the most uncertain alliance of the neighbouring commune, sufficiently important from a military point of view, whose popular regime seemed untrustworthy and unable to avoid that the imperial castle should become not only the redoubt of their enemies but the refuge of their own exiles.[29]

Between 1369 and 1370, thanks to the support of the Samminiatese Guelfs, some of whom came from the magnate class struggling with relatives of the Ghibelline allegiance, the siege of San Miniato was undertaken.[30] Taking advantage, therefore, of divisions in the local government and the scant protection conceded by the Visconti, the republican militia conquered the place and installed, immediately, a regime of occupation.[31]

---

[27] ASF, Dipl., 28 December 1368; and C. Guasti (ed.), *I Capitoli del comune di Firenze. Inventario e regesto*, I (Florence, 1866), p. 222, which refer to incursions by Samminiatese knights in the Florentine contado, actions for the which some magnates and their partisans were condemned to death or the confiscation of their goods; ASF, Cap. Pop., 152, 17r–20v (1368); ASF, EOG, 586, 80r–80v, 82r–85r; 587, 37r–v, 46v–49r; 589, 43v–44v, 78r–79r; 602, 15r–16v (1370); ASF, Pod., 2282, 8r–12r (1370).

[28] M. Luzzati, 'Firenze e l'area toscana', in G. Galasso (gen. ed.), *Storia d'Italia* (Turin, 1987), VII, p. 1, pp. 94ff., 659–62 and 679–80.

[29] In 1366–7 the republic had attempted to restore the popular regime at San Miniato. A pact with the Samminiatese exiles was sealed with a loan of 2,000 florins for which many pieces of land were given as security; Guasti (ed.), *I Capitoli*, I, pp. 218–24; ASF, PR, 56, 32r; ACSM, 2250, one loose folio.

[30] Some of the magnates had already declared themselves for the Florentines in 1365–6. The Florentines, moreover, weakened the local families and factions by inviting certain persons to Florence 'propter conservationem pacifici status terre Sancti Miniatis del Tedesco' for employment or to receive honours. The Ufficiali della Condotta were commanded to hire Piero dei Malpigli, Rodolfo Ciccioni and Iacopo dei Mangiadori for four months, with eleven knights and a monthly stipend of 96 lire common coinage for each of them; ASF, PR, 53, 131v–132r, 18 March 1365. In 1370–1 some of the Mangiadori allied with the Florentines were knighted (PR, 57, 159r, 170r). On the accords of 1367, which brought the city under Florentine control and transformed local institutions, see Guasti (ed.), *I Capitoli*, I, pp. 218–20.

[31] See the narration in Stefani, *Cronaca*, rubs. 708, 710–11, 713, 715–17, pp. 269–73; Bonincontri, *Annales*, pp. 16–18; Sercambi, *Croniche*, ed. S. Bongi (Rome, 1982), I,

These events only made anti-Florentine feelings more acute. The opposition was focused, as might have been predicted, on the fiscal contributions owed to the conquerors.[32] However, there was also resentment towards the officers sent by the ruling city, who lacked basic skills and were often corrupt.[33] A document brought to light by Giuliano Pinto relative to 1378 speaks eloquently to the situation. This was the condemnation by the Vicar – the new officer representing Florence – of a certain Taddeo di Francesco from San Miniato, for having stirred up the local population, referring explicitly to Florentine fiscal oppression, with the precise purpose of removing the town 'from the jurisdiction, dominion, power, will and obedience of the people and commune of Florence'.[34]

The Samminiatese, who were prostrated by the war to the point of asking their new rulers for regular shipments of grain,[35] obtained the deferment for about ten years of their payments to the Florentine estimo.[36] However, beginning with the early 1380s, they felt new fiscal pressures that provoked the malcontent of the less well-off classes. These were readily assisted by exiled magnates (above all from Pisa and Milan) and by certain of their *consortes* still active in the city.[37]

CCX, pp. 183–4; and the two contemporary letters edited in G. Lami, *Deliciae eruditorum seu veterum anekdoton opusculorum collectanea* (Florence, 1736–69), VIII, pp. 140–2 and 145–7.

[32] ACSM, 2253, 'Riformazione sopra le gabelle', 1374–5, 1r–6v. For the difficult financial situation of San Miniato and the problem of tax payments after the conquest, see C. M. de La Roncière, 'Indirect Taxes or "gabelles" at Florence in the Fourteenth Century: the Evolution of Tariffs and Problems of Collection', in Rubinstein (ed.), *Florentine Studies*, p. 185.

[33] G. Pinto, 'Alla periferia dello stato fiorentino: organizzazione dei primi vicariati e resistenze locali (1345–1378)', in Pinto, *Toscana medievale: paesaggi e realtà sociali* (Florence, 1993), pp. 51–65, esp. pp. 59–65. See also A. Zorzi, 'The Florentines and Their Public Offices in the Early Fifteenth Century', in E. Muir and G. Ruggiero (eds.), *History from Crime* (Baltimore, 1994), pp. 110–34.

[34] Pinto, 'Alla periferia', pp. 61–2. In the 'Atti criminali degli uffici forensi', which was Pinto's source, there are records of assaults on vicarial deputies (1370), attempts at revolt from Florence by the small communes once subject to San Miniato (1373), and measures to prohibit every 'gathering of armed men' (*raunata . . . di gente d'arme*) and every 'horse display' (*cavalcata*) by the inhabitants (1378); ASF, GA, 92, fasc. 6; fasc. 13, 12r, 13v and 18r). See too, ACSM, Ent. usc. vic., 1183, 2r (1371).

[35] For instance, ACSM, Delib., 2304, 32v (1388).

[36] Guasti (ed.), *I Capitoli*, I, p. 239.

[37] On the policy of fiscal exploitation pursued by Florence in her territory in this period, see M. B. Becker, 'Le trasformazioni della finanza e l'emergere dello Stato territoriale a Firenze nel Trecento', in G. Chittolini (ed.), *La crisi degli ordinamenti comunali e le origini dello Stato del Rinascimento* (Bologna, 1979), pp. 149–86, esp. pp. 178ff.; G. Petralia, 'Imposizione diretta e dominio territoriale nella Repubblica fiorentina del Quattrocento', in *Società, istituzioni, spiritualità: studi in onore di Cinzio*

Despite the confiscation of their estates, the exile of persons involved in the resistance and the complete redrawing of the anti-magnate norms,[38] certain members of the families that had been victims of the conquest began to plot to retake power, constantly preferring the avenue of revolt to one of accommodation with the popular government. The activity of these aristocrats, who, as a passage in Matteo Villani reveals, were seen in Florence as the persons behind the revolt of 1368, made them the ideal scapegoats for the normalisation promoted by the Florentines – the persons on whom to concentrate the repression, so as to separate them from the rest of the city.[39]

The victors introduced into the local *reggimento* strategies of domination that, in part, had already been tried out. At the beginning, they occupied fortified sites, and in particular the imperial castle, located at the highest point at the centre of the city (later entrusted to the magistracy known as the 'Six of San Miniato');[40] and then they reformed the statutes of the city. The nucleus of the intervention was the judicial system, at the head of which was appointed a Vicar, a Florentine citizen and agent of the central government, whose office was intended to replace and modify that of the former Podestà.[41]

Violante (Spoleto, 1994), pp. 639–52. On the discontent of the local communities with the structures of the Florentine dominion, see Zorzi, 'I Fiorentini e gli uffici', pp. 743–4; Zorzi, 'Giusdicenti e operatori di giustizia nello Stato territoriale fiorentino del XV secolo', *Ricerche storiche*, 19 (1989), p. 540. On the measures for compiling the estimo at San Miniato, see ASF, PR, 74, 94r; ACSM, 2254, 4 loose folios (*c.* 1380); and *ibid.*, 2257 and 2259 (1385–8).

[38] ACSM, 2255, 4 loose folios, 'Disposizioni del comune di Firenze per la cattura dei ribelli' (1375–80). The leaders in the struggle against Florence were publicly executed, as described in detail by Stefani, *Cronaca*, rub. 717, pp. 272–3. See also Guasti (ed.), *I Capitoli*, I, pp. 227ff.

[39] M. Villani, *Cronica*, IV, ch. 63–4.

[40] Guasti (ed.), *I Capitoli*, I, pp. 219, 231, 237, 239–41; ACSM, Delib., 2293, 124v; 2296, 100r; and also ACSM, Deliberazioni di Cigoli, 3963, 10r.

[41] Guasti (ed.), *I Capitoli*, I, pp. 225, 227–33; ACSM, 2251, 3 loose folios (pacts of submission); ACSM, Delib., 2293, 48r and 88v; 2298, 5r–7v; 2299, 12r. See also ASF, PR, 83, 4r, 37r; *Statuta Populi et Communis Florentiae publica auctoritate collecta, castigata et praeposita anno Salutis MCCCCXV* (Freiburg [Florence], 1778–81), II, bk V, rub. LIX, pp. 70–3; rub. LXXXI, p. 100; rub. LXXXII, pp. 101–3. On the powers of the Podestà, see ACSM, Dipl. SIL, 56, 5 September 1393; 60, 15 June and 21 July 1401. For this type of reform undertaken by Florence, see Benigni, 'L'organizzazione territoriale', p. 160; Zorzi, 'Giusdicenti', p. 524; Zorzi, 'Lo Stato territoriale fiorentino', pp. 804–7; S. Imbriaci, 'La giurisdizione criminale in alcune podesterie minori dello stato fiorentino alla fine del XIV secolo', *Ricerche storiche*, 21 (1991), pp. 418–19. On the Florentine Vicars, see Chittolini, 'Ricerche', pp. 299–302; A. Antoniella, 'Vicariati e vicari nell'organizzazione territoriale dello Stato fiorentino', in L. Borgia (ed.), *Gli stemmi del Palazzo d'Arnolfo di San Giovanni Valdarno* (Florence, 1986), pp. 13–22; Pinto, 'Alla periferia', pp. 53ff.; Zorzi, 'Lo

The sending of a Vicar in residence, one of the first governors with this characteristic created for the dominion, and the subsequent definition of his jurisdiction – the capital of which was San Miniato – constituted the elements of greatest novelty, and they also signified the cutting off of the Frederician district, through its subdivision into five *podesterie*.[42]

With the occupation of San Miniato, the Florentine government experimented with a technique of jurisdictional reform founded on the separation of contadi from their cities, which would be repeated with the annexations of Arezzo and Pisa.[43] The territory subject to the new officer, the Vicar of the lower Valdarno, included in fact 'the lands which once belonged to the Florentine San Miniato' (*terre quondam Sancti Miniati florentini*) and a few additional communes situated on the right bank of the Arno (Santa Croce, Castelfranco and Santa Maria a Monte).[44] In direct dependency on the Samminiatese magistrates there remained outside the walls only the city's old contado, made up of the settlements (*ville*) nearest to the chief city, which in earlier times had been annexed to the urban administrative wards (*contrade*).[45] But none of this was sufficient to secure the town's subjection.

Stato territoriale', pp. 806–7 and 815–17; Zorzi, 'Giusdicenti', pp. 519–20, and 521–4 (on their political role); Zorzi, 'L'organizzazione del territorio', pp. 331–2 and 348. See also E. Cristiani, 'Il ceto dirigente', in *La Toscana nel secolo XIV*, pp. 28–31.

[42] Compare Chittolini, 'Ricerche', pp. 300 and 339 n. 79. On the podesterie, see ACSM, Deliberazioni di Cigoli, 3953, 104r; Archivio Storico del Comune di Montaione, Codice di Statuti dal 1382 al 1492, I, 54v.

[43] Zorzi, 'Lo Stato territoriale', pp. 814–15; Chittolini, 'Ricerche', pp. 298–9 and 309–10.

[44] ASF, GA, 92, fasc. I, 1r; Guasti (ed.), *I Capitoli*, I, pp. 225, 229–30 and 232–4. For the beginnings of the activities of these vicars, see ASF, Tratte, 65, 18r ff. Compare also Chittolini, 'Ricerche', pp. 309ff.; Zorzi, 'Lo stato territoriale', pp. 802ff. and 814ff.

[45] Statuti del Comune, Intro., pp. 47–8; Guasti (ed.), *I Capitoli*, I, pp. 228, 231, 232, 234–6, 241, 243–53. For the Samminiatese resistance to these measures, see ACSM, Delib., 2293, 51v–53r, 87v; 2303, 50r–51v, 220r; 2310, 86v and 93r bis; ACSM, 2947, an agreement of *c.* 1400 for the autonomy of communes formerly subject to San Miniato. See also E. Conti, *La formazione della struttura agraria moderna nel contado fiorentino*, III, part 2a, *Monografie e tavole statistiche (secoli XV–XIX)* (Rome, 1965), p. 238; Chittolini, 'La formazione', pp. 300, 319–20; Pinto, 'Alla periferia', p. 64. Note that before the Florentine conquest, San Miniato's territory comprised a 'contado', directly tied to the city's *contrade* and including certain villas in the immediate vicinity, and a much greater 'distretto' that comprised tribute-paying communes and their jurisdictions. The distretto was especially extensive to the south, where it approached the territory of San Gimignano. See F. Salvestrini, 'Un territorio tra Valdelsa e Medio Valdarno: il dominio di San Miniato al Tedesco durante i secoli XIII–XV', *Miscellanea storica della Valdelsa*, 97(2–3) (1991), esp. pp. 159–65.

In general lines, it is possible to affirm that, faced with an economic situation that was difficult and had been worsened, as has been said, by the Florentine fisc and above all by the abolition of the highway gabelles that San Miniato had drawn from the road to Pisa,[46] so long as the old notable class survived in a manner to interpret the discontent of the inhabitants, it was not possible for the Florentines to pacify the city and begin negotiations with the local notables.

A first revolt, led by the magnates, took place in 1389, through the intervention of numerous exiles at Pisa, indirectly supported by Gian Galeazzo Visconti.[47] Notwithstanding the immediate Florentine suppression, in the mid 1390s there was another uprising, again in synchronicity with moments of hostility in the struggle between Florence and the potentates of northern Italy.[48] The plot's failure did not mean it would not be repeated. In fact, a last rebellion, again by work of the nobles and with the theoretical help of the lords of Milan, was attempted in 1432, on the occasion of the descent into Italy of the emperor Sigismund, although by now the question of Samminiatese independence seemed more like the internal affair of a very few knights (*milites*) belonging to magnate families.[49]

It seems evident that in a political climate not peaceful and still very fluid, during the first thirty years after the military conquest the Florentine republic had remained without adequate political contacts beyond the officers she sent to the town. As is shown, moreover, by the chasing out of the Vicar after the revolt of 1389, the Florentine magistrates worked in an atmosphere of wide and diffuse hostility, as well as in substantial and inevitable isolation. Eloquent testimony to this isolation is offered by Franco Sacchetti, Podestà at San Miniato in the 1390s, who, in certain of his personal letters, lamented the risks for Florentine officers who were sent to the riotous little town in the Valdarno.[50]

A lasting accord was not possible with the dissident members of the old ruling class, who were destined to reaffirm, after the conquest, the profound aversion for the popular regime. However, there was also lacking an alternative political class with the standing to begin a

---

[46] *Statuta Populi et Communis Florentiae*, III, bk V, rub. XXVII, pp. 413–16, 'De gabella passaggii, quod colligitur in curia de Empoli, & sanctae Gondae'.

[47] ACSM, Deliberazioni di Cigoli, 3962, 25r–v.

[48] Sercambi, *Croniche*, I, pp. 364–6 (CCCCXVIII–CCCCXIX); II, pp. 61–2 (DXXV–DXXVI).

[49] Bonincontri, *Annales*, pp. 139–40; Rondoni, *Memorie*, pp. 173–6.

[50] Franco Sacchetti, *I sermoni evangelici, le lettere ed altri scritti inediti o rari*, ed. O. Gigli (Florence, 1857), pp. 200–9 and 238–9. Indirect confirmation of the bellicosity of the Samminiatese is found also in his novellas: F. Sacchetti, *Il Trecentonovelle*, ed. A. Lanza (Florence, 1984), pp. 341–2 (CLVIII).

constructive dialogue that would permit the normalisation of the local context and loosen the bonds of the military occupation.

A clue of the uncertainty for the effects on San Miniato of the *pax florentina* that had been recently imposed was the situation of city property. It is known that the Florentine oligarchy consolidated its control over subject centres by means of a capillary-like penetration of land ownership. Land ownership guaranteed prominent Florentines the acquisition of local positions of power. And yet the fertile countryside of the Samminiatese territory, close to Florence and easily arrived at, were still in 1427, as is shown clearly from the catasto, hardly touched by the phenomenon. Florentine property was limited and concentrated only along the river Elsa, next to what had been the boundary with Empolese territory that had belonged for many years to the Florentine contado.[51] Confronted by the threats of revolt and repression, of passing troops, of population flight, landowners preferred not to invest in San Miniato and to wait for a future pacification.[52]

Given the impossibility of establishing an accord with the old ruling class, still bellicose and rebellious, still able to stir up the local population, the Florentines decided to strip it of its power and to provide, over a few decades, for its complete change. The most effective tools were those already mentioned: the execution and exile of the rebels, and above all the confiscation of their property.

Immediately after the conquest (1370–1), the Captains of the Guelf Party, on explicit command from the republic, requisitioned the goods of the so-called 'rebels', or rather of the Samminiatese who were animators of the resistance who had been previously condemned.[53] Among these were landowners of various extraction, but there stood

---

[51] In the community of Marcignana, at the mouth of the river, there were lands owned by Palla Strozzi; ASF, Catasto, 93, 248r; E. Conti, *I catasti agrari della Repubblica fiorentina e il catasto particellare toscano (secoli XIV–XIX)* (Rome, 1966), p. 53 n. 42. Deeper in Samminiatese territory, we know only of lands owned by Florentines in the commune of Vignale, possibly once the property of the Mangiadori, acquired by 'Giroçço de' Bardi' (ASF, Cat., 93, 589r).

[52] On the investments by city dwellers in the Tuscan countryside, see G. Pinto, *La Toscana nel Tardo Medio Evo: ambiente, economia rurale, società* (Florence, 1982), pp. 157–66; M. S. Mazzi and S. Raveggi, *Gli uomini e le cose nelle campagne fiorentine nel Quattrocento* (Florence, 1983), pp. 37–73. At Pisa, too, there was little Florentine investment in the decades immediately following the conquest, for reasons partially analogous with the situation at San Miniato. See Mallett, 'Pisa', pp. 418, 433–41.

[53] See *I Capitoli*, I: 218–19, 231–3, 236; ASF, PR, 57, 151r, 179r, 185r, 227r, 239r; PR, 58, 179r–180r, 182r–v; PR, 59, 142r; ASF, CPGNR, 5, 37r–38r; V. Mazzoni and F. Salvestrini, 'Strategie politiche e interessi economici nei rapporti tra la Parte Guelfa e il Comune di Firenze. La confisca patrimoniale ai "ribelli' di San Miniato (ca. 1368– ca. 1400)', *Archivio storico italiano*, 157 (1999), pp. 3–61.

out among them, as is obvious, certain of the Mangiadori, some of the Ciccioni, Ser Filippo Lazzerini of the consorteria of the Borromei, and, among the rural nobility, two of the counts of Collegalli. The Party confiscated their property in San Miniato, and the commune took over their property in Florence.[54] In San Miniato and its territory the residences of the magnates were also requisitioned – their 'towers' (torri) and 'strong-houses' (casseri), which served as an important sign of the lordly lifestyle.[55] The only magnates to escape this massive expropriation were those who had not resisted the Florentine intervention.[56]

The effects of this operation emerge clearly from the reading of the registers of the succeeding fiscal levies. For example, the Libra fiorentina of 1385 contained the names of six family heads of the Mangiadori and two belonging to the Ciccioni consorteria. Their total contributive capacity, in accordance with the parameters of the estimo, went from a maximum of 9 lire to a minimum of 7 soldi. These amounts cannot be ignored when one considers that in the later tax rolls of 1393, only 31.4 per cent of the Samminiatese populace were assigned a tax figure of 1 lira and only 1.9 per cent were assigned a levy of between 5 and 10 lire. These appear, however, much inferior to the assessments of certain notaries, rich merchants and other professionals, whose levies reached and even exceeded 20 lire.[57]

In the estimo of 1393, compiled at a distance of only a few years from the first anti-Florentine revolt, we find only one 'Anthonius de

---

[54] Among the goods, belonging above all to Filippo Lazzerini, that were confiscated in Florence from 1368, there figured monetary credits, commercial goods, some pieces of land, and a certain number of houses within the city walls or immediately outside; ASF, Bal., 11, 1r–15v. Part of the total was used to compensate Florentine creditors of Samminiatese citizens who were afraid of losing what was owed them in the war (ASF, PR, 56, 36r, 98v ff.). Some of Lazzerini's outstanding loans to inhabitants of the contado and distretto of Florence were also confiscated (ASF, Dipl., Monastero di S. Cristiana di S. Croce, 17 March 1371).

[55] Guasti (ed.), I Capitoli, I, pp. 230–1. According to a list of confiscated properties, composed in the mid-1370s and certainly fragmentary and partial, the Guelf Party took approximately 17,000 staiora of land, 140 buildings in the city and countryside, 8 towers, and certain other rural structures; ACSM, 2252. Until the 1320s the Party possessed barely 30 buildings and some 400 staiora of land; V. Mazzoni, 'Il patrimonio fondiario e le strategie insediative della Parte Guelfa di Firenze nel primo Trecento', Archivio storico italiano, 154 (1996), Appendix, notes 1–56.

[56] Guasti (ed.), I Capitoli, I, pp. 218–9; Bonincontri, Annales, p. 17.

[57] The Mangiadori were the brothers 'Johannes', 'Filippus' and 'Benedictus domini Bartolomei', 'dominus Domenichus', 'Agnolus domini Dominici' and 'Francischus del Serra'. The Ciccioni were 'Fenzo domini Pieri' and 'Antonius Marzuoli'. The assessments were, in order: 9 lire, 9 lire 14 soldi, 8 lire 14 soldi, 2 lire 10 soldi, 18 soldi 6 denari, 7 soldi (ASF, Estimo, 345, 6r–v, 7v). The names appear also in the records of the 'Capi di famiglia' of 1383, although with no indication of the properties assessed (ibid., 243, 1501r–v).

Malpigli' (another name of the Ciccioni), 20 years old, whose taxable property (*valsente*) was valued at a total of 600 lire. 'Dominus Filippus de Mangiadoribus' had instead wealth estimated at 700 lire.[58] Both men can be inserted in the 6 per cent of Samminiatese landowners with wealth above 500 lire, but among the 'rich' residents of the city and its ex-contado there were persons whose wealth was estimated above 4000 lire.[59]

Finally, it is interesting to note how the catasto of 1427 does not even include the name of Mangiadori. Even if the family was still in existence, it seems clear that it had lost any economic importance. According to what emerges from the first declarations or *campioni* of the catasto, the only three family heads of the Ciccioni to be mentioned presented a taxable patrimony that when added together did not surpass 600 florins; while there were spice merchants (*speziali*) whose wealth, individually, was estimated at above 1000 florins.[60]

After the attempted revolt of 1432, the landholding situation worsened even more, above all for a part of the *grandi di popolo* allied with the nobles in the struggle against Florence. The Bonincontri who remained in the city and certain of the Borromei had in fact supported the uprising of one of the Mangiadori and they were, in consequence, the most illustrious victims of a new confiscation ordered by the Guelf Party. It is important to note that, while the requisition of 1370 regarded large holdings of land, the one that took place in 1433 comprised especially moveable wealth (furnishings, agricultural tools, weapons, clothing, etc.). It seems clear that the old local patriciate no longer possessed the wealth of former years.[61]

---

[58] The other Mangiadori assessed that year, 'Benedictus domini Bartolomei', figured as the owner only of lands assessed at 250 lire in the contado; ASF, Estimo, 239, 553v, 698r, 701r.

[59] For instance, the *terziere* of Castelvecchio, the oldest and most central of the city, in which almost all of the magnates resided, hosted twenty-five contributors, most of them non-magnates, whose estates were assessed in a range between 500 and 4,000 lire. This same level of assessment was indicated for twenty-seven heads of household in the *terziere* of Fuoriporta and thirty-nine in the *terziere* of Poggighisi. The total number of hearths assessed in each *terziere* was, respectively, 85, 204 and 161. See ASF, Estimo, 239.

[60] ASF, Catasto, 167, 387r. The Ciccioni or Malpigli were the only such aristocratic consorteria evident before the sixteenth century; BNF, Poligrafo Gargani, 599, 31 and 41. Almost all of the Mangiadori went to Milan to enlist in the service of the Visconti; F. M. Galli Angelini, 'Messer Barone Mangiadori', *Bollettino dell'Accademia degli Euteleti*, 3, fasc. 1–2 (1921), pp. 42–3. On the spice merchants (*speziali*), who owned the largest estates, see ASF, Estimo, 249, 602v; 259, 102v and 111r; ASF, Catasto, 92, 740r, 776r–778r; 94, 420r–422r; 167, 368r, 368v, 376v, 385r.

[61] See ACSM, 2950, 'liber sive quaternus . . . bonorum . . . rebellium comunis Florentie et terre Sancti Miniatis pro crimine lese maiestatis . . .'. After this event, one group of the Borromei joined their relatives in Pisa, while another group went

The Florentines profited by counting on the exhaustion of the Samminiatese citizenry after the coups attempted by the *milites*, which only resulted in violent repression. They counted also on the desire manifested by the *nouveaux riches* of popular extraction, dedicated to economic and professional activities and undoubtedly damaged by the climate of instability. And so long as this last group enjoyed Florentine support, it received no concrete offers of participation in the government of the commune from the magnates.

The goods confiscated from the rebels in 1370 and in the 1430s passed over, as has been said, to the Guelf Party of Florence. The Party had rented out a conspicuous share of this property, most of it to tenant farmers or to intermediaries who were in good part Samminiatese.[62] Other lands, instead, had been quickly sold off (beginning, at least, in 1370), creating a strong dynamic in the land market and numerous opportunities for investment. Although there were few Florentines among the buyers, there were many Samminiatese and also residents of nearby communities, who in this way took the place of the former magnate elite.[63] The same renters, in the decades that followed, bought back from the Party the title to various lands, consolidating itself as a class of medium to small landholders.[64]

to Milan (where their descendants became famous). On the Bonincontri, see C. Grayson, 'Lorenzo Bonincontri', in *Dizionario biografico degli italiani*, XII (Rome, 1970), pp. 209–11.

[62] See, for instance, a lease conceded by the Party to the *sindaco* of Fucecchio of twenty-four parcels of land confiscated from Samminiatese exiles, many of them bordering on lands owned by Giovanni Mangiadori; ASF, Dipl., Comune di Fucecchio, 25 September 1374. For other such leases, see ASF, Dipl., Comune di San Miniato, 10 March 1374; 14 May 1374; 13 November 1374; 14 and 18 June 1379.

[63] Interesting in this regard is an act by which the Party sold to the *sindaco* of Stibbio, a community in the Samminiatese contado, a series of houses and lands in and around Stibbio that were 'de bonis olim Ser Filippi Laçerini ed hodie dicte Partis'; ASF, Dipl., S. Stefano di Empoli, 20 January 1376. For other examples of confiscated properties sold soon after by the Party, see ASF, Dipl., Monastero di S. Donato in Polverosa, 5 February 1376; *ibid.*, 23 September 1377. In 1370 the Party had received authorisation to sell confiscated lands of rebels that had been held for two years or more; ASF, PR, 58, 79r–v, 81r, 82r–v; ASF, CPGNR, 5, 41r–42v.

[64] See, for example, the decision of 1378 by which the city council proposed to the Florentine Priors to elect 'unus sindicus vel plures ad conducendum et recipiendum ad affictum . . . bona a dictis dominis capitaneis Partis Guelfe civitatis Florentie', so that Samminiatese citizens could receive them and afterwards exchange them; ACSM, Delib., 2298, 18v–22r. In 1427 a certain Niccolaio di Ser Michele da Rofia, from the contado of San Miniato, declared that he owned two parcels of land in this villa, acquired that same year from the Guelf Party of Florence; ASF, Catasto, 92, 573r. Purchases of land from the Party continued down to the early sixteenth century; ACSM, Dipl. SIL, 39, 10 May 1375; 50, 21 May 1386; ASF, DG, 5373 and 5374, *passim*.

These categories of persons owed to the new order the possibility of increasing their wealth, and they were favourable, as has been said, to the pacification of the city. They finished, therefore, by accepting the conquest, because by virtue of their new holdings they were better able to support the fiscal burden imposed by the conquerors, becoming progressively the political interlocutors with the Florentine government class who had previously been lacking.

The emerging families were called Gamucci, Rimbotti, Bonaparte, Grifoni, Salamoni and Roffia.[65] In the past these families had had only minimal contacts with the *grandi di popolo*. More often these were family lines that stemmed from obscure personages, figures who previously lacked family names and who even the popular regime had left in the shadows, but who in the course of the 1300s had enriched themselves through trade (although this is poorly documented), notarial work, usury and land rent;[66] and who now, in the 1400s, declared wealth for the tax rolls that was quite substantial.

In general, the richest part of the population transformed itself progressively into a class of notables, acquiring Florentine citizenship within a few years and serving frequently as the functionaries in the retinue (*familia*) of the Florentine Vicar.[67]

---

[65] On the new Samminiatese aristocracy, destined to establish itself in the following centuries, see A. Benvenuti, 'Classe dominante e strumenti del potere nel Vicariato di S. Miniato al Tedesco durante il governo di Cosimo I (1537–1574)', *Miscellanea storica della Valdelsa*, 77 (1975), pp. 159–228; P. Morelli, 'Classe dirigente e nobiltà a S. Miniato fra Cinque e Seicento', *Bollettino storico pisano*, 52 (1983), 211–25; B. Casini, 'I "Libri d'Oro" delle città di Volterra e S. Miniato', *Rassegna volterrana*, 61–2 (1985–6), pp. 391–429, esp. pp. 417–29; S. Nannipieri, 'Gostanza e la sua gente', in F. Cardini (ed.), *Gostanza, la strega di San Miniato: processo a una guaritrice nella Toscana medicea* (Bari, 1989), pp. 35–6 (on the Roffia); D. Stiaffini, 'Una grande famiglia di San Miniato: i Grifoni fra tardo Medioevo e prima età moderna', *Bollettino storico pisano*, 63 (1994), pp. 115–29; ASPi, Corporazioni religiose soppresse, S. Agostino di S. Miniato, 1995, esp. fasc. 19; ASPi, Archivio della famiglia Buonaparte di San Miniato, busta 1, esp. fasc. 1–3 (on the Bonaparte).

[66] Salvestrini, 'San Miniato al Tedesco', pp. 104–11; S. Mori, 'Il testamento di Ser Michele di Bindo: tra attività usurarie e opere pie', *Miscellanea storica della Valdelsa*, 98 (1992), pp. 7–35.

[67] Guasti (ed.), *I Capitoli*, I, pp. 227–8. The Bonaparte appear regularly among the Priors of the city in the deliberazioni from 1371 to 1399. The Salamoni, too, figure increasingly in the city's magistracies; ACSM, Delib., 2295, 5v). In 1427 Antonio di Gherardo Salamoni owned property assessed at 400 florins (ASF, Catasto, 167, 367v). A moneylender, Bindo di Vanni, was *camerario* of the Vicar in 1370–1. On him, and on other vicarial functionaries of local extraction, see ACSM, Dipl. SIL, 44, 29 January 1380; ACSM, Ent. usc. vic., 1183–1256 (for the years 1371–1492). See also Benvenuti, 'Classe dominante'; G. Nanni, 'Economia e società nel vicariato di S. Miniato al Tedesco durante il governo di Cosimo I (1537–1574)', *Miscellanea storica della Valdelsa*, 80–82 (1977), pp. 7–176. For the presence of Samminiatese

The new governing class, of 'bourgeois' extraction but quickly orientated towards oligarchic and elite social forms inspired by the Florentine patriciate, solidified its social position locally and also presented itself to the aristocracy of other subject centres by following precise choices of a matrimonial strategy.[68] As the ruling class of Florentine San Miniato, it conceived forms of self-presentation that were expressed in palaces and Renaissance residences styled after advanced urban building practices that were by now completely new with respect to the fortified structures that housed the 'Ghibelline' nobility.[69]

The new eminent class began quickly to concentrate its landowning around rural sites, favouring in this way the formation of substantial estates (*appoderamento*). In the meantime, the land investments of Florentines also increased, becoming more substantial in the 1450s.[70]

Certain persons from these emerging families established secure relations with the notables of the ruling city, creating therefore the bases for contacts of a clientelistic nature. It should be observed, however, that in the period before 1430, the ties of patronage that would have tended to permit a progressive normalisation must have been quite limited.[71] Then, as far as we can tell, they seem to have followed three channels. In the first place, there were the contacts with the Florentine Vicar, who was always from a leading Florentine family (Della Tosa, Adimari, Strozzi, Medici).[72] It has not been possible, however, to document personal relations between these Florentine magistrates and local figures during the period here considered. Still, it is possible that in a later period, once the climate of occupation had passed and the role of the Vicars was better defined (especially after the reform of 1424, which suppressed the Podesteria of San Miniato and left only the Vicariate),[73]

---

among the legal functionaries who accompanied Florentine rectors to their offices, see Zorzi, 'Giusdicenti', pp. 527 and 546.

[68] See the contribution of Oretta Muzzi to this volume. An analogous affirmation of a new local aristocracy closely tied with the Florentines, albeit without the drastic events that took place at San Miniato, was described at Pescia by Brown, *Pescia*, pp. 233–61.

[69] For the architectural evolution of San Miniato in this period, see M. L. Cristiani Testi, *San Miniato al Tedesco: saggio di storia urbanistica e architettonica* (Florence, 1967), pp. 115–27.

[70] Salvestrini, 'San Miniato al Tedesco', pp. 126–8; ASF, DG, 5650, 25r. See also Benvenuti, 'Classe dominante'.

[71] It is from this period that the phenomenon begins to be seen clearly in other parts of the Florentine territory; Zorzi, 'Lo stato territoriale', p. 811; Connell, 'Clientelismo', pp. 532ff.; Connell, 'Changing Patterns', p. 100.

[72] ACSM, Ent. usc. vic.; ASF, GA, 89, fasc. 3; Pinto, 'Alla periferia', p. 55.

[73] Chittolini, 'Ricerche', p. 301 n. 45, 334; Zorzi, 'Lo Stato territoriale', p. 817; Zorzi, 'Giusdicenti', p. 545 n. 100.

these officers undertook to create personal ties of a patronal nature with at least some of the local families. Moreover, the fact that certain members of the Florentine patriciate who were not interested in territorial office could avoid service meant that others occupied these offices more frequently and willingly, thus favouring the creation of personal clientele in the territory. This has been noted with respect to Pisan offices.[74] A prosopographical analysis of the Vicars sent to San Miniato in the fifteenth century would probably reveal analogous phenomena.

Less important were the contacts established with the citizen landowners who invested in San Miniato. Moreover, even in the Medici period, San Miniato did not figure among the smaller centres of the dominion that requested that Lorenzo the Magnificent appoint its salaried officers, such as, for example, Fucecchio or Galeata, who often engaged in exchanges of correspondence with the members of the leader's family and entourage.[75]

The mediation that was by far the most effective, at least till the end of the Albizzi period, was that which was realised by local figures who had long since moved to the capital city and played a significant social role in Florence, but who preserved lands and other interests – including networks of friends and clients – in their native town. These comprised, without doubt, the largest number of the 'Florentines' who purchased property in the territory of San Miniato in the first half of the fifteenth century.[76]

Among these, there was a family known variously as the Chellini or Samminiati, and especially a medical doctor who belonged to the family called Giovanni, who lived from 1370 through the first half of the fifteenth century.[77] He was also a merchant and a businessman who had

[74] Mallett, 'Pisa', pp. 439–40.

[75] Connell, 'Changing Patterns', pp. 96–7, Table II.

[76] In 1369–70 Samminiatese who had lived in the city for at least six months were allowed to hold Florentine offices; Guasti (ed.), I Capitoli, I, pp. 227–8. These city-dwellers were rich merchants and small to medium investors, who, once Florentine control was established over San Miniato, exercised the commercial expertise acquired in Florence in their native city. Thus Antonio di Manno, originally from San Miniato but now a wine merchant in Florence ('vinattieri in Firençe'), transformed a house within the San Miniato walls into an inn, the 'Albergho del Ghallo', while along the Pisan road he maintained another inn for travellers; ASF, Catasto, 92, 640r–641r.

[77] M. Battistini, 'Giovanni Chellini medico di San Miniato', Rivista di storia delle scienze mediche e naturali, 18(3–4) (1927), pp. 106–17; M. T. Sillano (ed.), Le ricordanze di Giovanni Chellini da San Miniato, medico, mercante e umanista (1425–1457) (Milan, 1984); S. Groppi, L'archivio Saminiati-Pazzi (Milan, 1990). For the family's origins and relations with San Miniato, see BNF, Passerini, 191, n. 38; BNF, Poligrafo Gargani, 577, fol. 1; 575, fols. 261, 275, 282, 283–5.

considerable economic resources,[78] and who was in contact with the most important Florentine families.[79] He acquired the lands and enterprises of Samminiatese magnates beginning in the 1420s.[80]

He does not seem to have influenced the choices of the ruling city with respect to local administration at San Miniato. Still, he favoured the establishment of socio-economic ties between the Samminiatese *nouveaux riches* and the leading classes of the capital city, calling, for example, some notaries to the city, or asking a spice merchant from the town to serve as witness to commercial contracts that were drawn up on his behalf in Florence and in the Valdarno. Giovanni also acted as a mediator by making loans to fellow townsmen (*conterranei*) or for the purchase of property by Florentines in San Miniato and its territory. Finally, as physician, humanist and protector, he hosted certain Samminiatese students in Florence, to encourage them in his own profession, or to insert them into the ranks of the notariate.[81]

From what has been said, it seems possible to conclude that, at the threshold of the modern age, Florentine control over San Miniato al Tedesco had become an accepted fact, along with the normalisation of relations between the central government and the class of local notables. However, it is also clear that this could have happened only after more than half a century after the definitive conquest, and only after the nearly total replacement of the former leading class of imperial ancestry. From this point of view the Samminiatese case, in the context of the policy followed by the republic in the process of the construction of its regional state, represents a model of able adaptation to the conditions present in each of its different cities. Florence did not consider it

---

[78] In the mid-1400s, he deposited 6,389 florins in the Florentine Monte; F. Di Trocchio, 'Chellini, Giovanni', in *Dizionario biografico degli italiani*, XXIV (Rome, 1980), p. 417.

[79] His 'ricordanze' show a privileged relationship with the Rucellai, but also mention exchanges of favours, land transactions, and other connections with members of the Strozzi, Salviati, Medici, Pitti and Capponi families of Florence; Sillano (ed.), *Le ricordanze*, pp. 94–5, 99, 103, 106, 119, 120, 140 and *passim*.

[80] *Ibid.*, pp. 39–40, 58, 62, 63. In the estimo of 1412 he was assessed 233 florins at San Miniato; ASF, Estimo, 249, 660v. After the mid-1400s he must have been the principal owner of lands in the Samminiatese but resident at Florence; ASF, Catasto, 826, 167r (1457).

[81] Sillano (ed.), *Le ricordanze*, pp. 64, 66, 69–70, 82, 84, 145–6, 154. On his relations with ecclesiastical institutions in San Miniato, see ACSM, Biblioteca di S. Iacopo, Cronaca del convento, 829, 40r. Generally on this type of patronage, see Kent and Kent, 'Two Vignettes'; and G. A. Brucker, 'The Structure of Patrician Society in Renaissance Florence', *Colloquium*, I (1964), pp. 2–11. The example of a Pisan family (the Gaetani), who moved to Florence but looked to acquire lands in the territory of their ancestral city, appears in Mallett, 'Pisa', p. 439.

sufficient merely to conquer San Miniato, the principal obstacle on the road to Pisa and the sea; rather it worked a transformation in the town's social structure, making possible an internal pacification and paving the way locally for the definitive success of a new order.

CHAPTER 13

THE SOCIAL CLASSES OF COLLE VALDELSA AND THE FORMATION OF THE DOMINION (FOURTEENTH– SIXTEENTH CENTURIES)

ORETTA MUZZI

The elevation of towns to cities from the late middle ages to the modern period is a theme that historians have only recently begun to study. Giorgio Chittolini has linked the general process of elevation to city that took place in Tuscany in the late middle ages to the reorganisation that followed the great territorial expansion of Florence in the early fifteenth century, and Elena Fasano Guarini has highlighted the particular significance of city status in the early modern period.[1]

I should like to investigate the possible motives of the local ruling classes to support the efforts to gain diocesan and city status. In particular, I should like to address the following questions. What was the relationship between the needs of the dominant city and the expectations of the towns themselves? What local interests were satisfied by the elevation of a town (*terra*) to the rank of 'city' (*civitas*)? And how and why did such interests find support in the dominant city only at certain key moments? I believe these are important questions, the answer to which will lead to a clearer understanding of the structure of the Florentine territorial state and of the changes resulting from the slow assimilation into a vast territorial entity of localities which had previously experienced periods of significant autonomy. I should like to clarify how the transformation from independent communes to com-

---

[1] G. Chittolini, ' "Quasi città". Borghi e terre in area lombarda nel tardo Medioevo', *Società e storia*, 47 (1990), pp. 3–26; Chittolini, 'Progetti di riordinamento ecclesiastico della Toscana agli inizi del Quattrocento', in S. Bertelli (ed.), *Forme e tecniche del potere nelle città (secoli XIV–XVII)* (Perugia, 1980), pp. 275–96; Chittolini, 'Centri minori e città fra Medioevo e Rinascimento nell'Italia centro-settentrionale', in P. Nencini (ed.), *Colle di Val d'Elsa. Diocesi e città tra '500 e '600* (hereafter *Diocesi e città*), (Castelfiorentino, 1994), pp. 11–37; E. Fasano Guarini, 'Nuove diocesi e nuove città nella Toscana del Cinque-Seicento', in *Diocesi e città*, pp. 39–63.

munities within a state affected the ruling groups, and how these ruling groups demonstrated a sufficiently strong awareness of their new standing to induce them to claim and obtain formal acknowledgment of a new rank in the hierarchy of subject communities.

With these aims in mind, I have chosen Colle Valdelsa as a case study, as it offers a good quantity and variety of source material. There are other particular reasons for concentrating on this locality. At the beginning of the fifteenth century the political scene and the socio-economic structure in Colle were not very different from other places with a similar demographic concentration, such as San Gimignano. A comparison between the two towns in terms of wealth, as shown in the catasto of 1427–30, reveals a less favourable situation in Colle.[2]

It was thus no coincidence that in this period Florence attempted to promote an ecclesiastical reorganisation that provided San Gimignano with the *honor civitatis*.[3] The different fortunes of the two places are evident in the pattern of urban building programmes: the late Renaissance palaces of Colle are testimony to a period of great socio-economic development and to the ability of the greater families for self-advertisement,[4] a trend which seems to bring Colle closer to Prato, Pescia, San Miniato and Borgo San Sepolcro.[5] In contrast, the towers of San Gimignano suggest that the growth did not continue beyond the fourteenth century.[6] The period in which their development differs

---

[2] O. Muzzi, 'Attività artigianali e cambiamenti politici a Colle Val d'Elsa prima e dopo la conquista fiorentina', in R. Ninci (ed.), *La società fiorentina nel basso Medioevo. Per Elio Conti* (Rome, 1995), pp. 224–5.

[3] Chittolini, 'Progetti di riordinamento', pp. 275–6.

[4] See in *Colle di Val d'Elsa nell'età dei granduchi medicei: 'La terra in città et la collegiata in cattedrale'* (Florence, 1992), the section on 'La città e l'architettura', with the contributions of G. C. Romby, N. Fargnoli and F. Rotundo; the contributions of the same authors, in *Diocesi e città*; G. C. Romby, 'Il rinnovamento edilizio nei centri minori della Toscana del Cinquecento: Colle Val d'Elsa e Montepulciano', in *La nascita della Toscana* (Florence, 1980), pp. 255–64. For general references, G. Spini, 'Intervento all'apertura del Convegno', in *Architettura e politica in Valdelsa al tempo dei Medici* (= *Miscellanea storica della Valdelsa*, 88 (1982)), pp. 161–5, and, in the same volume, the contributions of G. C. Romby and F. Parri.

[5] R. P. Ciardi, 'Architettura e arti figurative', in E. Fasano Guarini (ed.), *Prato. Storia di una città*, II, *Un microcosmo in movimento (1494–1818)*, (Florence, 1986), pp. 685–758; F. Angiolini, 'Il ceto dominante a Prato nell'età moderna', *ibid.*, pp. 343–427; J. C. Brown, *Pescia nel Rinascimento: all'ombra di Firenze* (Pescia, 1987); G. Spini, 'Introduzione generale', in Spini (ed.), *Architettura e politica da Cosimo I a Ferdinando I* (Florence, 1976), pp. 9–76; G. Pinto, 'Borgo San Sepolcro: un centro minore alla periferia dello stato', in Pinto, *Città e spazi economici nell'Italia comunale* (Bologna, 1996), pp. 223–36.

[6] E. Fiumi, *Storia economica e sociale di S. Gimignano*, 2nd edn (Florence, 1993 [1961]), pp. 15–16.

thus corresponds to the formation of the republican state, even though it becomes most evident well into the sixteenth century.

These preliminary considerations lead to issues requiring the analysis of institutional developments,[7] economic events and social changes. We need to deepen our understanding of local ruling groups and how they related to the regional ruling groups and to the regional bureaucracy. Individuals and families from Colle were well represented in important offices: from Bartolomeo Scala to Francesco Campana, from the Usimbardi to the Giusti, the Cini, the Beltramini, the Pacini and the Da Picchena.

This article will investigate the changes that took place among the economic, political and social elites at a local level and their relation to the process of formation of the Florentine state. These social and political changes will provide an insight into the evolution of the state and of the consequences that this had.

Our starting point must be the definition of these elite groups to ascertain whether wealth and social status were connected. This question is not difficult to answer: it is our aim to prove not only that there was a clear discrepancy between wealth and status, but also that their relationship proceeded in parallel to the main stages of state-building. We therefore need to examine local events over the span of the two-and-a-half centuries that elapsed between Florentine conquest and Colle's elevation to the status of a city-diocese. This chapter represents an initial analysis; for greater detail, I refer the reader to my forthcoming monograph, whose method of approach and main lines of investigation are described here.

ECONOMIC CLASSES

Four fiscal censuses provide information on wealth: the catasto of 1429,[8] the two estimi of 1473[9] and 1547[10] and the decima levied under the

---

[7] R. Ninci, 'Lineamenti dell'assetto istituzionale colligiano dalla fine del medioevo all'età moderna', in *Diocesi e città*, pp. 97–116, also in *Archivio storico italiano*, 152 (1994), pp. 701–33.

[8] ASF, Catasto, 211–12 (*portate* of 1429), 251 (*campioni* of 1430), 285 (*sommario* of the declarations of Colle and San Gimignano). For the delay in the fiscal returns, owing to the strong opposition to the catasto, see D. Herlihy and C. Klapisch, *I toscani e le loro famiglie: uno studio sul catasto fiorentino del 1427* (Bologna, 1988), pp. 53–6.

[9] ASS, Estimo delle comunità, 91–4.

[10] ASS, Estimo delle comunità, 96, 97. This fiscal census was analysed by L. Bonelli Conenna, 'Struttura fondiaria e mondo agricolo all'inizio dell'età moderna', in *Diocesi e città*, pp. 289–305.

Grand Duchy in 1577.[11] While the catasto of 1429 covers investment in industrial and commercial activities, the others are based solely on the value of real estate. This difference in the basis of the surveys can mean that it is dangerous to use these sources as evidence for the increase or decrease in the assets of individual families, but it does not undermine the validity of the rank order of wealth they show.

From the beginning of the fifteenth century to the end of the sixteenth no more than thirty-six families succeeded in reaching the highest ranks within the local economy, or had assets which could guarantee a comfortable standard of living: in 1429 thirty-seven households (*fuochi fiscali*), corresponding to thirty families, had taxable assets (*valsenti*) of more than 500 florins; in 1473 thirty-nine households, corresponding to thirty-one families, had a coefficient of estimo of more than 100 lire (a coefficient equal to 20 per cent of the value of their property, not counting the house in which they lived); in 1547 fifty-four households, corresponding to thirty-two families, valued their assets at more than 1000 lire; in 1577 the seventy-three households of more than 1000 florins belonged to thirty-six families. It is apparent from these figures that while the number of households which could boast a certain degree of comfort increased substantially, especially in the sixteenth century, the number of families did not – a clear indication of the concentration of wealth. Such concentration occurred even within families. In fact, significant differences in wealth are observable among individual family units bearing the same surname.

Notwithstanding the different basis of the surveys and the high inflation of the second half of the sixteenth century, the last census shows an overall increase in wealth. In fact, in 1429 the top seven contributors had a total *valsente* of little more than 10,000 florins (one florin = 80 soldi), while in 1577 the top seven households together had assets – of real estate alone – of almost 31,000 florins (one florin = 82 soldi). In each census, the richest level was represented by seven to ten households, i.e. 1 per cent or slightly more of the census, further proof of a highly unequal distribution of wealth. In the fifteenth and sixteenth centuries, around thirty families came to occupy the top level of wealth, at different points. An examination of their ups and downs, of the activities they undertook, of their social behaviour and their access to local political office, will enable us to tell whether social achievement and political success were based on economic status, or indeed what was the relationship between the two.

The nature of the assets covered by the 1429 catasto reveals that the

---

[11] ASF, DG, 7941–3.

greatest fortunes were linked not just to ownership of land, but above all to manufacturing activity. The possession of paper mills or a wool business is a regular feature of all the declarations of taxpayers worth 1000 florins or more and was frequent among those between 500 and 1000 florins. The latter level also included other tradesmen, such as shoemakers, leather workers, *speziali*,[12] merchants, a notary and at least four who farmed their own land.

In subsequent surveys only the ownership of water-powered buildings (paper, fulling and flour works) was declared, thus providing limited information on non-agricultural economic activity. But we also have notarial records and official documents, including the legislation of the council and priorate and the *Libri iurium* of the commune, which from the fourteenth century onwards give details of the administration of the gabelle and of communal property. These sources contribute to provide information, often in detail, about the activities undertaken by the families of Colle.

In 1473, the richest families in Colle owed their fortunes in large measure to the wool and paper industries. At the end of the fifteenth century and in the early decades of the sixteenth, alongside attempts at industrial redevelopment or the more efficient exploitation of water power,[13] new paper mills continued to be built and the productivity of existing ones was improved.[14] Such increased activity did not bypass the wool industry:[15] this sector experienced an expansion of its manufacturing infrastructure, a development that stemmed from the

---

[12] The *speziali* were apothecaries and pharmacists, but also sold miscellaneous merchandise, ranging from candles to paper and ink.

[13] Antonio del maestro Francesco applied to the commune for tax relief to set up an 'exercitio per condurre et lavorare acciaio, rami, ferro et altra ferrareccia'; ASS, Colle, 167, 40v–41r, 118r. For several years, the Vivini managed another foundry (*ferriera*) that produced muskets (*archibugi*) and springals (*spingarde*); *ibid.*, 97r–98r; Colle, 362, 12r; Colle, 353, 100v–102v, 115r, 117r–v, 192r; ASF, NA, 158, M, nos. 39, 40, 42, 44; NA, 20242, 120v. The commune granted Antonio Gozzini usage of the canals (*gore*) for an 'edificio per colare palle di ferro et una macina per macinar robbia et, per fare uno paio di pile da panni'; ASS, Colle, 169, 96r, 97v. In 1538 Raffaele Gozzini committed himself to deliver iron balls (*palleas ferreas*) to the commune of Città di Castello, ASF, NA, 8407, 182v; see also NA, 20266, no. 286; NA, 1556, 23v–24r; NA, 7233, E, no. 29.

[14] In 1517 one Maddali requested water rights to build a paper mill, ASS, Colle, 363, 197r–198r. During the same period a *bertesca* (bartizan) of the city walls was converted into a paper–drying facility, ASS, Colle, 156, 26r–28r.

[15] Iacopo Cerboni asked the commune for a tower to make a trimming shop, ASS, Colle, 361, 40r; Francesco del Fornarino obtained water rights for a fulling works, ASS, Colle, 363, 197r–198r. For the construction of new tentering works, see ASF, NA, 157, A, no. 4; NA, 20379, no. 222; NA, 19893, 116r–117v, 261v. For the restoration of the hall of the wool guild (*domus artis lane*), see ASF, NA, 11778, 7v.

utilisation of the industrial resources of Colle by Sienese and Florentine merchants.[16]

This was a period in which the building of new flour mills and oil presses revealed a sharp increase in the agricultural sector.[17] There was an attempt, albeit apparently not very successful, to introduce the cultivation of mulberry trees for the raising of silkworms.[18] At the same time the textile industry saw the substantial and long-lasting development of the linen manufacture, as witnessed by the presence of numerous linen weavers and by the growth of trade of raw materials, imported from Latium and Umbria.[19] This general revival of the economy of Colle, based on the expansion of traditional manufacturing activity as well as on the establishment of new enterprises, reinforced Colle's industrial character. Its economic structure became comparable to that of Borgo San Sepolcro or Prato, even though there was a difference in scale because of the difference in population. Nevertheless, it appears that few 'quasi-cities' of the Florentine dominion had, at the end of the fifteenth century, so many and such well-established economic ventures: at Pescia the cultivation of silkworms and the paper manufacture became important only in the mid-sixteenth century, while San Gimignano was never an industrial centre.

---

[16] ASF, NA, 7233, A, no. 20 (Sienese who got their fulling done at Colle); NA, 8535, no. 112 (the Orlandini of Florence made use of the wool guild's tentering works).

[17] It is possible to trace the stages in the construction of a mill at Buonriposo (near Gracciano) on a farm belonging to the friars of Sant' Agostino, with capital provided by a prosperous farrier in ASF, NA, 9115, nos. 162, 164, 165; NA, 9116, nos.1, 18, 59 (first lease of 1501); the construction of a new mill by the parish of Santi Ippolito e Cassiano on the river Fosci in 1525–6, ASF, NA, 19893, 92r–94r, 107r, 163v–164r, 189v–192v, 200r–202r; enlargement of the mill of the dean at Caldane (near Gracciano), ASS, Colle, 353, 16v; Colle, 361, 31r; the building of an oil press in the town of Colle (terziere of Borgo) ASF, NA, 19892, 165r–166r, 199r–200r. The revival of agriculture is evidenced, for example, by a farm at Quartaia 'de novo culturatum et desodatum' (ASF, NA, 20379, no. 259); by the contractual obligation to clear land ('desodare terram') (ASF, NA, 157, H, nos. 21, 38, 39; NA, 17569, 178r); by the new wine presses (ASF, NA, 13759, no. 45; NA, 8397, 166v; ASS, Colle, 361, 31r). On the estates of the Hospital of the Commune the land was divided into farms to increase productivity (ASS, Colle, 351, 18r–19r; Colle, 167, 75, 85r–86v).

[18] For the purchase of leaves for silkworms, ASF, NA, 20266, no. 322; and ASS, Colle, 2107, a register titled 'Raccolta e tiratura dell'arte della seta'.

[19] See, for example, on the import of linen bolsinensis, ASF, NA, 8397, 112r; of linen viterbensis, ibid., 178r–179r; of linen de Patrimonio, NA, 8406, 406r. In 1580 the wool guild of Florence claimed the right to matriculate the wool makers/traders from Colle (ASS, Colle, 189, 112r), a claim which would have made no sense had the number of local tradesmen not greatly increased, although during those years the privileges and the exemptions granted to the territories of the dominion had been drastically reduced, including those concerning the organisation of arts and trades.

We must not forget that even for Colle agriculture remained the main economic activity and it is the significant expansion of this activity that helps to account for the increased investment in land. From the early years of the sixteenth century, there was an obvious concentration of land in the hands of a few families who, seemingly as a deliberate strategy, bought up the majority of farms and pieces of land for sale. Thus it was that the Sabolini, Beltramini, Ranieri (alias Rinieri alias Renieri), Banchini, Guidotti, Del Cegna and Tommasi found themselves among the wealthiest in Colle in the estimi of 1547 and 1577. The concentration of wealth was in direct proportion to the concentration of landownership. This is also shown by the change in the composition of the larger estates in the century-and-a-half between the first and last tax censuses. In 1429 the Vivini, the richest family in Colle, possessed assets made up in almost equal parts of investments in industrial activities (tanning, paper-making and fulling to the tune of about 700 florins) and in land (821 florins).[20]

In 1577, the Sabolini, the largest taxpayers in Colle and divided into five households, declared assets of 16,947 florins solely in real estate.[21] It is true that the basis of the survey distorts the resultant comparison, but the fact remains that almost none of the owners of industrial buildings appear in the highest positions in 1577. Prospero Tommasi (whose whole family was divided into seven households, with a total taxable estate of 9534) had assets of 992 florins, of which 610 were tied up in a paper mill: he occupied fifth place in the rank order of wealth within his family.[22] Thus it is easy to see why no owners of industrial buildings (such as the Lupardi, Morozzi and Porzi) appear even in the top thirty tax-paying families in Colle. The preference for investing in land siphoned capital away from manufacturing industries, especially paper production, as Sabbatini has shown.[23]

On the other hand, the investment in agriculture and the transformation of many families essentially into rentiers led to the notable enhancement of the professional class during the sixteenth century.

---

[20] ASF, Catasto, 212, 378r–392r; Catasto, 251, 552r–560r.
[21] ASF, DG, 7941, 300v–305v, 338r–347r, 513r–v, 514v–515r, 722r–725v; DG, 7943, 141r–143v, 161r–165v, 240r, 245r, 344r–345r.
[22] ASF, DG, 7941, 54r–55r, 198r–202v, 212v–215r, 269v–273r, 536r–536v, 619r, 851r–854r; DG, 7943, 27r, 97v, 102v–103v, 126r–128r, 256r–256v, 295r–296r, 413r–414r.
[23] R. Sabbatini, 'Di bianco lin candida prole'. La manifattura della carta in età moderna e il caso toscano (Milan, 1990); Sabbatini, 'Una manifattura in cerca di protezione, capitali, capacità imprenditoriale: le cartiere di Colle dalla riforma dei Capitoli alla fine dell'Appalto (1548–1749)', in Diocesi e città, pp. 307–40.

As early as the mid-fifteenth century the sources show many families encouraging their sons to become notaries.[24] This was one way to succeed and elevate oneself socially; new members of the profession came from families of humble origins (sons of craftsmen and agricultural labourers[25]), as well as from those families who had traditionally followed the profession. Whereas in the first decades of the fifteenth century fewer than ten notaries, all belonging to different families, were active in Colle, in 1506 there were at least forty-five from more than twenty different families.[26] Thus not only was there an increase in the total number of notaries, but the number of families involved had doubled in spite of their tendency to specialise and to establish veritable notarial dynasties. This social phenomenon became even more marked in the sixteenth century. By then the range of professions had opened to even more prestigious careers, including those of *legum et utriusque iuris doctores*, of graduates in canon law and of physicians. To get an idea of the numbers involved, the estimo of 1577 is helpful: at least thirty-five tax returns are filed by notaries, thirty-eight by *messeri* (doctors of canon and civil law, physicians and clergymen) while the title of *maestro* (schoolmasters and surgeons) was submitted by six households. It is worth noting the wording of three of these underlining the offices held: 'il vescovo Beltramini',[27] 'monsignor vescovo de' Pacini',[28] 'capitano Bartolomeo detto Baiosso (Guidotti)'.[29] Ecclesiastical and military careers had in fact become one of the preferred means of social climbing (the Beltramini were notaries and paper manufacturers, the Pacini were tradesmen). The significance of the numbers involved in these professions and careers is clear if we consider that the population of Colle was around 3000 and the entire podesteria consisted of little more than

---

24 A list of notaries who came from Colle can be found in the 'Inventari del Notarile Antecosimiano' in the Florentine State Archive, where the records of 113 active notaries are preserved from the beginning of the fifteenth century to 1569. The Ferrosi, Pasci, Ranieri, Da Picchena, Tolosani and Usimbardi were all notarial families.

25 Simone Fulvi (alias 'Brami') was the grandson of Bramo di Mone da San Gimignano, a carpenter who had obtained citizenship in 1425 (ASS, Colle, 146, 105r); Girolamo Pieralla was the son of an immigrant from Poppi, citizen at least since 1454 (ASS, Colle, 157, 6r); Simone Fanucci was the son of farmers.

26 So many were the notaries who could be employed in civil and penal trials in the court of the Podestà, ASF, Tratte, 1466, 'Riforme degli uffici di Colle', 379r–380r.

27 ASF, DG, 7941, 477v: Messer Beltramo was Bishop of Terracina. Beltramo was preceded in the same office by Francesco Beltramini.

28 *Ibid.*, 373v–377r, regarding Messer Salvatore, Bishop of Chiusi.

29 ASF, DG, 7942, 863r–865v. Locally, he was referred to as 'capitan Baiosso', becoming so famous that a piazza ('Piazza Baios') was named after him.

4000.[30] The large number of graduates is an outstanding characteristic of Colle throughout the sixteenth century. Material gathered by Franco Angiolini on doctorates granted by the University of Pisa places Colle, with its ninety-two graduates in the period 1543–99, in fifth place among local centres in the Grand Duchy. Colle was surpassed only by four cities – Florence, Pistoia, Arezzo and Pisa – and did far better than Volterra or Prato.[31] This explains the lively intellectual and cultural life in the Valdelsa in the late Renaissance[32] and provides a solid explanation for the numbers of highly qualified citizens of Colle to be found in the state bureaucracy.

FROM COMMUNE TO COMMUNITY: ECONOMIC ACTIVITY, WEALTH AND SOCIAL MOBILITY

One of the most interesting points to emerge from an examination of the distribution of wealth is that there was a significant change among the wealthiest families. Not only did the relative position of many individual families change, but new families made their appearance in the topmost ranks. Some families originating from Colle itself had seen a rapid rise in fortune; others were descendants of newcomers. There was a marked mobility at all levels, but particularly at the middle to lower end of the economic scale. This trend was closely linked to the industrial side of the economy of Colle. From the fourteenth century the manufacture of woollen cloth, paper and iron had attracted a steady influx of immigrant workers who, once they had obtained citizenship, often became part of the ruling class.[33] Emigration was low, while, with the growth of the regional state, it became a phenomenon closely connected with the expansion of the city beyond its original boundaries and with the process of integration of new areas into the state. The consequences were clear in the sixteenth century, when a large crowd

---

[30] According to E. Repetti, *Dizionario geografico fisico storico della Toscana*, I (Florence, 1833), p. 760, in 1551 Colle had 3,370 inhabitants, while the podesteria, which included the town (*terra*), had 4,440. Ten years later, after the war against Siena, the town appears to have had only 2,087 inhabitants and the podesteria 3,723; R. Stopani, 'La distribuzione della popolazione e le tipologie insediative nel Cinque-Seicento', in *Diocesi e città*, p. 349. In 1577 the households in the census were 485 (*terra* and district).

[31] Angiolini, 'Il ceto dominante a Prato', pp. 391–3.

[32] L. Rossi, 'Aspetti della cultura colligiana tra la fine del Quattrocento e la prima metà del Seicento', in *Colle di Val d'Elsa nell'età dei granduchi*, pp. 243–57, with bibliography; G. Fioravanti, 'La cultura a Colle tra XV e XVI secolo', in *Diocesi e città*, pp. 421–8, and the contributions of L. Rossi, D. Pitadella and C. Bastianoni in the same volume.

[33] Muzzi, 'Attività artigianali', pp. 241–4.

of professionals from Colle made their appearance, not in response to local needs, but to meet the administrative requirements of the Medicean state. What had clearly emerged was a regional patriciate whose members, despite the deep and enduring roots they retained with their place of origin, maintained a multiplicity of ties, above all with the dominant city, and then with kindred social groups from other centres in the dominion (the Ferrosi in Cortona, Bardini in Piombino, Usimbardi, Beltramini, Dini and Cini in Florence, Da Picchena in Volterra, and Borgo San Sepolcro, Sabolini and Pasci in San Miniato). Thus from the sixteenth century it would be incorrect to refer to them as 'the local economic elite', as their wealth and political careers went well beyond the narrow confines of the distretto of Colle. These families still wanted to build family palaces in Colle itself, displaying, significantly, the coat of arms of the Medici family beside their own.[34] This was a way of acknowledging the role of the Grand Dukes in their own success and underlining their belonging to the regional elite.

This is the general trend over the centuries; it is possible to refine the analysis by identifying at least four periods each with its own characteristic features: (1) from the submission to Florence to the years of the catasto (1349–1429); (2) from the catasto to the Aragonese conquest (1430–80); (3) from the 1480s to the beginning of the principate (1481–1531); (4) from the 1530s to the establishment of the diocese (1532–92).

1 From the submission to Florence to the years of the catasto (1349–1429)

The long and hard-fought process of submission to Florence, begun in 1331, was finally formalised in January 1349. Then a period of drastic social upheavals began, caused by both demographic change and political events (plagues, wars and the consequent financial pressures, and opposition to Florentine rule, which manifested itself in guerrilla warfare for the rest of the century). The economy underwent huge changes. Some of the industrial and commercial sectors experienced a significant contraction, as evidenced by the disappearance of the guild of haberdashers, grocers and speziali, organised under their own statutes at the beginning of the century,[35] and by the temporary disappearance

---

[34] For example, the Grand Duke's architect Bernardino Renieri in 1580 had a coat of arms removed from the façade of his palace to substitute it with the arms of the Grand Duke, ASS, Colle, 189, 140r.

[35] A. Castellani, 'Gli Statuti dell'arte dei merciai, pizzicaioli e speziali di Colle di Valdelsa (1345)', Studi linguistici italiani, 20 (1994), pp. 3–39.

of the shoemakers' guild (reorganised in 1428).[36] At the same time there was a strong expansion of the paper industry, as witnessed by the formation of its own guild which received its first statutes in 1415.[37] The 'political economy' of the commune was also transformed; it focused ever more on food supplies through tighter control of flour mills, with the commune taking over the mills or increasing its share holding. At the same time the financial strain endured by the commune opened the way to the privatisation of some of its industrial buildings, starting with the paper mills, which by 1429 were all in private hands.[38]

From the socio-political viewpoint, the key event was the ending of the political influence of the majority of the oldest families (significantly, the only families in the fourteenth century to be known by their surname). These were the families who had ruled the commune in the thirteenth century and who had headed the factional struggles in the first years of the fourteenth. They were 'magnates' – the Tancredi, Trinchi (alias Trinci) and Ruggeri, and certain branches of the Guidotti and of the Da Picchena. A few offshoots of these families remained and managed to be made *popolari*: for example Francesco Ruggeri in 1354[39] and Piero Trinchi in 1374.[40] The fortunes of these two exemplify the contrasting destinies or rather the political divisions that continued to characterise the two families. Ruggeri was unable to adapt to the new political scene and was probably the leader of the uprising that took place in 1375, to which the Albertani, Ferrosi and Buonaccorsi responded by murdering him.[41] On the contrary Piero di Cione di Trincuccio de' Trinchi successfully joined the ruling group (he was prior five times) and became a shareholder in the company which administered the mills of the commune. He was sometimes referred to as *lanaiolo* and was an active contractor for the communal gabelle. His son, Meo, followed in his father's footsteps, but his tax return of 270 florins in 1429 put him in one of the lower ranks in terms of wealth. The other son, the notary Gaddo with a tax return of 58 florins shared a place with the poorest in Colle.[42]

[36] ASS, Colle, 148, 78v–79r; Colle, 154, 82v.
[37] Muzzi, 'Attività artigianali', p. 250.
[38] Most of the industrial buildings, paper mills, fulling works, 'wheels' for forging iron, and flour mills, belonged to companies in which the commune was one of the two major partners prior to becoming the majority shareholder; Muzzi, 'Attività artigianali', pp. 235–6.
[39] ASS, Colle, 97, 10r.   [40] ASS, Colle, 120, 71r–72r.
[41] Four years later his murderers were pardoned, with the agreement of the Florentine Signoria; ASS, Colle, 120, 8v–10r.
[42] ASF, Catasto, 211, 711r; Catasto, 212, 444r–449r; Catasto, 251, 339v–340r,

The magnates who kept a place in the higher economic echelons in Colle were the descendants of the judge Bartolomeo Guidotti and of Monaldo di Messer Usimbardo Da Picchena. In the second half of the fourteenth century judge Bartolomeo Guidotti followed a career characteristic of his social class – he was Podestà in Asti[43] – and steadfastly maintained his distance from the rebellions fomented by his relatives, descended from the lines of the knights Messer Sgrana and Messer Michele.[44] A prior on various occasions, his views were often solicited by the executive, and he was a regular member of commissions (balìe) elected to decide specific issues. The political careers of the Da Picchena family followed similar lines. The Guidotti and Da Picchena became some of the prominent wool merchants[45] and their economic success is proved by the fact that their sons and grandsons in 1429 occupied third and second place among the highest taxpayers in Colle – Agostino di Messer Bartolomeo with a tax return of 1654 florins and Antonio di Nanni di Monaldo with one of 2072 florins.[46]

Another significant group in late fourteenth- and early fifteenth-century society in Colle were those families who appear to have had no major role in the life of the commune before, and who came to prominence in this period. They were not yet known by a family surname; when they began to be, in the second half of the fifteenth century, they acknowledged a common descent from people who had lived at the end of the thirteenth and beginning of the fourteenth century (Vivini, Dini, Ranieri, Cerboni, Galganetti, Ferrosi, Albertani, Tolosani). Alongside these were some completely new families, who had moved to Colle and been made terrigenae at the beginning of the fourteenth century (Sabolini)[47] or who had obtained citizenship after

---

536v–540v. Their poverty is also shown by the fact that they were continually in tax arrears; ASS, Colle, 150, 216r–217r; Colle, 153, 9v.

[43] On 8 September 1370, a 'petitio domini Bartholomei Augustini de Colle ad presens potestatis civitatis de Asti' was presented to the Council; ASS, Colle, 113, 35v–37r.

[44] See the criminal career of Iacopo di Messer Michele (Guidotti) in ASS, Colle, 120, 61r–62r.

[45] Many contracts in the name of Giovanni di Monaldo da Picchena for the sale of wool cloth can be found in ASF, NA, 5855, 63v; NA, 5866, part I, 202r; NA, 5866, part II, 5r and passim.

[46] ASF, Catasto, 211, 12r–26r, 47r–57r; Catasto, 251, 4r–13r, 13v–19v.

[47] ASS, Colle, 86, 9r, citizenship granted in 1337 to Ser Giovanni Campori da Lucca, although in 1341 he was said to be citizen of Staggia (ASF, NA, 2911, 42v). His son Bartolomeo and grandson Piero di Bartolomeo lived in Colle from the late fourteenth century and did business with the Galganetti; ASF, NA, 2195, 2, 14r; Catasto, 212, 692r–699r; Catasto, 251, 690r–693r.

1350 (Manzoni,[48] Lupardi, Morozzi,[49] Viviani[50]). The first group provided the majority of the leaders of the commune especially in the second half of the fourteenth century, but from the beginning of the fifteenth century they began to share power with new arrivals who, with few exceptions, succeeded in having their names put into the election bags and frequently filled the highest offices (Priorate, Captains of the Guelf Party, Standard Bearers of the Militia). Steps taken to restrict access to public office to those who had obtained citizenship *a tempore mortalitatis citra* soon proved to be futile.[51]

Though they all participated in the lively industrial and commercial activities (having almost all become involved in the paper and wool industries or dealing as *speziali*), the families of these two groups were set apart by significant differences in wealth, resulting from the degree of diversification of their investments: the richest, such as the Vivini, had invested in all the main manufacturing concerns.

This was the most 'democratic' period in the political life of Colle. Access to the Priorate was achieved by numerous craftsmen whose assets placed them in lowest local ranks in 1429 (less than 50 florins). They benefited from the statute of 1387 that lowered the age and the qualifying estimo level necessary for entry to office.[52] It was a democracy that owed its existence to the falling population and to the general level of poverty,[53] caused, among other things, by the large demands for money and troops on the part of Florence. Its position on the border with Siena meant that Colle had the further burden of heavy defence costs, such as the fortification of Paurano, especially during the innumerable wars with the Visconti. The main thoroughfares between Siena and Pisa and between Florence and the Maremma, which passed through Colle, exposed its territory to marauding mercenaries and to the bandits who were based in the Sienese contado.[54] A form of democracy could, at

---

[48] Fabiano di Giovanni, known as Manzone, was registered in the *terra* of Colle in 1389; he was originally from Onci where he was a miller at the local mill, ASS, Colle, 129, 69v.

[49] See Muzzi, 'Attività artigianali', notes 76 and 82.

[50] ASS, Colle, 95, 206r.

[51] ASS, Colle, 95, 233r–235r (reforms of 1361); Colle, 116, 78r–81r (reforms of 1374).

[52] ASS, Colle, 127, 79r–91r.

[53] See Muzzi, 'Attività artigianali', p. 224, for a comparison of the wealth of Colle and San Gimignano.

[54] As shown by the description of the crimes committed by Battista Cambi da Colle and his associates, who, from their base at Castiglioncello in Sienese territory ('locum inimicum communis Florentiae'), blackmailed and robbed persons in the Colle district; ASF, Cap. Pop., 1847, 45r–46v. The document was mentioned by G. Brucker, *The Civic World of Early Renaissance Florence* (Princeton, 1977), p. 143 n. 207.

least to some extent, be seen as a necessary means of widening the social basis of consent for the policies of the ruling city. On the other hand, becoming part of the Florentine Republic was not completely detrimental. Florence, at least indirectly, supported the development of the paper industry, and by bringing Colle within the compass of the regional market it gave new opportunities to the wool business.[55]

2 From the catasto to the Aragonese conquest (1430–80)

There began to be signs of a slow but perceptible economic revival, spurred by the easing of the financial pressure from Florence. Petitions from the commune to Florence for tax relief and a reduction of the gabelle[56] were supported by a network of Florentine citizens who were 'friends' of the commune, led by Bartolomeo Scala.[57] This meant a more favourable spending forecast and a more effective 'budget'. Extraordinary taxes were less of a burden on the population and it even became possible to reduce the communal debts. An exemption (gratia) was obtained in 1460, removing the gabelle on the movement of cloth, livestock and oil, and before that the Florentine Republic had allowed greater freedom of trade with Siena and its territory.[58] In 1461 Colle was granted exemption from the provision that goods coming from Pisa were all subject to the Florentine customs office.[59] The importance of these provisions for Colle is underlined by the establishment of the office of the Six Defenders of the Exemption (Sei conservatori della grazia).[60] Moreover, the privileges thus obtained and renewed with remarkable consistency impelled the 'ingenuous' people of Colle to ensure that their mercatus remained liber.[61]

The exemptions had a positive impact on the economy of Colle: the

---

[55] Muzzi, 'Attività artigianali', pp. 252–3.

[56] ASS, Colle, 157, part III, 52v; Colle, 158, 124r, 157v; Colle,159, 33v, 36r; Colle, 162, 88v–89r.

[57] A. Brown, Bartolomeo Scala (1430–1497) (Florence, 1990). Scala's relatives in Colle received many political ackowledgements, thanks to the chancellor's interventions in favour of the commune; ASS, Colle, 163, 188v. For honours to Scala himself, see also Colle, 346, 117r; Colle, 162,169v–170v.

[58] ASS, Colle, 8, Statuti, 31r–34r; Colle, 345, 11v–13r, 23v. See also Colle,158, 273r; Colle, 159, 70v, 74v, 88r–99r; Colle, 344, 36r; Colle, 161, 91r.

[59] ASS, Colle, 345, 105r, 110r.   [60] ASS, Colle, 162, 21v.

[61] On the border between Florence and Lucca, at Santa Gonda, some pigs that had been bought in Colle by a Lucchese dealer were impounded by Florentine customs officers. Colle sent an envoy to the Signoria and to the customs officers to request that the provision be reversed, 'since the market of the town of Colle is free' (cum mercatus terre Collis sit liber), but they did not receive a favourable response ('bonum responsum'); ASS, Colle, 169, 77v–79r.

wool guild increased its productive capacity by expanding the dying works at the expense of the communal brothel;[62] there were also attempts to install new paper mills.[63] The cattle merchants hastened to buy grazing rights in the Maremma,[64] leading to an expansion of the livestock and leather trades, which, as became clear in the succeeding decades, were beginning to rank as among the most lucrative businesses.[65] The tanneries attracted a large crowd of shoemakers, especially from Lombardy[66] but even from France:[67] for example, one Piero di Giovanni from Lyons, who in 1470 established a shoelace business (*exercitio di fare le stringhe*), building up a lively trade with places in the Maremma.[68]

The economic vitality of Colle is also reflected in the printing works set up by the Frenchman maestro Bono and the Dutchman Giovanni di Mademblinch,[69] and in the presence of other immigrants from the north of Italy and northern Europe, who often had particular skills such as *magistri murorum, magistri formarum, velectarii*, kiln workers, cutlers, hat makers and tailors. There were also the families involved in trade (the Squarcialupi from Florence,[70] the Banchini from Poggibonsi[71] and the Pacini from Casole[72]), or in the professions (the Malingegni from Milan, physicians;[73] the Giusti from Volterrra, physi-

---

[62] ASS, Colle, 346, 162r.

[63] *Ibid.*, 107v–108v.

[64] ASF, NA, 8751, 21r.

[65] ASS, Colle, 153, 28r; Colle, 1052, Gabella dei contratti, 72v; Colle, 154, 57v, 67r, 80r; Colle, 342, 295r; Colle,158, 270v; ASF, NA, 8749, 2v; NA, 20379, no. 62; NA, 9667, no. 114, 1r.

[66] ASF, NA, 1485, 30v–33v; NA, 8397, 2r–8v, 53v–57v; NA, 9120, no. 226.

[67] ASS, Colle, 346, 4v, 6r.

[68] Suvereto, Bibbona, Pomarance; ASF, NA, 8753, 13r.

[69] F. Dini, 'Maestro Bono di Bethun stampatore in Colle', *Archivio storico italiano*, ser. 5, 31 (1903), pp. 177–97. Also ASF, NA, 11778, 35r; NA, 157, A, no. 12. Maestro Bono's application for citizenship in 1480, granted 'considerata qualitate dicti magistri Boni et qualiter magnam utilitatem confert terre Collis mediante eius arte', ASS, Colle, 350, 22v–23r. He died soon afterwards, between June and September 1481 (ASF, NA, 1484, 58v; NA, 20379, n. 145), leaving in Colle a *torculator*, previously his employee (*ibid.*).

[70] ASF, NA, 8532, A, n. 9; NA, 7438, 48r–50r; ASS, Colle, 1054, Gabella dei contratti, 28v. Citizenship in 1456: ASS, Colle, 158, 26v–27r.

[71] Maestro Silvestro di Nanni in 1427 already lived in Colle (ASS, Colle, 1052, Gabella dei contratti, 15v), he did not appear in the Catasto of 1429, but before 1437 had obtained citizenship (*ibid.*, 105r–106v).

[72] Giovanni di Pacino da Casole obtained citizenship in 1443; ASS, Colle, 152, 145r.

[73] Maestro Gabriello di Giovanni de' Malingegni da Milano married a Lupardi in 1480, becoming then a 'native' (*terrigena*); ASS, Colle, 1054, Gabella dei contratti, 227r; ASF, NA, 20264, no. 92.

cians and notaries;[74] and the Della Rena from Florence, notaries and physicians[75]) all of whom obtained citizenship and settled permanently in Colle.

The siege and occupation of the city by the Aragonese in the years 1479–80, together with the epidemics of 1476 and 1478,[76] must have contributed, albeit temporarily, to a slowing down of the economic recovery. It could hardly have been otherwise with the destruction of so many industrial buildings and of almost the whole of the Borgo district, with its resultant depopulation.

From the social point of view this period saw the amalgamation of families who had come to Colle during the fourteenth century with the indigenous families, an integration which took place thanks to family ties and joint commercial and industrial undertakings. This socio-economic elite, who at that time occupied the great majority of political offices, acted to consolidate their own position by excluding from the principal offices, in the statute of 1462, those who had not succeeded in obtaining office since 1400.[77] This statute is evidence of the formation of a tightly knit social group which was fully aware of its own identity and whose members were seeking a means of excluding outsiders, even though there were vast differences in wealth between the families who were part of that group. From then on, only a few of those families that had immigrated had access to communal offices. This was the period when wealth and socio-political status diverged the most (or at least it is the moment in which the phenomenon is easiest to pinpoint). Wealth became secondary in social and political advancement; in this respect, Colle mirrored a trend noticeable in Florence and throughout the state.

---

[74] Ser Giusto di Bartolomeo arrived in Colle as a grammar teacher ('magister grammatice') in 1451 and taught for nine years (ASS, Colle, 342, 333r–v; Colle, 343, 143v–144r; Colle, 160, 88v–89r). Later he became chancellor, from 1460 to 1482 (with a brief interruption), and married a Vivini. His son, the physician Pierfrancesco, was employed by the Commune as soon as he graduated (ASS, Colle, 353, 198r–199r), and he was granted citizenship in 1511.

[75] Maestro Giuliano de Arena, a physician, was the adopted son of Ser Martino di Piero da Firenze, chancellor in Colle at the beginning of the century, and of Ginevra Mati. He adopted Giovanbattista, son of Andrea di Luca da Firenze (ASS, Colle, 1055, Gabella dei contratti,150v–151r); Giovanbattista was the grandfather of Messer Giulio, the husband of Aspasia, who was the daughter of Aonio Paleario (ASF, NA, 16341, 60v). Giovanbattista was granted citizenship in 1492, ASS, Colle, 352, 223v, 230r.

[76] ASS, Colle, 164, 15r, 17r. The plague of 1478 was very serious: the chancellor fled and for six months the business of the commune was interrupted. The ordinary drawing of lots was stopped and offices were filled by co-opted candidates. There is a vivid account of this episode written by the chancellor on his return to Colle, ibid., 71r.

[77] ASS, Colle, 6, Statuti, 13v; Colle, 163, 188v, 190r; Colle, 164, 87r.

One has only to reflect on the career of Messer Bartolomeo Scala, the miller's son, and, later on, that of Messer Francesco Campana, who was the grandson of a bell ringer employed by the commune at the beginning of the fifteenth century.[78] The careers such men enjoyed in the ruling city opened the prospect of public office to their relatives back in Colle.[79] Another significant and well-known example of the story, retold so many times in the sixteenth century, of professional and political fortunes at the 'centre' and at the 'periphery' was that of the Usimbardi family,[80] and in some respects the histories of the Giusti, the Pacini, the Cini and the Luci (Luchi) were the same.

3 From the 1480s to the beginning of the principate (1481–1531)

The economic trends that had begun to emerge in the earlier period gained strength. The new submission agreements with Florence,[81] drawn up once Ferdinand of Aragon's occupation had ended, confirmed substantial tax relief (the ordinary tax of 430 *fiorini di sugello* was reduced to 100 *fiorini larghi* and the salary of the Podestà was halved for six years). In addition, the people of Colle were allowed to practise any craft within the area of Florentine jurisdiction without paying the matriculation fee. It is no accident, therefore, that we find paper manufacturers from Colle in business in Prato[82] and Pescia.[83] On top of all this,

---

[78] F. Dini, 'Francesco Campana e i suoi', *Archivio storico italiano*, ser 5, 23 (1989), pp. 289–323, and 24 (1899), pp. 13–22; M. G. Cruciani Troncarelli, 'Campana Francesco', in *Dizionario biografico degli italiani*, 17 (1974), pp. 341–5, with bibliography. A certificate of the origin and the social standing of the family, requested in 1580 by 'Messer Cosimo del magnifico Messer Camillo di Messer Giovanbattista', written by the chancellor of Colle, did not go beyond his grandfather and his grandmother (a Staccini), since otherwise it would have been difficult to certify that he descended 'da casate nobili di questa terra', ASS, Colle, 189, 152r. Regarding nobilisation, R. Bizzocchi, 'Cultura di città, cultura nobiliare nella Toscana del Cinquecento', in *Diocesi e città*, pp. 83–96; M. Fantoni, *La corte del granduca: forme e simboli del potere mediceo tra Cinque e Seicento* (Rome, 1994).

[79] Brown, *Bartolomeo Scala*, pp. 155–67 and note 57 above.

[80] Fantoni, *La corte del granduca*, pp. 139–68; M. Fantoni, 'Dalla provincia alla capitale: gli Usimbardi di Colle alla corte medicea', in *Diocesi e città*, pp. 117–38.

[81] ASS, Colle, 8, Statuti, 47r–58r.

[82] ASF, NA, 8532, E, n. 20; NA, 20250, 11r, Piero di Sacchetto da Colle, paper maker who lived in Prato (1468); NA, 157, A, n. 24, Tommaso and Francesco di Giovanni Bartoli da Colle, who lived in Prato (1485); NA, 1487, part II, 25r–26r (1496); Francesco di Giovanni from Prato in 1526 was nicknamed Francesco 'del Cartaio', NA, 8401, 219r.

[83] Nepo di Giovanni Bartoli da Colle (brother of emigrants to Prato and of Brunellesco, who owned a paper mill in Colle) lived in Pescia in 1486; ASF, NA, 157, A, n. 37; NA, 8535, n. 216. Andrea di Iacopo Lippi (Porzi) in 1537 married a woman from Pescia; NA, 8407, 72r. The immigration of people from Colle to Pescia may also

Florence undertook to contribute to the reconstruction of the city to the tune of 500 florins a year for ten years.

The reconstruction works attracted another wave of *magistri murorum* and ironworkers to Colle, particularly from Lombardy. Industry and commerce, especially the livestock industry[84] – encouraged by the fact that Colle was on one of the favourite cattle drives into the Maremma – experienced a considerable revival,[85] just like agriculture, as we have seen. Ceramic manufactures were established alongside the traditional manufacturing industries.[86] These produced goods for everyday use which, judging by a workshop inventory that listed 1600 items of crockery, were destined for more than just the local market.[87] They must also have been manufacturing luxury items, given that the Manzoni brothers engaged a worker to design and paint these articles.[88]

The favourable economic climate was one of the factors behind the ruling group's applying for the first time, in collaboration with dean Francesco Rucellai, for a bishopric.[89] Promoting the *maternam terram* to *episcopalem civitatem* would have implied freeing the people of Colle from their conflictual connection with the bishop of Volterra. However, it did not have the support of the entire ruling group. Quite the opposite: between December 1498 and the following February the conflict between those who were in favour of the proposal and those who were against assumed the proportions of a *pestifera seditio*, threatening the social cohesion of the whole town.[90] The extraordinary

have been encouraged by the presence of a chancellor who came from Colle; ASS, Colle, 342, 363r. For many years the paper industry in Pescia depended on labour from Colle; Brown, *Pescia*, p. 159.

[84] For example, see the significant purchases of livestock from Sienese merchants, among them a Chigi, ASF, NA, 9121, part II , 80r–84r.

[85] Before 1442 there is no evidence for transhumance either in the public documents or in notarial records. After that year, however, references begin to multiply and regulations were drawn up for the *vergarii* (shepherds) who were responsible for damaging property en route through Colle territory, ASS, Colle, 152, 21r–22v; Colle, 154, 80r; Colle, 156, 9v. In 1483 a 'Lex pro bestiis forensibus transeuntibus' granted relief from the gabella del passo if shepherds stayed in Colle and sold at least 200 fleeces there, ASS, Colle, 165, 126v–127v.

[86] Probably books continued to be printed, since 'Simonem Geraddi de Flandia impressorem librorum', who had been Maestro Bono's *torculator*, settled down in Colle after Bono's death and married the daughter of a paper maker, ASS, Colle, 1054, Gabella dei contratti, 238v; Colle, 1053, Gabella dei contratti, 72v. Regarding trade in other products, such as 'plura genera armorum', see ASS, Colle, 163, 134v–135v.

[87] ASF, NA, 8404, 304r.   [88] ASF, NA, 9125, no. 140.

[89] P. Nencini, 'Le origini della diocesi di Colle', in *Diocesi e città*, p. 225.

[90] ASS, Colle, 168, 122v–127r; 128v–129r.

nature of this episode and of the conflict within the ruling group is vividly documented in the report compiled by the chancellor and preserved in the records of the Council's deliberations. It took the intervention of the Florentine Signoria and its envoys to settle the dispute. At first patiently but then with increasing irritation, the Florentine priors ordered a *parlamento* of all those with political rights to be summoned, so that they could decide by majority and 'reach a consensus as to whether they wanted or did not want the said bishop'. There were 178 people assembled and those opposed to the scheme were defeated by a narrow majority (ninety against the bishopric, seventy-nine for, nine abstentions). This did nothing to ease the tension; they had to send four spokesmen for each faction to Florence, in a further attempt to restore peace. Representing those in favour were a Da Picchena, a Della Torre/Luchi, a Porzi and a Guidotti; against were an Albertani, a Mingozzi, another Da Picchena and a Pasci. This episode is important in two different ways: on the one hand, it helps to explain the phenomenon of the internal struggles of the nineties and the first decade of the sixteenth century, and on the other it highlights the fact that behind the conflict stood the interests of social classes who had very different objectives. One social class aimed at ennobling the *terra* as a way of conferring distinction on the individual or the family and another class wanted to direct policy and local energy towards more concrete, perhaps more limited, ends – perhaps to support local productivity. We shall return to this shortly.

Conflictuality was the chief characteristic of the little town in the Valdelsa, as witnessed by the numerous truces, sworn by the families of Colle before the Podestà or his judge. The struggles within the ruling group began in 1475 when the conflict turned on the election of the chancellor,[91] while in 1486 the criteria for the filling of the electoral bags[92] were the focus of fierce antagonism, not to mention again the election of a chancellor. In this instance, it was necessary for Bartolomeo Scala to intervene and for Antonio Nobili to be sent as the Signoria's commissioner in order to produce a settlement.[93] The problems connected with the administration of the commune became mixed up with the feud between the Viviani and the Tolosani, which bloodied the

---

[91] See the documentation by Ser Giusto (Giusti, as in note 74 above) da Volterra, who returned to his office on 27 March 1476; ASS, Colle, 164, 1v–2r.

[92] These were the bags containing the names of those who could be elected to public office. The names were then extracted at random.

[93] ASS, Colle, 166, 216v, 222v, 225v–226v, 228v–229r; Colle, 352, 5v–7r.

streets of Colle for twenty years besides embroiling other families.[94]
Even Lucrezia de' Medici was dragged in to restore peace.[95]

The difficult issue of the bishopric was thus broached in a period
already vexed by internal upheavals. The Florentine Signoria was forced
to intervene time and again to impose truces, frequently ignored, and it
was sometimes involved in episodes leading inevitably to disagreements,
as in the case of the Ferrosi and Bardini, which was serious enough to
'turn the land upside down', given that both their families had vast
connections and had men come in from Siena and Piombino.[96] The
Signoria first sought to mediate between the contending parties, then
imposed a truce on the Bardini and Bolognini.[97] Meanwhile the
struggles between the Bertini and the Agostini impelled three brothers
of the latter family to leave 'se non teneri pro delicto alterius' and for
each one of them to respond only 'de eorum stirpe et consorteria per
lineam masculinam'.[98]

The application for the bishopric was the incident that brought to the
surface other and more profound tensions generated by social change.
Although this is not obvious from the names known to us in each social
faction, which do not correspond to different social classes, this period is
characterised by the conflict between families who based their standing
mainly on trade and manufacturing industry and those, generally
immigrants, with small or recently acquired means, who, thanks to the
professions or to a career and benefices in the church, succeeded in
establishing or confirming a status based on a very different political,
cultural and ideological perspective. This group was less and less tied to
the local scene, drawing its vital force rather from a regional and supra-
regional orbit, the latter opened up to it as a result of connections with
the Roman curia.[99] Hence the importance of acquiring, in the eyes of
'foreigners', the prestige of coming from a 'city', instead of a mere town
(terra). A complex interaction of cause and effect associated, at least in
the chronology of events, these political and social developments to the
advancement of these families, which were now on the way to growing

---

[94] ASF, NA, 20264, nos. 2, 119; NA, 8752, 115v; NA, 1484, 19r, 82v; NA, 8753, 96v.
[95] ASS, Colle, 350, 7v.
[96] ASF, NA, 20266, nos. 126, 128; NA, 158, N, no. 32; NA, 5162, 210r.
[97] ASF, NA, 7233, F, no. 14.   [98] ASF, NA, 20266, no. 115.
[99] There is much evidence of the importance of Rome and the papal states in providing
offices and commercial opportunities for the people of Colle, not to speak of
appointments to benefices. As an example, we can consider the fact that, at the
beginning of the sixteenth century, Rome often appeared in the notarial formulary
among the places in which obligations could be repaid, ASF, NA, 5162, 15r; NA,
8397, 7r–8v; NA,19893, 359r. During the sixteenth century, a large group of 'nostri
compatrioti' was in the Roman curia, ASS, Colle, 189, 46v–47r.

out of their traditional structure, already loosened by the increasing independence of the separate branches. And this in itself led to conflict as, for example, in the case of the Galganetti and the Bolognini,[100] whose quarrel was arbitrated by citizens of Florence, not to mention the case of Broccialdo Cini and his brother,[101] the physician Antonio,[102] and the long quarrel between the various branches of the Albertani family.[103]

Further evidence of the transformation that was underway in this period was the practice of changing family names. Surnames became common in Colle from the second half of the fifteenth century. Previously families identified by surname were remarkably few; not counting magnates, we find some de Albertanis, de Tolosendis, de Beltraminis and de Vivinis, but very few others. The usual practice among notarial and chancery documents was to refer to individuals by their baptismal name followed by the patronymic and the name of the grandfather. Even the procedure for filling the electoral bags followed this form, which was only abandoned in the scrutinies dating from the sixteenth century when the family name in both Latin and Italian was included.[104]

To trace individual family histories we have to reconstruct their genealogies – not an easy task, given that the third name often does not correspond with that of the grandfather but could be an invariable patronymic, a primitive form of real surname. And even when the surname appears to have been fixed and its use adopted in documents, what we are presented with in many cases is a new version of the same name. Sometimes we are dealing with a name which came later to identify a particular branch of a family, for example Luchi/della Torre, de Liurottis/de Guidottis, or with a nickname for the surname: 'de Scottinis alias del Cipolla', 'de Cionis alias del Mela', or 'del Taglia de Cerboneschis'. In these instances it is easy to conclude that the layering of surnames is evidence of the process of differentiation of branches of the family, which gave rise to as many 'new' families: for example the Galganetti and the Tommasi from the *terzo* of Castello[105] were descendants of the Mati.[106] Such differentiation was established also by

---

[100] ASF, NA, 7233, E, no. 33.
[101] ASF, NA, 17387, 35v–36r; NA, 19893, 10r–11r.
[102] ASF, NA, 20244, 177v.
[103] ASF, NA, 20264, nos. 127, 128; NA, 1484, 108r; NA, 1485, 30v–33v.
[104] ASF, Tratte, 1466.
[105] Not to be confused with the Tommasi of the district of Piano.
[106] One of the most significant documents was ASF, NA, 7233, E, no. 33.

adopting a surname that does not even seem to derive from a common ancestor, as in the case of the Carletti, a branch of the Cini. For some a change of surname was a way of achieving noble status, as in the case of the de Baccelli, who rediscovered their remote ancestry in the magnates Tancredi and adopted their surname,[107] similarly the Del Porco exchanged theirs for the more honorific de Portiis/Porzi.

It is more difficult to establish the significance of a change when it involved all branches of a family, as happened with the Tolosani, called de Nirghiantibus/de Nirglantis for twenty years before they went back to their previous surname or with the Del Nero/Cagnarelli later Bolognini. The examples could be multiplied. The process involved large numbers of families from Colle, even those of humble status: the Del Colunna/Giancolonna were agricultural labourers; the Paragliasini/Ceccarelli were also agricultural labourers; the Calafati/Pachini were blacksmiths.

A variety of motives – the division of families, ennoblement or a simple desire for self-advertisement or social prominence – could be at the bottom of this chaotic phase in the development of surnames, which, so far as I am aware, has only been highlighted by Carocci for Tivoli,[108] where, however, it is linked solely to attempts to achieve nobility. In Colle the underlying significance of the phenomenon can be explained in relation to the local conflicts of this period. It is another piece of the jigsaw depicting a transition phase, a 'crisis' in social and cultural development, whereby a new set of values is established, involving a different concept of family. It is not without its contradictions, however: alongside families in which the bonds of solidarity and shared responsibility do not seem to go beyond two generations[109] we find the formal reunification of families, involving numerous branches of uncles and cousins, who 'submitted' to the authority of the head of the *domus*, or

---

[107] The notary Ludovico Tancredi used both surnames at first, but later only the last, ASF, NA, 19892–19906.

[108] S. Carocci, *Tivoli nel basso medioevo: società cittadina ed economia agraria* (Rome, 1988), pp. 79–80. Some changes of family names in Arezzo are mentioned, but not analysed, by R. Black, 'Umanesimo aretino nella commedia senese, 1516: il Parthenio di G. Pollastra allo Studio di Siena', *Atti e memorie della Accademia Petrarca di Lettere, Arti e Scienze*, 56 (1994), pp. 117–18.

[109] As witnessed by a contested separation between the Bolognini, father and sons, which required the intervention of the Signoria (ASF, NA, 8397,149v–150v; NA, 9120, no. 19), and separations between the Viviani (*ibid.*, 15v–18r), between the Albertani (NA, 20264, nos. 127–128; NA, 1484,108v; NA, 1485 30v–33v), and between the Da Picchena (which also required the intervention of the Signoria; NA, 20266, nos. 202, 203; NA, 7233, A, no. 26).

decided to return to live under the same roof, or to pool their economic resources.[110]

There is no doubt that at the end of the fifteenth century new values were beginning to prevail. First there was the new importance attached to education, perceived as *honor et virtus* to the extent that it lent prestige not just to the person studying but indeed to the whole family.[111] This perception became widespread and was the moving force behind all those families who sent their offspring to university in Siena, Pisa,[112] Lucca, Bologna,[113] Perugia[114] and as far as Naples and Padua.[115] At the same time, the wider opportunities for employment in the bureaucracy of the state or of the church provided a more concrete incentive for the love of learning. The public institutions of Colle did not finance scholarships as happened in Prato, nor have I yet found any reference to bequests for this purpose. But anyone who applied to the Community obtained financial support to which the Ospedale del Ricovero also contributed, often with the stipulation that this be repaid at the end of the period of study, sometimes without security.[116] Again, it is significant that such applications become more numerous in the late fifteenth century[117] – a sign of how widespread the phenomenon had become and of how quickly public institutions responded to new social demands.

---

[110] Thus did the Vivaldi da Calcinaia (ASF, NA, 8535, nos. 181, 248, 300, 312), the Cennini (NA, 8397, 67r–68r), a family of tenant farmers (NA,17569,192r–193v).

[111] When in 1486 the brothers Amerigo and Bartolomeo Sabolini separated, they chose not to calculate the costs incurred to support 'in studium in arte fisice magistrum Tommaxium olim filium dicti Amerigi et nepotem dicti Bartholomei in civitate Senarum et in civitate Pisarum', because the expenses where relative to 'aquirendum honorem et virtutem et quod hoc veniebat in honorem totius domus eorum'; ASF, NA, 157, A, no. 31.

[112] Gregorio Tolosendi studied canon law; ASS, Colle, 345, 66r, 68r; Colle, 346, 18v–19r.

[113] Messer Antonio Pasci, student in Florence, Bologna and Lucca, 'causa aquirendi litteras et virtutes'; ASF, NA,1559,128r–135r.

[114] Messer Alberto Pocciatti studied in Florence, Perugia and Pisa; ASS, Colle, 165, 20r–21v.

[115] For example, Francesco Tommasi; M. Berengo, 'Un agronomo toscano del Cinquecento. Francesco Tommasi da Colle Val d'Elsa', in *Studi di storia medievale e moderna per Ernesto Sestan*, II (Florence, 1980), pp. 495–518, at p. 502.

[116] The commune lent Francesco Franzesi 60 florins to graduate in civil law in Siena and Padua; ASS, Colle, 346, 186r.

[117] See notes 110, 112 and 114 above; and ASS, Colle, 167, 31r–v; Colle, 361, 20r–21v. In the financial records of the commune for 1485, 25 lire appears to have gone to Messer Giovanbattista Campana (Francesco's father) to 'andare allo Studio'; ASS, Colle, 166, 120r–122v. The motivation of this financial help given 'cupientibus venire ad virtutes et se conferre ad studia' is extremely significant: because this 'vertitur in honorem Comunis', ASS, Colle, 167, 79v–80v.

The process of aristocratisation becomes evident in this period. It involved all the major families, not only the wealthiest and more powerful, but also those who, thanks to marriage connections and professional careers, had managed to become part of the ruling group and were actively concerned in all the various economic activities of the commune, without having become particularly rich. The Cioni/ Del Mela/de Trincucci/de Trinchi or Cini/Carletti and the Lupardi/ de Bucionis, the Luchi/Della Torre, Allegretti/Capobianchi/Franca-lancia and Bardini/Puccinelli fall into this category. In fact, the truly rich were beginning to differentiate themselves above all by their significant investment in land; while not giving up industrial and commercial activity completely, their clear preference for owning land became another sign of the aristocratisation of society. Further support for such aristocratisation, which we have already seen in the establish-ment of surnames, is to be found in the decidedly new use of the terms *nobilis vir*, *spectabilis vir* and *discretus vir*, which ever more often preceded the names of individuals.[118] The history of the Sabolini family (but also of the Usimbardi and Ranieri) serves as an example of this pattern. The Sabolini's forebear, Ser Giovanni Campori da Lucca, had obtained citizenship as early as 1337[119] and his son and grandson established lucrative *speziale* and paper businesses, which made Piero di Bartolomeo one of the richest men in Colle in 1429 (a *valsente* of almost 1000 florins).[120] Piero, however, did not boast any particular claim to social distinction and did not use a surname. The desire to obtain noble status became irresistible at the end of the century; the *nobilis vir* 'Amerigo di Piero de Sabolinorum de Luca' appointed notaries and legitimised natural children by virtue of a privilege which went back to Charles IV,[121] and after a few years he became a count palatine.[122] His son Piero adorned himself with the title 'count' (*comes*), while the new self-consciousness of the family led to a search for a well-connected and wealthy wife for his brother Niccolò. He married one of the Grifoni of San Miniato, who were an old noble family from that area and who provided two deacons for the parish of Colle. The grandson of the *comes* Piero, Messer Amerigo, became coadjutor to the dean and prepared the ground for the subsequent accession of his nephew as deacon, Messer Niccolò, who was the champion of Colle's

---

[118] For example, regarding the Da Picchena, Ranieri, Pasci; ASF, NA, 8533, nos. 327, 436; NA, 20383, 40r.
[119] See note 47 above.
[120] ASF, Catasto, 212, 692r–699r; Catasto, 251, 690r–693r.
[121] ASF, NA, 1484, 109v, 182v–184v; NA, 5161, 182r.
[122] ASF, NA, 20266, no. 72.

elevation to diocesan status (1592) but who never became bishop himself. From the beginning of the sixteenth century, while continuing to maintain their *apotheca*,[123] the Sabolini were distinguishing themselves for their careers in the church and for their military careers at the service of the Medici. The order of Santo Stefano, obtained during the 1580s, set the seal on their noble status and coincided with their retreat from trade.[124]

The process of ennoblement was helped by the building of new family chapels or the expansion of existing ones in the major churches (the parish church of Sant'Alberto, raised to the status of collegiate church in 1520 with the privilege *nullius diocesis*, Sant'Agostino, Sant'Iacopo, San Francesco, Santa Caterina) as well as by the construction, finished in 1513, of the church of Santa Maria delle Grazie,[125] which was backed by the shoemakers Luchi and the woollen cloth dealers Bertini in conjunction with the commune.[126] Further joint public and private initiatives lay behind the embellishments and overall improvements made in Colle:[127] social services were reformed and expanded with the founding of the convent dedicated to Saints Mary Magdalene and Catherine,[128] to provide a home for women who could not be married off; the ancient Ospedale del Comune was relocated and rebuilt and the public baths (*stufa*) were constructed.[129] Even marriage alliances assumed different connotations. Up to this point people in Colle had for the most part married within their own circle, thus weaving a close network of *parentadi*, as witnessed by the requests for dispensations for marrying within the prohibited degree;[130] from the

---

[123] ASF, NA, 158, N, nos. 39, 40.

[124] For certifications of their trade as wool merchants and *speziali* until 1533, see ASF, NA, 8405, 79v, 252r. In 1538 the palace was completely rebuilt in a manner different from their previous home ('casa vecchia'); NA, 21212, part IV, 33r–35r, 36v–39r.

[125] ASS, Colle, 361, 20r.

[126] ASF, NA, 20265, no. 199; NA, 5162, 135r; NA, 5163, 76r; NA, 5161, 152v–153r; NA, 7256, no. 78.

[127] Note the windows with glass, the new choir and the travertine architrave in Sant' Agostino (ASF, NA, 9115, no. 132; NA, 7233, E, no. 9; NA, 8400,127r); and the window 'inginocchiata' and the commune's coat of arms (a 'horse's neck') carved for the priors' palace, which had windows of glass (ASS, Colle, 351, 113r, 137r, 140v, 200r; Colle, 352, 106r–107v).

[128] *Ibid.*, 22r–24r, 74r, 77r–78r.

[129] ASF, NA, 20379, no. 244; NA, 9117, no. 34; NA, 20266, no. 2; NA, 8397, 96r.

[130] ASF, NA, 20266, nos. 28 (Cini-Ferrosi), 305 (Albertani-Allegretti); NA, 19893, 89v–90v, 103r–104v (Ricci-Cerboni); *ibid.*, 166r–168r (Squarcialupi-Guidotti); 169r–172r (Guidotti-Ranieri); NA 8397, 155r–156v (Vivini-Vivini); NA 8403, 55r–56v (Albertani-Ranieri).

late fifteenth century, many offspring, male and female, sought marriages in other towns in the dominion, besides Florence and Siena. The
choice of partner was dictated generally by social connections, but there
is also evidence of a tendency to favour particular places: Volterra, San
Gimignano, Certaldo, Castelfiorentino, Cortona, Piombino, San
Miniato, Pescia and Prato. There seems thus to have been a parallel
hierarchy of smaller towns, ranked according to social ties, other than
the usual financial criteria. This might have been a way, besides the
much more compelling one of professional standing (notaries and judges
approaching members of rectors' retinues, or rectors approaching other
rectors), through which the exclusive attachment to one's own
commune (*campanilismo*) was overcome and replaced by the awareness
of belonging to a wider cultural area – that of the region.

4 From the 1530s to the establishment of the diocese (1532–92)

In these final sixty years the first effects of an economic recession began
to be felt, shown initially by the ending of the period of industrial
expansion: significantly there were no applications to the General
Council (*Consiglio generale*) to establish new industrial buildings.
Furthermore some of the most important structures for milling and
cloth fulling were 'nationalised' by the ducal *Gran Camera*. I have yet to
discover the precise mechanism for this,[131] but it seems that the transfer
to the treasury after the conquest of Siena of the ownership of five
manufacturing structures worth at least 6700 florins (at 82 soldi to the
florin)[132] followed from the need to promote the integration of the 'old
state' with the new. In fact only the mills and fulling works in the
neighbourhood of Gracciano or the ones nearest to its boundary passed
under the control of the *Camera*, while those in the suburbs of the *terra*
of Colle remained with their previous owners. The 'privatised' facilities
had always been heavily used by subjects of the republic of Siena,
especially by people from Casole, Monteguidi and Radicondoli,[133]
but also by Sienese citizens, one of whom tried, in vain, to take

---

[131] So far I have not been able to examine the archive of the *Camera*. Only one piece of
evidence comes from the notaries of Colle, a document of 1564 in which the
provveditore della gabella for flour in Florence acquired shares in the mill of Calcinaia;
ASF, NA, 1553, 45r. Clearly, the mills of Colle were recognised as having an
important function in the provision of corn and in contributing to Florentine
finances with the taxes they paid.

[132] ASF, DG, 7943, 537r.

[133] ASS, Colle, 343, 10r; ASF, NA, 157, C, no. 14; Muzzi, 'Attività artigianali',
pp. 239–40.

over some 'shares' in them.[134] All of this led to a long series of disputes
and difficulties at the time of the wars between Siena and Florence,
reflected in the impossibility of gaining access to these works and in the
great increase in the gabelle.[135] Although such central control benefited
the Grand Duchy's new subjects, the families and ecclesiastical bodies
who had owned them before paid a heavy price. Among these families
the Vivaldi and the Pelagalli, both from Calcinaia, who had earlier
figured high in the ranks of taxpayers,[136] were now, in 1577, among the
poorest and some of the Vivaldi had emigrated.[137]

The expansion of the state, on the other hand, meant that investments were more secure and allowed for an increase in land ownership
outside the narrow confines of the territory of Colle. Many families,
including the Giusti, Sabolini and Galganetti, rushed to buy land and
graze their cattle on Sienese territory;[138] professionals, such as notaries
and judges, now had the chance of carrying on their profession there.[139]

The aristocratisation of society begun in the earlier period was
accompanied by the 'ennoblement' of local offices. These were already
restricted by law and in practice to a narrow oligarchy and further
discrimination was sought by means of minute codes covering dress,
shoes, hats and colours to be worn – not only during office hours, but
also whenever the officeholder was outside his own front door.[140] The
rules of precedence, the reserved pews in church, added to the manners
and symbols which united the ruling group and allowed them to
differentiate themselves from the rest of the population. In addition, the
ousting of the commune's traditional patron saints in favour of new
civic cults more in keeping with the role that Colle now enjoyed in the

---

[134] In 1533 Girolamo Tancredi da Siena, in order to circumvent the statutory
prohibitions still in force (and valid for Florentines too) against foreigners (forenses)
acquiring land in the territory of Colle, employed a nominee, but without success;
ASF, NA,10936, 37r, 38r.

[135] See ASS, Colle, 343, 10r–11r, with provisions in the contract for the letting of mills
that set a lower rent if the Sienese could not use them. Also ASF, NA, 7233, A, no.
55; NA, 7229, 12r; NA, 13759, no. 199; NA, 8403, 391r–392r. For problems with
the excise duties, see ASS, Colle, 163, 12v; Colle, 164, 47v; Colle,167, 85r–v.

[136] ASS, Estimo del contado, 94, 7r, 64r.

[137] ASF, DG, 7941, 266r; DG, 7942, 654r; DG, 7943, 124r, 311r.

[138] ASF, NA, 12838, 223r; NA,12839, 30r; NA,143, 113v; NA, 16341, 39r; NA,1559,
103v.

[139] For the numerous notaries 'de Colle' who exercised their profession in Sienese
territory from the second half of the sixteenth century, see S. Fineschi and
G. Catoni (eds.), Archivio notarile, 1221–1864: inventario (Rome, 1975), for the
Sienese State Archive. For Niccolò Beltramini's career, see E. Fasano Guarini, 'La
Maremma Senese nel Granducato Mediceo', in Contadini e proprietari nella Toscana
moderna, 2 vols. (Florence, 1979–81), I, pp. 422–423.

[140] Ninci, 'Lineamenti dell'assetto istituzionale', p. 116.

grand-ducal arena saw the city moving ever further into the shadow of Florence.[141]

In this milieu of social exclusivity, it became impossible – even having one of the greatest fortunes and sharing property with families in the oligarchy or forging bonds of kinship with them – to receive full political recognition, that is, to participate in all the advantages enjoyed by the patriciate of Colle. This was true of the Del Cegna, of the Bimbi and of the Montegabbro, who had been among the richest families since the beginning of the century.[142] They all maintained residences in Colle but still were not granted citizenship and it was perhaps this sleight-of-hand that prevented the descendants of *laboratores terrarum* from associating with the ruling group, in stark contrast to the practice of the preceding century. On the other hand, from the middle of the sixteenth century the law had indicated exactly which tradesmen were barred from public office: the great variety of craftsmen and tradesmen, who had enlivened the economic life of Colle until a few decades earlier, were now definitively excluded from the administration of the affairs of the commune.[143]

One economically and socially homogeneous group, who had achieved dominance over the middle classes, ruled the commune of Colle. It was this controlling class that renewed the application, successfully at last, for a bishopric and the status of 'city' (*civitas*). Victory was due in part to the fact that the application coincided with orders from the Council, aimed at eliminating the areas of privilege reflected in the exemptions enjoyed by local churches.

Within the oligarchy, there were no opponents, nor could there have been, given its strong cohesion. The application for the bishopric and its failure in the previous century came, significantly, in a period of economic development, of social upheaval and of the arrival of new families into the ruling class, that is, in a period when society contained enough class conflict to splinter the ruling group. Then, the 'insidiatoris

---

141 O. Muzzi, ' "Tenere la città abbondante, unito il popolo e la nobiltà onorata". Tre secoli di feste a Colle tra Medioevo e Età Moderna', in *Diocesi e città*, pp. 187–210. Regarding symbols and the places of power, Fantoni, 'La corte del granduca'.

142 Luca di Cegna da Campiglia in 1473 had landed property worth more than 12,000 lire; in 1494 his lands alone exceeded 14,000 lire, and he had houses worth 118 lire; ASS, Estimo del Contado, 94, 72r ff. In 1547 the four Del Cegna households were worth 8,068 lire: Bonelli Conenna, 'Struttura fondiaria', p. 294. In 1577 Piero di Bartolomeo alone was worth 5,280 florins, ASF, DG, 7941, 385r–396r; DG, 7943, 186r–191v. For the Bimbi in 1547 see Bonelli Conenna, 'Struttura fondiaria'; in 1577 two households of this family exceeded 7,000 florins; ASF, DG, 7941,128r–134r; 158r–165r; DG, 7943, 79r–82r, 443r–444r.

143 See a passage from the reforms in Ninci, 'Lineamenti dell'assetto istituzionale'.

humani generis perversitas' divided the hearts of the people of Colle and produced antagonism that was enough to feed long-lasting hostilities and to undermine the cohesion of families themselves. At the end of the fifteenth century, society had another reason for dividing into two factions: whether or not they wanted the bishopric.[144] At that point those who believed that the strength of the community lay in commerce and industry prevailed. On the other hand, for those groups of rentiers and of state and ecclesiastical bureaucrats who had the job of leading the government and society of Colle at the end of the sixteenth century, it was much more important to obtain the bishopric: the final, formal acknowledgment of their social and political status. We are not yet faced with that 'impoverished nobility' which became a feature of the eighteenth century, but the signs were there to indicate the path of the future evolution.[145]

In the end the issue of the bishopric was coherently pursued not just locally, but also in cooperation with those people from Colle who were 'abroad', in the Roman curia and in the central government, whose intervention and mediation provided evidence that local needs and aspirations could only be met when close ties existed with the real centres of power. From this point of view, the commune had truly been supplanted. The commune itself openly accepted that it now belonged to the regional state; their cohesion had been borne out of the many and widespread social ties forged between the ruling classes of the 'quasi-cities'.[146]

---

[144] Biadi, who first noticed the split in the ruling class, post-dated the events of 1498–9 by a century: L. Biadi, *Storia di della città di Colle Valdelsa*, repr. (Rome, 1971), p. 207. It seems that his mistake was due not so much to his confusion as to his having deliberately changed the dates; indeed, he cited the number of those for and against exactly as they appeared in the summary of 1498, omitting only those absent. On the problematic nature of other aspects of Biadi's work, see Fasano Guarini, 'Nuove diocesi e nuove città', pp. 59–60.

[145] M. Cassandro, 'Colle di Val d'Elsa nel quadro dell'economia toscana tra Cinque e Seicento', in *Diocesi e città*, p. 285.

[146] Note that Francesco Tommasi was proud to be 'colligiano, fiorentino, toscano'; Berengo, 'Un agronomo toscano', p. 502.

CHAPTER 14

AREZZO, THE MEDICI AND THE FLORENTINE REGIME

ROBERT BLACK

On 4 June 1502 the city of Arezzo rebelled against Florentine rule, maintaining an independent government until 25 August. Since the establishment of Florentine dominion in 1384, there had been a number of attempts to restore independence to Arezzo. At the core was normally a group of malcontented patricians, resentful of Florentine dominance, of the loss of communal liberty and of exploitative taxation. In 1502 there were several problems which rendered Florentine control over Arezzo particularly precarious. Florentine territorial authority was seriously weakened by the successful rebellion of Pisa in 1494, followed the next year – and even closer to Arezzo – by the loss of Montepulciano to Siena. Attempts to regain these dominions exhausted Florentine resources, and, moreover, there is documentary evidence that Pisa and Montepulciano provided examples for Arezzo in 1502. Another problem was that in 1502 grain was in short supply in Florentine dominions and it had been necessary previously to move substantial stocks to feed Florentine troops lodged near Borgo San Sepolcro and needed to protect against a possible attack from hostile forces in Umbria; there was considerable anxiety among the Aretine populace lest the Florentines should do this again and leave Arezzo to starve. Another difficulty for Florence was the weakness of local support. It is true that several Florentine families had established political and economic power bases in Arezzo – most notably the Canigiani and the Pazzi; indeed, the latter included Messer Guglielmo de' Pazzi, who was a prominent defender of Aretine interests in the 1490s, and his son Cosimo, who was the resident bishop of Arezzo in 1502. Moreover, the Florentines had cultivated clients among the Aretine citizenry; most prominent here were the Albergotti, who were favoured, according to one Aretine source, with privileges and even Florentine citizenship. However, a number of supporters of the Florentine regime in Arezzo were *gente nuova*, newly arrived citizens such as the Tondinelli from

Todi without the political clout of established Aretine patricians. More-over, a few hitherto reliable Aretines – such as the Camaiani family – were showing distinct signs of hostility to Florentine rule. Most notable among previously philo-Florentine families were the Accolti, one branch of whom had become Florentine citizens in 1459. Indeed, Jacopo di Michele Accolti, a member of this branch, actually played a prominent part in the military campaigns of 1502 on behalf of the Aretine rebels. In the case of the Accolti, there is little doubt that their desertion of the Florentine regime was inspired by what for them was a higher loyalty – to the Medici family, expelled from Florence in 1494. In fact, Jacopo Accolti's uncle, Bernardo, the famous poet, known as 'L'unico aretino', actually contributed 200 florins to the pro-Medici conspiracy of 1497 and was declared a Florentine rebel as a result. The Medici were probably the greatest internal problem for the Florentine regime in Arezzo in 1502, to such an extent that one Aretine chronicler commented that the Medici name was 'much loved by the Aretines' (*molto amato dagli Aretini*) in 1502; indeed, in the rebellion cries not only of liberty (*libertà*) but also of balls (*palle*, the Medici emblem) were used to rouse the populace against the Florentine authorities.[1]

The events of the 1502 rebellion make it clear therefore that, by the end of the fifteenth century, the Aretine province, so to speak, of the Florentine territorial state consisted not merely of two but rather of three elements: lord (Florence), subject (Arezzo) and the Medici. This triangular structure was founded on the powerful network of patronage and clientage which the Medici, particularly under Lorenzo di Piero, had woven in Arezzo during the fifteenth century.

For Florentine subjects a voice at the centre was essential, and it is no surprise to learn that throughout the fifteenth century Aretines sought protectors and benefactors in Florence. Indeed from the earliest days of Florentine rule, patronage by leading Florentines was recognised as a necessity of political life; as the Aretine general council resolved in 1387:

> In the past the commune of Arezzo has sent many ambassadors to the city of Florence, but rarely with any positive outcome. Moreover, the Aretine commune is too poor to meet the expense of maintaining ambassadors in lodgings in Florence. But since there are many Florentine citizens who, as friends of this city and of its citizens, desire the honour and welfare of our commune, it is decided that the priors and captains and four citizens from each half of the city should be authorised to elect a

---

[1] See R. Black and L. G. Clubb, *Romance and Aretine Humanism in Sienese Comedy, 1516: Pollastra's Parthenio at the Studio di Siena* (Siena, 1993), pp. 73ff.

number of honourable Florentine citizens as protectors and defenders of the said commune of Arezzo, with appropriate recompense or salary.[2]

For the most part, Florentines were the patrons who dispensed the favours sought by their Aretine clients, but the Aretines could reciprocate. There were a number of communal offices to which not insubstantial revenues were attached, and throughout the fifteenth century these were frequently sought by prominent Florentines for their friends and clients. The most lucrative of these Aretine placements was the notariate *dei danni dati* (of damage inflicted), charged with punishing damage to the country property, mainly, of town citizens. Because of his role as an adjudicator of property disputes between town and country, the *notaio dei danni dati* was meant to be a non-Aretine, like the Captain and Podestà, and it was laid down by statute that he had to come from Florence or its *vecchio contado* (ancient domain). Since it had therefore to be filled by a Florentine notary, the office was particularly susceptible to Florentine patronage, and appointments were often made as gestures of goodwill to Florentine rectors in Arezzo who could place one of their clients, dependants, former colleagues or friends in the magistracy; however, Aretines were also frequently able to oblige their patrons among the Florentine patriciate with this office as a gift for a notarial client or friend, and increasingly in the years after 1434 Aretines used the *danni dati* to repay debts of gratitude to important Florentines.[3]

In view of his role as leader of the Florentine regime after 1434, it was inevitable that Cosimo de' Medici should have emerged as a significant patron in Arezzo; moreover, Cosimo was not the only member of the Medici family to emerge as an Aretine patron in the years before 1434. Particularly active was Filippo, bishop of Arezzo between 1457 and 1461, but the most significant Medici patrons apart from Cosimo before 1464 were his two legitimate sons, who developed

---

[2] ASA, Provv. 1, 106v (11 December 1387): 'Cum per comune Aretii iam pluries multis temporibus elapsis fuerint transmissi quam plures ambasciatores ad civitatem Florentie . . . et raro fuerit obtemptum quicquid quisitorum . . . tum propter impossibilitatem et inpotentiam nostri comunis Aretii et ambasciatorum nostrorum standi in hospitiis cum quam plures cives civitati[s] florentine sint amatores et amici huius comunitatis et singularum personarum eiusdem qui ad honorem et utilitatem nostri comunis atenderent . . . [it is decided] . . . quod priores et capitanei . . . et quatuor cives pro quolibet mezzo eligendi per prefatos domini priores . . . habeant . . . autoritatem . . . eligendi . . . plures nobiles cives florentinos . . . in protectores et defensores dicti comunis Aretii . . . cum provisione seu salario . . .'.

[3] See R. Black, 'Cosimo de' Medici and Arezzo', in F. Ames-Lewis (ed.), *Cosimo 'il vecchio' de' Medici, 1389–1464* (Oxford, 1992), pp. 36–7.

relatively distinct roles in their connections with Arezzo. When Piero
became Florentine Standard Bearer of Justice in January and February
1461, Aretines were quick to seek his favour; it was even declared that
their ambasssador was 'daily at the feet of the gonfalonier on account of
the pressing needs of the Aretine commune'. Nevertheless, what is
interesting about this pattern of patronage is that Cosimo and his family
were by no means unique among their fellow Florentine patricians as
influential figures in Arezzo. Indeed, archival sources suggest that
Florentine patronage in Arezzo was shared among leading figures and
families during Cosimo's pre-eminence. During Cosimo's lifetime, in
fact, the pre-eminent Florentine patron in Arezzo was Luca Pitti.[4]

During the first two years of Piero's personal ascendancy, Aretine
relations with Florence, the Florentine patriciate and the Medici in
particular remained much as they had been in the last few years of
Cosimo's life. The Florentine patrician most frequently mentioned in
the Aretine provisions remained Luca Pitti, but the increasing interest in
Arezzo taken by the Medici under Piero's leadership is demonstrated by
the prominence of Piero himself. In fact, the most important new figure
to emerge between 1464 and 1466 was Piero's young son, Lorenzo,
who was referred to seven times between 1464 and 1466. With the
change in Florentine internal politics after the collapse of the challenge
to Medici predominance in 1466, Florentine patrons in Arezzo connected with the opposition to Piero now almost entirely disappeared
from the scene: there were no more references to Luca Pitti, and Piero
now strode forth as the leading Florentine figure in Arezzo.[5]

A significant difference between Lorenzo's style of predominance in
Arezzo and that of his father Piero was the development of an almost
complete monopoly of Aretine patronage. Once he had ousted Luca
Pitti, Piero had emerged as the supreme patron of Arezzo, mentioned
almost three times as often in the Aretine communal provisions
between 1466 and 1469 as his nearest rival, Giovanni di Antonio
Serristori. Like his father, Lorenzo was at first content to yield some of
the limelight: by the mid-1480s, however, the names of other Florentine patricians disappear almost completely from the Aretine communal provisions. After this time there seems to have been something
more than rhetorical hyperbole present when the Aretines described
Lorenzo as their 'unique benefactor'.[6]

[4] *Ibid.*, pp. 37ff.
[5] See R. Black, 'Piero de' Medici and Arezzo', in A. Beyer and B. Boucher (eds.), *Piero
de' Medici 'il Gottoso'* (Berlin, 1993), pp. 24ff.
[6] See R. Black, 'Lorenzo and Arezzo', in M. Mallett and N. Mann (eds.), *Lorenzo the
Magnificent, Culture and Politics* (London, 1996), pp. 221–2.

The main exception to this pattern was the emergence of Lorenzo's son Piero in the 1490s to a position of almost equal prominence to that of his father, although it must be said that his patronage efforts did not at this time meet with the same unqualified success as his father's. Another interesting figure to emerge in the late 1480s was the powerful Florentine notary of the Riformagioni and close collaborator with Lorenzo, Ser Giovanni Guidi, who was approached by Arezzo regarding an imminent *balzello*; he seems to have given the Aretines some help but interestingly he painted a vivid picture of limitations:

> I have heard about your wishes regarding the extraordinary levy (*balzello*), and they are certainly justifiable [he wrote to the commune]. But the difficulty of the matter requires greater help than I am able to offer. It seems to me that you will have to send an ambassador to the Magnificent Lorenzo [de' Medici]; if he is favourable to making some changes on your behalf, I shall do everything I can, but without his backing, and it will have to be considerable, nothing can be done.

By the mid-1480s, Arezzo had become exclusively the preserve of Medici patronage, and it was 'hands off' to everyone else.[7]

One interesting feature in this story of Florentine patronage in Arezzo between 1434 and 1494 is that the Medici only gradually assumed a pre-eminent and ultimately almost exclusive role. Their slow start there seems to have been largely due to Cosimo's indifference or antipathy to Arezzo. A particularly notable example is the appointment to the bishopric of Arezzo in 1457. The Aretines mounted a strong campaign for their favourite – Ugolino Giugni, a cathedral canon in Arezzo – but all their efforts were in vain. Cosimo was determined to have his relative, Filippo de' Medici, as the next bishop, overriding the expressed wishes of the Aretine government. Cosimo's coolness to Arezzo was in part due to his preoccupation with Pisa, whereas he had neither property in the Aretino nor apparently any investments in Aretine business. It is noteworthy that the Aretines managed to obtain the support of the Florentine Signoria (government) for their candidate to the Aretine episcopate in 1457. The years 1455–8 marked the nadir of Medici influence in Cosimian Florence, and Aretine success with a Signoria of this period is a measure of the gap between Arezzo and Cosimo.[8]

The Aretine problem with Cosimo may have been a legacy of an earlier regime. Up to the mid-1420s Florentine patrons in Arezzo came principally from the established oligarchy, including prominent figures

---

[7] *Ibid.*, p. 222.   [8] Black, 'Cosimo', pp. 41–2.

such as Bindaccio Ricasoli,[9] Maso degli Albizzi,[10] Giovanni Bucelli[11] and Filippo Corsini;[12] in this early period, the only prominent future Medici partisan was Giuliano Davanzati.[13] As the temperature of factional conflict rose later in the decade, a number of Medici adherents now began to emerge as patrons in Arezzo; the key year here seems to have been 1428, when a series of Mediceans appeared as Aretine patrons, including Giovanni di Bicci Medici,[14] his sons Cosimo[15] and Lorenzo,[16] Luca di Maso degli Albizi,[17] Martino Martini,[18] Zanobi Arnolfi,[19] Giovanni Carducci[20] and Francesco di Michele Nardi,[21] not to mention a reappearance by Giuliano di Niccolò Davanzati.[22] The Aretines were clearly playing both sides of the field: simultaneously in 1428 they also appealed to leading anti-Mediceans, including Rinaldo di Maso Albizi,[23] Tinoro Guasconi,[24] Palla Strozzi,[25] Matteo Solosmei[26] and Duccio di Paolo Mancini.[27] In the end, Arezzo seems to have chosen the initial winners: after 1428, Mediceans completely disappear from the Aretine communal deliberations, while names such as Ricasoli[28] and Niccolò da Uzzano[29] are still to be found. Possibly significant in influencing Aretine allegiances was the position taken by their compatriot, Leonardo Bruni, who had acted as a patron for Arezzo

[9] ASA, Provv., 2, 116r (3 March 1390, ab inc.) See D. Kent, *The Rise of the Medici* (Oxford, 1978), p. 357.

[10] ASA, Provv., 3, 151v (11 January 1397, ab inc.); Provv., 4, 125v (29 September 1407). See Kent, *The Rise of the Medici*, pp. 179–80, 214.

[11] ASA, Provv., 4, 118v (12 July 1407). See Kent, *The Rise of the Medici*, pp. 248, 345n.

[12] ASA, Provv., 5, 79r (20 October 1412). See Kent, *The Rise of the Medici*, p. 248.

[13] ASA, Provv., 5, 223r (21 December 1417). See Kent, *The Rise of the Medici*, p. 352.

[14] ASA, Provv., 6, 14v (26 September 1428).

[15] *Ibid.*, 15v (7 October 1428); 24r (27 December 1428).

[16] *Ibid.*, 15v (7 October 1428).

[17] *Ibid.*, 17v (17 October 1428). See Kent, *The Rise of the Medici*, p. 352.

[18] ASA, Provv., 6, 24r (27 December 1428). See Kent, *The Rise of the Medici*, p. 353.

[19] ASA, Provv., 6, 14v (26 September 1428). See Kent, *The Rise of the Medici*, pp. 328, 352.

[20] ASA, Provv., 6, 14v (26 September 1428). See Kent, *The Rise of the Medici*, p. 352.

[21] ASA, Provv., 6, 14v (26 September 1428). See Kent, *The Rise of the Medici*, p. 226.

[22] ASA, Provv., 6, 24r (27 December 1428).

[23] *Ibid.*, 12v (17 September 1428).

[24] *Ibid.*, 14v (26 September 1428). See Kent, *The Rise of the Medici*, p. 356.

[25] ASA, Provv., 6, 15v (7 October 1428); 17v (17 October 1428). See Kent, *The Rise of the Medici*, p. 357.

[26] ASA, Provv., 6, 15v (7 October 1428). See Kent, *The Rise of the Medici*, p. 357.

[27] ASA, Provv., 6, 17v (17 October 1428). See Kent, *The Rise of the Medici*, pp. 318–19.

[28] ASA, Provv., 6, 62v (21 July 1429).

[29] *Ibid.* See Kent, *The Rise of the Medici*, p. 236.

while a papal secretary in Rome in 1411:[30] he figures prominently in 1429[31] and 1430,[32] the period when not only the Aretine commune seems to have been articulating an anti-Medicean stance; indeed, 1431 saw the marriage alliance between Bruni's son, Donato, and Alesssandra, daughter of Messer Michele di Messer Vanni Castellani,[33] one of the most prominent families to be exiled by the Medici in 1434.[34] During September 1434, moreover, while Florence was paralysed by political deadlock marking the confrontation between pro- and anti-Mediceans, the Aretines flaunted their close connection with the Albizzi family, recalling in a letter to Rinaldo degli Albizzi's son Maso the benefactions of his ancestors.[35] It is perhaps not entirely surprising that Cosimo never completely overcame his distaste for a city that not only demonstrated disloyalty to the Medici faction at the height of their battle for survival after 1428 but also brazenly embraced the family of his mortal enemy.

Medicean interest in Arezzo was enhanced with Piero de' Medici's emergence as a major political figure in his own right in the early 1460s, but while Cosimo lived the development was gradual and tentative. Piero favoured Arezzo with the restoration of the annual fair, but the Aretines believed this benefaction was really due to their ex-bishop, Filippo de' Medici. When the Aretines finally gained the temporary suspension of their Podestà in 1462, the Medici were not even listed among the benefactors to be thanked. Moreover, Piero did not persist in giving full backing to the Aretine fair. The neighbouring town of Cortona, also a Florentine subject city, objected to the Aretine fair on

---

[30] ASA, Provv., 5, 48v (29 November 1411): 'Supradictis magnificis dominis prioribus [et] capitaneis partis guelfe civitatis Aretii fuerunt distinate quedam littere pro parte egregi[i] viri Domini Leonardi de Aretio, in effectu continentes circa negotia Domini Benedicti abbatis de Roti aretine diocesis, quod ipse iam superiori tempore deffendit eum in iure sui monasteri. Nunc vero non patitur honestas pro ipso defendendo suo solito et usitato more [ut] interponere possit, quia non est e(n)i(m) honestum sibi familiari pape eum defendere qui sic turpiter de papa loquatur, et non pertinet ad ipsum determinare ac dicere contra determinationem factam Pisis per tot doctores et tot magistros in sacra cheologia ac cardinales et excusat se si dictus abbas amictit benefitium suum abbatie de Rota etc.'.

[31] ASA, Provv., 6, 62v (21 July 1429).

[32] Ibid., 78v (23 January 1429, ab inc.).

[33] L. Martines, The Social World of the Florentine Humanists (London, 1963), pp. 200–1.

[34] Ibid., pp. 200–10; Kent, The Rise of the Medici, pp. 137–8, 154, 332, 356. For an exciting unknown confirmation of Bruni's support for the oligarchic regime and his possibly clandestine opposition to the Medici regime, see the important article by Arthur Field, 'Leonardo Bruni, Florentine Traitor? Bruni, the Medici, and an Aretine Conspiracy of 1437', Renaissance Quarterly, 51 (1998), pp. 1109–50.

[35] ASA, Provv., 6, 184r (11 September 1434): 'opera facta et secuta tam per magnificum militem Dominum Masium de Albizis olim avum dicti Masi Domini Rinaldi quam per ipsos consortes et de domo de Albizis erga comune Aretii et eius cives'.

the grounds that it took place at the same time as their own fair, but Piero sided with Cortona, so that in the end the Aretines had to change the date of their fair.[36]

It seems to have been the crisis of 1465–6 that changed Medici attitudes to Arezzo, clearly demonstrating the potential military support that Aretines could offer. When the confrontation came to a head in August–September 1466, Piero turned to his network of Aretine *amici* (allies), headed by Ser Giovanbattista Lamberti and Morello da Pantaneto, who not only secured the official backing of the commune for Piero but also led a private contingent of well above sixty men, not to mention the 200-strong communal force, towards Florence in aid of the Medici. Arezzo's allegiance had hitherto hung in the balance between Luca Pitti and Piero, but now it was recognised as a fully committed Medici town and was suitably rewarded by Piero in the wake of the events of summer 1466.[37]

Loyalty and support seem to account for the growing Medicean role in Arezzo under Piero, but, as far as Arezzo is concerned, *figura* (standing) seems to have preoccupied Lorenzo. Lorenzo tended to see problems in personal and political terms, reflecting his own *stato* (standing) and position, not in their legal or formal dimension: thus when his secretary, Ser Giovannantonio di Maestro Guglielmo, who had been given the *danni dati* as a six-year sinecure from 1484 to 1490, complained that he was having trouble gaining reconfirmation for his *locum tenens*, Lorenzo penned an irritated letter to Arezzo, showing his impatience with the formalities of sindication and demonstrating his feeling that such technical difficulties derogated his *stato*:

> I understand that the affairs of my Ser Giovannantonio for some time have not been conducted in your city by some people in the way that his needs and my pleasure would require. In particular, you want the consignment of some books regarding the conduct of his office. This would be the greatest detriment to him, since he has not yet finished his term of office. I beseech you, out of regard for me, to treat him as my loyal follower, considering his interests as though they were my own; indeed, every friendly action towards him and his concerns will win the greatest possible favour from me.

In their letter of explanation to Lorenzo, the Aretines explained the requirements of sindication which Lorenzo had overlooked; it was not, as Lorenzo had understood, 'to deviate from the affection which the entirety of this completely devoted people shows towards your magnificence'.[38]

---

[36] Black, 'Cosimo', p. 42.   [37] Black, 'Piero', pp. 25ff.
[38] Black, 'Lorenzo', pp. 223–4.

Preoccupied as he was with his standing, Lorenzo not only installed clients of foreign rulers in the *danni dati*, but also effectively ousted all other Florentine patrons, none of whose nominees ever served a full term after 1473 (and the last non-Medicean occupant served less than a month in July 1477).[39] Another factor that led to the concentration of patronage in late fifteenth-century Arezzo was the rise of household government under Lorenzo. The growing prominence of Medicean chancery and secretarial figures in Florentine government at this time needs no comment, but it is worth noting that this trend spilled over into Arezzo. In 1482 Lorenzo nominated his secretary, Ser Giovannan-tonio di Maestro Guglielmo, to the *danni dati* as an absentee magistrate for a six-year term from 1484 to 1490. Towards the end of his life, moreover, Lorenzo was moving, *vis-à-vis* Arezzo, from jobs for the boys to outright nepotism with the appointment of his relative, Giuliano di Mariotto di Averardo de' Medici, to succeed Ser Giovannantonio, in the *danni dati* for ten years.[40]

Lorenzo's monopoly of patronage, and particularly his use of the *danni dati*, was not an entirely happy development, at least as far as the Aretines themselves were concerned. This office clearly had a substantial revenue, becoming as it did a highly sought-after honour, not only by Florentine but also by foreign patrons for not only Florentine but also foreign clients. The Aretines wanted to turn some of this income to public use and so, beginning in 1470, they put forward schemes to appoint to the *danni dati* a local builder, Bartolomeo Serragli, who would in exchange repair various public works, especially some local fountains. At first Serraglio, as he was called, encountered obstacles in Florence to the confirmation of his appointment on these terms, but when on 16 April 1471 the Aretines wrote a pleading letter to Lorenzo in support of this scheme, six days later a *bullettino* (order) from the *Otto di guardia* arrived in Arezzo requiring Serraglio's appointment and he duly served in the *danni dati* for the following six-month term.[41]

The Aretines succeeded in gaining Lorenzo's approval for a tax on the *danni dati* for the restoration of their cathedral; as he wrote, 'the allocation for your cathedral is a great pleasure to me, and I commend this plan and the provision to finish the building work as something praiseworthy, religious and holy; I should desire much more warmly to support this enterprise than to obstruct it in any possible way'. This declaration was certainly in harmony with the spirit of Serraglio's appointment to the *danni dati* for six years from 1478 to 1484; not only did he make the required contribution to the *vescovado* (cathedral) but

---

[39] *Ibid.*, pp. 222–3, 225–6.   [40] *Ibid.*, p. 226.   [41] *Ibid.*, p. 225.

he also completed the repairs to various Aretine fountains and aqueducts. It is possible that Lorenzo felt he had gone too far with the *danni dati* in the early 1470s, not only installing foreigners but effectively ousting all other Florentine patrons, none of whose nominees, as has already been pointed out, ever served a full term after 1473.[42]

However, Lorenzo had other calls upon his patronage than public works in Arezzo. In 1482 he nominated his secretary, Ser Giovannantonio di Maestro Guglielmo, to the *danni dati* to be an absentee magistrate; although the tax payable by the incumbent to the cathedral building project had been raised to 100 florins per annum, Lorenzo insisted that his secretary pay only the 64 florins disbursed by Serraglio. Provision for his household here took precedence over any higher purpose for Lorenzo, who wrote that 'the tax of 100 ducats a year would be impossible for him to pay, given that I want him to stay with me and earn something besides'. Similarly, the commune elected Serraglio to succeed Ser Giovannantonio in 1490, this time for ten years, not only with a contribution of 100 florins per annum to the cathedral but also of a further 50 florins to the commune. Again this did not suit Lorenzo, who had the *danni dati* given instead to his relative, Giuliano di Mariotto di Averardo de' Medici, for ten years.[43]

It is not surprising, therefore, that Ser Giovannantonio was a less than popular figure in Arezzo during the 1480s. He was himself actually an Aretine citizen, the son of a French schoolmaster, Maestro Guglielmo da Bourges, who had first come to Arezzo in 1440 and taught there for a total of eighteen years until his death in 1477. Guglielmo probably had some kind of Medici affiliation from the beginning, having been recommended to Arezzo by Cosimo's intimate confidant, Carlo Marsuppini, the Aretine first chancellor of Florence. Certainly, when Guglielmo transferred to the roll of the university of Florence from 1466 to 1473, his extraordinarily high annual salaries of 200 and later of 150 florins for a grammar teacher indicate a strong Medici connection. Giovannantonio assisted his father as coadiutor in the Aretine grammar school in the 1470s, although he was already preoccupied with *faccende* (affairs) outside Arezzo, so that he had sometimes to substitute his brother Matteo in his place; some of his activities may already have had to do with the Medici regime, as a leading Medicean and the number-two Florentine in Arezzo, Giovanni Serristori, intervened on his behalf with the Aretine commune in 1478.[44]

The Aretines congratulated Giovannantonio on his appointment as Lorenzo's secretary in August 1480, but there was from the beginning a

---

[42] *Ibid.*, pp. 225–6.   [43] *Ibid.*, p. 226.   [44] *Ibid.*, pp. 226–7.

distance between him and his native city, possibly the result of his French ancestry and evident in his failure to matriculate in the Aretine college of notaries and even more in the astonishing near absence of requests from Arezzo for interventions from him with Lorenzo. When he was appointed to the *danni dati*, there was *obstinatio populi* (popular resistance) because of the reduced contributions to the cathedral, and there was a late attempt to pay him off and to 'recuperate' the *danni dati*, as they declared, *pro comuni Aretii*. There were complaints about the *locum tenentes*, often foreigners, who substituted for him, requests that the office should be restored to the commune after he had got out of it what he wanted, and laments that under his regime the residents of the *cortine* (the area of the countryside immediately adjacent to the city) 'have been so oppressed that little or nothing remains for them'; indeed, his complaints to Lorenzo about his treatment in Arezzo have already been noted. It is clear that by the end of Giovannantonio's term there was little common interest left between Lorenzo and Arezzo *vis-à-vis* the *danni dati*, and it is not surprising that when Lorenzo moved from jobs for the boys to outright nepotism with the appointment of Giuliano de' Medici as the next official of the *danni dati*, he encountered opposition and counter-proposals to his arrangements.[45]

The three poles of political life in Arezzo (the commune, Florence and the Medici) can be seen fully active in the later years of Lorenzo's life. The central question, as always, was the financial contribution made by Arezzo and Aretines to Florence. As a source of revenue to Florence and Florentines, Arezzo's main contribution was indirect taxation, realised through numerous gabelles administered by a Florentine provisor in Arezzo; through direct taxation, which was largely diverted to pay the salaries of the Florentine Captain and Podestà as well as their establishments, and through occasional but heavy *balzelli* or lump-sum contributions to the Florentine fisc. In these areas, Arezzo tried to mitigate such demands by attempting to maintain and extend their privilege of a week-long gabelle-free fair every September, to eliminate the office and hence salary of the Podestà and reduce, mitigate and even gain exemption from individual *balzelli*. Lorenzo's policy in these areas was to balance, on the one hand, the heavy pressures from the Florentine government in its attempt to save the Florentine treasury from total insolvency, with, on the other, his attempt to enhance the power base of his regime in Arezzo by granting financial relief to the notoriously impoverished Aretine people.[46]

The fair, established in 1461 under the patronage of Lorenzo's father,

---

[45] *Ibid.*, pp. 227–8. [46] *Ibid.*, p. 228.

Piero, was threatened by the *Dieci Ufficiali dello Accrescimento dell'Entrate del Comune di Firenze* (ten officers charged with increasing the revenues of the Florentine commune) in the winter of 1471–2 but was reprieved, only to be entirely suspended by Florence in February 1476, despite pathetic pleas to Lorenzo to imitate his father's munificence. The fair was a dead issue in Arezzo until the autumn of 1483, when Lorenzo, amidst his unpopular insistence on Ser Giovannantonio's appointment to the *danni dati*, appears to have decided to give the Aretines back their fair, possibly to obviate the opprobrium gained over his policy of sinecures for his secretariat. But Lorenzo's skill in balancing one interest against another here is nothing short of remarkable, as he conceded the fair but without the full privileges it had enjoyed since Piero's special dispensation of 1466–7. Lorenzo thus succeeded in mollifying the Florentine financial establishment while also temporarily pacifying the Aretines. The Aretines attempted to regain the fair's full privileges over the next year or so, but their efforts were always blocked; finally in 1490 they decided that this reduced fair was worse than no fair at all and so they petitioned to have the fair permanently cancelled.[47]

There was a similar story with the office of Podestà, a lucrative honour for Florentine patricians. Arezzo and its contado had suffered heavy losses and damage during the Pazzi war and in compensation it seems they were granted the suspension of their Podestà, beginning in January 1480, not least through the efforts of Giovanni Guidi, who was particularly thanked *pro impetrandis gratiis* (for seeking favours). The original dispensation was for five years, with the possibility of extension for a further two, and when approached, Lorenzo, always keen to balance competing interests, advised taking the two-year extension rather than pressing for a full five-year renewal. The unpopularity of this *vacatio Potestatis* (suspension of the Podestà) in Florence is suggested by Lorenzo's subsequent request to the Aretines to postpone their campaign for renewal until after the widely disliked 1484 scrutiny. In the end, Arezzo once more lost out to the pressures of the Florentine patriciate, when the office of Podestà was reinstated in January 1487, although Lorenzo was thanked for his efforts, 'however unsuccessful'.[48]

The Aretines did a little, but not very much, better with the *balzello*. These were better times than the earlier decades of the fifteenth century when such demands were incessant; Lorenzo's ascendancy saw only two, in 1480–1 and 1488. To the first, Lorenzo, at the height of his authority after the treaty with Naples, was able to obtain complete

---

[47] *Ibid.*, pp. 228–9.   [48] *Ibid.*, p. 229.

dispensation for the city of Arezzo (the only time this may have occurred since 1384) although the *cortine* had to pay 500 florins and the Aretine communal charitable fraternity 350 florins. Such an unprecedented favour was not to be repeated in 1488. A particularly stern, it seems, team of Florentine officials decided to impose the *balzello*, which overall was to raise 40,000 florins, not on communities but rather on individuals, throughout Florentine subject territories. This appears not only to have threatened a higher levy for Arezzo as a whole but also to have endangered the immunities enjoyed by the Aretine poor. After repeated interventions with Lorenzo, the Aretines managed to obtain a change in the law so that they had to pay as a commune 1000 florins and they gained exemption or reductions for 112 *impotenti* (indigents) in addition to their *miserabili* (destitute). The brevity of payment time – thirty days – was still harsh, to say the least, so that an enormous direct tax (*dazio*) of 20 lire per lira assessed had to be paid, possibly the highest single *dazio* of the fifteenth century in Arezzo. Nevertheless, they were so grateful to Lorenzo that they presented him and his family in perpetuity with a house in the city of Arezzo, particularly for the use of his son Piero 'so that he might be encouraged some time during the year to come and recognise our servitude and have direct knowledge of the state to which his most loving people have been reduced'.[49]

One might wonder whether there was a touch of irony in this donation, and whether the Aretines really wanted the Medici to see for themselves how low they had been reduced by their servitude to Florence and by the enormous *balzello* of 1488. At the end of his ascendancy, Lorenzo seems to have succumbed to pressure from the Florentine state and to the demands of patronage from his household and family; for Arezzo, the halcyon days of Medici bounty in the early 1480s – with the suspension of the Podestà, with the *danni dati* under Serraglio and used for public works, with the exemption from the 1481 *balzello* – were long past. Given the less than happy end of Lorenzo's predominance for Arezzo, it may seem strange that the *nome de' Medici* was still much loved by the Aretines in 1502.[50]

In the later fourteenth and earlier fifteenth centuries, there had been simply two elements between Arezzo and Florence: subject and lord. In fact, the pre-Medicean regime had shown leanings, as far as Arezzo was concerned, towards centralization and even severity. Thus, when the Florentine regime was first established in Arezzo, a number of important offices were restricted to Florentine citizens, including the Captain, the Podestà and the chancellor. The last-mentioned office was finally

[49] *Ibid.*, p. 229–30.   [50] *Ibid.*, p. 230.

restored to the Aretines in 1395,[51] but they had more problems with notariate of the *danni dati*. Up to the turn of the fifteenth century, appointment to the *danni dati* remained in the hands of the Aretine commune,[52] but by 1406 the Aretines had lost control of the office for some time.[53] In 1414 the functions of the *danni dati* were being exercised by one of the notaries of the Aretine Podestà,[54] and by 1428 the restoration of this office to the commune had become a major preoccupation of Aretine lobbying in Florence.[55] Indeed by the autumn of that year even the Podestà no longer had a *notaio de' danni dati* in his entourage, which led to complaints that 'the properties of Aretine citizens have been and are going to ruin every day since this officer has been lacking in the city of Arezzo'.[56] Early in 1429 they continued their campaign to regain the *danni dati*, declaring that

[51] After 1384, 'debet dictus cancellarius esse originaliter de Florentia et non aliunde quoquo modo': ASA, Provv., 1, 35v (18 July 1386). The last Florentine to exercise the Aretine chancellorship was 'Ricchardus filius Bernardi Ricchardini civis et notarius florentinus . . . generalis cancellarius . . . civitatis Aretii . . .', whose six-month term began on 15 May 1395: Provv., 3, 62r. The first Aretine citizen and notary to act as chancellor under Florentine rule was 'Jacobus Ser Johannis Ser Torris civis et notarius aretinus pro magnifico comuni Florentie cancellarius et reformationum scriba comunis Aretii ac priorum eiusdem comunis et populis notarius': Provv. 3 (24 November 1395).

[52] Cf. Provv., 1, 33r, 35r; Provv., 2, 108r, 109v, 119v, 121r, 121v, 143v, 150v–151r, 160r; Provv., 3, 9r, 10v–11v, 13r–v, 26v, 31v, 37v, 43v, 49v, 53v, 54v–55r, 59v, 84r–v.

[53] Provv., 4, 83r (22 July 1406): 'Cum per aliquos cives aretinos fidedignos dictum et assertum fuerit dominis prioribus quod magnifici et potentes domini nostri domini priores artium et vexillifer iustitie populi et comunis Florentie una cum eorum collegiis habeant auctoritatem a consiliis opportunis concedendi quod comune Aretii eligat offitialem dampnorum datorum plani civitatis Aretii, ut iam aliquo tempore deinde comune Aretii eligit . . . [it is decided] quod domini priores possint . . . mictere unum bonum et sapientem virum Florentiam.'

[54] Provv., 5, 118r–v (6 April 1414): 'Cum . . . Pierus quondam Bartolomey de Caponibus de Florentia . . . potestas civitatis Aretii et eius comitatus . . . die ultimo mensis martii suum deposuerit officium, cumque ipsi et dicti sui officiales, videlicet Dominus Petrus de Vico Pisano eius iudex et vicarius, Ser Jacobus Domini Bartolomei Torigina Castri Sancti Johannis milex sotius, Ser Antonius Francisci de Bibiena notarius plani et dampnorum datorum et Ser Franciscus Antonii de Sancto Geminiano eius notarius.'

[55] Provv., 6, 4v (8 July 1428): 'Qui etiam oratores . . . debeant omni solerti cura procurare . . . hec omnia infrascripta, videlicet: Quod per consilium et comune Aretii possit in fucturum eligere nominare et deputare semel et pluries unum notarium dannorum datorum et custodem bonorum civium et comitatinorum pro tempore, modis, conditionibus et aliis quibuscumque prout viderint convenire et voluerint et prout fuerit dictis oratoribus commixum per presentes dominos priores civitatis Aretii.'

[56] Provv., 6, 18r (17 October 1428): 'e beni de' cittadini d'Arezo . . . vadino in ruina

residents of the countryside with their animals and workers are ruining the property of citizens, damaging their goods and possessions, and there is no one to guard the property of citizens, so that they are not receiving income from their possessions; therefore it would be useful to be able to appoint, on behalf of the Aretine commune, a foreign notary to act as *notaio de' danni dati.* [57]

This finally resulted in the restoration of the *danni dati* to one of the Podestà's notaries.[58] However, this concession did not satisfy the Aretines, who resented that their commune could not 'elect a *notaio de' danni dati* according to former custom and just like the city of Cortona and other Florentine subject towns'.[59]

The authority to elect a *notaio de' danni dati* was finally restored to the commune in September 1433,[60] a favour possibly related to Aretine support for or acquiescence in the triumph of the Albizzi that month; indeed, at the same time the Aretines were granted the *gratia*[61] of a temporary suspension of the office of Podestà.[62] However, the oligarchic regime still tended to be wary of granting too much autonomy to its subject territories, 'considering that', as the Aretines complained, 'this concession of electing a *notaio de' danni dati* carried with it such a miserable salary and poor conditions that no one could be found to accept the appointment'.[63] The office was not effectively reinstated until 1435, owing not to the intervention of Cosimo de' Medici, who was not thanked in this connection, but rather to the efforts of another important Florentine political figure, Antonio di Ser Tommaso Masi.[64]

. . . come oggi dì vanno e sono andati, da poi è manchato il detto ufficiale nella detta città d'Arezo'.

[57] Provv., 6, 27v (12 January 1428, ab inc.): 'cum comitatini cum eorum bestiis et personis devastent bona civium et eis dampnum inferant et dent in eorum bonis et possessionibus, et cum non sit aliquis qui custodiat bona dictorum civium propter quod cives non recipiunt fructus ex eorum possessionibus, utile esset habere et eligere posse et quod eligeretur et deputaretur per comune Aretii unus notarius forensis dampnorum datorum pro dampnis datis'.

[58] ASA, Atti del danno dato, 2 (1429), 55r, NN: 'tempore . . . Lapi olim Johannis de Bucellis de Florentia . . . potestatis . . . Aretii . . . per . . . Jacobum Marci Jacobi de Pistorio . . . officialem dannorum datorum'. Volumes 3, 4, 5 and 6 of the same series contain similar acts compiled by a notary of the Podestà.

[59] ASA, Provv., 6, 156v (15 July 1433): 'eligere notarium dannorum datorum prout alias fuit consuetum et prout possint facere comunitas Cortone et alie supposite dominationi florentine'.

[60] *Ibid.*, 159v (2 October 1433).   [61] *Ibid.*, 162v (16 December 1433).

[62] *Ibid.*, 159v–160r (2 October 1433).

[63] *Ibid.*, 162v (2 December 1433): 'considerato quod huiusmodi concessio eligendi [notarium dannorum datorum] alias facta tribuit tam miserum salarium et tot habet conditiones quod non invenitur qui velit talem electionem acceptare'.

[64] *Ibid.*, 203v (25 August 1435), 205v (27 September 1435).

Nevertheless, it seems clear that Arezzo was in greater favour after the triumph of Rinaldo degli Albizzi in September 1433 than at any time in the previous fifty years of Florentine rule. Not only were the Aretines allowed the above-mentioned temporary unification of the offices of Captain and Podestà and the restoration in principle of their *danni dati*, but the Florentines also granted a visitation to Arezzo in December 1433 by two Florentine citizens 'commissioned to investigate and inform themselves with regard to the indigence and poverty of the commune of Arezzo and its people'.[65] Such a level of favour to Arezzo was not to be seen again in Florence until the aftermath of the Aretine demonstrations of loyalty to the Medici in 1466 and 1480. In many respects the Medici would follow precedents established by Rinaldo degli Albizzi's regime of 1433–4,[66] and, on the evidence of developments in Arezzo, it seems that this pattern extended to the territorial state as well.

However, despite the new direction of Florentine policy towards Arezzo under Rinaldo degli Albizzi between September 1433 and September 1434, the previous fifty years of Florentine rule had tended to severity and limitation of local autonomy. Characteristic was Florentine reaction to the civic unrest in Arezzo provoked by Florence's deteriorating relations with Ladislas of Naples in 1408 and 1409. A policy of exiling large numbers of potential rebels had been used to underpin Florentine rule in Pisa since 1407, and in 1408 a similar policy was suggested for Arezzo. It was rejected then as counterproductive, but the events of 1409 led the Florentines to change their minds. As Ladislas prepared an invasion force against Florence at the beginning of the year, Florentine intelligence uncovered allegedly treasonable activities by a number of friars and at least one layman in Arezzo. In May 1409 Ladislas appeared before the walls of Arezzo with his army but the major insurrection for which he had hoped failed to occur; a plot to betray Arezzo to him was uncovered, resulting in the execution of one conspirator. A more important result was that the Florentine regime now introduced the policy of mass exile used in Pisa, turning at least a hundred Aretines out of their homes. Exile on this scale led to incidents of injustice, mistaken identity, rapine and fornication, and growing

---

[65] *Ibid.*, 163v (20 December 1433): 'cum commissione ut investigarent et se informarent de egestatibus et paupertatibus comunis Aretii et seu etiam personarum eiusdem'. See also *ibid.*, 161v (30 November 1433), 162r (2 December 1433), 162v (16 December 1433).

[66] See N. Rubinstein, *The Government of Florence under the Medici* (Oxford, 1966), pp. 4ff.

hostility to Florentine rule provoked two large-scale conspiracies in Arezzo: the first in September 1409 was led by the Bostoli family, the second in December by the Albergotti. Both plots failed and were followed by numerous executions; Florence then continued the policy of exiling potential rebels until 1414 when, with Ladislas' death, the danger to Florentine rule in Arezzo once again receded. The bitterness that was the legacy of these years, however, lived on in the memories of Aretines and was at least in part responsible for another attempt to overthrow Florentine rule in Arezzo twenty years later in 1431. A prominent Aretine from a feudal family, Conte Mariotto di Biagio Griffolini, who had been one of Arezzo's most eminent citizens and merchants in the 1420s, attempted in 1431 to betray the city to the forces of the Duke of Milan. Griffolini's declared motives for conspiring against Florence were oppressive tax burdens and fear of renewed mass exile in Arezzo. Once again, however, the conspiracy failed and Griffolini and a number of his associates were apprehended and summarily executed.[67]

After the suppression of the Aretine rebellion of 1502, the Florentine regime returned to the earlier, pre-Medicean policy of severity and restriction of local autonomy. About eighty Aretines from leading families went into exile in Siena, including the philo-Medicean humanist and communal grammar teacher, Giovanni Pollastra,[68] and a number of supporters of the insurrection, including Matteo, the brother of Lorenzo's secretary Giovannantonio (who had died in September 1492),[69] were declared rebels and suffered confiscation of their property.[70] The most prominent among communal offices lost to the Aretines was the chancellorship, which was held from 1503 to 1514 by a foreigner, Girolamo di Ciriaco Palamedi from Borgo Sansepolcro.[71]

It was only with the return of the Medici to Florence and the pontificate of Leo X that the Aretines regained their communal autonomies, restored in fact through the direct intervention of the pope himself with this brief to his nephew, Lorenzo:

> The Aretines have informed us that various honours, offices and emoluments which they enjoyed before 1502 have not yet been restored. We are fully aware of the affection and loyalty which that city and its

---

[67] See R. Black, *Benedetto Accolti and the Florentine Renaissance* (Cambridge, 1985), pp. 4–5.
[68] See Black and Clubb, *Romance*, pp. 81ff.
[69] See Black, 'Lorenzo', p. 228 note 100.
[70] ASA, Provv., 17, 81v (15 March 1515, ab inc.).
[71] See ASA, Provv., 15 and 16, *passim*.

citizens have always and at all times demonstrated towards us and our family, as well as of those things which that city and its citizens experienced out of consideration for our family; therefore, we make known our intention that all benefits enjoyed before that time should be restored. Consequently we urge you to see to it that the office of chancellor of the priors and of the notary of gabelles and other offices and emoluments which they enjoyed before that time should be restored; that their statutes in force at that time should be reaffirmed; and that in all things you should show yourself to be favourable to that community and its citizens. All this will give us great pleasure. Dated Rome at St Peter's, 27 March 1514, in the second year of our pontificate.[72]

Little more than a month later, in May 1514, the chancellorship was returned to the Aretines, with Ser Andrea del fu Messer Guillichino di Lodovico Guillichini elected as the first restored Aretine chancellor.[73]

The triangular relationship among Florence, Arezzo and the Medici had finally come to fruition. In the fifteenth century, the benefits of loyalty to the Medici had been relative and perceived rather than substantial: in comparison to the pre-1433 regime the Medici assumed the role of benefactors, although the actual concrete advantages gained by the Aretines, even under Lorenzo di Piero, were negligible and temporary. After their overt demonstration of loyalty to the Medici in 1502, however, Arezzo was recognised universally as a Medicean city: hence, the severity of the regime established there by the Florentines after 1502. This was the papal view too, and with the restoration of communal autonomies in May 1514, there could be no more doubts about the benefits of Medicean loyalty. What may be particularly significant is that the triangular structure possibly worked to impede the

---

[72] ASA, Provv., 17, 7v: 'Copia brevis. Dilecte fili. Exponi nobis fecerunt aretini quod ad quosdam honores et officia et quaedam alia emolumenta, quos et quae de anno milleximo quingentesimo secundo gaudebant et potiebantur, hactenus civitas ipsa restituta non fuit. Quia attendentes dilectionem et fidelitatem, quam erga nos et domum nostram semper et omni tempore civitas ipsa et cives habuit et habuerunt, et deinde quae ipsa et ipsi domus nostrae intuitu sustinuit et sustinuere, de quibus ad plenum informati fidem facimus et attestamur, et mentis et intentionis nostrae esset, ut ad omnia quibus dicto tempore potiebantur et gaudebant restituerentur. Igitur hortamur nobilitatem tuam, ut omni cura studio et diligentia procures et cum effectu facias, ut praefata civitas et cives ipsi ad officium cancellariatus priorum dictae civitatis et notariatus gabellae et alia officia honores et emulumenta, quae dicto tempore habebant gaudebantque reintegrentur ac restituantur, et statutorum quae tunc temporis in usu erant, confirmationem in forma valida ottineant, ac eisdem civibus et communitati in omnibus te gratum exhibeas, quod erit nobis admodum gratum. Datum Romae apud Sanctum Petrum. Die XXVII marzii M. D. XIIII, pontificatus nostri anno secundo. A tergo vero: Dilecto filio Laurentio Medices Florentiae.'

[73] ASA, Provv., 17, 15r ff.

growth of direct Florentine control and to lessen the decline of local autonomy in Arezzo. The effect of Medicean influence in the fifteenth century and particularly after 1514, as far as Arezzo is concerned, appears to have counteracted the centralising tendencies of previous republican regimes in the territorial state.

CHAPTER 15

RUBRICS AND REQUESTS: STATUTORY DIVISION AND SUPRA-COMMUNAL CLIENTAGE IN FIFTEENTH-CENTURY PISTOIA

STEPHEN J. MILNER

In the twentieth chapter of *The Prince*, Machiavelli famously observed: 'Our ancestors and those who were considered wise used to claim that it was necessary to hold Pistoia with factions and Pisa with fortresses, and consequently nurtured differences in several subject cities in order to keep hold of them more securely.'[1] What this assertion masks is a fundamental difference in the manner by which these so-called *parte* were managed during the course of the fifteenth century, for almost continuously between 1376 and 1457 Pistoia's offices were equally divided by statute between the societies of San Paolo and San Giovanni. The purpose was to secure civic peace through the equitable distribution of honours as enshrined in legislation. With the establishment of Medicean hegemony in Florence, however, the dissolution of the statutory 'parte' in Pistoia meant that communal peace was dependent on the impartiality of the Medici and their agents in their role as patron/arbitrators between competing elements within the Pistoiese elite. An examination of the Pistoiese case sheds interesting light on the changing nature of power brokerage within and between both Pistoiese and Florentine elites during the course of the Quattrocento.

RECONFIGURING THE POLITICAL LANDSCAPE

In 1376 Florentine ambassadors annulled the Pistoiese's own civic reforms in an attempt to pacify the city, and mandated four commissioners to carry out a new reform to last six years, doubling the number

---

[1] Niccolò Machiavelli, *The Prince and Other Political Writings*, ed. and trans. S. J. Milner (London, 1995), p. 109. Part of the research cited in this article was made possible by a grant from the University of Bristol Research Fund.

of bags for the major civic offices from four bags per office, one per quarter, to eight. This reform applied to the Standard Bearer of Justice, the Elders (*Anziani*), Twelve Good Men and General Council (*Consiglio generale*), the idea being that each quarter had two bags: one for the company of San Paolo, associated by contemporary commentators with the Panciatichi, and one for the company of San Giovanni, considered synonymous with Cancellieri interests.[2] This provision was maintained in the subsequent Florentine reform of Pistoia's offices in 1383 and endured almost unbroken until the reform of 1457.[3] The formal institution of a divided polity as a means of securing peace by guaranteeing the respective sides a share of civic offices had previously been practised elsewhere, but was in stark contrast to developments within Florence itself during the late Trecento, where the constitutional structure and communal rhetoric sought to preclude internal division and establish government based on the values of consensus and unity.[4] Although initially a response to divisions within the commune itself, it is undoubtedly the case that the statutory division of the commune by the Florentines actually contributed to the longevity of factional solidarity.

The eventual abolition of the practice of dividing the city's bags between the respective societies of San Paolo and San Giovanni was part of a radical reconfiguration of the political landscape which fundamentally altered power relations within Pistoia, with formal governmental structures being cleared and a political marketplace established where benefits were secured through negotiation, exchange and the peddling of influence. The abolition was proposed by the twenty reformers elected according to the rubric established in the Florentine provision of 5 May 1455 formulated by Alessandro degli Alessandri who had been sent to Pistoia as commissioner to settle the disorders in the city. Their suggestion was forwarded to the city's Podestà, Bartolomeo Lenzi, in March 1457.[5] Conscious of the potential political ramifications of such an innovation, Lenzi wrote to Cosimo de' Medici that same month seeking guidance,

---

[2] See C. Guasti (ed.), *I Capitoli del comune di Firenze. Inventario e registro*, I (Florence, 1866), pp. 19–21.

[3] Guasti (ed.), *Capitoli*, I, pp. 22–4.

[4] See, for example, D. Waley, 'Guelfs and Ghibellines at San Gimignano, c.1260–c.1320: A Political Experiment', *Bulletin of the John Rylands Library*, 72 (1990), pp. 199–212. For Florence, see J. Najemy, *Corporatism and Consensus in Florentine Electoral Politics, 1280–1400* (Chapel Hill, 1982), pp. 263–74.

[5] ASF, PR, 146, 98r–99v.

It has come to my attention that some of these citizens elected to
undertake the said reform are keen to use four bags in the scrutiny, one
per quarter, where previously the custom has been to use two, one for
the Panciatichi and one for the Cancellieri. The purpose, it is claimed, is
to ensure that citizens are more free and not constrained by any
individual or concerned with currying favour . . . I request that you be
so kind as to advise me of your opinion on this matter, namely whether I
should agree to the use of four bags as mentioned above or follow the
customary procedure. Your advice would be more than welcome to
me.[6]

The policy obviously received Cosimo's approval as the subsequent
reform dispensed with the practice of electoral division of the city's
offices, requiring names to be placed in the relevant bags 'with the
whole city and every society included'.[7] The removal of the statutory
division of offices meant that civic harmony was increasingly dependent
on Florentine negotiation and arbitration. As an historically divided
commune the newly configured political field post-1457 was extremely
sensitive, for the Pistoiese were proven experts in reading shifts in
favour and quick to react to overt partiality from the centre.

Even prior to this significant innovation, the Pistoiese had benefited
from the alteration in the style of government within Florence, securing
significant concessions from the Florentines at the communal level. In
December 1454 they successfully petitioned the Priors and Colleges for
the confirmation of a recently approved Pistoiese statutory rubric which
forbade Pistoiese from initiating proceedings through a variety of Florentine offices which had jurisdiction over the territories. These included
the Defenders of the Laws, Five of the Contado, the Officers of the
Tower, the Regulators of the Florentine Treasury, the Night Officers
and all other Florentine magistracies, with the exception of the Signoria
and its Colleges, the Eight of Custody, the Ten of *Balìa*, the Officers for
Orphans, and the Six of the *Mercanzia*. The confirmed statute also
prevented the listed magistracies from seeking to intercede through

---

[6] ASF, MAP, XII, no. 231, 4 April 1457; 'sento che alchuno di questi cittadini eletti a
detta riforma vorebbero fare de' decti squittini quattro borse in nome di quattro porti
dove prima s'è usato fare due borse una per Panciatichi e altra per Chancellieri e
questo dichono fanno perché gli uomini sieno più liberi e non siano sottoposti a
persone e non s'attenda a chareggiare . . . vi priegho siate chontento chonsigliarmi e
dire da vostro parte cioè se è da chonsentire fare quattro borse chome di sopra si dice
o fare al modo usate e me ne farete singhulare piacere'.

[7] ASPt, Com. Otto Riformatori, 99, 16v: 'et per tota civitate et omnibus societatibus
mixti'. See also the undifferentiated 1458 lists in ASF, Tratte, 1495, 17r–22r.

Pistoia's *rettori*, the penalty being examination by the Florentine Defenders of the Laws.[8] These privileges were confirmed again in 1484.[9]

The reduction in the number of Florentine territorial agencies with jurisdiction over Pistoiese affairs constituted a significant concession both symbolically and jurisdictionally. It also defined the charismatic centre more clearly, with authority channelled through fewer offices administered by a narrowing elite within Florence. This tendency towards concentration and centralisation was in keeping with alterations in Florence itself where Medicean pre-eminence was established through the systematic manipulation of the city's electoral procedures and the exploitation of strong patronage networks. However, whilst the Medici had to be mindful of the republican values enshrined within the constitutional and rhetorical frameworks when operating inside Florence, they were less subject to constraint beyond the city walls. There was therefore greater scope for the evolution of government based on the culture of requests, with the Medici exercising influence over Pistoiese affairs through the use of patronage as an instrument of rule.

The abiding difficulty of managing Pistoia during the late medieval and Renaissance periods was to avoid decisions that would crystallise factional solidarity. The keystone of Florentine policy prior to, and during, Medicean hegemony was therefore to maintain both sides within the political realm as a necessary precondition of government. Whilst constitutional division ensured a sharing of the spoils of political office in the first half of the century, Medici management in the second half successfully established Pistoiese dependency upon their mediation. Although Medici sympathies seem to have shifted from a pro-Cancellieri stance under Cosimo and Giovanni di Cosimo to a marked partiality for the Panciatichi under Lorenzo, the realignment was insufficient to induce rebellion. Enough requests were met to maintain fidelity and nurture the hope of preferment, and divisions did not always break down the same fault lines.

In analysing the relations between the two communes, the use of the

---

8 ASF, SCAS, 598, 28r–v. For these provisions see also W. J. Connell, 'Clientelismo e stato territoriale. Il potere fiorentino a Pistoia nel XV secolo', *Società e storia*, 14 (1991), pp. 526–7.

9 For the reconfirmation see, ASPt, Com., SO, 31, 3r–4r, 19 December 1484. See ASPt, Com., Provv. e rif., 48, 80r, 22 December 1484, for the commune's acknowledgement: 'una dichiaratione . . . molto utilissime per la vostra città che in effecto contiene che e Conservatori delle Leggi, Cinque del Contado, Regulatori e simili officii non hanno cognitione nella vostra città: Ma solo l'anno la Signoria, Collegi e Dieci'.

terms 'Florence' and 'Pistoia' suggests a homogeneity that was at odds with the fluctuating fortunes of political groupings within the respective cities. Whilst Florentine intervention resulted in certain administrative and procedural changes that affected Pistoiese political life, the durability of those changes was conditional upon how the respective factions perceived their influence within Florence. The political elite within Pistoia was clearly aware that Florence itself was governed by an elite. Only twice in the fifteenth century was the tenuous equilibrium lost. These two episodes, posted at either end of the Quattrocento, are crucial in understanding the changing nature of the balance achieved in the intervening century.

The 1401 crisis was a result of Florentine anxieties concerning the fidelity of the Cancellieri faction in the face of Visconti aggression, whilst the civil dissension that consumed Pistoia post-1498 was clearly a consequence of the Medici's exile four years previously. Focusing specifically on the events preceding both of these crises will help chart the interrelation between patronage groups that transcended communal structures and ideologies, and their importance in fashioning the political landscape of Renaissance Tuscany.

SUPRA–COMMUNAL CLIENTAGE AND THE REBELLION OF 1401

The characterisation of the relation between Florence and Pistoia as one between dominant and subject denies the possibility of developments within Pistoia influencing Florentine affairs. Historically this was far from true. According to the Florentine chronicle and historiographical tradition Pistoia was held responsible for the introduction of factions into Florence at the beginning of the fourteenth century and the subsequent plague of civil dissension that ravaged the city. Stefani noted how, in attempting to deal with the split within the Cancellieri family, the Florentines ordered the heads of the two branches, termed the 'Whites' (*Bianchi*) and 'Blacks' (*Neri*), to the city to control the feuding. The result was the division of Florence itself along partisan lines as the Cancellieri were not only a rich and numerous family but also 'closely bound by ties of friendship', having both friends and relations amongst the most powerful Florentine citizens. The account describes how the Bianchi collected at the house of the Cerchi in the Garbo, whilst the Neri assembled at the house of the Frescobaldi in the Fondaccio near the bridge of Santa Trinita.[10] Stefani's account echoes that of the

---

[10] Marchionne di Coppo Stefani, *Cronaca fiorentina*, ed. N. Rodolico, in *Rerum italicarum scriptores*, 2nd edn, XXX, part 1 (Città di Castello, 1903–13), rubric I, p. 3.

anonymous author of the *Storie pistoresi* and is similar to Villani's and Ptolemy of Lucca's, the latter stating that the whole of Tuscany was divided according to 'friendships' (*amicitiae*) and that both Florence and Lucca were brought to the brink of civil war as a consequence: 'In this manner the house became divided between Whites and Blacks with the result that the whole city and the whole of Tuscany were split according to the ties of friendship that people held in that town, and this was especially true in Florence and Lucca where these ties are still maintained to this day.'[11]

Such explanations illustrate the importance of ties that transcended individual communes in this period, emphasising the strength of associational bonds based on kinship, friendship and mutual interest in a period when the communal sphere was yet to be consolidated. To speak of the relation between Pistoia and Florence as autonomous communes ignores the interrelation and cooperation between factions within both cities. Prior to the Florentine-negotiated *capitoli* of 1329, Pistoiese factions sought support from allies in Lucca, Pisa, Bologna and Florence. The cumulative effect of subsequent Florentine interventions and diplomatic arbitration during the Trecento was to establish Florence as the charismatic centre to the exclusion of other Tuscan towns. The assurance of Pistoiese fidelity, irrespective of the constitution of the ruling elite within Florence, constituted a significant simplification in the relationship between the two towns. When Pistoia was divided, the relative combatants were encouraged or prevented from seeking redress against their opponents by calling on allies beyond Florence, Pistoiese divisions being either absorbed or reconciled by the Florentines. What the 1401 rebellion of Ricciardo Cancellieri illustrates is how easily Florence's own security could be threatened as a result of alterations in the balance of power between competing clientage networks which transcended both Pistoia and Florence.

Events prior to the rebellion of Ricciardo Cancellieri in 1401 suggest that the tenuous equilibrium that existed within Pistoia was strained and that Florentine intervention was under considerable scrutiny as to its impartiality. Once the Cancellieri perceived that the Panciatichi allies within Florence were gaining political ascendancy they feared for their position within their own town. For those within Florence, the potential financial and strategic impact of losing Pistoia at that particular

---

[11] See *Storie Pistoresi (1300–1348)*, ed. S. A Barbi, in *Rerum italicarum scriptores*, 2nd edn, XI, part 5 (Città di Castello, 1907–27), p. 6; and Ptolemy of Lucca, *Die Annalen des Tholomeus von Lucca*, in *Scriptores rerum germanicarum*, ed. B. Schmeidler, n.s. (Berlin, 1930), p. 210.

time is testified by the regular and comprehensive discussions within the *consulte* during these early years of the Quattrocento. Morelli in his *Ricordi* is quite emphatic about the impact of the rebellion on Florentine exiles in the surrounding communes, implying that Ricciardo's actions provided a catalyst for the uprising of exiled Ghibellines in the Mugello, Arezzo, Prato and Volterra. He notes that if the Duke of Milan had left Bologna and ridden into the Florentine contado he would have been able to seize all the surrounding territory.[12]

That tension between the factions in Pistoia was running high during the second half of the 1390s is clear from contemporary chronicles and archival documents. Twice within four years, one of the foremost leaders of the Cancellieri faction had been subject to a ban (*banno*) and expelled from the city, only being reinstated through the intervention of the Signoria and Colleges in Florence. The extent of the division this caused is clear from the correspondence between Luigi di Piero Canigiani, commissioner in Pistoia, and the Signoria (the Priors and Standard Bearer of Justice) in Florence in 1396 concerning the *ribandimento* of Niccolò Pandragoni dei Cancellieri, one of the leaders of the Cancellieri faction. On 3 December the Pistoiese General Council was split 62:62, and despite repeated attempts, 'again and again the votes were divided equally in two halves'. The matter was eventually resolved in mid-January when a majority of the Council elected to devolve the decision to the Signoria in Florence by granting it the authority held by the Pistoiese councils. In this case, the Florentine policy of instituting two bags for all offices necessitated a call for Florentine intervention to break the deadlock. Both sides, however, maintained that they would never depart from the will of the Florentines. While those who spoke on behalf of the Company of San Giovanni claimed that 'their party would never disobey any orders given them by their masters in Florence', the representative for the Company of San Paolo asserted three times 'that their party was the one which never departed from the will of the Florentine commune'.[13]

Niccolò Pandragoni dei Cancellieri was again at the centre of factional tensions in the months immediately prior to Ricciardo Cancellieri's rebellion. This time it related to the contested marriage of Datina

---

[12] Giovanni Morelli, *Ricordi*, in V. Branca (ed.), *Mercanti scrittori: ricordi nella Firenze tra Medioevo e Rinascimento* (Milan, 1986), p. 263.

[13] See the diplomatic correspondence in ASF, SCLCRROF, 1, 5v–7r, 23 November 1396 to 18 January 1397: 'più volte e sempre le fave anno medesimo modo per metà'; 'mai la loro parte non si deviò da chosa che per la loro Signoria da Firenze fosse loro comandato'; 'che 'lla parte loro era quella che mai non si deviò dalla voluntà del comune di Firenze'.

Guazzalotti from Prato to Bichecco Bracciolini. Such was the force of his intervention that he was, once again, banned by the then Podestà of Pistoia, and Bracciolini's marriage was confirmed. Once more his reinstatement was only through the agency of the Florentine commissioner under instructions from the Florentine authorities.[14]

There can be little doubt that Ricciardo's actions were a result of the perceived weakness of the Cancellieri's allies in Florence relative to those of the Panciatichi. That such connections existed is clear not only from marriage alliances between the major families in both towns, but also from the records of the surety payments made to the Executors of Justice between 1389 and 1403 to secure declared rebels living in the contado or distretto of Pistoia.[15] Here we find the Ardinghelli, Rinaldeschi, Strada, Barducci, Frescobaldi, Arrighi, Gianfigliazzi, Adimari, Guasconi, Giugni, Vecchietti, Tornaquinci, Tosinghi, Medici, Albizzi, Canigiani and Soderini, to name the most prominent, all standing surety for former *banditi* of the commune of Pistoia and its surrounding territory. The growing influence of the Panciatichi was symbolised in April 1388, when both Giovanni di Giovanni and Bandini di Bandino Panciatichi were made knights by the Florentines with much pageantry and celebration.[16]

At the same time, the political fortunes of the Florentine families connected with the Cancellieri were on the wane. According to the Pistoiese chronicler Luca Dominici, the Panciatichi faction, composed mainly of mercantile and trading families, secured advantageous marriage alliances with the Albizzi, as well as enjoying close ties with the Pitti, Castellani, Buondelmonti, Vettori and Guasconi, whilst the Cancellieri were related to the Ricci, Acciaiuoli and Medici and a series of families of either magnate or recently granted popular status such as the Frescobaldi, Cavalcanti, Bardi, Tornabuoni and Tornaquinci.[17] The Acciaiuoli, Ricci and Medici had all had family members exiled or disqualified from office as a result of a number of plots against the regime, the most recent in 1400 resulting in three of the Ricci and two of the Medici being declared outlaws.[18] That Ricciardo Cancellieri was

---

[14] For the cancellation of the ban see ASPt, Com., Provv. e rif., 27, 9v–10v, 15 March 1401; and E. Conti (ed.), *Le 'Consulte' e 'Pratiche' della repubblica fiorentina nel Quattrocento*, I (Pisa, 1981), p. 71.

[15] ASF, CPGNR, 59, 1r–59v, 2 August 1389 to 2 October 1403.

[16] See the report of three days of celebration in Florence in A. Molho and F. Sznura (eds.), *Alle bocche della piazza. Diario di Anonimo Fiorentino (1382–1401)* (Florence, 1986), pp. 79–80.

[17] Luca Dominici, *Cronache*, ed. G. C. Gigliotti, 2 vols. (Pistoia, 1933–9) II, pp. 10–12.

[18] See G. Brucker, *The Civic World of Early Renaissance Florence* (Princeton, 1977),

serving in Bologna prior to the plot only adds to the probability that he was aware of developments within Florence through contact with exiled members of the families mentioned above, and may well have been aware of their enemy Bonaccorso Pitti's role in securing Florentine imperial jurisdiction over Pistoia.[19]

The confessions of the conspirators reveal that Ricciardo was not responsible for initiating the plot. It was devised in the first instance by other members of the faction, not surprisingly one Niccolò Pandragoni dei Cancellieri, together with Bartolomeo Camaggiore and Giovanni and Lazero Cantansanti who sought to murder Giovanni Panciatichi and his sons. Before they acted, however, they sought clearance for their plan from Ricciardo in Bologna, who subsequently joined them in Pistoia.[20] Once the plot had been discovered, Ricciardo fled to the safety of the fortress of Sambuca in the north-eastern tip of the Pistoiese mountains, where he remained until the fort was eventually rendered in 1403 subsequent to negotiations with the Florentine authorities.

Despite calls to punish the rebels and confiscate and destroy their property, the eventual outcome of Ricciardo's actions some three years later involved a general amnesty for all rebels which was finally declared in October 1403. The price of reintegrating the Cancellieri into Pistoiese civic life was the total absolution of Ricciardo Cancellieri and his family and followers from all judicial sentences against them. In addition, individuals were prevented from proceeding against any former *bandito* in either the civil or criminal courts on account of crimes committed between August 1401 and October 1403. The only exception related to murders and thefts carried out within the Pistoiese walls in the preceding year, although even in this instance Ricciardo Cancellieri and the other Cancellieri *ribanniti* were exempted. Furthermore, additional concessions were granted to the former rebels. There was also a promise to meet the cost of the rebuilding of Ricciardo Cancellieri's house and the repair of the family stronghold outside Pistoia.[21]

The Florentines' inability to punish the rebels and their humiliation at having to reintegrate the banned Cancellieri families back into Pistoiese political life, pay testimony to the intractable problem of

---

pp. 96–100, 157–65 and 171–7. Brucker notes that Donato Acciaiuoli in particular had many enemies in Pistoia, p. 98.

[19] This was certainly the case after the uprising, Dominici noting that 'si diceva a Firenze che Ser Niccolao di Pandragone et gli usciti di Firenze aveano ragionato et ordinato volere pigliare Pistoia et tenerla, o almeno disfarla con nuovi avisi et modi'; Dominici, *Cronache*, II, p. 93.

[20] ASF, Pod., 3821, 66r–70v and 81v–82r, 5–8 November 1401.

[21] ASF, Capitoli, 57, 9r–13v, 30 October 1403.

securing a split commune. However, the custom of dividing the city's electoral bags seemed to work, and between 1406 and 1455 Pistoia was relatively peaceful. The termination of this practice, and the increasing reliance on the mediation of Medici agents reintroduced an element of volatility into Pistoiese life which finally erupted in 1498, when Cancellieri resentment boiled over as a result of the first contested election in Pistoia subsequent to the Medici exile. How this resentment accumulated is apparent from a brief examination of patronage relations between the Medici and leading players within Pistoia.

THE MEDICI AND THE TRAFFIC IN REQUESTS

The alteration in the style of government under the Medici is clearly reflected in the volume of correspondence between Pistoia and the Medici family, most markedly during the pre-eminence of Lorenzo the Magnificent. Although Florentine officials still served in Pistoia and commissioners continued to be sent, most of these officers were themselves Medicean clients facilitating the process. As the established charismatic centre within Florence, responsibility for maintaining political equilibrium within Pistoia increasingly became the task of the Medici themselves, rather than being enshrined and executed via the traditional organs of government associated with the territorial state.[22] Crucially, there seems to have been a consensus within the rival elements of the Pistoiese elite, if only grudgingly at times, concerning the family's role as communal patrons. This did not mean there was an absence of resistance to increased intervention, or even an absence of patronage networks with other members of the Florentine elite, but solely that at a communal level the city became dependent upon the intervention of the Medici to mediate when divisions arose.[23] It was within this context that the weight of correspondence passing through the official governmental organs declined relative to the letters directed to the Medici themselves.

Yet within this newly configured patronal arena the Medici were not

---

[22] See P. Salvadori, 'Rapporti personali, rapporti di potere nella corrispondenza di Lorenzo dei Medici', in G. C. Garfagnini (ed.), *Lorenzo il Magnifico e il suo tempo* (Florence, 1992), pp. 125–45, and W. J. Connell, 'Changing Patterns of Medicean Patronage: The Florentine Dominion during the Fifteenth Century', in G. C. Garfagnini (ed.), *Lorenzo il Magnifico e il suo mondo* (Florence, 1994), pp. 87–107.

[23] For Piero Baldinotti's attempted murder of Lorenzo see A. Chiti, *Di un tentativo di congiura contro Lorenzo il Magnifico* (Pistoia, 1898), and W. J. Connell, 'Clientelismo e stato territoriale', pp. 540–1.

the sole beneficiaries. For patronage as a process is premised on the notion of reciprocity and mutual benefit. Other players possessed forms of symbolic capital, for example as judicial officials, controllers of civic patronage or dispensers of charity. In order to trade successfully, some form of currency was required, in addition to proximity to the key patronal centres.[24] In this context, the roles of giver and receiver were never fixed, but ever fluid, one man's client being another's patron in relationships that were periodically reversed. The clear hierarchical relation implicit within the terminology of patron and client suggests a rigidity at odds with the ever changing alignments within the market-place of favours. To describe the relation between Medici and the Pistoia as that of patron and client is to rob the Pistoiese of agency, or at least underestimate the political leverage possessed by clients. For, as noted, the Pistoiese also benefited from the alteration in the style of government, securing important communal privileges. Although the Medici benefited from, and facilitated, the clearing of bureaucratic structures, they also had to assume the role of arbitrator in the regulation of factional disputes within the Pistoiese elite. Pistoia presented the challenge of maintaining impartiality whilst operating a system of government premised on favouritism, a challenge previously met through the statutory division of political offices.

Medici involvement in the civic life of Pistoia only became signifi-cant after the second quarter of the fifteenth century. The Medici held positions within the territories including Pistoia during the early part of the century, as Captain of Custody and Podestà of Pistoia on seven occasions between 1352 and 1452, although only twice subsequent to Giovanni di Bicci's period of office as Podestà in 1407, namely in 1443 and 1452 when Orlando di Guccio de' Medici and Niccolò di Vieri de' Medici, father of Pistoia's Bishop Donato de' Medici, both served as Captain. Although it was not until the return of the Medici to Florence in 1512 that one of their number again assumed such a post when Antonio di Lorenzo became Captain, this absence from such posts during the greater part of the fifteenth century belies the increasing significance of the family in Pistoiese civic life.[25] The first honours afforded the Medici family on the part of the commune were granted

---

[24] The terminology of 'field' and 'symbolic capital' are drawn from Pierre Bourdieu, *Outline of a Theory of Practice*, trans. R. Nice (Cambridge, 1977), pp. 171–83; Bourdieu, 'Sur le pouvoir symbolique', *Annales*, 32–33 (1977), pp. 405–11, and Bourdieu, 'La représentation politique. Eléments pour une théorie du champ politique', *Actes de la recherche en sciences sociales*, 36–7 (1981), pp. 3–24.

[25] For the lists of Medicean Captains and Podestà at Pistoia, see ASF, Manoscritti, 496, fols. 402, 407, 409, 416. Antonio di Lorenzo held the post of Captain in 1525.

on the death of Giovanni di Bicci. In February 1429 the Priors of Pistoia wrote to Averardo de' Medici recalling Giovanni's period as Podestà with affection, and concluding: 'For this reason we have decided that your house be permitted to freely assume and carry the *insignia* and arms of our commune as you please.'[26] Throughout the remainder of the century, Pistoiese recognition and acceptance of Medicean pre-eminence is clearly documented in the city's provisions and records. Gifts were sent by the commune to family members, ambassadors were sent to honour them when visiting the city and its surrounding area, hospitality was arranged when they stayed in the town and whilst marriages and promotions to Cardinal were celebrated, orators were sent to offer condolences to family members and money was voted by the General Council to honour the departed.[27] This respect is reflected in the terminology used in the provisions themselves to describe the nature of the relationship between the Medici as patrons and protectors of Pistoia and the city as client, a terminology redolent of the language of Medicean apologists in Florence. That their relation was

---

[26] ASF, MAP, II, no. 231, 21 February 1429: 'E per questa cagione abbiamo deliberato che a voi sia licite et possiate tutte insegne e arme del nostro comune avere e portare liberamente a ogni vostro bene placito'.

[27] On 3 November 1463 a provision was passed by 75 to 8 to spend up to 400 lire to send orators to Florence to honour the memory of Giovanni di Cosimo and offer condolence to his father and Piero his brother; ASPt, Com., Provv. e rif., 42, 46r. Similarly on 18 May 1478, 300 lire were voted to honour the memory of Giuliano de' Medici and four citizens elected to represent the city at his funeral; *ibid.*, 44, 74r. Lorenzo's pre-eminence is reflected in the fact that three citizens were granted authority to spend 'ogni quantità di pecunia che alloro paresse per honorare el corpo della sua Magnificenza'; *ibid.*, 48, 344r. The commune paid homage to visiting members of the family, for example in early September 1476, when four orators were elected to honour Giuliano de' Medici with an honorarium of 100 lire as he was visiting the Pistoiese baths; see *ibid.*, 44, 2r–v. On 20 September 1476, when the commune invited Lorenzo to stay in the Palace of the Priors on his visit to Pistoia, electing four citizens to honour him on 23 September 1476; see *ibid.*, 44, 9v. On 12 August 1478, when Lorenzo's wife and part of the family came to stay in Pistoia the Council deputised citizens to oversee the provision of a house for the duration of their stay; see *ibid.*, 44, 79r. On 21 July 1485, four citizens were elected to honour Lorenzo on the occasion of his attendance at the Feast of San Jacopo; see *ibid.*, 46, 134v and *ibid.*, 48, 106r. On 1–2 April 1487, three citizens were elected to oversee the organisation of the celebrations for 'la buona nuova del parentado contracto non molto giorni sono fra la Santità di Nostro Signore et la Magnificenzia di Lorenzo'; *ibid.*, 48, 145v; whilst on 12–13 March 1489 four citizens were elected to honour Giovanni di Lorenzo de' Medici upon his election to Cardinal; *ibid.*, 48, 209r. The Medici also required Pistoiese attendance at Florentine festivals, for example *ibid.*, 42, 100r, 21 June 1464, where 25 lire were raised from gate taxes to meet Piero di Cosimo's requested Pistoiese attendance at the celebrations of the forthcoming Feast of San Giovanni.

one of patron and client is clear. On Giovanni di Cosimo's death, the commune noted the 'many benefits received by the commune of Pistoia from his father Cosimo and brother Pietro'.[28] In June 1464 Piero de' Medici is referred to as 'father of the city of Pistoia', whilst in September 1476 the Medici house is cited as 'protector of the city of Pistoia and of all men'.[29] The extent of Pistoiese indebtedness was noted in the preamble to the granting of the right to Lorenzo and Giuliano di Piero to place their insignia in the Great Hall of the Palace of the Priors in March 1478: '. . . so great have been the continual graces, favours and kindnesses received at different times and in various instances by your city from the magnificent and generous house of the Medici, that it would be almost impossible, given the constraints of time, to be able to list them in a manner that would do them justice'.[30] That these patterns of patronage were well established is clear from another preamble to a request for the granting of citizenship to a client of Piero di Lorenzo in July 1488: 'It has always been your practice to be accommodating, dear and prudent citizens, and especially in relation to the house of Medici and with good reason. For you have always turned to that house in times of difficulty as a reliable guardian and partisan of your community.'[31] The nominating, in Pistoiese council minutes, of the Medici family members as 'fathers' and 'protectors' of the commune demonstrates the less cautious use of such terminology in the territories in comparison to within Florence itself, where only Cosimo was ever officially addressed in such terms.[32]

The extent to which the culture of requests became a means of government under the Medici is illustrated by an examination of the correspondence between Pistoia and the Medici. One thousand two hundred and thirty-one letters have been identified in the *Mediceo avanti*

---

[28] *Ibid.*, 42, 46r, 3 November 1463; 'multa benefitia que comunitatis Pistorii reportavit a Cosimo eius patre et Petro eius frate'.

[29] *Ibid.*, 42, 100r, 21 June 1464: 'pater civitatis Pistorii', and *ibid.*, 44, 2r–v, 3 September 1476: 'protectorem civitatis Pistorii et omnis hominus [*sic*]'.

[30] *Ibid.*, 44, 68r–v: 'tante anche siano sempre state le gratie favori e beneficii in diversi tempi e vari casi ricevuti per la vostra città dala Magnifica e generosa casa de' Medici . . . sarebbe quasi impossibile cum brevità di tempo poterli a sufficientia narrare'.

[31] *Ibid.*, 48, 187v, 18–22 July 1488: 'Egli è stato sempre vostra usanza carissimi prudentissimi compiacere et maxime alla casa de' Medici meritamente perché quella è suta sempre ogni vostro refugio particulare e buona protectrice e fautrice della vostra comunità'.

[32] See N. Rubinstein, *The Government of Florence under the Medici (1434–1494)*, 2nd edn (Oxford, 1997), pp. 250–2.

Table 15.1. *Distribution of letters to the Medici by decade (1400s-1530s)*

Yr	1400	1410	1420	1430	1440	1450	1460	1470	1480	1490	1500	1510	1520	1530
Total	1	1	8	18	12	78	213	600	25	92	4	140	6	2

il Principato archive spanning the period 1405–1538 (Table 15.1).[33] The vast majority of these letters are addressed to members of the Medici family or their notaries, only thirty-four being sent to other individuals, and of this total, only five were jointly addressed to two members of the family. Included in this number are all letters sent by Pistoiese institutions or councils, letters by prominent Pistoiese citizens and clerics irrespective of whether sent from Pistoia itself, and all letters sent by Florentine officials resident or visiting Pistoia. Also included are letters from smaller communes, individuals and officials within the Pistoiese contado and distretto.

A brief statistical analysis of the chronological distribution of letters sent to the Medici illustrates the volume and importance of letters of request, furnishing interesting indications concerning the perceived centres of influence and the periods of most patron/client activity. An analysis of the letters themselves reveals far more concerning the processes of negotiation and the rhetorics of deferral deployed by both the addressees and the correspondents. Figure 15.1 illustrates the distribution of these letters between the start of the fifteenth century and the late 1530s, with thirty-two letters undated. The clearest conclusion to be drawn from this information regards the marked increase in the volume of correspondence during the first half of the Laurentian period, the years immediately preceding the exile of the Medici in 1494 and the years immediately following their return from exile in 1512. All but four of the letters written during the 1490s were from the first four years of the decade. An examination of the recipients of the letters also illustrates the perceived locus of authority within the Medici family on the part of the correspondents (see Table 15.2). Lorenzo's pre-eminence

---

[33] See F. Morandini and A. d'Addario (eds.), *Mediceo avanti il principato*, 4 vols. (Rome, 1951–7). For Lorenzo's correspondence with the Pistoiese see Lorenzo de' Medici, *Lettere* , I–VII, ed. R. Fubini, N. Rubinstein and M. Mallett (Florence, 1977–98); M. del Piazzo (ed.), *Protocolli del carteggio di Lorenzo il Magnifico per gli anni 1473–74, 1477–92* (Florence, 1956); P. G. Ricci and N. Rubinstein, *Censimento delle lettere di Lorenzo di Piero de' Medici* (Florence, 1964), pp. 3, 20, 72, 161, 167 and 180; and E. Bindi, 'Tre lettere inedite di Lorenzo il Magnifico agli operai di S. Iacopo e allo spedalingo del Ceppo', *Archivio storico italiano*, Appendice II (1845), pp. 55–62.

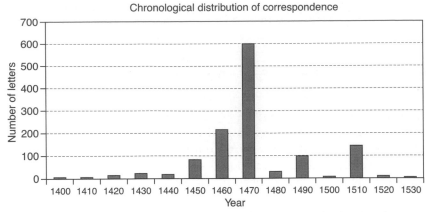

Fig. 15.1 Bar chart of distribution of letters to the Medici by decade
(1400s–1530s)

Table 15.2. *Numerical and percentage distribution of letters to Medici family*

Recipient	Letters sent	Percentage of total
Lorenzo *il magnifico*	669	54.34%
Giovanni di Cosimo	120	9.75%
Piero di Lorenzo	74	6.01%
Lorenzo di Piero di Lorenzo	74	6.01%
Piero di Cosimo	65	5.28%
Cosimo *il vecchio*	24	1.94%
Medici women	21	1.7%
Medici notaries/secretaries	94	7.63%

Table 15.3. *Distribution of letters by four-year periods to leading Medici*

Years	'36	'44	'48	'52	'56	'60	'64	'68	'72	'76	'80	'84	'88	'92	'94
Cosimo	16	0	0	0	0	5	1								
Piero		2	1	3	3	4	17	29	7						
Giovanni		1	7	10	18	41	37	1							
Lorenzo							2	59	115	223	242	2	3	18	
Piero														34	38

is amply illustrated by these figures, as is the role of Giovanni di Cosimo as the Medici contact for Pistoia rather than Cosimo. An examination of the chronological distribution of these letters to the respective recipients is also revealing. Lorenzo seemed to break the Medicean tradition of schooling their offspring in clientage in the territorial state, for whereas both Piero di Cosimo and Lorenzo were obviously introduced relatively early to the role of managing clients in the territories, he kept his son Piero from such tasks until such a responsibility was thrust upon him on Lorenzo's demise in 1492, only six letters being directed to Piero prior to the year of his father's death.

Letters were sent by leading members of the competing elements of the Pistoiese governing elite to secure his favourable intervention on their behalf, whether it concerned inclusion in the bags for the forthcoming elections or protests against perceived mistreatment by opponents. There was also a regular traffic of gifts between the town and the Medici table. The commune itself also turned to the Medici to protect its fiscal interests against the contado, to prevent the inclusion of old magnate families in the electoral process, and to lobby on its behalf when the commune fell behind with its payments to the Florentine Treasury (*Camera del comune*).[34] Whilst Giovanni di Cosimo and Piero di Cosimo were regular recipients of missives from Pistoia and its surrounding communes prior to Lorenzo's pre-eminence, the process of centralisation was accelerated by *Il Magnifico* during the 1470s with the aid of local agents. Effective control was secured by 1477 when a more restricted *Consiglio dei graduati* was instituted in Pistoia with authority to decided questions of political eligibility in conjunction with Florentine commissioners.[35]

THE LOSS OF PATRONAL CONSENSUS

The arbitrational role assumed by the Florentines in the Trecento initially instituted division into the constitutional structure of the Pistoiese commune. However, the replacement of such a statutory provision with the paternalistic government of the Medici left the commune dangerously dependent on the impartiality and virtuous rule of its patrons. Given that patronage as a practice was fundamentally

---

34 See S. J. Milner, 'Lorenzo and Pistoia: Peacemaker or Partisan?', in M. Mallett and N. Mann (eds), *Lorenzo the Magnificent: Culture and Politics* (London, 1996), pp. 235–52.

35 BFPt, FF, B 169, 22r–23r, rub. XXIIII. For a *volgare* version, see ASF, Tratte, 44, 279r–286v.

premised upon the exchange of favours, Pistoia proved vulnerable to changes in political fortune. Even prior to the exile of the Medici in 1494, discontent was evident in Pistoia and the surrounding country-side, with Florentine commissioners in almost permanent residence from 1490 onwards subsequent to the murder of the leading Medicean agent in Pistoia, Mariano Panichi, in 1488.[36] Maintaining its symbiotic relationship with Florentine developments, the exile of the Medici in 1494 left Pistoia as well as Florence in a state of suspension. As in 1401, the struggles for pre-eminence within the competing elements of the Florentine *reggimento* were replicated within Pistoia as a result of patronal and kinship links between the two cities. Disunity in one fuelled disunity in its neighbour. As a leader of the Cancellieri faction, Jacopo Melocchi, lamented:

> This all came about due to the lack of any provision from Florence, for they were in disagreement amongst themselves and without their own government on account of both the war with Pisa and the factions that were circulating at that time of Fra Girolamo, a monk of San Domenico of the order of Saint Mark, who had been burnt as a heretic together with two of his fellow monks. This had caused great division within Florence and when the head suffers, the members weaken, and for this reason poor Pistoia grew weak and was ruined.[37]

In this instance the lack of a unified response from Florence meant that Pistoiese divisions were exacerbated by tensions within the Florentine *reggimento*, a point stressed by Guicciardini in his *Storie fiorentine*, Niccolò Valori in his *Ricordanze* and Piero Vaglienti in his *Storia dei suoi tempi*.[38]

---

[36] For the 1490 commissioners' correspondence see BNF, F.P., II.III.246; and their official papers in ASF, Pratica segreta di Pistoia e Pontremoli, 1, 1r–136v; and ASPt, Capitano di custodia, poi commissario, IIIa serie, 34, 1r–79r.

[37] Jacopo Melocchi, 'De' casi di Pistoia', in Biblioteca Marciana di Venezia, MS, Cl. It., VI. 197 [5803], i, 4v. For the original manuscript see ASF, Acquisti e Doni, 8: 'tutto avenne perché da Firenze non veniva rimedio alcuno, perché erano mal d'accordo et senza governo loro per conto della guerra di Pisa, et delle sette che infra di loro giravano di frate Girolamo frate di San Domenico dell'ordine di San Marco, il quale era stato abbruciato per heretico con duoi suoi altri frati, il quale haveva messo Firenze in gran divisione et cum caput dolet, caetera membra languent, et però la povera Pistoia languette, et è rimasta disfatta'.

[38] Francesco Guicciardini, *Storie fiorentine dal 1378 al 1509*, ed. R. Palmarocchi (Bari, 1931), p. 202. Valori acted as commissioner to Pistoia in 1501, securing a peace which he believed would endure 'se da nostri cittadini non saranno nutrite, et riaccese, come sono sute insino a qui'. See N. Valori, 'Ricordanze', in BNF, Panciatichi, 134, 12v. Buoni, commenting upon the maltreatment of certain Panciatichi ordered to Florence in the summer of 1500, states, 'nacque questo caso in nella città di Firenze per ordine di certi cittadini fiorentini, et de' primi, et benché io

The fusion of internal division and external threat only compounded the instability.

The consequence of Lorenzo's partiality towards the Panciatichi, therefore, was the increasing marginalisation of the Cancellieri leadership from the beginning of the 1470s onwards, and the gradual accumulation of resentment at imprisonment, exclusion from office and the deprivation of patrimonies. The events of 1498 onwards witnessed an exact reversal of the pattern set in 1401, with the effective exile of the Panciatichi from the city, their exclusion from its offices and the unification of predominant Florentine interests with those of the Cancellieri.[39] In this instance the process of pacification and reintegration of those exiled proved far more difficult with no policing power with sufficient authority to enforce the headings of peace. As the Florentines contended with rebellions elsewhere in the *dominio*, notably Arezzo in 1502, repeated attempts to secure peace in Pistoia proved fruitless, a whole series of *capitoli* passing unheeded despite the efforts of Florentine commissioners and officials.[40] Managing Pistoia's factions through patronage rendered the stability of the commune dependent upon the political fortunes of the Medici. This is reflected in the relationship between recurring factional crises in Pistoia and the position of the Medici within Florence during the first three decades of the sixteenth century, for it was not until the advent of the Medici principate that Pistoia's factions were finally rendered impotent.[41]

The exile of the Medici in 1494 resulted in a patronal vacuum in

---

sappia il nome, non li voglio nominare, et erano quelli che favorivano e Canciglieri'; Bastiano Buoni, 'De' casi di Pistoia dal 1499 insino al 1504', in Biblioteca Marciana di Venezia, MS, Cl. It., VI., 197 [5803], ii, 3r. In recounting the violence of May 1499, Vaglienti remarks, 'e perché e Panciatichi erano sfavoriti dalla nostra città, ne hano el pego'. See P. Vaglienti, 'Storia dei suoi tempi', in BNF, F.P., II.IV.42, 67v. For an examination of the relations between Florentines and Pistoiese in this case see W. J. Connell, ' "I fautori delle parti". Citizen interest and the treatment of a subject town, c.1500', in C. Lamioni (ed.), *Istituzioni e società in Toscana nell' età moderna* 2 vols. (Rome, 1994), I, pp. 118–47.

[39] See ASPt, Com., SO, 31, 23v–24r for the list of Panciatichi banned from the city in October 1500. For the deliberations of the committees of between six to eight citizens elected to oversee the defence of Cancellieri-controlled Pistoia see BFPt, FF, E 375., 1r–40r. The inner circle is composed of the Melocchi, Tonti, Dondoli, Bracali, Bellucci, Tarati, Fioravanti, Baglioni, Ambruogi, Dal Gallo, Baldinotti and Forteguerri.

[40] 'Headings for Peace' were drawn up by the Florentines on 2 October 1500, 28 April 1501, 21 August 1501, 16 April 1502, and 24–25 August 1502. See ASPt, Com., SO, 31, 22v–24r, 25r–29r, 29v–32r, BFPt, FF, E 389a, 1r–9r; and E 389, fasc. 5, 1r–4r.

[41] M. Dedola, ' "Tener Pistoia con le Parti". Governo fiorentino e fazioni Pistoiesi all'inizio del '500', *Ricerche storiche*, 22 (1992), pp. 239–59.

Pistoia, leaving the city searching for a new charismatic centre. The effect of granting privileges to the Pistoiese commune was to reverse the process of Florentine bureaucratisation in the Pistoiese case, thereby reducing the machinery of rule and respect for formal governmental institutions. This weakening of the communal sphere was accompanied by a growing realisation that effective power was administered through the agency of the Medici. With their departure, however, the cost of such dependency in terms of civic peace became clear. The lack of respect for a clearly articulated and constituted communal structure, combined with the size of the respective sides and the nature of the historical division, precluded the possibility of one group establishing hegemony, as even the fiction of consensus was unrealisable. Consequently each sought to legitimate itself through the territorial occupation of the communal realm, excluding their opponents from any share in the government and administration of civic patrimony. In Pistoia's case, therefore, the faction that remained within the city represented the commune solely on grounds of territorial occupation.

The Pistoiese case may well have been in the forefront of Machiavelli's mind when writing Chapter 11 of the first book of his *Discorsi*. The maxims cited concerning the danger of relying on the benevolence of a communal patron could easily have been drawn from the Pistoiese experience of the previous half-century:

> Kingdoms that depend solely upon the *virtù* of one man are not long lasting, since upon his death that *virtù* is gone; and it rarely comes about that it is restored through succession, as Dante prudently observes,
>
> > Through the branches of a family,
> > Rarely does human *virtù* travel,
> > And this is the wish of He who grants it,
> > In order that it is recognised as His gift
>
> The health of a republic – or a kingdom – therefore, does not lie in having a prince who governs prudently whilst alive, but rather in having a prince who constitutes it in such a way that it maintains itself upon his death.[42]

CONCLUSION

Pistoia's assimilation into the Florentine territorial state and its subsequent management requires the fusion of three historiographical narra-

[42] Machiavelli, *Discorsi*, in *Opere complete*, ed. S. Bertelli, 8 vols. (Milan, 1968), I, p. 128. Author's translation.

tives which have, to date, largely evolved autonomously, namely those of the emerging modern state, of social and political patronage and of so-called civic republicanism.[43] As well as showing their interrelation, the Pistoiese case also questions the traditional parameters of all three discourses. In terms of established narratives of the emerging bureaucratic state, which are often based on the quantative analysis of civic offices instituted to oversee territorial administration, the Pistoiese case seems to problematise the notion of a linear progression from medieval forms of patrimonialism to the precocious modernity of the Florentine state. The removal of administrative structures and the deployment of patronage as a means of government during the second half of the century demonstrate how such a transition was far from seamless. In relation to the historiography of patronage, there seems to be a need for a change in focus, moving beyond an examination of informal relations within communes to examine the role played by supra-communal patronage-based power blocs in shaping the political geography of late medieval and Renaissance Tuscany. Increased study of how such groups cooperated in appropriating communal structures in their relative communes would in turn illustrate the vulnerability of the public sphere in such pre-modern states.

Finally, Pistoia's incorporation into the Florentine *dominio* illustrates the limited applicability of civic republicanism outside Florence, demonstrating the extent to which studies of the evolution of the political rhetoric of *libertà* have remained untroubled by the simultaneous creation of what the Florentines themselves referred to as their *imperio*. Whilst the subject territories described the Florentine commune geographically as all that lay within the city's walls, they also aided in

---

[43] See the comments of J. Kirshner, 'Introduction: The State Is "Back In"', in Kirshner (ed.), *The Origins of the State in Italy, 1300–1600* (Chicago, 1996), pp. 1–10 and A. Brown, 'Florence, Renaissance and Early Modern State: Reappraisals', *The Journal of Modern History*, 56 (1984), pp. 285–300. On the growth of staff in the territorial state see for example G. Chittolini, *La formazione dello stato regionale e le istituzioni del contado: secoli XIV e XV* (Turin, 1979), and the essays collected in G. Chittolini (ed.), *La crisi degli ordinamenti comunali e le origini dello stato del Rinascimento* (Bologna, 1979). For Pistoia see E. Magliozzi, 'Istituzioni comunali a Pistoia prima e dopo l'inizio della dominazione fiorentina', in *Egemonia fiorentina ed autonomie locali nella Toscana nord-occidentale del primo Rinascimento: vita, arte, cultura* (Pistoia, 1978), pp. 171–205. Studies on political patronage within communes have focused in particular on the identification of ruling elites, as, for example, in the essays collected in *I ceti dirigenti nella Toscana del tardo comunale* (Florence, 1983), and *I ceti dirigenti nella Toscana del Quattrocento* (Florence, 1987). On the tradition of Florentine civic republicanism see the overview of J. Hankins, 'The "Baron Thesis" after Forty Years and some Recent Studies of Leonardo Bruni', *The Journal of the History of Ideas*, 56 (1995), pp. 309–38.

the evolution of a distinct sense of *fiorentinità* through their symbolic participation in Florentine civic ritual in their role as subjects. Yet in the process of helping fashion an objective manifestation of the Florentine commune, they were simultaneously denied an autonomous voice and thereby silenced, rhetorically and ideologically.

CHAPTER 16

A COMMENT

GIORGIO CHITTOLINI

I

A first observation is prompted by the wealth of current research on the Florentine territorial state.[1] Gene Brucker, when discussing the present studies, stated that in the 1950s or 1960s a theme like this would have been unthinkable for a conference or a seminar. I can say that the same was true of the beginnings of the 1970s, when Marvin Becker was one of the very few scholars to combine an interest in the territory and the history of the state. *Vice versa*, when today we survey the field, we encounter a great quantity of work that exists in finished form, numerous scholars who in the past twenty years have worked intensely on the Florentine territorial state, and an even greater number of scholars who are just beginning their work on the subject. They are working, moreover, on themes that until the 1970s were largely ignored and were not comprised in the usual array of subjects traditionally studied by Florentinists. Today, indeed, research on the territorial state makes up the great share of ongoing work in *fiorentinistica*; and, more importantly, studies on the territory have offered a kind of basic historical perspective that serves to situate all of the quite diverse ongoing research into different aspects of the history of Florence. All of this activity might easily have suggested a seminar, and a volume on the theme of the Florentine territorial state, and, fortunately, what we have here is the first collection of historical essays ever specifically and integrally organised to discuss the territorial state of the republic of Florence.

---

[1] This comment was delivered at the seminar 'Lo Stato territoriale fiorentino (secoli XIV–XV). Ricerche, linguaggi, confronti', held by the Centro di studi sulla civiltà del tardo Medioevo, in San Miniato, Italy, at which most (but not all) of the essays here published were discussed in earlier draft form.

It is interesting to note that the organisers, for reasons to which we have already alluded, have turned to a group of scholars who, while highly diversified among themselves in their nationalities and historical schools, are in large part homogeneous with respect to their ages. These scholars belong to the new generation of Florentinists for whom the theme of the Florentine territorial state has seemed a more natural field for research than others that might easily have been suggested by a historical tradition that has by now become as burdensome as it is illustrious. Thus, in addition to the work of the past three decades on urban social and political life, civic institutions, families and patronage networks, political and literary culture, and civic humanism, there has emerged in Florentine historiography a strong group of studies – consonant with historical work on the Duchy of Milan and the Venetian *Terraferma* – that is intent on examining the forms and apparatuses for territorial control, the relations between Florence and her subject cities, the connections between Florentine families and families of the dominion, and the political culture that comprised these phenomena. And this has been done with a view to understanding the system of political and governmental relations that were fundamental to the construction of a new territorial state under two aspects already indicated as characteristic of this sort of state formation by research on the states of Milan and Venice, namely, the affirmation of new modes of governing, and the recognition of existing territorial and political entities.

This is also a generation of scholars that has confronted the theme of the organisation of a Renaissance state (and, more generally, of the 'history of the state') in terms that are new with respect to twenty years ago. Political history has, in the meantime, been profoundly renewed, broadening itself from a perspective that was largely 'administrative' and 'institutional' to achieve a more ample understanding of political developments. It has been enriched by interpretive and analytical tools developed in other fields, for example in economic history, sociology and anthropology. Its work is now more likely (when compared with research that used methodologies of the past) to discern in historical sources the elements of discontinuity and possible alternative directions. These essays, therefore, offer an occasion for looking again at Florentine historiography. They reveal both the fecundity of a subject with which we are by now on quite familiar terms, and the progress that has ensued from the introduction of new agenda for research.

The main title of this seminar was 'The Florentine Territorial State'; and the category 'state', or 'state-ness' (*statualità*), remains central throughout this book. By this, I mean that the perspective of the state is always present – that the chapters consider a quite diverse series of social and political phenomena from the unifying perspective of the Florentine dominion. This was not, moreover, simply a geographical or 'regional' perspective: it was also the political perspective determined by a specific system of government established by the republic of Florence.

This said, we proceed necessarily to inquire about the theoretical characteristics of the state that has been evoked as both the inspiring motive and delimiting boundary for these essays. To which model of the state are they referring? The answer is certainly not univocal, since there are language differences, different disciplinary reference points, and differences of historical school and method, as the scholars themselves are aware. But if one were to look for a characterising element, I would say that for the majority of the writers there has been a tendency towards defining the state in 'negative' terms with respect to a 'previous historiographical tradition'. 'I speak of the "state"', many have said, 'but of course I don't speak of centralisation, rationalisation, or planning.' It is as though they were trying to keep their distance from a tradition which was received as burdensome or distracting by proposing a definition that is 'negative' or reductive with respect to so-called 'high' models of the state and the qualities usually attributed to it – but it is this definition that itself also becomes reductive with respect to a more neutral conception of the state. The polemic against this tradition has become repeated and insistent – more so than is warranted in a field that has substantially renewed itself. But it is interesting evidence of how strongly felt is the need to oppose a model that is perceived as still very strong and still in need of exorcism.

Conversely, we have also been offered in these essays a number of 'concrete' or 'material' elements (as has often been emphasised) in order better to understand the constructive process that took place in the Florentine dominion and how it functioned in practice. The resulting picture is both complex and carefully articulated.

On the one hand, it seems evident that there has taken place a broadening of attention to a series of protagonists, practices and organising structures that were 'non-institutional' or 'sub-institutional', rather than fixtures of the public apparatuses of government. These phenomena – along with public institutions – are now seen as essential components in the building of the state. This is an historical gain of great importance when one considers that these elements were once understood – for example in the long historiographical tradition relative to the Sforza duchy – as 'checks or brakes', or as 'neutral or negative residuals, the elimination or the overcoming of which was essential to the affirmation of the state', rather than as constitutive elements of the state itself.

On the other hand, in these studies there has been an attempt to avoid studying historical phenomena as resulting from the realisation of predetermined models; rather, there has been an attempt to trace the 'construction of the state' as evinced in its daily activity, on its often uncertain and contradictory path, following the necessities and contingencies of the moment more often than long-term plans. Stress has been placed, for example, on a rich and varied group of 'practices', which did not necessarily consist in the activities of magistracies and institutional bodies, nor were they carried out in accordance with norms and procedures under laws and legality. But they comprised a vast range of collective and single actions, linked, often, to branching networks of patronage.

Vice versa, these studies have diminished the importance of the administrative measures taken by public magistracies (once a privileged area of study), and they have emphasised the haphazard nature of legislation and other government actions that were once taken as evidence of firm plans. Thus, we now learn that fiscal policy did not reach a highpoint with the catasto of 1427 – that the catasto should no longer be seen as evidence of careful and strategic planning on the part of the Florentine state. In similar fashion, the judicial apparatus in the Florentine dominion is described as having little importance and meaning; more important by far were the sub-judicial practices, both public and private, for the arbitration of conflicts. Even the strong measures that Florence took in her territory are not ascribed to a desire to assert strong authority, or to the capacity to use effective means of coercion, but rather to a system of consensus that the work of negotiation and mediation are said to have produced.

III

To illustrate how this new framework has come about – and this is the other element I should like to emphasise – there is an evident preference in many of these studies to make use of a lexicon that is more customary in the social sciences than in the history of the state. It is a vocabulary that is more characteristic of anthropology and sociology than of institutional history or public law. I am referring to such terms as 'practices', 'legitimation', 'negotiation', words that are now pregnant with the strong meanings they have derived from the various disciplinary fields in which they have been used: terms that have been used in various essays for describing political and governmental actions and to define institutional structures and dynamics.

Thus, for example, it has become preferable to use the term 'negotiation' to indicate the various types of treaties and agreements between Florence and the communities of the dominion; whereas a long historiographical and archival tradition referred to these same agreements with words of a more specific institutional force that were also closer to the language of the time, by calling them 'articles' (*capitoli*) or 'surrender pacts' (*patti di dedizione*).

The term 'legitimation' has often been used to indicate the 'recognition' of bodies or persons as institutional interlocutors with the Florentine government, for instance through the concession of privileges, the approval of statutes, the receiving of embassies. This emphasis on a 'recognition' that is really the reflexive concomitant of legitimacy, risks perhaps diminishing the significant formal aspects and the juridical and institutional content of what the legal tradition knew as *recognitio*. Or again, terms from the language of clientelism and patronage have been used not only to indicate the relations between persons, but also to define the relations between public entities, which, in accordance with a long tradition, have been generally discussed instead with the language of public law – which, if it is here employed, is done so through quotations of others, or is often substituted with a 'weak' or less demanding vocabulary.

IV

Many of the contributors, therefore, are trying to exit – even at the level of language and lexicon – from the rigid cages of a statist tradition, and to use tools less subject to conditioning (in the worst sense) by an 'institutional' approach. They are thus better suited to treat that plurality and complexity of structures I have already mentioned.

It is therefore a rich framework, which offers many points for discussion. I would prefer to limit myself to touching on a few points, connected among themselves, the least common denominator of which can be found perhaps in the impression of 'pallid statehood' that the Florentine regional state seems to offer us. 'Pallid statehood' is the expression of Gian Maria Varanini, and I should like to adopt it here, without pretending to give it precisely the same meaning.

A first question regards the impact and capacity for government shown by the Florentine state: an impact and a capacity which, it seems to me, certain authors have intended to diminish or perhaps set aside, in so far as the accent has been placed on legitimising practices, negotiating and coming to terms, rather than on the objectives that the government proposed for itself, and on the extent to which it achieved those objectives. This is a possible path to liberation from the problematics of the 'origins of the modern state', which often implied – out of the necessity of measuring the progress of the state's action with respect to centralisation and absolutism – a certain overvaluation of the capacities of central government, attributing therefore to its actions not only a strong and coherent planning function, but also responsibility for historical achievements that were not always verified in a concrete way. There is no doubt but that, in effect, one of the most characteristic aspects of the action of the Florentine state – as with the Milanese and Venetian states, as has already been said – consisted, during this historical phase, not so much in a desire for the direct and sweeping exercise of government functions, as in the ability to coordinate and mediate among great variety of political forces at different levels of power.

This does *not* signify, however, it seems to me, that such a complex political construct as the 'state', supported on the one hand by a claim of new authority and on the other hand by a more traditional foundation of accords and pacts, based on a connection between the direct exercise of power and the delegation of fairly broad competencies to local entities and 'bodies' (*corpi*) – that all of the complicated and apparently contradictory structure of the regional state – fills and exhausts its historical purposes in the simple creation of a higher level of coordination among diverse forces, without also establishing its own, historically new, ends of government. Nor does it signify, even if the state limited itself to a neutral *function* of *coordination* among 'other' powers 'at the level of the state', that the possibility of the concrete exercise of governmental power on the part of the state should have been precluded. Nor can it mean that the state in this period was somehow unable to realise its various objectives (with respect to fiscal matters, for example, or judicial policy, or the maintaining of 'public order', or ecclesiastical policy), and therefore did not determine changes in society. The Florentine state, in effect, has often been recognised to have been especially efficient and innovative in its political action, and to have made a significant impact in comparison with other states of the Quattrocento.

It seems to me that the realisation (not new) of the importance of mediation and consensus in the construction of the regional states should not preclude – in the name of excessive caution towards attributing 'pre-modern' authority and efficiency to Quattrocento states – a recognition of the *consequences* of these various acts of consensus, which were sometimes to the advantage of one, sometimes to others among the parties involved: although perhaps in the case of the Florentine state they were more often to the advantage of the controlling class of the ruling city. Nor should we fail to recognise the other associated problem of which of the classes and social groups involved in this often harsh game of negotiations and conflicts were the winners, and which were the losers.

V

A second question might regard the problem, if it is a problem, of focusing better on the type or model of state which, in consonance with the declared acceptance of the category of 'the state', is here discussed. It should be more than a negative model – a state which does *not* have the characteristics of the 'modern state' – but positive, in the sense that it helps us to understand the specific characters and content of this state when compared with others, or with other forms of political organisation in other contexts and historical periods.

I have already said of the perspective adopted here that it is attentive above all, and polemically so, to realities and practices that were 'extra-institutional' or 'sub-state', so as to bring light to the materiality of the structure, the concreteness of the system of power. And I have said of the language adopted here that, in its desire to express distance from a conception and model of the state that use modernising concepts and terms, and also from a conception too reliant on public law and often deformed by subsequent experience, and in its desire to free itself from the interpretive cage implicit in these conceptions, it has shown a preference for a linguistic toolkit that is not strongly connotative but rather neutral (in terms of the theory of the state and public law). This vocabulary attempts to describe aggregative structures, ties and practices in their elementary substance, as they might be perceived from the perspective of a 'society without a state', thus avoiding the distorting lexical and interpretive filters that stem from the public-law tradition on these themes.

All of this, even if it presents the positive aspects mentioned above, still seems to me not to help us to focus on the characteristics of the 'state-ness' that has been referred to, while indeed it risks impoverishing the discussion of some of its distinctive elements. The use of anthropological and sociological lenses, in effect, if it helps us to overcome the abstractness and formalism of institutional phenomenologies (the laws and the procedures they prescribe, councils, offices, magistracies, representation, governing apparatuses – all with their own abstract geometries), and also helps to grasp, behind these phenomena, the concreteness and the multiplicity of the forms of social aggregation, of the relations and ties between groups, of the ways for exercising power and government, risks nonetheless, in certain respects, distracting our attention from the *specific form* in which a system for the organisation of power takes shape in a society such as Florentine Tuscany in the Quattrocento. Florentine society had its own unmistakable characteristics, and expressed itself through a particular political and institutional culture. Certainly, a 'lens' of a different type – such as the legal tradition or that of the state in the old manner – risks concentrating attention above all on external aspects, while cancelling or flattening other aspects. But perhaps we need to examine whether by favouring the eyeglasses offered by the social sciences, which indeed show us things that are new, we do not also blur and impoverish our vision of other things. Let me try to explain myself by way of a pair of examples.

When the various aggregative structures into which the society of the Florentine dominion was organised are examined, and one tries to grasp both the variety and the specificity of those structures, it is certainly just and necessary not to limit oneself to the structures that have been formalised and institutionalised by the laws of the commune of Florence, or of the subject communities (definable according to the parameters of the state or of public law). And one cannot not take into account forms of social aggregation based on blood and marriage ties, factions, client networks, neighbourhoods and villages, etc., which were all so many functioning political societies, both small and large, operating according to their own political and social logics that variously intersected with one another. Innumerable studies have shown in recent years the essential role played by such groupings in the social landscape and political dynamics of the Florentine state. The importance of these phenomena is inescapable for whoever seeks to understand the type of society and state we are considering. Yet, it would seem to me mistaken if it were not also understood that certain of these historical structures of aggregation had a physiognomy quite different with respect to other forms of aggregation – that special characteristics, for example, pertained to governing councils and communities as organisations under public law, and this ensured them a heightened importance when compared with other social formations, such as patronal, blood and factional groupings. And this, above all, was because the Florentine state recognised in its 'constitution' (*Verfassung* in the sense of Otto Brunner: not only in written norms but in the collective political consciousness) the value and importance of these structures, and provided for them in its laws. And as strong and important elements of the constitution they also belonged to the collective consciousness and were fundamental to a widely accepted political language. And yet these ideas, so integral to the Florentine dominion, are resistant to description according to the more generic and 'neutral' concepts and definitions that social scientists use to characterise political groups.

The concept 'community', for example, has a specific and strong meaning that cannot be treated as though it simply dissolves in the context of such sub-communitarian groupings as the neighbourhood, parish or family or such supra-communitarian groupings as the faction, kin group or lineage. This was a concept that the Florentines and their subjects understood as in large measure structuring their political practices and their systems of interaction. It was the primary element of identification in the self-articulation of local political societies. With respect to patronal ties to the great Florentine families, there was a great difference if the interlocutor was a 'community', instead of a faction or a local family. The relations that were established in these cases seem to me to have been undertaken differently and expressed in words of a different language.

VI

The risk of overlooking signifying elements can perhaps be accentuated by the language used in the study of relations between a central government and local groups. The use of concepts such as 'negotiation' or 'legitimation' permits a new attention to a whole series of new phenomena, and it sheds more light, for example, on the plurality of the protagonists and of the diverse elements on which the construction of the regional state is based: the complexity of the relations according to which the political society is organised, the great extent to which power was 'shared' rather than concentrated, the fluidity among the levels of power itself, etc. And yet, I ask myself whether the scarce consideration that this language reserves for the forms and the specific occasions through which these negotiations took place (pacts for the surrender of cities, the concession of a privilege, or letters, or more informal accords or contacts) and for the precise juridical and institutional content of these accords and concessions (the meaning of fiscal privilege, of a jurisdictional concession, the content of an immunity or an exemption) do not indicate a scarce consideration for the precise meaning that those negotiations and those legitimations assumed in the system of relations that the Florentine 'constitution' supposed, and whether they do not indicate a scarce consideration for their meanings and outcomes, which were, moreover, essential elements for defining the articulation of powers, competencies, the differing degrees of legitimation, the different qualities of the relations and the positions of the different actors.

A practice such as that expressed by the term 'negotiation' is enriched in meaning if consideration and importance are attributed to the determined form in which the negotiation was undertaken (legally, informally, through generic discussions), if attention is paid to the quality of the protagonists and actors (community, family, individual), to the specific object of the negotiation: all of them elements which in form and substance pertain with a specific value to the total organisation of the society and define its 'constitution'.

Analogously, the meaning that the term legitimation intends to express I believe can also be enriched in meaning if it can be seen and analysed in the juridical and constitutional forms through which these legitimations in fact expressed themselves: in surrender pacts, the concessions of privileges, the ability to make statutes, and feudal investitures. These are forms of legitimation that carry meaning from the specific juridical language in which they were formulated, in order to express a precise institutional relationship, rather than a vague and generic connection.

These are thus the terms and concepts of a language that is 'constitutional' – again in the Brunnerian sense – which were used to define, in a meaningful and pregnant way, the practices and institutions that, in the eyes of contemporaries and of the historical actors themselves, required a particular and specific lexicon, to express a certain quality or the precise meaning of powers, relationships, etc.: a sort of 'language of the state', that broadly drew upon the political and institutional culture of the time; a language that was surely manipulated and manipulable, but which contemporaries themselves – not latter-day historians of the 'modern state'! – thought was essential for expressing a certain idea of the whole of a political organisation.

This was a language that should be interpreted and read correctly. Read 'correctly', not only in the sense that it should be stripped of the encrustations and distortions added by readers of later centuries, but also in the sense that terms and concepts need to be historically contextualised within a specific political, juridical and institutional language. This was a language, for example, that made use of the vocabulary not only of public law, but also of 'private law' (according to the categories of today), that was nonetheless adapted to express ideas and concepts relative to the state. This 'language', I believe, is important, because it offers us not only a theoretical, abstract model, but also the idea that was generally accepted at the time of what a complete political entity was with respect to its logic and its internal coherence. And the consensus concerning this idea of the complete political entity differentiated this language from others, becoming an important condition for the maintenance and functioning of the state. The refusal to take into account a constitutional and institutional vocabulary ('institutional' in the broad sense as recognised, for example, by Santi Romano and Giovanni Tabacco) can only make it more difficult to understand a complex social construction like the Florentine state in this period – a construction that was quite different and distant from a 'stateless society'.

VII

From this there also derives the impression I have had of a strong dissonance between the image of a 'pallid statehood' evident in some of these essays and the results of so many other research efforts, both recent and less recent, that have also been conducted on the processes of state construction in Florence in the Quattrocento. These were studies that drew upon an old and illustrious scholarly tradition, and were often orientated towards showing the modernity of the Florentine regime and its capacity to anticipate new political practices, new institutions and new forms of the state. Here I am referring to the work of such scholars as Alison Brown or Riccardo Fubini, to mention two of the historians who have participated vigorously in the discussions of this seminar, and also to the work of others present, such as James Grubb and Anthony Molho, who have noted the importance of these institutional perspectives. Fubini, in particular, has not refrained from stating his conviction that we cannot speak of the 'territorial state' – or whatever we wish to call it – without taking into account the doctrinal elaboration that accompanied its practices, the relationship between practice and doctrine, the high degree of theoretical understanding shared by the persons involved, and, most importantly, the strong and new conception of the state that inspired contemporary political action.

The decision not to focus particular attention on problems of ideological elaboration and theoretical reflection on the themes of politics and the state in these essays was, in truth, a precise choice on the part of the organisers. It was a decision motivated both by the fact that there had been much discussion of those themes in past years, and also by a perceived need to work through certain new themes and problems. Still, with hindsight, and precisely because of the novelty and scope of the subjects here studied, it might be said that the decision to omit these aspects – the ideological and cultural dimension of the 'system' of the

Florentine dominion, in the sense that even the language of the Florentine state at the beginning of the Quattrocento, as was said above – has risked making it more difficult to establish a dialogue with an important sector of research, accentuating the impression of an opposition or a divergence of perspectives.

Objective elements of dissent are not lacking – even among the writers of these essays. The researches of Fubini, who is often cited in this volume, propose, in effect, an image of statehood and modernity that is quite strong. It is a modernity that was established above all on a foundation of new authority, expressed in terms of sovereignty, rather than the medieval concept of the commune, the system of the *res publica*, or corporatism, in a divorce from practices and concepts that for centuries had furnished an ideal for government of the medieval commune.

This new concept of authority was evident not just in theoretical works and treatises: it was also demonstrated in the formulae used in chanceries, and in the new political practices that were inspired by a strong conception of authority/sovereignty. These included the system of *balìe*, the tendency to identify the government with the regime (*reggimento*), and the exercise of a more authoritarian power than in the past, especially in urban contexts. From this perspective, Florence in the fifteenth century seems to offer strong anticipations of the modern state, of a strong power that radiated outward from the *civitas potens*. The new Florentine system, from this point of view, was quite removed from the 'Mediterranean system of power', based on the relationship of patron and client and on the culture it expressed, a 'Mediterranean system' within which numerous studies have attempted to circumscribe the Florentine experience. One does not need to deny that there was clientelism, but it appeared as a secondary phenomenon, an instrumental but not a defining practice, when compared for example with the 'statist' conception that inspired the political actions of Cosimo de' Medici. In this approach, the historian accents, above all, the model of the state and the concept of authority or sovereignty that lay behind it. And this is done from the perspective of the long history of models of the state, of the different understandings of power that evolved during the long itinerary from the medieval commune to the modern state. Seen from this perspective, the instruments of Florentine government that were concretely put into service, above all in the territory, appear much closer to concepts associated with the idea of a 'modern' state (the development of a class of functionaries, the ability of rectors to exercise authoritarian powers) than is suggested by some of these studies. The power claimed by the commune seemed naturally to translate itself into the strong exercise of authority, according to new procedures that corresponded to a growth in territorial power.

With respect to this idea of the state, the contrast with many of these studies is clear. It is a contrast that derives not only from disagreement over objective matters, on factual data, but also from the perspective of the research – a difference that is accentuated perhaps by a tendency to look at 'material' and 'concrete' situations, rather than seek the full logic and language of the Florentine state.

And yet, the attention to the 'materiality' of the structure, to those aspects that were 'extra-statist' or 'sub-statist', and to the actual practices of government, and the underlining of the meaning of contingent developments in the process of constructing the state, of initiatives born in response to particular situations (rather than as organic projects or systems), permits us, certainly, to see better how the edifice of the Florentine state was actually constructed and what were certain important elements of its functioning. And all of this is deserving of further examination. But now, after all of these acquisitions, we need also to ask ourselves if it would not be opportune to broaden the investigative field so as to recover not only the phenomena that help us to understand the Florentine state as an elementary system of power – too similar and ill-distinguishable from other generic systems of power – but also those that were specific to the Florentine dominion, and to its 'state-ness', in these other aspects, in the political panorama of Renaissance Italy.

INDEX

The politics of ritual kinship
Confraternities and the social order in early modern Italy
Edited by NICHOLAS TERPSTRA

War, diplomacy and the rise of Savoy, 1690–1720
CHRISTOPHER STORRS

Politics and diplomacy in early modern Italy
The structure of diplomatic practice, 1450–1800
Edited by DANIELA FRIGO

The politics of exile in Renaissance Italy
CHRISTINE SHAW

Florentine Tuscany
Structures and practices of power
Edited by WILLIAM J. CONNELL and ANDREA ZORZI

Naples in the eighteenth century
The birth and death of a nation state
Edited by GIROLAMO IMBRUGLIA